Who Stole Cinderella?

The Art of 'Happily Ever After'

DENISE RENNER

Who Stole Cinderella?
The Art of 'Happily Ever After'
ISBN: 978-0-9903247-2-0
Copyright © 2014 by Denise Renner
8316 E. 73rd St.
Tulsa, Oklahoma 74133

Published by Harrison House Publishers
Shippensburg, PA 17257-2914
www.harrisonhouse.com

6 7 8 9 10 11 / 25 24 23 22 21

Editorial Consultant: Rebecca L. Gilbert
Cover design: Debbie Pullman, www.ZoeLifeCreative.com
Text design: Lisa Simpson, www.SimpsonProductions.net

DEDICATION

I dedicate *Who Stole Cinderella?* to all the women whose real stories are shared in the pages of this book. These wives gave their best as they embraced the teachings that you're about to read. Some of these women experienced great trials and difficulties. But as you will read, they did what was hard at the time, and God saved their marriages as a result of their heartfelt obedience. Today these women are godly heroes who are reaping the harvest of fruitful marriages because of their trust in God and His Word.

Thank you for your stories and your willingness to share your weaknesses, your mistakes, and what you learned for the benefit of others. Your stories will encourage many and serve as an inspiration to wives everywhere who still believe in "happily ever after."

TABLE OF CONTENTS

ACKNOWLEDGMENTS

First of all, I want to thank the Lord Jesus Christ and His wonderful Spirit, whose power enabled me to walk out this journey so that I could even have a story of victory to tell.

I want to express my thankfulness to my husband Rick for his loving support and patience as I worked on this project and for the great wisdom and insight he provided as he read and reviewed the manuscript with me.

I want to thank Beth Parker, our executive assistant, for her help in the various stages of this project. Beth was always there to help when I needed to share my thoughts about the book, dictate some notes or manuscript revisions, ask her to proofread, etc. I also want to acknowledge my dear friend, Carol Holderness, for her excellent contributions to the manuscript as she read each word. I'm deeply grateful for Carol's expertise and her heart to see my story get into print.

I am grateful to Debbie Pullman for using her superb creative skills to develop the beautiful cover design for this book.

A big thank you to Michal Taylor for her editorial skill and the ingenious way she took so much raw material and helped weave together the pieces into a seamless testimony of God's goodness that can now bless many with its message.

I am so very grateful to Becky Gilbert as the primary editor on this book for her many hours of diligent labor and her heart and expert skill to beautify, clarify, and augment the truths contained in these pages. With both professionalism and passion, Becky was able to draw out and accentuate the lessons I learned along this journey so that others can take hold of the divine principles found in my story and walk them out in their own lives.

I want to thank Cindy Hansen for lending her seasoned editorial touch to my manuscript as well. I am also very grateful for the wonderful encouragement both Cindy and Andrell Corbin gave me to make sure this story was told on the printed page. These two women lovingly "pulled" out of me the details of my journey and made sure the most important elements were articulated and included. At times when I needed it most, they encouraged me that I had a story to tell and needed to tell it.

And now you hold that story in your hands! I give all glory and honor to Jesus, who helped me each step of the way and didn't let me stop moving toward the healing and wholeness He had planned all along for my life and my marriage!

FOREWORD BY RICK RENNER

I am honored that Denise asked me to write the foreword to this book. When she first told me of her decision to write *Who Stole Cinderella?*, I was certain she would ask one of her many well-known female friends to write the foreword — so when she asked me instead, I took her request very seriously. I have carefully read every word of this book, more than a few times, because I wanted to be able to write this foreword with absolute certainty that I believed in what I was about to endorse.

As I read, especially the first three chapters of this book, I felt every word deeply, having personally walked with Denise through the many years she tells about in her story. No one was closer to that story than I was. But even for me, her transparency about her own struggles and her frankness about what God required of her is almost disarming. As a reader, you should prepare yourself to hear honesty from a real woman of God who has lived at the Cross and in the power of the resurrection as long as I've known her.

Throughout the more than three decades Denise and I have been blessed to be each other's spouse, I have seen my wife do whatever the Lord asked of her. She has always been determined to make whatever changes He required of her and to follow Him in every act of obedience He asked of her. Those acts have spanned a great variety of experiences — from changes in attitude to moving our entire family to very foreign soil at one of the most difficult moments in the history of the USSR. As her observing husband, I tell you that her willingness to change, to obey, and to be whatever God wanted her to be has always left me in awe. I witness that what she has written in this book is not theoretical writing. What you are about to read is the true testimony of what Denise has lived and her continual willingness to do whatever is necessary to become the woman God has destined her to be.

Some years ago, Denise took to heart the biblical commandment that older women should teach the younger women (*see* Titus 2:4,5). She sensed the need to begin imparting to other women the truths she had learned through her years of walking with the Lord. As a result, Denise began conducting a weekly two-hour session in Moscow for women who want to see change in their marriages — change that is often drastic and very dramatic. In the years Denise has conducted this intense discipleship program, hundreds of women have attended. Countless marriages have been healed and strengthened, and many "hopeless" marriages have been saved. The impact of her weekly discipleship program is simply incalculable. This powerful ministry to women has provided an inestimable contribution to the marital and family health of our entire congregation.

As you read this book, know that it has been written seriously and thoughtfully and that it has been scoured again and again to make sure it correctly represents what Denise believes the Word of God teaches to women about marriage. I encourage you not to read it quickly; rather, take it in deeply and let each word impact your heart. Let it sink in before you decide whether or not you accept its validity. This teaching — like precious pearls — has been obtained by diving into the deep to learn of God and His ways over the course of many years. It is yours for the reading — but believe me when I tell you that it has cost Denise extravagantly.

One more thing — don't skip the introduction, for it is there that Denise introduces her beautiful description of Cinderella and Prince Charming, which leads to the question: WHO STOLE CINDERELLA?

Now… start your journey with Denise as you read the following pages!

Rick Renner

PREFACE

This book is based on my teachings to Russian women in marriage seminars I hold in the former Soviet Union. Sprinkled throughout these pages are true stories of transformations that have occurred in the marriages of many of those who've attended these seminars. These women took what they learned from God's Word, humbled their hearts to apply it, and allowed the Holy Spirit to guide them on a journey of recovery and restoration so they could experience fulfillment in their marriages as God intends.

Culturally, most of the women in Russia today were taught as young women to be strong, controlling, and in charge in their relationships and their homes. This trend began as a condition of war when during World War II, the male population of the Soviet Union was greatly reduced by the ravages of battle. In the Battle of Stalingrad alone, which lasted about 200 days, more Soviet soldiers died than all the American soldiers lost during the entire war. It was a bitter tragedy.

Because of the widespread destruction of residential areas in wartime, many families began living in small, one-room flats. People often had no clean water and no food — in fact, a large percentage of the population was literally experiencing starvation. Rather than attend school and work and go about normal, everyday activities of "home and family," the people in this region of the world were focused for years on fighting the enemy and on survival. This continued onslaught changed them profoundly, altering the family dynamic of an entire population of people.[1] The women who suffered through this horrific period were strong, heroic, and brave.

The grandmothers of the women I teach in these marriage seminars came through the war very strong, and they passed that characteristic on to their daughters, who then passed it on to *their* daughters. These women were forced to be both mother and father. (This fact remains true in most cultures where husbands and fathers have given their lives on the battlefield. Women have been left to continue the work in the factories, running and operating heavy machinery, as well as run their households.)

Even with this heritage and the difficult and challenging culture that surrounds them today, it has been amazing to see the positive changes in Russian women who have attended these marriage seminars and embraced the teaching we've presented. I've seen these women wonderfully transformed, and I've witnessed the principles they've learned work for them time and time again. Some of their testimonies are presented in this book. These women have been bold and brave in describing the dramatic changes in their lives and in their struggling marriages as they received the truth of God's Word into their hearts. Often their turnaround happened in a very short period of time after they began practicing the teaching they heard.

The principles I teach in this book are universal and will work for all women everywhere, whether in Russia, the United States, or any country of the world. God's Word crosses the boundaries of cultural differences to answer the heart's cry of women, whether they're seeking answers for their struggling marriages or greater fulfillment in their already satisfying marriages.

Isaiah 10:27 (*KJV*) says, "…The yoke shall be destroyed because of the anointing," and that is true for women who carry a heavy yoke of burden or bondage, no matter where they live. The material in this book, including the testimonies, provides the tools and the inspiration to help women draw on the wisdom, grace, and power of God to experience similar results for themselves, beyond anything they might expect or even conceive is possible.

I learned these principles on my personal journey of growth that began in 1991. Rick and I took a bold step to follow God on a daunting, yet exciting adventure by moving our family of five to the Soviet Union on the eve of its collapse. It was a wonderful decision that we've never regretted, but we had no idea just how challenging those early years would be. We faced difficulties and pressures we'd never imagined. But as issues in our marriage began to surface, I went to the Lord in search of solutions. And that's when the real adventure began as I embarked upon my own journey of change.

The change the Lord has brought about in me by the transforming work of His Word and His Spirit has not only deepened my relationship with Him, but it has also deepened my relationship with Rick. God has also used these experiences to establish great unity in our marriage and to build a husband-and-wife ministry team that has ministered effectively to hundreds of thousands of people and has stood the test of time. By His grace, this ministry has had an enormous impact throughout the entire former USSR as well as in the United States. And it continues to grow. But had I not learned and applied the principles I share in this book, my effectiveness would have been greatly reduced and the far-reaching influence of our ministry hindered.

The path I've walked hasn't been an easy one, but it has been a fruitful one, and I'm so glad I stayed with the journey. As you read this book, may the Holy Spirit speak to your heart and show you where the "Cinderella" in you is hiding. God's will is to work in you to help bring about the peaceful and fulfilling marriage that you desire — your *happily ever after*.

I want to specially recognize the teachings of Helen Andelin, author of *Fascinating Womanhood*. [2] I read her book years ago and was deeply inspired as I drew concepts from her insights, which formed the framework of the teachings I've developed in my own journey. As I build on what I learned from this author many years ago, I continue to benefit from her wisdom. Her writings are reflected in my experiences and my teachings today.

Denise Renner
Moscow, Russia

Introduction

CINDERELLA AND PRINCE CHARMING— IT'S STILL A LOVE STORY

In so many marriages, a wife begins her journey as Cinderella. She glides down the aisle in her beautiful white gown to marry Prince Charming and to become his crown of joy and glory as the wife of his dreams. But in time, Cinderella can find herself knee deep in housework and tasked with changing diapers and refereeing arguing children. She may deal with sickness and setbacks in the family, ailing parents, a husband who works too little or too much, and a number of other challenging circumstances along the way in her "happily ever after."

Imperfections — in ourselves, in our husbands, and in our circumstances — have the potential to crowd out all those initial wonderful feelings in marriage and replace them with disappointment, fear, disillusionment, and even a negative, critical attitude. Instead of living *happily ever after* like Cinderella and Prince Charming, we're not even sure where Cinderella and Prince Charming went! It's as if our dream was stolen, and we question whether recovering it is worth the pain. How can a wife be a crowning joy to her husband when life and circumstances can be so unfair? Even if she wanted to support her husband unwaveringly, what happens if a wife believes in a husband who doesn't believe in himself? What are the chances of her success — even if she musters the strength to keep trying — when his efforts seem halfhearted and lukewarm?

Proverbs 12:4 (*AMP*) tells us, "A virtuous and worthy wife [earnest and strong in character] is a crowning joy to her husband...." Could we be telling ourselves that this kind of character is just going to *appear* without any struggle, problems, or price — or that we'll glide through our "happily ever after" as easily and gracefully as our walk down the aisle?

None of us truly arrives at the point of being a perfect wife. After several decades of marriage, I'm still on my journey — and so are you. But each of us as believers can draw from a perfect Heavenly Father and a wonderful Savior, who supply all the strength and compassion we need to make it and to thrive. And we have the Holy Spirit, our Helper and Guide, to successfully guide us on our happily-ever-after journey. God knows exactly what to do to make the journey glorious and to bring about the transformation in our lives that He desires.

Titus 2:3-5 instructs us that older women in the faith should teach the younger women to love their husbands. The sense of "love" in this passage is that of *being a friend*. Well, what does that look like in everyday life? I hope that in reading this book, you will find some of the answers you seek. I certainly don't think of myself as old, but I do have years of experience. I've done many things wrong over the years, but with an open, honest heart to learn from my mistakes and to align myself with God's Word, I'm doing more and more things right! In this book, I desire to see women of all ages benefit from the lessons I've learned through my years of marriage and through the guidance of the Holy Spirit. It's possible — and I believe it's God's desire — to prevent women from losing out on years of happiness because of mistakes similar to mine that can be corrected, beginning *now*!

Those big learning years of my marriage were still very good, but in some ways, they were very difficult too. It is my prayer that God will use my experiences to break the cycle of struggling and suffering for wives who are honestly looking for godly change and biblical solutions to the problems they face.

Proverbs 14:1 says, "The wise woman builds her house, but the foolish pulls it down with her hands." By applying the practical wisdom of the Holy Spirit that I share in this book, you can learn how to build your house — a solid, strong, and fulfilling marriage — on the solid foundation of Jesus Christ. As you experience this transforming process, I believe you will see fruit not only in yourself, but also in your husband and your children.

This book contains my personal illustrations, teaching from God's Word, and testimonies of women who sought God in their imperfections for guidance on their own journeys of growth and change. (In order to protect their privacy, I changed the names and identifying details of these women.) If you're discouraged and feel like you want to run from your situation, I want to encourage you that there is still hope for your marriage! I want to help you run *to the Lord* with your dreams that seem lost, so please join me on this journey. It's not a journey of perfection that's free of struggle, but it *can* be one of great beauty, contentment, and victory.

Chapter One

My Story

A story of faith turning to sight is often *not* a story of overnight success. In fact, it's most likely that the journey to your "happily ever after" will consist of some struggling along the way. There may even be times when you feel darkness all around you as you anticipate by faith seeing the radiant light of day — the time when what you've asked God and trusted Him for finally comes to pass.

Just as a seed planted deep into the soil of the earth must take firm root and then struggle to wind its way upward through the dark, so many of our victories in life are about the *process* — the *journey*. Jesus said, "Most assuredly, I say to you, unless a grain of wheat falls into the ground and dies, it remains alone; but if it dies, it produces much grain" (John 12:24). How true this becomes in our lives when we finally make the decision to bear peaceable fruits of righteousness (*see* Hebrews 12:11) where there has been desolation or very little fruit. We come to realize that we must "die" to doing things the same unhealthy way we've been doing them.

Those old ways of doing things might include a pattern of trying to control others so we can feel a measure of comfort ourselves. Or it might require us to return our gaze toward Jesus when we've looked away and have fixed our focus on someone else to help us. As long as these patterns are allowed to influence our lives and our relationships, our brokenness will remain undealt with and unsubmitted to Jesus' Cross and His resurrection life. And nothing good of eternal value can come out of that.

Jesus, the Word of God who was made flesh, was "buried" as a seed for three days — but He rose from the dead, bringing us to new life with Him. Because of His great sacrifice and act of redemption, we can take His Word into our lives and allow Him to bring forth from the darkness something new that never existed before. Whether it's healing from our brokenness, deliverance from our shame, or freedom to love without fear, God's Word and His Spirit are powerful to transform our lives — to do in us what we could not possibly do for ourselves.

That is my story. Yes, it's one of pain and struggle, but it's also one of great fruitfulness. Although your story is no doubt different than mine, perhaps you will see hidden in these pages a similar picture of yourself as you face your own unique challenges. If you do, I pray you find the courage you need to pursue God's path of victory for *you* and your own journey of "happily ever after."

Only One True Rock

Often women set themselves up for failure from the very beginning of their married lives because they want their relationship with the man they love to meet the needs of their heart that only Jesus can provide. Psalm 18:1,2 says, "I will love You, O Lord, my strength. The Lord is my rock and my fortress and my deliverer; my God, my strength, in whom I will trust; my shield and the horn of my salvation, my stronghold."

Notice verse 2 *doesn't* say, "*My husband* is my rock, my fortress, my deliverer, my strength, my shield, the horn of my salvation, and my stronghold." *Whew!* That would be a lot of responsibility for one man's shoulders! As wonderful as our husband might be, his shoulders are simply not that big, and our false expectation that he can meet our every need sets us up for undue disappointment.

Our journey of growth that leads to a deeply fulfilling relationship with our husband always places Jesus firmly at the center of the marriage. *Jesus* is our Rock and Fortress — *only Him*. When we enter marriage with all our imperfections and insecurities, we have an opportunity to allow God to lead us to a place of security in Jesus rather than try to gain that security from our husband.

Shortly after moving to the former Soviet Union to launch a new phase of our ministry, I began the struggle of my life with my emotions. Engrossed with everything that comes with embarking on a new assignment from God, Rick quickly poured himself into the work we had come to do. I started and directed the praise and worship of our church, which included about 30 people. I helped Rick in the TV ministry — and I was blessed to be the stay-at-home mom of three wonderful little boys, whom I even home-schooled for a time. I was engaged in helping in the ministry and in serving by Rick's side. But as his responsibilities and vision kept increasing, I began to fear that I was losing the place in my husband's heart that belonged to me as his wife, and I became resentful.

The vision Rick carried in his heart at that time would prove to have a vast impact on that entire region of the world, but it took an enormous amount of time and attention as the foundation was being laid in those early days. To get the job done and fulfill that phase of the call, Rick had to intently focus not only on constructing a physical church building in Riga, the capital city of Latvia, but also on raising up church leaders and developing the foundation of what was to become a huge ministry. I began to harbor feelings of resentment and unforgiveness toward him because I felt so left out of his life.

Before I knew it, my negative feelings had so consumed me that I began to experience some troubling symptoms in my body. At times my hands and feet would go almost completely numb. Also, my unforgiveness opened the door to a great deal of fear in my life, including panic attacks at times. I remember thinking to myself, *I'm a Christian — this is NOT supposed to be happening to me!*

After much time spent genuinely seeking God in prayer, I came to the difficult but life-changing realization that, although my emotions were directed toward my husband, *I* was the source of my own bitterness and frustration.

As women, we have great hopes for a marriage that's always peaceful and happy, but often life brings just the right circumstances that cause us to see in full color some of the ugliness inside us that disrupts that happiness and peace. When we feel vulnerable and become needy toward others, that hidden ugliness floats right up to the surface. Although we want to escape from our issues, if we don't bring them to God and find *His* way of escape, they will continue to raise their ugly heads again and again.

Often it's in our desperation that we discover the truth that our only real means of escape and freedom are found in God — through turning to Him and sincerely seeking His face. James 4:8 says, "Draw near to God and He will draw near to you...." Only when we draw near to God will we find the true security we desire that no person can provide for us, no matter how hard he or she may try.

As I struggled with all of those negative emotions concerning Rick and our marriage, I was in a desperate place to draw near to God. I really needed Him to draw near to me because I knew that when God draws near, He doesn't come empty-handed. He comes with power, grace, and the answers we seek.

THE TRAP OF ISOLATION

I want to share with you a little bit about how traps are set to capture our lives — traps designed to bind us up and *keep* us bound so that we fail to find joy and fulfillment on the path God has called us to walk and in the life He has called us to live.

Just as a trap designed to catch a wild animal is usually hidden from sight, the traps the enemy sets for us are not always obvious. They often start as one small

Only when we draw near to God will we find the true security we desire that no person can provide for us, no matter how hard he or she may try.

thought, feeling, or suggestion that can seem very good, right, and reasonable at first, especially if we feel someone has wronged us in some way or that life's circumstances have been unkind and unfair. In times like these, it's so easy to begin feeling sorry for ourselves — and it's in those weak moments, the enemy moves in with negative thoughts that serve no other purpose than to keep us stuck in that one place, unable to move forward.

That's what happened to me when we moved to the former Soviet Union. Because Rick was so focused on fulfilling the vision God had given him for our ministry — *as he needed to be* — I didn't feel I was as important to him as the people he had to give time and attention to in those early days. I felt as though I had been left on the side of the road! In fact, that's how my lonely road of isolation and despair began — with one negative feeling!

Perhaps you've felt that way before — like your husband is loaded down with responsibilities, and you're just another one of those many responsibilities. Maybe you feel like just another spinning plate among many that your husband has to deal with so that everything doesn't come crashing down around him. If you lived in a perfect world, your husband could do it all and still love you the way you think he should. But it's not a perfect world, and sometimes in marriage, there will be seasons when he has more than his fair share of responsibilities and problems to deal with in his job or vocation. I want to encourage you that more than likely, your husband is doing the best he can and probably feels overwhelmed at times because of all the things that clamor for his attention.

During the times when we're vulnerable and afraid — and even when we feel like lashing out in anger — it's Jesus, not our husband, whom we need more than ever. We need the Master Artist to paint on the canvas of our soul the answers and instructions we need to take us through our journey without becoming self-focused and believing the wrong things. That kind of inward focus and wrong believing will bring us to the wrong conclusions, paint a wrong picture on our soul, and eventually destroy us emotionally. That's why we have to recognize that *Jesus* is our Rock, Fortress, Deliverer, and Strength. We can safely draw near to Him. We can put our trust in Him.

Proverbs 3:5,6 says, "Trust in the Lord with all your heart, and lean not on your own understanding; in all your ways acknowledge Him, and He shall direct your paths." Of course, I knew this passage when I began struggling with wrong feelings and emotions toward my husband, but I didn't have the wisdom I needed at that time to put into practice what I'm describing here. Instead, I nurtured hurt feelings, believed wrong thoughts, and became very isolated and discouraged — *trapped* — as a result.

What happened to me during those long months of struggling emotionally was no one's fault but my own. I not only fell into the trap of nurturing wrong thoughts and feelings, but I also failed to do the things necessary to avoid being isolated. I didn't speak the Russian language very well. I could have spent more time learning it, but I made excuses for not studying. I didn't have any friends, but I could have been bolder and less fearful to step out of my comfort zone and speak the little Russian I *had* learned so that I could meet people and get to know them better.

You may ask, "Denise, how could you do that? How could you allow all that to happen?" Although I faced an onslaught of negative emotions during this time of transition in ministry, I wasn't fully aware at each moment that I was responding so poorly. Each negative response that caused me to plunge deeper and deeper into despair was very subtle. I didn't notice right away what was happening as I shrunk away into isolation, resentment, unforgiveness, and shame.

Have you ever isolated and hidden yourself because you couldn't seem to shed the extra pounds on your body that you loathed? Or have you tried to do something significant — maybe involving church, work, or school — and things didn't go exactly the way you thought they would, so you gave up? Rather than boldly facing your challenge or setback, did you withdraw in discouragement or hide your "failure" behind someone else you could blame?

Life is challenging, and we have an enemy who tries to stop us cold. But we have to push forward, *past* the challenges. Otherwise we can become stuck in life, captive to fear, discouragement, and depression, or even to resenting and blaming others. I'm not proud that I had all these emotional challenges to deal with. But I am grateful to God for the deep healing and delivering work He did in my heart as I sought Him honestly for the truth. I share the details of my situation not to embarrass myself, but rather to help *you*. If you find yourself stuck in life in any way, my prayer is that from my story, you will see the danger in the trap of isolation and avoid that serious pitfall.

ESCAPING THE TRAP OF NEGATIVITY AND FEAR

As time passed during our time of new beginnings in the former Soviet Union, I became more and more isolated and withdrawn, and let me tell you: *Isolation is a terrible and lonely trap!* Everyone needs others to talk to, and that is especially true for women. But I had no one to talk to so that I could be encouraged and strengthened while Rick was away doing the work of the ministry. I couldn't expose the negative parts of my soul — my fears, my resentment, and my pain — because I didn't want to dishonor my husband. So I chose to say nothing. I kept all my feelings to myself, and I thought about them day in and day out, again and again and again. I was alone, stuck with just me, and I wasn't very happy.

Many women can relate to my situation. They want to escape what they're going through, but they can't because they can't seem to escape from *themselves!* They allow themselves to become trapped by their negative emotions and begin to believe the lie that there is nowhere to turn and their situation is hopeless.

I didn't know who I could turn to in my situation. As a pastor's wife, I knew it wasn't wise to talk to anyone in our congregation about challenges I was experiencing relating to my husband. And at that time, I couldn't see that my problem was with me and not Rick — that I was expecting way too much of him. *No one* could fill my bill of request — only Jesus. But I wasn't looking to Jesus; I was looking to Rick. And because I was expecting so much of him, I was disappointed with him on a regular basis.

As Rick was striving diligently and with joy to meet his challenges head-on, I was shrinking back with fear and intimidation. While he was filled with conviction and resolve to fulfill God's vision for our lives, I was struggling more and more deeply with bitterness and resentment.

Insecurity, new or unpleasant surroundings, and the isolation that can result are a bad combination, often leading to loneliness, fear, neediness, and even bitterness. In my case, Rick couldn't totally understand my situation because he had embraced this new step in our calling with excitement and enthusiasm. His attention was riveted on the vision — on building the church and raising up leaders as God had asked him to do.

I should have stood beside Rick in a different way than I did to help shoulder the load of those difficult first steps in a brand-new country. But I was ill-prepared emotionally to handle the onslaught of thoughts and feelings that I was constantly barraged with. This huge, new part of our assignment and my own fears and insecurities created a "perfect storm" to bring me to a place with the Lord I had never been before. I had to learn to allow *Jesus*, not Rick, to become my comfort, shelter, and source of help. Before I could reach that place, however, I had to move past the bitterness and unforgiveness I'd allowed to fester in my soul.

REMEMBER, IT'S A *PROCESS*

A journey to growth and change doesn't happen overnight. (Take comfort, dear one — Moses was in the wilderness 40 years. I have comforted myself with this thought many times!) I wasn't looking for a quick fix or instant deliverance. The bitterness and unforgiveness that had been building up in my heart for two years wasn't going to just go away in a moment.

In fact, bitterness and unforgiveness cause their damage and destruction over a period of time. They carry roots that grow deep into the recesses of our soul. The thoughts and feelings that strengthened those roots in my own life and caused them to grow so powerful had become habitual. Tormenting thoughts did their dark work beneath the surface in me and brought a ravaging root system of destruction in my already weakened soul. And it began to affect our marriage.

Bitterness and unforgiveness cause their damage and destruction over a period of time. They carry roots that grow deep into the recesses of our soul.

Matthew 18:34 speaks of a servant who suffered at the hands of "the tormentors" because he refused to forgive his fellow servant a very small debt. I used to wonder who the tormentors were until bitterness and unforgiveness took hold in me! For almost two years, I was tormented with sleepless nights, symptoms of sickness and disease, and nagging fear. There came a time when I simply had to deal with it. And when I finally surrendered my will to let go of the pain, it still took several months

of consistently yielding to the Holy Spirit so He could work through the damage that had been done and bring me to a place of healing.

IN SEARCH OF THE TRUTH

When we allow something ugly or unseemly to grow inside us, we often justify ourselves by blaming someone else as the source of our problems and pain. This closes the door to our much-needed healing. Our mind searches for a place to put the guilt because we can't bear the thought that the problem could possibly be with us! We can't seem to grasp how anything in us could possibly cause offense in others. We see *ourselves* as the victims, and we think, *Lord, I know what my problem is. It's that HUSBAND you gave me!*

The problem with this kind of thinking is that it's not based on the truth, and if we succumb to it, we become trapped by false, circular reasoning. Just like a little hamster that runs and runs on a wheel in its cage, we keep running through the same wrong thoughts over and over again — and *justifying* them. The devil and our flesh will keep us running endlessly on that hamster wheel of toxic thoughts *unless* we find and yield to the answer that brings deliverance and renew our mind with God's true and right thoughts about the matter.

In every circumstance of life, there has to be an answer that brings deliverance, and *there is!* But deliverance doesn't always come quickly or overnight. Sometimes it takes time to come to a place of understanding with the Holy Spirit's help that our biggest problems are not the result of what someone else is doing or has done to us. Our biggest problems have to do with *us* and how we respond to the situations and circumstances of life. We have to be willing to ask, "*What am I doing wrong?*" and, "*How can I change?*" In other words, we must ask God for help and then take responsibility to humbly receive and submit to whatever He tells us.

Every married couple should be experiencing an ongoing journey of growth and change. When a man and a woman make a covenant in marriage, the Bible says they "become one flesh" (Ephesians 5:31). The word "become" includes in its meaning the idea of *something engaged in an ongoing process.* In other words, a husband and wife do not just become "one flesh" the moment they experience physical intimacy together. That physical oneness happens in a short time, but genuine oneness takes a lifetime.

I remember the time just days before our wedding in 1981 when Rick and I sat before our pastor and received this very counsel. We listened attentively and pondered what he meant by his statement, "It will take you a lifetime to become one." Then our journey as husband and wife began, and I can tell you that through every season of our lives together, we've come to value more and more our pastor's wise words.

Many of us as women enter marriage expecting that our husband will be everything we'll need him to be — and that we'll be the perfect helpmate who will complete his life. However, it doesn't take long to realize that we're not perfect, and neither is our husband. At the marriage altar, we actually say, "I do" to a host of our husband's imperfections — and our husband says, "I do" to our faults and shortcomings too.

We may not see all the imperfections in ourselves or in our spouse in the beginning, but those imperfections will show up in time. Along life's journey, we will begin to see the "imperfect," because life has a way of uncovering the worst in each of us. The question is, *what will we do?* Will we focus only on what's imperfect at the expense of our relationship? Will we run away and hide? Will we throw in the towel and forget the words of the covenant we made in our pretty white gown — "...*for better or worse, for richer, for poorer, in sickness and in health, to love and to cherish...until death do us part*"? Or will we choose to run to the Lord for wisdom and counsel and remain steadfast on the path in our journey?

Perhaps you feel as if you're in a laboratory with just the right mix of components — your weaknesses, your husband's weaknesses, disappointment and discouragement — to cause you to believe that your marriage will never change. We all deal with these same components at different times in our lives, although our situations vary. Or maybe some of your "laboratory" ingredients are more staggering, such as childhood abuse, and you've never dealt with the damaging emotional fallout. My friend, the transforming power of the love of God through His Word and His Spirit can make you whole again. But if your wounded emotions aren't dealt with and healed, you may find yourself creating something very toxic, volatile, and unhealthy in the laboratory of your life, and it will adversely affect every relationship you have.

However, when we focus on *Jesus* and give all the components of our brokenness to Him, they become the perfect setup for Him to do His best work in us and in our family. And the best part of

If your wounded emotions aren't dealt with and healed, you may find yourself creating something very toxic, volatile, and unhealthy in the laboratory of your life, and it will adversely affect every relationship you have.

those inner workings is the new image of ourselves that we come away with. We begin to see ourselves as God's precious daughters who are humble, pliable, and yielded to the Holy Spirit as He creates something wonderful in each of us — a beautiful, teachable spirit that will cause blessing to come to us and our family for a lifetime.

STAND YOUR GROUND AGAINST THE ENEMY OF YOUR SOUL

James 4:7 (*KJV*) says, "Submit yourselves therefore to God. Resist the devil, and he will flee from you." Before we can effectively resist the devil, we must first submit ourselves to God. If we're not submitting ourselves to God, His Word, and His Spirit — and to His process of transformation in our lives — we won't be able to stand against our enemy Satan.

The enemy knows this. And he knows that when we persevere to the end of our test or trial, we'll come into a great victory. So what does he do? He tries to distract us on our journey or stop us altogether. In the heat of our battle, the devil will try to intimidate us. He will attempt to get us off-track by pushing us in areas where we're vulnerable — bringing up difficulties we faced growing up or through other events and mistakes from our past. He will revisit us with the negative effects those situations had on our lives, trying to paralyze us with fear so that we won't press forward. He may even try to make us think we're weak or to believe that *others* think we're weak so we become overly preoccupied and concerned with how others see us.

After all, this is the very same enemy who attacked Eve's mind in the Garden of Eden, saying, "Did God *really* say that?" (*see* Genesis 3:1). Anytime we're engaged in spiritual warfare, contending for what's ours in Jesus Christ and for what's right in the eyes of God, the enemy will be right there, accusing us and trying to make us feel confused, condemned, embarrassed, or ashamed. But First Peter 5:9 says these kinds of spiritual attacks and sufferings are being waged against all the brethren — and that means *all of us* who are in Christ.

I'm not telling you these things to discourage you, but to let you know what's coming the minute you make a firm decision to overcome the negativity of the past. Second Corinthians 2:11 says we're not ignorant of Satan's devices or schemes. We're supposed to recognize him when he comes with his negative thoughts and tries to play on our emotions. We're to maintain our position of victory, knowing that the battle we're in is a *good* one — it's the *good* fight of faith (*see* 1 Timothy 6:12)!

Another thing that will help you win your fight of faith for a victorious marriage is understanding the truth that our battle is not against flesh and blood. Ephesians 6:12 (*KJV*) tells us, "For we wrestle not against flesh and blood, but against principalities, against powers, against the rulers of the darkness of this world, against spiritual wickedness in high places."

My battle wasn't against Rick. I was in a battle against the enemy in an area of my life — an area of my *flesh* — where insecurity had reigned for a long time. After all that time, there I was in my "happily-ever-after" marriage, wanting my comfort and security to come from Rick. Although I didn't realize it at the time, I wanted to depend on him instead of on Jesus. That was too much pressure to put on one person, especially on my husband whom I deeply loved. The part of my flesh that kept rising up to try to make Rick my security — and to give him the place in my life that was reserved for Christ alone — was going to have to die. I was going to have to grow up in Christ.

But the question was, *how?* The Lord was faithful and gracious to show me the way out of that dark place and time in my life. It wasn't an easy journey, but He brought me out in a powerful way. And the story of my journey is what I am sharing in this book.

'I'M A WORK IN PROGRESS'

When I fell in love with Rick, I knew he was the man I'd wanted all my life, the one I could depend and lean on. But God never intended for any of us to be totally dependent on another human being! He wants our dependence to be on *Him*. So I had it wrong from the very beginning of my marriage in that I was putting too much pressure on Rick, expecting that *he* would meet all my needs.

Perhaps you don't overly depend on your husband, and you can't totally relate to what I'm saying. But it could be that you have an inordinate dependence on your money, your friends, your children, your career, your beauty, your reputation, etc. The point I'm making is that Jesus wants us to trust Him with all our heart and to place our dependence completely on *Him*.

Many of us get married thinking, *My husband is going to make me so happy. He'll be there for me to meet my emotional needs. This is it — now my life is good!* That's actually a selfish way to start a marriage, but, unfortunately, it happens that way for many of us. In the early days of my own marriage, I didn't have a full awareness that I was supposed to be in the marriage for my husband. I mainly held the belief that he would be there for me at all times and would hold the answers to all my needs.

My attitude and focus needed to change. Instead of being centered on me and my needs, I needed to focus more on Rick and *his* needs. Over time I realized that the Holy Spirit is the only One I should depend on to meet all my needs; I didn't need to constantly look to Rick. Once I settled that in my heart and allowed God to do a transforming work in me, I began to concentrate more and more on what I could do for Rick instead of on what he could do for me.

When I was able to take my eyes off my husband as the supplier of all my needs and look to the Lord instead, I was free to enjoy Rick in a fresh, new way. It also gave him the freedom to enjoy our journey through life together in a way he'd never been able to before. I was finally able to give to him without wanting anything in return because of the secure, confident place I'd reached with the Lord.

What Is 'the Journey'?

When I fell in love with Rick, it was in an instant. But it took a process of time for me to develop into the person God wanted me to be in our marriage. I was a work in progress, and I still am. You are too. We're all in different places in our journey, but as long as we're alive on earth, we're still on the journey.

When you're on a journey, naturally speaking, whether you're traveling by plane, automobile, or even on foot, it's easy to track your progress by measuring the distance you've traveled. But when you're on a spiritual journey, you're being changed on the inside by the work of the Holy Spirit, and you can't necessarily measure your progress from day to day. So when I talk about the "journey," I'm talking about a *process*. I'm talking about God doing such a work in us that we can't describe *how* He's doing it; we just know He *is* doing it and that He's going to complete the work He began in us if *we* won't give up and quit. We can't always chart our progress so that we know where we are on that journey on a given day. But we know by faith — *because we're committed to this journey for the long haul* — that we're continually making progress and moving forward.

In my situation, sometimes I felt like I was taking two steps forward and three steps back! But it's important for us to maintain the attitude that we will keep moving forward with God in complete trust. We have to open the door of our heart and trust in His love, allowing Him to do a work on the inside of us.

Philippians 1:6 (*NIV*) states, "Being confident of this, that he who began a good work in you will carry it on to completion until the day of Christ Jesus." According to this verse of Scripture, God has begun a good work in you and in me. And we are in the middle of that operation — somewhere between the beginning and the end. We are on a path with Christ, and His work in us is in progress. And *He* is the One who's doing it! Our job is to submit and yield to Him as He carries His activity in us to completion.

JESUS UNDERSTANDS THE PAIN OF BETRAYAL

The journey to real change is a path on which God can do such a work inside you that you know it's beyond your own strength, intelligence, or ability. You may have felt insecure and tried to find your own solution, whether it was to look for help in a special book or seminar — or to lean heavily on someone you thought would make you feel secure. Or you may have even had a minister lay hands on you for deliverance and healing. I'm thankful for books and seminars and the prayers of others, but Jesus is the only One who can truly proclaim Himself as Deliverer and

Peace-Giver. He will take you by the hand and lead you on the right path if you'll let Him — and He will never fail!

There's only One who paid the complete price for our deliverance with His precious blood, and that is Jesus. He alone is our Deliverer from all fears, insecurities, and bondages. Isaiah 53:5 says, "…He was wounded for our transgressions, He was bruised for our iniquities; *the chastisement for our peace was upon Him*, and by His stripes we are healed." Jesus bore everything that would take our peace from us. He took it *all*.

How did Jesus take it all? He took the tearing of our soul when we struggle to do God's will by forgiving someone who has hurt us, despite our suffering and pain. Jesus experienced this struggle to obey the will of God as He agonized in the Garden of Gethsemane — to the point of His sweat turning to blood!

Jesus also took upon Himself the deep pain of betrayal we feel over the decisions of others who wound us. A wife who suddenly discovers that her husband has broken his marriage vows and forsaken his pledge to be faithful feels this kind of soul-piercing pain. Jesus Himself experienced a similar betrayal when He was given up by His "friend" to the religious rulers who sought to take His life.

Jesus also bore our shame. As He hung naked on the Cross in front of onlookers, including His own mother, He took upon Himself all the shame we would ever feel. Jesus is touched with the feelings of shame a wife experiences when her marriage is failing and she is exposed to humiliation and the judgment of others. Yet with every soul-wrenching emotional blow she receives, Jesus is there to help her see that He took her place and bore all her rejection and pain.

Hebrews 4:14,15 (*KJV*) says, "Seeing then that we have a great high priest, that is passed into the heavens, Jesus the Son of God, let us hold fast our profession. For we have not an high priest which cannot be touched with the feeling of our infirmities; but was in all points tempted like as we are, yet without sin." Truly, Jesus bore it all. He took our judgment for every bit of sin and wrongdoing we would ever commit. He bore the punishment of it all. Then Jesus arose victoriously over it all to give you and me a new nature and His Spirit as our Helper. He did all this so we could become godly, peaceful, and loving women, wives, mothers — and, most importantly, daughters of our Heavenly Father. His Word says that even today Jesus saves "…to the uttermost [those] that come unto God by him, seeing he ever liveth to make intercession for them" (Hebrews 7:25 *KJV*).

God wants to be our only God, with no other "gods" before Him. He doesn't want us to have idols in our lives — things we cling to and trust in instead of looking to Him. He is a jealous God, who plainly states, "You shall have no other gods before Me" (Exodus 20:3). And He has a right to say that! He made us and then He bought us back through His plan of redemption, which was consummated with Jesus' own blood — a covenant He made with us and sealed it with His very life.

When we put *anything* else before God, it grieves the Holy Spirit in much the same way someone is grieved who discovers his or her spouse has committed adultery. The Holy Spirit has strong feelings about putting our love for other people or things ahead of our love for Him.

Overcoming Those 'Sinking Feelings'

During the course of my journey, God told me so sweetly, *Denise, you have to get your eyes on Me, not on Rick, to meet your needs.* We know from Psalm 18:2 that the Lord is our Rock, our Fortress, and our Deliverer. He is more than enough to supply whatever we need in life!

I used to spend many hours consumed with thoughts about what Rick did or didn't do for me, but God revealed to me that doing that was a form of idol worship. I hadn't realized that I had set up as an idol the expectation that my husband would be my source of security. But when I considered this honestly and sincerely, I saw that it was true.

Once I understood what God wanted — to bring change to my life — a season of my journey began that lasted several months. I fasted for the first two weeks, and I hardly took my nose out of the Word of God! Of course the enemy came to intimidate me. He pressed me with thoughts like, *You're not going to make it. Give up — the pain isn't worth it.*

My flesh also fought against me to stop. As I made the decision to let go of the bitterness and unforgiveness I'd allowed to lodge in me, in a sense, I felt lonelier than ever before. I was learning not to look to Rick to make me feel secure. But as I was learning to look to the Lord instead, my emotions would get the best of me at times. God was healing my emotions, but in order for Him to do that, I had to let go of all the pain, hurt feelings, and resentment that had been my toxic "friends" for so long.

You'd think you would feel instantly better the minute you made the decision to let go of your negative attitudes and receive healing in your emotions. But when the Holy Spirit begins to

> When the Holy Spirit begins to open your eyes and you see your brokenness in full color, it can be very painful. Yet it's a necessary part of the process.

open your eyes and you see your brokenness in full color, it can be very painful. Yet it's a necessary part of the process. Jesus was healing my emotions, but it was as if the healing came in waves. With every new wave of healing, something old had to be washed away, and it didn't always feel pleasant. In fact, it was very uncomfortable and scary because I was in uncharted waters — a place I'd never been before and was unfamiliar with. I was tempted at times to run back to my old, comfortable way of doing things that made me feel better in my flesh for the moment. But the truth was, those old ways made me miserable, and I'm sure they made Rick miserable at times too.

During those first several months of my journey to healing, Rick and I were doing some extensive traveling for the ministry. God had been doing a powerful work in me, but I had moments when I felt weak and crippled with fear as thoughts bombarded my mind that I would *never* see the breakthrough I desired. One night, I got up in the middle of the night and went into the bathroom of the hotel where we were staying. Behind the closed door of that bathroom, I felt like falling in a heap on the floor. I was practically breathless with fear, as if someone had punched me in the stomach. Clutching the sides of the sink, I held on tightly as if clinging for life to Jesus Himself, and I cried, "Lord! I don't understand everything You're doing, but *I will not let You go!*"

Through the tears, I continued, "I know You have an answer for me, and I am not going to stop seeking You! I will not move from this place of waiting on You because Your Word says, 'They that wait upon the Lord shall renew their strength'" (Isaiah 40:31). I quoted that verse and prayed that prayer many times on my journey, and each time I did, the Lord would always give me the strength to continue.

As I called out to Jesus, seeking His help day and night, He delivered me. On one particular occasion, the Lord spoke to me and said, *"Within 24 hours, you will wake up in a new world."* On the day He said that to me, for the first time in two years, I was able to come to an understanding of my problem and to articulate heartfelt forgiveness. After all that praying and waiting upon the Lord, my answer was finally being manifested. And just as the Lord had said, within 24 hours, I woke up in a new world. His awesome power of deliverance came to my heart, and deep within my soul, where no human could touch, it was as if Jesus reached in with an invisible hand and pulled out every root and trace of the bitterness and unforgiveness that had entangled me.

From that time on, I could finally put my complete trust in God as my security. The symptoms in my body — the numbness in my hands and feet — left immediately. The fear that had gripped my mind abruptly stopped. *I was free! No more torment.* It was indeed as if I had awakened in a brand-new world. God had touched me and delivered me, and I knew it! That was many years ago, yet thanksgiving and adoration still well up within my heart each time I think of how Jesus delivered me from that horrible prison of unforgiveness.

IT'S TIME TO DRAW NEAR

This type of deliverance usually doesn't come through someone laying hands on us, and it usually doesn't come overnight, although both are possible. We usually receive this kind of deliverance through a process of seeking and drawing near to the Lord Jesus Christ. The Word tells us that if we seek the Lord with all of our heart, we will find Him (Deuteronomy 4:29; Jeremiah 29:13), and when we draw near to God, He will draw near to us (James 4:8).

If you are bound in any way, you do not have to be stuck in the place where you are today. The Word of God can bring deliverance, growth, change, and a solid foundation of knowing who you are in Jesus. You can go to Him and let Him free you from the chains that have bound you — chains that may even have to do with someone else's choices.

Regardless of our circumstances, each of us is responsible for the condition of our own heart. Our deliverance has been completely paid for by the horrendous suffering and sacrificial death of our Lord Jesus Christ. But *we* must each make the decision to accept the freedom and healing that He has provided for us.

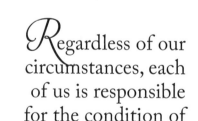

Regardless of our circumstances, each of us is responsible for the condition of our own heart.

The following is a testimony of one woman who experienced this freedom and victory in her own marriage through the power of forgiveness.

Rada

Marriage Restored Through Forgiveness

I married in my late 20s. I waited for my future husband, telling everyone that I was waiting for God to bring the best man for me. Everyone said I wouldn't find a husband because I worked a lot in the church, and that was not a place where I could find him. But I did find him. We met at church, and it was so perfect when we dated.

But everything changed after we married. We could not communicate the right way. Our feelings for each other became dull and dead. Our baby was born, and it became one more trial. We drifted apart more and more. Although I never was sick before, I began to be sick and even went to the hospital.

I understood I could not cope with my marriage problems on my own. I felt I was at a wall and could not go through. Going to these seminars was my last hope. I saw that when we gathered, it was a great support. I was grateful to be encouraged and prayed for. The speakers opened their hearts and served us through their testimonies. It is difficult to go through these things alone, but when we are together, we are strong.

After I finished the last marriage seminar, I was so deeply touched I could not move from my chair. I closed my eyes, and God showed me that I had to forgive my father! As a Christian, I understood that I need to honor my parents. I do love them, but I had no easy relationship with my father. I did not want to communicate with him. It was not in my heart. I had tried to do it, but it was just outward behavior. I knew the offenses I had against him were my weak place. I had tried to forgive him many times, but in a practical way, nothing came out of my trying. But as I sat there in that moment after that seminar, I realized God somehow had done something in my heart! At that moment, the process of forgiveness began. I understood that I could do it — with God's help, of course; I couldn't do it by my own efforts.

For sure, all of this reflected on my relationship with my husband. I hadn't realized it before, but I became offended by him and judged him the same way I had judged my father. God worked in me, and I was able to forgive my husband and to ask him to forgive me for the way I had treated him. And now it's easier for me to receive him as he is. Our situation has *changed*.

Before those seminars, I might not speak with my husband for several days, and I'd use other wrong ways to show my displeasure and disgust with him. When I wasn't silent, I would speak rudely to him and on purpose do exactly what he didn't like or didn't want me to do.

For example, if I left the house — and my husband would stay at home with our daughter — when I came back and saw that he was watching TV, I would act badly. Everywhere the house was a mess, and he would leave our daughter to her own resources. I would tell myself over and over that I would not act badly if my husband didn't handle things the way I wanted — or that I would at least keep silent. But because that unforgiveness had a hold on me, when I would see these things, I couldn't control myself. Those bitter feelings I had toward my father were dictating my actions toward my husband! Even without speaking, I would demonstrate my displeasure with bitter silence and harsh, abrupt movements.

Sometimes my husband tried to do good things for me, but because he was not able to do everything right, I became irritated at the wrong things instead of praising him for what he did right! I understood my actions were wrong, but I didn't know how to change them. I couldn't deal with it on my own.

My father lives in Siberia, and we would go to see him once a year. Before, it was very difficult for me to stay with him. I tried to do what I could for him, but very often I left being at odds with him. But after releasing my father at the seminar, the bitterness in my heart left and things really changed in our relationship. Even a word or tiny disapproval from him would bring pain in the past, and I would react negatively. But now, although he still does some criticizing, I hardly notice, and *it does not hurt me*. I react in peace because of the grace of God on my life.

Similar things have happened concerning my husband. Now when he does things I don't like, I don't consider that he purposely did them against me, and it's much easier to forgive him. Before I forgave my father, there was little peace and joy in my home. After I forgave him, I was able to see the good in my husband. I began to accept my husband as he is and enjoy him.

My husband loves to play football. And every day off from work that he had, he went to play football. I could have gone with him to watch him play — I know he dreamed of me going to watch him — but I was discouraged because the others on his team were unbelievers who used bad language. It was not nice to hear how they talked to each other. And for sure I did not want our daughter to hear it. I actually resented my husband playing football. I understood that football meant a lot to him, but I got angry thinking that he would not even miss it one time. Sometimes I demanded that he make a choice of either going to the football game or doing something for his family.

When I started accepting him as he was and stopped trying to change him, I told him that I would like to go to his games, but I was honest and told him why I hadn't gone in the past — because of the bad language. Can you imagine — my husband was so kind to me that he asked his team not to say bad words because of his wife and daughter! And they do it much less now. My daughter and I go to the football games now, and my husband is really happy!

When I went to that last marriage seminar, my husband was away on business. When he came back, I was different — more loving and a great deal more peaceful. God's grace had already started working. I saw that he had another attitude toward me — a good, changed attitude. He did things for me that he'd never done before. He asked me how he could help me and even took our daughter and me to the park. We spent the best time in my life there together!

Through these teachings, I began to see my mistakes, and I can honestly testify that hope and grace came into my heart I hadn't known before. As a result, there have been permanent changes in me and my marriage.

I often minister to women who have been abused and betrayed by someone close to them. Their lives have been broken and shattered — but, thank God, many of them find the help and hope that's available in Jesus!

The Lord can redeem any life in any situation. And we can be confident that whether our pain came as a result of verbal and mental abuse, physical abuse, betrayal, deception, loss, or even our own negative thoughts, the devil is the ultimate source of all distress. He tries to create chains of bondage to stop what God is doing in our lives. The enemy wants to break our hearts and destroy our families. But he ultimately cannot stop what God is doing, because greater is He who is in us than he that is in the world (1 John 4:4)!

Be encouraged that the power of the Holy Spirit in you is greater than *anything* that comes against you. You can be an overcomer, regardless of the decisions of others that have negatively affected your life.

THE UNCHANGING ROCK
WHEN EVERYTHING ELSE IS SHAKING

Sometimes we run into a rock-bottom place where it looks as if there's no way out. But when we feel that way, we need to realize that there is *another* Rock — the Solid Rock, Jesus Christ — upon whom we can depend. And He lives inside us through the Person of the Holy Spirit! When we come to the end of ourselves — when we feel there's no hope and nowhere to turn — if we're truly searching for Jesus, we can come to a place of assurance that He is there and will *remain* right there with us. And He is the Way, the Truth, and the Life (John 14:6). Not only is Jesus the only way to the Father — He's the way out of whatever problem or prison in life that we're facing, even if it's a problem or prison of our own making.

Jesus is the Rock of our salvation — immovable, unshakable, and unchanging. Second Corinthians 4:18 says, "…We do not look at the things which are seen, but at the things which are not seen. For the things which are seen are temporary, but the things which are not seen are eternal." So to find our power, we must ask ourselves, *What has my attention? What am I looking at?* Our power in the hard places is found only in our riveted gaze upon Him.

Studies have shown that when drivers place their attention on something else besides the road, their instincts are to steer the vehicle in the direction of the object that drew their attention. Of course, if drivers allowed themselves to be distracted long enough, they would probably cause a wreck.

Similarly, what we are constantly looking at and focusing on is where we will go in life. If we're not looking at the Word of God, our emotions will be very unsteady and unstable and will lead us astray, causing emotional havoc and wreckage in our lives.

Jesus is the Rock that will not move or change! Everything around us is temporal and will change, but Jesus and His Word are eternal. When we put our focus on Him, it holds us steady and firmly in place. He alone provides a place of security that's absolutely trustworthy, different than any place of safety and protection we've ever known. His gift of deliverance and freedom is deeper, wider, and higher than any pain or affliction that comes our way. Jesus is our High Tower, our Fortress, our Bridegroom, and our absolute security.

There's an old song I used to sing in the church where Rick and I met, and some of the lyrics are still my favorite: "When my heart is overwhelmed, lead me to the Rock that is higher than I. For Thou hast been a shelter for me and a strong tower from the enemy." I like this song from Psalm 61:3 because it speaks of our dependence on Jesus when we're feeling overwhelmed, undone, and powerless in our own strength to help ourselves.

That is exactly how we have to approach our journey to change. Our growth in Christ will only happen as we choose to respond to

Him and His Word with faith and humility, even when we feel we've been wronged or treated unfairly. I'm not saying it will always be easy, but it will be worth all we do to yield to His Spirit's work in us. We will enjoy the fruit of the effort we sowed to become free.

Many times we say that we want to grow in Christ — yet we also want a quick way out of every test, trial, and feeling of discomfort! When trouble comes to each one of us and presses hard against our faith, we are presented with an opportunity for *growth*, not a quick fix! As we stand our ground and witness His faithfulness to see us through and bless us, we are changed.

*O*ur growth in Christ will only happen as we choose to respond to Him and His Word with faith and humility, even when we feel we've been wronged or treated unfairly.

James 1:4 (*KJV*) says, "But let patience have her perfect work, that ye may be perfect and entire, wanting nothing." God works while you're trusting Him. And through His working, He causes you to walk in more patience and peace, regardless of your circumstances and the actions of others. *That's powerful!* Trouble may come, but as you hold fast to your trust in Jesus, you will come out on the other side of it sweeter, stronger, and steadier — and knowing Him better!

PREPARED FOR THE NEXT SEASON

My deliverance came at a crucial time, just before we moved from Riga, Latvia, to Moscow, Russia, where we live today. In order to be fully prepared to walk into that next phase of the vision God had given us — and to be able to go through other tests that were to come — I needed to have put behind me the years of insecurity, bitterness, and unforgiveness that would have hindered my future ministry. It wasn't a painless journey, but it was a victorious one. Jesus did in me what I could have never done in myself, and *no one else* could have done it in me. It was worth all the pain and struggle I went through to make the change from bitterness to forgiveness — and from being so needy of others to putting more of my trust in Jesus.

You may think you're failing just because you're going through something difficult. That is absolutely not the truth! The only way you can truly fail is if you quit! No matter how deep the pain or how great the trial, if you'll just dig in and remain at your place of determined faith — "...not moved away from the hope of the gospel..." (Colossians 1:23) — Jesus will reveal Himself to you. You may feel as if you're not going to make it, but I encourage you to persist in the faith. As you do, Christ will reveal *to* you and *in* you just how faithful He really is. In fact, He will do "...exceedingly abundantly above all that we ask or think, according to the power that works in us" (Ephesians 3:20)! He'll do it in your circumstances, but He'll especially do it in your heart. That power is working in you right now.

BEGIN YOUR OWN JOURNEY TO CHANGE

Anytime we're going through some trouble or test and we're crying out to God for His help, it's important to answer some difficult questions honestly and humbly as He begins to deal with our hearts. The Holy Spirit is right there to help us. His ministry is to reveal Jesus to us more fully and to help us become conformed more and more to His wonderful image. But the Spirit of God always works in our lives from the inside out, and He's looking for our cooperation — our willingness to yield to and obey Him. He is faithful to walk us through whatever it is we're facing, and He will make us into someone we could never have become on our own if we'll trust Him and let Him lead the way.

That was my experience. We all face unique circumstances and walk very different paths in life. But I'm sure you can relate on some level to my struggles and the pain I endured until I allowed Jesus to show me the way out of the emotional prison I lived in for so long.

And now I must ask you:

- If you're married, do you expect your husband to meet emotional needs that only Jesus can satisfy as you depend on Him and allow Him to heal all the broken places in your life?

- Are you hurt, nursing emotional wounds and feelings of resentment because your husband isn't fulfilling the role you thought he would in your life?

- Is your expectation of him based on the Word of God or on pain and old mindsets from the past?

- Can you recognize any idols that have set themselves up in your life to control you and hinder you from walking in God's highest and best?

Some of these idols could include *fear*, *jealousy*, *insecurity*, *resentment*, and *anger* — anything you run to and depend on instead of Jesus. I pray that you identify these things, whatever they may be, and give them to Him. Whatever familiar emotion you "run to" first that replaces your trust in the Lord, He wants to redirect you to run to *Him*. He gave His life for your complete freedom. You can trust Him; just ask Him for help.

Practical Steps To Begin Your Journey To Change

1. Stop blaming the other person.

   Judge not, that you be not judged. For with what judgment you judge, you will be judged; and with the measure you use, it will be measured back to you. And why do you look at the speck in your brother's eye, but do not consider the plank in your own eye? Or how can you say to your brother, 'Let me remove the speck from your eye'; and look, a plank is in your own eye? Hypocrite! First remove the plank from your own eye, and then you will see clearly to remove the speck from your brother's eye.

   Matthew 7:1-5

2. Be willing to ask God about your wrong choices. Allow Him to show you where you missed it or what you need to do so that, together, you can work on healing and rebuilding the broken-down places in your emotions that misguided you to begin with.

3. Make a change in your schedule *and put God in it*! If you don't already do so, read the Bible when you get up every day and when you go to bed. Read, study, and meditate on the Word of God at every opportunity, every day (Joshua 1:8).

   Give attention to my words; incline your ear to my sayings. Do not let them depart from your eyes; keep them in the midst of your heart; for they are life to those who find them, and health to all their flesh. Keep your heart with all diligence, for out of it spring the issues of life.

   Proverbs 4:20-23

4. Make a time during your day just to be quiet in His presence, with no interruptions or distractions. The Holy Spirit lives in

you. He wants to speak to your heart so you can hear Him and He can quiet the waters of your soul.

Be still, and know that I am God; I will be exalted among the nations, I will be exalted in the earth!

Psalm 46:10

Chapter Two

DRIPPING FAUCET
OR RUNNING SEWAGE?

The Bible tells us that the husband is to love the wife and the wife is to respect the husband: "Nevertheless let each one of you in particular so love his own wife as himself, and let the wife see that she respects her husband" (Ephesians 5:33). In the following pages, I share from the Word of God and from my experience what it means to respect your husband. But first, what does *dis*respect look like?

One way we show disrespect to our husband is by trying to control him. Feeling in control can give us a sense of security and power. But in a relationship, trying to control another person to gain the security we desperately desire creates the opposite effect. The more we try to control our husband, the more he wants to escape from us to find peace.

Proverbs 19:13 says, "…The contentions of a wife are a continual dripping." Have you ever had a dripping faucet — or a leak somewhere in your house — that you couldn't stop? Most people would react to that situation the same way: "That is so annoying! Please shut that water *off*!"

Similarly, it really hits home to realize that God likens that kind of continual dripping to *us* if we complain or are ungrateful, critical, faultfinding, or argumentative toward our husband. To our husband, we're like a dripping faucet that he just wants to shut off!

In one Russian translation, Proverbs 19:13 is even stronger. It says that a complaining, griping, faultfinding, argumentative woman is like *running sewage*! Oh, that *really* hits home!

Let's think about sewage for a moment. It's not a pleasant subject, but it will help you understand this aspect of disrespect more clearly. No one likes to be around sewage. No one says, "Let's go have a picnic next to the sewage plant." Why not? Sewage has a bad odor. It carries toxins and poisons. If you were to get sewage on your clothes, it would be hard to get out and would probably leave a stain. Sewage can have a long-lasting negative effect. If you've ever been around sewage, you certainly don't look back on that experience with fond memories!

In much the same way that sewage can affect us, the dangerous habit of criticizing, judging, or complaining to our husband can bring a foul odor into our marriage that's long-lasting and hard to get rid of. When I first read Proverbs 19:13, I was horrified that "sweet little me" could have something as ugly, stinky, and toxin-filled as sewage flowing out of my character. I began asking God how it could be that His beautiful creation, *woman* — His specially crafted one — could be capable of such sickening and repulsive behavior.

Of course, we know that our fleshly nature must be placed in submission to our recreated spirit after the new birth. That's why the apostle Paul told us in Romans 12:2, "...Do not be conformed to this world, but be transformed by the renewing of your mind, that you may prove what is that good and acceptable and perfect will of God." Jesus said, "Apart from Me, you can do nothing"

(John 15:5 *NIV*). Without the Word of God in our lives, we will not be able to "put on the new man" and live out of our born-again spirit. Instead, we'll be subject to our old ways of thinking and acting — right back at that stinky sewage plant!

JESUS CAN CHANGE
UNHEALTHY GENERATIONAL PATTERNS!

Have you ever been tempted to try to control your husband and nag him like a continually leaky faucet — or running sewage? Is it possible you do this in your marriage because it's what you saw your mother do? If so, did you ever ask yourself what your mother's nagging and complaining ever accomplished? Did your father change? Was their communication sweet? Did he love and adore her and feel grateful toward his bride for her attempts to change and control him?

We've identified the problem of trying to control others. It's a form of disrespect, and it is not only annoying, it also stinks like sewage! Now what is the answer? We know where our help comes from, and the good news is that *we can change*. We do not have to repeat the mistakes of the past — even mistakes from past generations.

Now, I'm not criticizing mothers of past generations. If our precious mothers made mistakes, we can learn from them and go on with the Lord. Most of the time, they did what they did simply because they didn't know how to deal with things any other way.

Perhaps your grandmother set the course for the behavior of your mother. Your mom followed *her* mom's example, and now here you are at a crossroad: You can follow the negative aspects of your mom's example and continue that unhealthy course from the past, or you can take Jesus by the hand and let Him show you the better way.

Perhaps your mother truly adored your father and kept her complaints confined to her prayer closet. Then follow her example — she left you a good one! Enjoy the fruit of her works and thank God *and your mother* that the way to peace and prosperity in your marriage was paved for you from the past.

THE UGLY TRUTH ABOUT OUR NEED TO CONTROL

Trying to control our spouse is one example of idolatry — of trying to make our flesh feel better temporarily instead of dealing with the issues of our soul through our faith and trust in Christ.

Trying to control our spouse is one example of idolatry — of trying to make our flesh feel better temporarily instead of dealing with the issues of our soul through our faith and trust in Christ. When we try to control someone else, we're depending on something — *or someone* — other than the Lord to make us feel better for the moment. But even if it "works" and we feel better temporarily, what have we really gained? Nothing at all. In fact, we are slowly destroying that precious relationship God has given us.

Trying to control our husband breaks down the intimacy the Lord intended for us to enjoy together within the marriage relationship. Yet as women, we tend to want to control. It is a *big* temptation for us, and the hidden reason behind it is *fear*. *What will happen if I let my husband take the lead?*

The dynamic of wives trying to control their husbands began as a result of the Fall in the Garden of Eden. Genesis 3:16 (*NLT*) states: "Then he [God] said to the woman, 'I will sharpen the pain of your pregnancy, and in pain you will give birth. And you will desire to control your husband, but he will rule over you.'"

A wife will desire to control her husband, but he will rule over her. This tension is often the source of great problems in marriage.

MARRIAGE IN REDEMPTION

I want to stop here for a moment and talk about one of the greatest truths known pertaining to the marriage relationship — and, for our purposes, one of the greatest truths to help us as wives. Jesus became a curse for us so that on the Cross, He could take this terrible curse that seems to hang over all marriages: *that the wife wants to control her husband, yet he is going to rule over her.*

The curse we're confronted with is our temptation to control our husband. But we need to realize that this temptation is simply fear trying to push us around. We're afraid we won't get what we want. We also need to realize the great truth that Jesus has redeemed us from this curse by becoming a curse for us. This is the message of Galatians 3:13,14: "Christ has redeemed us from the curse of the law, having become a curse for us (for it is written, 'Cursed is everyone who hangs on a tree')."

So what does it mean that this curse is broken? How was it broken? What does Jesus' sacrificial death have to do with your marriage?

Everything. Think for a moment about the temptation every married woman faces to try to control — teach, correct, or change — her husband. Think about the horrible damage that her actions bring to her marriage if she yields to that temptation and her attitudes and actions are left unchecked.

As a wife, you have probably thought to yourself, *I really don't want to correct my husband. I know he hates it when I do that!* But then out of your mouth, faster than you can stop it, comes a slight hint of a teaching — or an outright correction with the boldness of a lion! After all, you *have* to teach him because you just know he'll never make it without your input to improve him!

Does this sound familiar?

When I began to meditate on Galatians 3:13, I thought, *Wait a minute. Jesus was cursed in my place. He took this curse for me. Just as He was cursed so I could experience salvation for my spirit, healing for my body, and peace and soundness for my mind — He also took away this curse of my desire to control my husband!* I had received all those other marvelous benefits of the Cross — salvation, healing, and peace — so why should I live under the curse of wanting to teach, correct, and change my husband? Why should I have to carry a chain of bondage around my neck by fostering this attitude of complaining, criticizing, and faultfinding toward my husband?

The truth is, we *don't* have to carry this bondage! Jesus bore this curse and broke this chain. For unbelievers — those who are outside of Christ — that curse is working a great, negative effect in their marriages. In the United States, the divorce rate has been estimated to be as high as 50 percent. In Russia, it's even higher than that. In years past, the rate of divorce has been as high as 63 percent. More recent statistics reveal that 53 percent of marriages in 2012 failed in the nation of Russia. At that rate, it is a sobering thought that when women in Russia make their commitment to marriage, more than 5 out of 10 of them, statistically speaking, will experience divorce![1]

But for those marriages in which the husband and wife are Christians and attend church together, the rate of divorce is significantly decreased to 42 percent.[2] In other words, a full 58 percent of marriages do *not* end in divorce! Research also shows that Americans who attend religious services several times per month were about 35 percent less likely to divorce than those with no religious affiliation![3]

Why such a difference in these statistics? Unbelievers are forced to struggle in their marriages because of the curse. But couples who believe God together and actively trust Him to help and to lead and guide them are not operating under the curse, but under His blessing.

What about the other part of the curse we read about in Genesis 3:16 — that a woman's husband will rule over her? Jesus redeemed husbands and wives from that part of the curse too! That curse is broken over the wife, so now, instead of being imprisoned by an inner drive to control her husband, she desires to be Spirit-controlled and conformed to the image of Christ. She wants to honor, respect, and obey her husband.

Although the husband has been ordained and commissioned by God to be the head of his house, there's no place for the heavy hand of control in a marriage by either the husband *or* the wife. Jesus never intended for marriage to be a battle of the wills, but rather a beautiful, peaceful, and godly relationship in which the wife willingly respects and submits to her husband — and the husband willingly loves and cherishes his wife (*see* Ephesians 5:33). But it's still true that when all the wife wants is to honor, respect, and obey her husband, she makes it easy for her husband to feel no need to demand control over her.

The curse that results from violating God's law has been broken over our lives. We must praise Jesus and glorify Him for the horrendous suffering He endured on the Cross. Through His suffering, He purchased our freedom from the curse. And among the many benefits bestowed on us by Jesus' great gift of redemption is this one: *The wife is free from the need to control her husband, and the husband is free from the need to rule over his wife.*

LET THE HOLY SPIRIT HAVE CONTROL

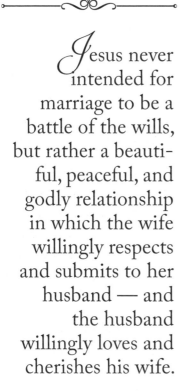

Jesus never intended for marriage to be a battle of the wills, but rather a beautiful, peaceful, and godly relationship in which the wife willingly respects and submits to her husband — and the husband willingly loves and cherishes his wife.

When we try to teach and control our husband, we're actually trying to take on the role of the Holy Spirit. But it's possible to relinquish that fleshly desire as we draw on the power of the Holy Spirit and allow *Him* to bring about the necessary change in us.

A wife's desire to control may rear its head in the area of financial budgeting and spending, child-raising, running a household, etc. I'll give you one example of a way I tried to control Rick in the earliest days of our marriage. After we were married, I soon discovered that our diets were very different from one another. I was raised to eat a certain way, and he was raised to eat an entirely different way. I wanted to convert him to my style of eating, which I thought would be much better for him! So I prepared our meals a certain way and then explained to Rick, "It's for your own good that I do this."

Certainly, it's good to want the very best for someone you love. And if I had only said that once, it would have been okay. But I said it repeatedly — *over and over and over again*!

I'm not at all saying that in marriage, you should never tell your husband when something bothers you. But I *am* saying that you should say it in a rational manner, not with incessant nagging, and then *drop it*. Leave it with him to process what you said and decide what to do with it.

Do you know what the Holy Spirit said to me years ago about Rick's diet? He said, "If he eats this way all his life, it's none of your business"!

It's a deception for us as women to think we're going to change something in our husband. We can't change him! Let me say that to you one more time: We'll never be able to change anything in our husband. Change is up to the Holy Spirit; change is *His* job.

Tensions arise and problems come when we start believing that we're commissioned and appointed to change our husband. This wrong belief causes so much conflict. Our husband may hear us the first time — and maybe even the second time. But by the *third, fourth, tenth, thirtieth, and forty-fifth time*, we sound to him like a dripping faucet. Not only is he unable to hear us because of our nagging, but he also wants to just shut off the noise!

ROOTS OF INSECURITY HINDER
OUR ABILITY TO BEAR GOOD FRUIT

In my case, the Holy Spirit revealed to me that much of my desire to control my husband, as well as gain security from him, was rooted in the insecurity I felt relating to my father as I was growing up. My dad was really precious and I loved him. Now he's in Heaven and is made perfect, but before that, he constantly felt a great deal of pressure as a salesman to sell enough product to support his family (he sold Electrolux® vacuum cleaners for 58 years). So my father was always very serious.

My father lived through the Great Depression as a young person, and that experience contributed to his very serious attitude and personality. In fact, I think his experience affected him with *unusual* pressure and fear. As a young boy, he also suffered the loss of two family homes that burned to the ground!

The enemy worked really hard to steal my dad's joy. Even though he was born again, I rarely saw my dad smile — and even more rarely did I see him laugh. He was unable to show emotions to communicate how much he treasured his little girl. Although I know now that he did the best he could, at the time, I was left with a longing for the kind of attention and affection that lets a daughter know she's prized and cherished by her father. That same longing remained with me into adulthood, and I assumed I would receive from my husband all those feelings I missed growing up. What an unreasonable pressure and expectation to place on Rick and our marriage.

Now I understand so much more about my father's struggles. But as a child, I understood only the absence of his approval and affirmation. It was on my journey of growth and change as a married woman that I began to understand, with the Holy Spirit's help, why I wanted so badly for Rick to fill up this longing in my soul.

THERE'S A MAN ON THE ROOF!

Proverbs 21:9 says, "Better to dwell in a corner of a housetop, than in a house shared with a contentious woman." When I first read this verse as a newly married woman, I thought to myself, *Could I be a contentious woman?* I already understood some of the issues I was dealing with from my childhood insecurities, but as I studied this verse, I also discovered that at times I was indeed contentious — critical, faultfinding, and argumentative! There were times when that description actually fit me very well.

That was a very painful discovery at first. But I made the choice *not* to be contentious. With the Holy Spirit's help, I made the necessary changes in my heart, and it has made all the difference in my marriage. I'm not saying that I'm perfect, but I am saying that I have greatly improved! Now I can look back without experiencing those painful feelings, and I can even joke about where I was before the Lord helped me grow in that area of my life. I jokingly say, "Picture me in the house back then. The phone rings, and I answer it. The person on the other line says, 'May I speak to Rick?' and I say, 'I'm sorry, you'll have to wait a moment. He's on the roof'!"

There were probably times in our marriage back then when Rick wished he could have been on the roof alone rather than in the house with me. It might have been "safer" for him in the snow and subzero temperatures outside than to be exposed to the emotional fallout inside. *Imagine that* — safer for my husband on the roof in freezing temperatures than in the house with me!

How about *your* husband? Is he "on the roof," hiding from you?

It sounds somewhat comical that the Lord said in His Word, "Better to dwell in a corner of a housetop, than in a house shared with a contentious woman." It may sound humorous, but the living reality of that principle is not funny at all. God is trying to give wives serious guidance about how dangerous our immature or underdeveloped character can be. It has the potential to chase our husband out of the house — and it can certainly cause him to close off part of his heart to us.

CONTINUING THE JOURNEY TO CHANGE

Do you see that you have a desire to control your husband out of insecurity or a fear of loss of security? This is your opportunity to recognize issues and motives that may have been hidden from you until now. If you see yourself in this chapter, I encourage you to allow the Holy Spirit to flood you with His love and grace. He will fill that void inside you and help you overcome every sense of insecurity.

Practical Suggestions
for 'Unlearning' the Habit of Disrespect

1. Buy duct tape. Apply to mouth. (Just kidding!)

    The Bible says we're to put a guard over our mouth, so make it your practice to think before speaking. Ask yourself, *Does Jesus want me to say this? Will what I want to say be constructive or destructive?* It is always appropriate to pray before you speak! Proverbs 16:23 says that a wise man's heart guides his mouth.

    He who guards his mouth preserves his life, but he who opens wide his lips shall have destruction.

    Proverbs 13:3

2. Make a choice this week to purposely say seven uplifting and encouraging things to your husband — one heartfelt compliment or gesture of kindness for each day of the week!

3. Memorize Proverbs 3:3-6. Sometimes it helps to write down the verses that you want to memorize.

    Let not mercy and truth forsake you; bind them around your neck, write them on the tablet of your heart, and so find favor and high esteem in the sight of God and man. Trust in the Lord with all your heart, and lean not on your own understanding; in all your ways acknowledge Him, and He shall direct your paths.

    Proverbs 3:3-6

4. Tell a friend about this chapter, "Dripping Faucet or Running Sewage?" Sharing with others what you're learning helps it become more real to you — and it may be just what they need to hear!

Chapter Three

'HOW CAN I RESPECT HIM? LET ME COUNT THE WAYS'

In Chapter Two, we read Ephesians 5:33, which says, "Nevertheless let each one of you in particular so love his own wife as himself, and let the wife see that she respects her husband." We saw from this verse that as a wife, our biggest need is to be *loved*. And for our husband, his biggest need is to be *respected*.

There is so much meaning in this word "respect," and many marriages fail because we don't have the true knowledge of its meaning. Hosea 4:6 tells us, "My people are destroyed for lack of knowledge...." And we know from John 8:32 that truth from the Lord brings us freedom: "And you shall know the truth, and the truth shall make you free."

GET KNOWLEDGE, AND DRAW ON WISDOM

A wife has a great deal of power in her home. Proverbs 14:1 tells us that through wisdom, she builds her house, but through foolishness, she can pull it down. As a wife gains knowledge about the different ways she can follow after God's wisdom and show respect to her husband, she will build him up and also help build their lives together into something wonderful.

By nature, women are nurturers. If you're a mother, you know what you'll give up for your children. You'll give up sleep. You'll give up food. You'll buy something for them to wear even if it means not getting something you need for yourself. You'll instinctively hone in on your children's needs, and when they're hurting — whether it's physically or emotionally — you'll skillfully bind up their wounds.

But just as women are nurturers by nature with their children, it seems the opposite is true when it comes to respecting their husband. *That* does not come naturally!

Respect for our husband is something beautiful that God develops in us as a wife by changing us through the power of the Holy Spirit. As we give our attention to the Word of God and determine to live a surrendered, obedient life unto the Lord, little by little we can become more and more respectful and fulfill one of the greatest needs of our husband.

The book of Proverbs provides light for the path of the wife who wants to build her home rather than tear it down with wrong attitudes and words.

> **The fear of the Lord is the beginning of wisdom, and the knowledge of the Holy One is understanding.**
>
> **Proverbs 9:10**

> **By humility and the fear of the Lord are riches and honor and life.**
>
> **Proverbs 22:4**

Wise women receive correction through the Word of God and are open to allowing themselves to be changed. They're humble and willing to change when presented with the knowledge of the truth.

Another characteristic of wise women is the ability to control their emotions. Foolish women can tear down what they're building with just a few angry words.

If we have to be the one who wins every argument, we're not operating in the wisdom of God. I'll say it a different way: If we think we have to be right all the time, we're being foolish. No one is right all the time. We all have room for improvement.

Before you allow the condemnation of the enemy to come in, stop right now and be encouraged: If you're reading this book in search of answers, you are a wise woman! You're seeking godly understanding and instruction, and that shows wisdom. On the other hand, a foolish woman might say, "The solution to our marriage problems is that my husband needs to change and appreciate who I am. I don't need to learn anything about how to change and improve myself. *He's* the one who needs to read a book on how to love his wife!"

Wisdom Can Be Taught

In Titus 2:3-5, God commands the older women who have grown in wisdom to teach the younger women in the church. If these younger women are not taught according to the Word, they will probably do exactly what they saw their own mothers do. Of course, for those with mothers who correctly demonstrated how to love their husbands and children, that's a good thing. But if they didn't have good examples, they will still likely imitate their mothers — who probably imitated *their* mothers. As a result, this younger generation of women will perpetuate ways of doing things that will not lead to success in their homes.

I've heard some women say, "I couldn't stand the way my mother treated my dad — I'll never be like her!" But the truth is, a woman who had that kind of experience will be *exactly* like her mother if she harbors unforgiveness in her heart toward her mother.

Forgiveness sets us free and opens us up to what God wants to give us and what He wants to do in our lives. But harboring unforgiveness is like being bound by invisible chains. It shackles us to our bad behavior.

We chain ourselves to a spiritual and emotional prison if we refuse to forgive. I wrote in my book *The Gift of Forgiveness*: "Unforgiveness opens a huge door to the devil to come and bring great sorrow to our lives.... Unforgiveness that isn't dealt with sinks deep down inside a person and becomes a root of bitterness.... Like a malignant tree, its evil roots spread out and dig their way deeper and deeper into a person's soul...[and] keeps on producing its terrible harvest of fear, judgmental attitudes, sickness, lack of peace, anger, envy, and jealousy."[1]

> *Harboring unforgiveness is like being bound by invisible chains. It shackles us to our bad behavior.*

But here's the good news: If we choose to forgive, we release the supernatural, delivering power of God into our own lives and the lives of others!

If your mother treated your father with disrespect and provided you with a wrong example, it's time to forgive her if you haven't already done so. The simple decision to forgive is part of the great wisdom with which you will build and *continue to build* your happy home.

There will be plenty of opportunities to forgive others along life's journey — and to *be forgiven by* others. Ephesians 4:32 says, "And be kind to one another, tenderhearted, forgiving one another, even as God in Christ forgave you." God has forgiven you, and I'm sure you don't want anything pulling you back into your own past. You want freshness in your soul, and that's what forgiveness brings. God in Christ has forgiven you, so if you need to forgive your mother, your father, or your husband — or someone else who has hurt you — simply acknowledge your need before God. Humbly and genuinely seek His presence and His power to forgive that person. The freedom you'll experience as you release that burden of unforgiveness will transform you and affect *all* of your relationships.

RESPECT HIM IN HIS ROLE AS LEADER

There are three primary aspects of respecting our husband: 1) humbling ourselves and being willing to see our own faults (that's a big one); 2) accepting him just as he is (that's another big one); and 3) appreciating and admiring him as leader of the home (that's a *huge* aspect of showing respect).

I'll begin with the last one — appreciating and admiring our husband in his role as leader. Seeing your husband in his role as leader of the home and as provider — and allowing him to function in that role — is a vital and integral part of showing him your respect.

God has established an order for the home: "But I would have you know, that the head of every man is Christ; and the head of the woman is the man; and the head of Christ is God" (1 Corinthians 11:3 *KJV*). The order that God recognizes is *God the Father*, *Christ the Head of the Church*; *husband*; *wife*. One reason we can cause all kinds of problems for our marriage when we try to control or rule over our husband is that it creates chaos where God intended there to be order. As we saw in Genesis 3:16, we will desire to control our husband, but he will rule over us. That's the curse — but Jesus took that curse upon Himself so we could live free from it through the power of His blood.

When we try to take charge over our husband, we are getting things out of order. The order then becomes God, Christ, *wife*, husband. That plan will not work. God is not going to bless that plan because His order is God, Christ, *husband*, wife.

Then what is our part? Our place is to respect and cherish our husband — *not* to try to rule over him.

God did not design the husband to be a dictator, but to be the head of his home and a strong leader. He speaks as final authority where decisions are to be made that will affect the family and the general direction of the home. He is an overseer. Of course, in the case of single-parent families in which the mom is raising her children alone, *she* becomes the head of the home under Christ.

In the home of a married couple, there's only one head in the family, and it isn't the wife. It's the husband. It's important to keep in mind that your husband was appointed by God to this position as leader in the home. It wasn't his idea, but God's. Just as Jesus submitted to the plan of God and kept the divine order of the Father first and the Son second, we're taught to follow His example and keep God's plan of order as well.

So instead of trying to reverse the order between husband and wife, we should honor our husband in his position as leader and head of the home. If our husband isn't a Christian, he is still the head of the home.

I want to encourage you that God is our Father, and He only wants the best for His daughters. He will perfect that which concerns us and give us what's best through the order of the husband as the head of the home. He set up that plan of order, so He can certainly work through it to give us His best!

It's good for single women to learn this principle as well. The following testimony beautifully illustrates this truth.

Nadeshda

'I Put This Into Practice as a Single Woman'

I'm not married, but decided to attend these seminars to help me prepare to be a "Cinderella" bride and wife one day. I am a Christian, but my father is a devout follower of another faith. Ever since I became a Christian, our relationship has been strained. So I decided to put the truths I was learning at the marriage seminars to work at home in my relationship with my father.

My father and I argued a lot, and at first it was difficult for me to walk in a humble spirit of gentleness, respect, and honor. But I did it. Gradually he began to notice a change in me. In the past, I would argue belligerently when he said something that went against my faith and my values. But I started giving a "soft answer" to my father — the kind of answer that turns away wrath (Proverbs 15:1). It didn't work immediately, but I stayed with it, and finally my father began to respond peacefully and graciously to the "new" me.

My father didn't like the fact that I was going to the church I attended. I just began to humble myself before him and simply say to him, "Dad, I respect you. I understand your point of view." And something began to happen. Our relationship became less and less strained, and joy even returned to the relationship. He stopped complaining about my faith and about my church. And in a culture where marriages are sometimes arranged, my father actually said to me, "I don't believe like you do. But it would be okay with me if you met and married one of those gentlemen in the church you attend"!

This turnaround in my father's behavior was nothing short of miraculous! And I know it was because I stopped arguing and started respecting. The best part is that I learned some very precious, invaluable truths that will help me when I marry and begin a family of my own.

LET HIM HAVE THE REINS

When you honor your husband, whether he's saved or not saved, you're honoring the Lord. You're honoring His plan and design, and in doing that, you keep yourself under an "umbrella" of protection as you submit to your husband's leadership. Of course, if your husband wants you to do something that goes against God's Word — something that's immoral or illegal — you are not required to obey that. You can obey Christ as your Head in that case. But it's important not to look for excuses for rejecting your husband's leadership. Even if you don't agree with his decisions, that place of submission to him is a very powerful place to be. So I encourage you to turn control of your home over to your husband, where it belongs. Let him have the reins of the family and watch God work His will in your marriage and your home.

Respecting your husband as a leader includes being adaptable, and that means staying flexible where his likes and dislikes are concerned. For example, your husband may want a certain kind of car, sofa, or food, and you might be tempted to jump in and say something like, "No, you're not going to have that!" But acting that way dishonors your husband's leadership, and it's out of order. His tastes in furniture or food are not moral issues, so it would be better to say, "Okay, Honey, let's do that." Even if you don't agree, being adaptable and submissive will bring so much peace and calm to your home. It will certainly save you an argument over something that isn't really that important.

The following statement sounds elementary, like basic common sense, but it's still necessary to say: Simply being *sweet* can go a long, long way in securing peace in your home!

A wife can be tempted to take the reins and start telling her husband what he is and isn't going to do. *But there's no blessing in doing that!* We can't go against God's Word and His order and expect Him to bless us. On the other hand, we can't go wrong trusting Him. If we'll obey Him and His Word, a blessing will come to us. It may look very scary as we step out to obey Him when every fiber of our being is crying, *I don't like this!* But God will be with us, and what's better or greater than that? The Lord will protect us because we're trusting Him as we're honoring our husband.

The world will not tell you this, but *this* is the truth we need to build our lives on. When we build wisely — with the truth of God's Word — we'll enjoy homes and families that can't be torn down by the foolishness of the world.

A MATTER OF ORDER

Any organization has to have a head. This is a matter of order. If there's no head, there's no order. The same is certainly true of the "organization" of home and family. By nature and temperament, a man is a leader. But more than that, honoring the man as leader in his home is a matter of following God's plan. When we follow God's pattern and plan, things simply go better for us.

I'm in awe when I think about how perfectly God does everything. After all, He made the universe and the heavens, and they are still doing very well! God also created the institution of marriage. He made it, and He knows how to make it work!

It's a husband's natural bent to be the leader. And he will usually lead — *if* his wife allows him to lead. But when a wife uses her power in a wrong way, he could shrink back and allow her to have the reins of their marriage. If this happens, confusion and chaos will be the result because that family is out of God's divine order and plan.

If that describes you, things might look a little scary for a while as you allow your husband to take the lead in your home. But if you'll trust God, you will produce good fruit.

I want to add a note here. If you are a strong woman and leader, it's wonderful that God gave you that kind of strength and character. It's a gift, but according to the Scripture, your husband is still the head of your home. You may have to work harder at keeping yourself in check than others, but don't use your leadership skills to control or disrespect your husband.

Sometimes a man will lead by strong feelings and not by reason. You may think, *What he's doing doesn't make any sense! I just don't agree!* Perhaps you don't understand your husband's decision, or you may have your own opinion about the way things should go — and that's okay. But realize that he is probably doing something a certain way because he feels very strongly about it. So rather than try to rule over him and take control, determine to honor God's order and be submissive to your husband's leadership. As you do, you will be able to confidently and respectfully say, "I'll go with what you're feeling."

When I talk about submitting to your husband's leadership in the home, I'm not saying that you will always agree with every decision he makes — or that you'll always *want* to submit. But choosing to submit to your husband's leadership and to God's divine order is for your own benefit and good. It will keep you under the umbrella of divine protection, and God will bless you for your humility and obedience.

WHO'S FOLLOWING WHOM?
(WHY PRINCE CHARMING ISN'T ATTRACTED TO SUPERWOMAN)

Perhaps you're a wife who is holding tightly to the reins in your marriage, trying to do everything in your home your own way. I had to work on this because when Rick was away ministering during the early years of our marriage, I was in charge of the home — but when he came back, I had to consciously switch gears and let *him* be in charge.

Today I'm over the women's ministry in our church, and at times I'll realize that I've started making plans without even telling Rick. God has made women strong and capable. But we have to train ourselves not to take over our husband's leadership role, even if we're in charge of something. We need to train ourselves to articulate our plans courteously. For example, instead of giving him orders about something that needs to be done, we could say, "Sweetheart, if it's okay with you, this is something I'd like to do." Projecting a supportive and respectful attitude honors his leadership role.

THE EMPTINESS OF HAVING IT YOUR WAY

Have you ever pressured your husband about something, nagging him until he gave up resisting? After you repeatedly nagged and pressured him, he finally said, "Go ahead — have it your way."

I confess that I have done this too! I remember one incident years ago when we lived in the United States. I'd seen a certain dress in a store that I really wanted. Rick saw it and said, "Denise, we can't get that right now." I thought, *Well, okay, maybe it will go on sale.*

A couple of weeks later, we were in the area of town where that store was located. I said, "Rick, can we just drive by the store? I'll run in to see if that dress is on sale."

He reluctantly said, "Okay." We drove to the store, but the dress still wasn't on sale.

I kept on with the desire for that dress, and I questioned and questioned Rick about it until, really, it became a form of arguing and rebellion. I was, in reality, dishonoring my husband. And I was manipulating him. But I wasn't consciously thinking like that — I just wanted the dress and wouldn't stop thinking and talking about it.

Finally, after my much nagging, Rick bought me the dress. I didn't apologize for all the commotion I'd caused over it. I only thought, *Good! I got the dress!* I finally had the dress I'd pushed for. But after I wore it once, I decided I didn't really like it — and I ended up giving it away!

I had gotten my way through manipulation. I should have simply submitted to Rick, respecting his decision not to buy the dress at the time I wanted it. There would have been a blessing for me in doing that, but I forfeited that blessing through my impatience. Instead, I pushed and pushed and finally got my way, but I did it at the cost of dishonoring Rick as leader. And after all that pushing and manipulating, I ended up not even wanting what I'd fought so hard to obtain!

Another thing wives sometimes do that dishonors their husbands is doubting their ability to lead by asking questions, questions, and more questions! For example, a wife may ask her husband to do something and then very shortly afterward ask him:

- "Did you do it?"

- "Are you sure you did it?"

- "Did you do it the way I asked you to do it?"

- "Did you finish it?"

- "Are you sure?"

- "Can I see it?"

A wife may be asking those questions innocently because she values excellence, but her questions show mistrust. She's dishonoring her husband by questioning his abilities and even his character, and she's disrespecting his leadership.

We wouldn't want someone to treat us that way. If someone asked us to do something, and we agreed to do it, we wouldn't want that person asking us 15 questions about where we're at on the project, how we're doing on the project, and so forth. We would feel mistrusted, and we wouldn't like it. Likewise, if we do that to our husband, it breaks down the mutual trust that's so important in a marriage.

Giving unwanted advice to your husband also creates the impression that you don't think he's providing leadership that can be trusted. If your husband wants to know what you think, that's great. You should tell him. But if you habitually give him unsolicited advice, that's like telling him you don't think *he's* smart enough for the job, but *you* are!

Also, if you cut your husband off in conversation and break in with your ideas and opinions without waiting to hear his point of view, you might come across like "Superwoman" with all the solutions to his problems and challenges. Your husband may say to himself, *Why should I even speak? She's got this handled and doesn't need my input.* As a result, you can miss the help you need from your Prince Charming because you're so intent on swooping into the situation like Superwoman with the attitude, "Never fear — *I* am here!"

CALLING HIM 'LEADER'

How should a wife respond when she believes her husband is making a wrong decision? First Peter 3:4-6 (*AMP*) gives us an answer: "...Let it [your adornment] be the hidden person of the heart, with the incorruptible beauty of a gentle and quiet spirit, which is very precious in the sight of God. For in this manner, in former times, the holy women who trusted in God also adorned themselves, being submissive to their own husbands, as Sarah obeyed Abraham, calling him lord, whose daughters you are if you do good and are not afraid with any terror."

There were times when Abraham had the wrong idea about how to handle things, yet Sarah submitted to her husband's leadership and authority, and God honored her. We should respond to our own husbands in a similar way.

Genesis 12:11-20 gives the account of Abraham (then *Abram*) telling Pharaoh that Sarah (then *Sarai*) was his sister. Sarah was so beautiful that Abraham was afraid Pharaoh would take her and have him killed. So he told Egypt's leader that she was his sister, and Pharaoh took Sarah into his house. Sarah didn't argue with Abraham; she submitted to the situation he had created by lying, and God protected her. Great plagues came upon Pharaoh's house because of Sarah, and Pharaoh said to Abraham, "...'What is this you have done to me? Why did you not tell me that she was your wife?'" (v. 18). Pharaoh returned her safely to Abraham and sent them both away.

Now, I'm not at all condoning lying. The Word of God is very clear on that subject. The point I'm making is that when we honor our husband because we want to please God, God sees our heart toward *Him*, and He blesses our humility and our willingness to comply rather than argue and fight.

I had an opportunity years ago to criticize and question Rick's leadership when I felt a decision he was making for us wasn't right. Rick paid a man, who said he was an architect and a contractor, to build a house for us in Latvia. Naturally speaking, there was no reason to distrust this man because his family members had been instrumental in the success of our early ministry in the former Soviet Union. They also played a huge part in the opening of the first-ever Bible school in this part of the world. In addition to that, this family had been a great influence in the effectiveness of a large crusade we held in which approximately 32,000 people attended. We were the first ministry to have a Christian television network in the former USSR, and this family played a key part in that as well. In fact, they had been the "door" for many Christians to enter through to minister in Latvia. So we had no reason to believe that anything could be wrong with a business deal this family member offered us.

Right after this man proposed the deal, he wanted to meet with us late one night, at about midnight, to show us the property where he wanted to build our house. We agreed, and when we arrived at the proposed site, we saw that a foundation was already in place! I had great doubts and feelings of caution about the whole situation. I said to Rick, "I don't think this is right." But from our history with this man and his family, there was no apparent reason to distrust him. Rick felt it was the right decision to pay him the money to build our house.

As time went on, we would return to the site to see the building progress, but for a long time, there was no progress at all. Finally, the house did get built, but it was so poorly constructed that we couldn't get from one side of the house to the other without first going outside! Also, the house didn't have a roof!

As it turned out, this man wasn't an architect at all, but rather a criminal. We learned about his criminal activities when Rick read in the paper that he'd been arrested for holding a gun to someone's head and demanding a ransom. It was very disappointing to learn he wasn't trustworthy, and our financial loss was a hard thing to walk through.

The whole ordeal affected Rick so greatly that he went into seclusion in our bedroom and didn't come out for five days. But the Holy Spirit turned the situation around in a number of ways. On the fifth day of his seclusion, Rick had a divine encounter with God. The Holy Spirit supernaturally showed him a map of the entire former Soviet Union and said, *"I will give this to you."*

Rick quickly left our house, went to the office, and on a large map of the former USSR, he began circling huge regions where we would expand the reach of our TV broadcasting. *Wow!* That was more than two decades ago, and we are still broadcasting in these regions today!

The Holy Spirit turned our challenging situation around for good. The house we bought after that one was so huge that it later became an orphanage. I remember saying about the new house when we first saw it, "It has a roof!" But it was a wonderful home to replace what we had lost — a 3,500-square-foot house with three floors and a basement. We lived in that beautiful replacement home for four years. Then when we were getting ready to move to Riga and needed to sell it, it became an even bigger blessing when another large ministry bought it and turned it into an orphanage.

Although I didn't think Rick's decision was right to pay that "architect" to build our house, I supported him and submitted to his leadership. And look how the Holy Spirit worked in that situation! He turned it into a blessing not only for us, but also for another ministry to positively impact the lives and eternal destinies of many children! God also made up for the money we lost.

I encourage you to have a trusting attitude toward your husband about even the big things. Let him lead in those matters. He may make mistakes, but learn to trust God that He will work in each situation to turn it around for good. Don't argue with your husband or try to take over if you disagree with his decision. And if something goes wrong, be gracious. Don't say, "I told you so" or rub his nose in his mistakes. That would be an example of "tearing down your house" with wrong words and attitudes.

Instead, encourage your husband that at least he took the lead and gained wisdom from the experience.

Sometimes this level of trust can be frightening when you feel like you know what's right, yet your husband is going a different direction. He may be sincere, or he may be motivated by selfishness, vanity, and pride. But if you try to control him and cut off his leadership, you'll make him feel weak, and he will not appreciate how you made him feel or the fact that you took the leadership role from him. So save yourself not only from an argument with your husband, but also from your own feelings of failure or guilt because you weren't as supportive as you needed to be!

It's important that a wife try to understand *why* her husband does what he does. If it looks like he's failing in a certain area, it's usually not because he's weak or incompetent — or because he *wants* to do things irresponsibly. So it's important for a wife to ask God *why* in order to understand the heart of her husband. Often when she understands why, it helps her have compassion for her husband instead of judgment.

If your husband is leading your family into a life-threatening, immoral, or illegal direction, in that case, it would be wise to talk to a professional counselor or pastor.

Again I want to say that if your husband is leading your family into a life-threatening, immoral, or illegal direction, in that case, it would be wise to talk to a professional counselor or pastor. You're in a very difficult situation, and you need to talk to and seek the wisdom of someone else who is qualified to help you.

Obedience and submission are so important. Heeding and obeying our husband's counsel and instruction will work out well for us as we do it in faith before God. And we must do it with a willing attitude! If we yield to our husband with a good attitude, God will bless that. But if we obey, yet complain the whole time we're doing it, there will be no blessing. We need to obey God and submit to our husband with a sweet spirit and a willing heart. God will bless us, and He'll bring more and more sweetness into our relationship. Our husband will notice and appreciate our yielded spirit.

On the other hand, a wife who refuses to honor and obey her husband causes serious problems in her marriage. As we've already read, Proverbs 14:1 says, "The wise woman builds her house, but the foolish pulls it down with her hands." Actually, if we're not practicing this level of obedience and submission to our husband, our heart has a wrong attitude and we're in rebellion, which is sin. We need to go to God and repent.

Every husband is different and will ask for different things from his wife. Your husband might make a simple request from time to time that you help him by calling someone on his behalf, for example. You may not want to do it, but if you really want to help your husband, you'll help in ways that are meaningful to *him*, not just in ways *you* want to help.

Perhaps it's really important for your husband to be on time for appointments and activities, so he requests that you be punctual as well. You may not see it as important, but if punctuality is a priority for him, it will be a great blessing both to your husband and to your marriage if you place it at the top of *your* list of priorities. I encourage you to consider his request as important to him — because it is — and then submit to it with a good attitude.

YOUR HUSBAND NEEDS YOU!

Respecting your husband's role as leader and appreciating and admiring him in that role is a very big part of your own role as a wife. I know that Rick is a strong leader and is extremely gifted. He has a huge call on his life, and he fulfills that call with so much grace and strength. He's amazing! I admire and appreciate all of those things about him — *and I also know how essential my supportive role is in his life.*

Your husband may never tell you how much he needs you, but he does need you. Your support is essential for his success. He feels it if you withdraw or separate yourself emotionally, just as he feels it when you connect yourself to what God has called him to do. As husband and wife, you are not just two people coexisting. You are *one*, and your husband desperately needs your support. Your wholehearted support of your husband strengthens him and helps him accomplish what he is called to do in life.

Our supportive role as a wife is very powerful. Our support helps our husband have confidence to do what he needs to do. It helps him believe he can succeed. He thinks, *My wife is with me, and because she's with me, I can do this.* He may never put that thought into words, but it's true. So we should never minimize our role as a support to our husband.

As husband and wife, you are not just two people coexisting. You are one, and your husband desperately needs your support.

Sometimes the ideas you have are invaluable to your husband and to your success together. I don't mean you should be telling him what to do, but if he asks you, "What do you think?" — it's important to answer him! Don't minimize your ideas — they may be divinely inspired! You can state your thoughts in a way that doesn't sound controlling. In other words, you don't have to say, "I have the answer. I know *just the way* we should do this"! Instead, you could say, "I have an idea I'd like to share." This is received much more easily than if you said, "We're going to do it *this* way!"

Your husband doesn't want to hear you complain about the way he approaches things or talk to him as if you're trying to take over his role as leader. When you speak to him that way, it seems to him like you think he doesn't know what he's doing. But when your husband asks for your ideas, he wants to hear them! He needs your input. So share your ideas generously and with grace. When the two of you have times of exchanging thoughts and ideas like this, it becomes a beautiful moment in which the one-flesh relationship is working: You're two people working together as one, and it is a very fulfilling experience.

Sometimes wives struggle with seeing their value in a marriage, and I've heard some women say, "I don't tell my husband my thoughts and ideas. He probably doesn't want to hear them, anyway."

These women have been listening to wrong thoughts in their mind — thoughts from the enemy who's trying to oppose them and work against them and their marriage. He's the one who injects thoughts into their mind, saying, *Your idea is no good. You don't know what you're talking about. He doesn't want to hear from you.*

If a woman gives attention to these lies of the enemy, she won't be what she needs to be for her husband when he asks her, "What do you think?" She will close up and won't talk to him about her ideas, and he will be left without the input his wife should have provided. He doesn't benefit from her ideas because she's been listening to a wrong voice.

If you struggle with those kinds of thoughts, make the decision today that you're never going to receive and listen to those lies again! Those thoughts are born out of rejection, and you need to put them down. Your husband *does* need you. He doesn't want to be controlled by you, but he needs you! You are valuable and precious to him. So refuse to listen to the enemy's lies one day longer!

HIS BURDEN TO LEAD AND PROVIDE

So much rests on your husband's shoulders for which he is responsible. Your responsibility lies in understanding and supporting him.

Men don't often talk about it, but most husbands carry a burden of leading and providing. Generally speaking, men carry a great sense of responsibility, thinking about matters that many wives perhaps don't think about. Even after the children are grown and leave home, husbands who provided for the family all those years still carry the load of leading and providing in other arenas of life.

Rick and I are not changing diapers anymore or driving our children all over town to their lessons and special activities, but we're still carrying on with life beyond the child-raising years! We have seven grandchildren at the time of this writing, and we enjoy the time we get to spend with them and with our sons and their wives. But our sons have their own lives, as do Rick and I. We've raised a family, but we're still called to the ministry. We're still functioning in our office, and Rick is still at the helm of our church, an international ministry, multiple programs and outreaches, and our home. His "burden" to lead and provide continues.

We need to recognize everything our husband does for us. There's power in understanding our own role as a wife, but when we understand and acknowledge our husband's role, we are filled with gratitude to him and to God, and we're able to show compassion for him because of the great responsibility that has been assigned to him as the head of the home.

You should appreciate and honor your husband for what he does for you, but you should *not* take the responsibility away from him for leading. That responsibility is his. Your support and your love and care for your husband cause him to remain strong. If you take his God-given responsibility away from him, you can cause him to become weak. You are a big part of your husband's success in life — and *his* success is *your* success.

Your husband probably works to provide a living for his family. You may work, too, but it's different for a man because his identity is tied to his work. Maybe he's experiencing conflict at work or his boss is being hard on him or he doesn't receive a good paycheck on a particular payday. When you surround him with honor and respect, he knows he's coming home from work to a wife who loves him and helps him face his challenges fearlessly. When you let him know how grateful for and proud of him you are, he will become even stronger. You'll be sowing toward his future and yours too. As you grow older together, you'll have a strong man standing by your side.

HONORING YOUR 'PRINCE CHARMING' IN FRONT OF YOUR CHILDREN

One very powerful way of showing respect to our husband is to learn to be a better follower. It's so important to honor our husband's position as the head of the family and to teach our children to do the same. The way we honor our husband is the way our children will honor us. So if we're disrespectful to our husband, we'll train our children to be disrespectful to us. With our attitudes and our actions, we're setting an example for them to follow.

> The way we honor our husband is the way our children will honor us.

When we were raising our sons, Rick and I always demonstrated before them that we were in agreement. Doing that was a way for me to show honor to Rick as the head of the family. If one of the boys came to me and asked if he could do something, I would respond by saying, "What did your dad say?" Rick would say something similar, such as, "Go ask your mom." I would often say, "Go tell your dad that I said we'll do what he says."

Our children are watching us! It's important that husbands and wives maintain a united front where our children are concerned. It will bring great stability and blessing to our children if we do. Anything less will cause confusion in the children and chaos in the home. This kind of confusion will open the door to upset the balance of peace and order that God ordained for our families.

We should also avoid arguing in front of our children. Of course, we're human and we will have disagreements. But when you find yourself in a disagreement with your husband in the presence of your children, you can simply say to your husband in a calm, rational tone, "Could we go into another room?" Of course, your husband may be the one to take the disagreement into another room, away from the children. But if he doesn't, it's certainly okay to make a simple request to move the conversation to a place where you'll have privacy, and young hearts and minds won't be affected or confused.

Even if you think your children are right about something that your husband disagrees with, it will not work for you to take their side when they are in the presence of you and your husband! You might think you're being a great mediator and peacemaker who can make their father see the light and change his mind. But the truth is, things will probably turn out the opposite of what you were hoping for. Your husband may become even more reluctant to yield to you if he thinks you're playing his children against him.

Siding with the children against your husband dishonors him and his leadership. Even if he does change his mind and lets you and the kids have your way, the long-term results will not be positive. Your motives may be pure — you may simply be trying to get your husband to see their viewpoint and understand how they feel. But doing this without discretion can embarrass and dishonor him in front of his children, and he will not appreciate your maneuver even if your intentions were right. It would be far better to find a time when you and your husband are alone to communicate with him on behalf of the children.

When children see Mom honoring and supporting Dad, they take that as an example to follow. It helps them learn to honor both of their parents and submit to their authority.

The reverse is true as well. In one family I know, the wife continually dishonored her husband by lying to him. In turn, when their children were teenagers, they dishonored their parents and brought much heartache to them both. Proverbs 17:25 (*NLT*) states, "Foolish children bring grief to their father and bitterness to the one who gave them birth." That wife's actions of lying and deceiving her husband were seeds sown inside her children. Those seeds grew up and produced an ugly harvest that caused pain and grief for the whole family.

> *If you have shown dishonor to your husband in front of your children, it's not too late to begin turning your situation around.*

If you have shown dishonor to your husband in front of your children, it's not too late to begin turning your situation around. First, apologize to your children and tell them that your actions were wrong. Your repentance can abort those seeds of dishonor, especially if you begin sowing the *right* seeds into the hearts of your family members.

When we plant seeds of obedience and honor into our young children, by the time they're teenagers, those seeds will have started to grow and we can begin to see a harvest of respectful behavior. But regardless of where you are on your journey, *right now* is the right time to begin sowing God's Word into your own heart and into your precious family! It's never too late to reap a harvest of blessing from the good seeds you've sown, *but you have to start!*

Marina's short testimony that follows will encourage you that it's never too late just to *start* doing what's right.

Marina

Our Child Followed My Example

My husband is a very good man, but pride, rivalry, and even malice were inside me. In the teaching seminars I attended, I saw that all my problems I created myself by manipulating and nagging my husband.

Now when my husband comes home, I meet him at the door and ask how he is. I prepare a tasty dinner especially for him and try to pay more attention to him. I also began to listen to my husband and really hear him. I tried to be more silent.

I stand under his umbrella of protection. It was not and is still not easy for me — pride has prevented me from doing the right things — but I just began to work on it. The seminars gave me direction on how to go forward, how to say things better to my husband, and when to be in silence. Seeing the way I am with my husband, our child has become more obedient with less talking back.

I began to do what my husband says in order to support him. And I saw that he really understands me and sees through me. Now he is the best advisor and friend I could ever have!

Reverse the Pattern
of Manipulation and Control

Among today's Russian women, many of their mothers were heads of their homes. Through no fault of their mothers and grandmothers, these modern-day women didn't have a good example to follow. Their mothers would have done better, but they didn't know how. So much of those family dynamics happened because of the casualties of World War II. Because women were forced to be independent and strong, their daughters learned from the only example they saw.

The consequences of that today — and it can be true in *any* culture — are that strong, independent women are taking the reins from their husbands in the home. These wives feel they need to be the savior of the home. That may sound noble and good, but it can leave men feeling like they're nothing — worthless.

Many men grow up with a terrible lack of self-worth and turn to alcohol, drugs, or other things looking for comfort and an escape from their emptiness and pain. A wife certainly can't fix what happened because of her husband's upbringing — only God can do that. But a woman's role is still so very powerful in the home. When she honors her husband as the leader of the home — showing appreciation for his role and respecting him — it can actually enable him to fulfill and excel in the role that God created for him. A wife can use her "super powers" to take charge and contribute to the disorder in the home, or she can use her strength to strengthen her husband in his God-given role. By relinquishing control, she gives God room to work to establish peace and a "happily-ever-after" atmosphere in her home.

So how do we turn the control of the home back over to our husband? What are ways we can start letting him have leadership of the family?

I have a friend in Ukraine whose story helps answer those questions. She is an example of someone who let God teach her His ways in a difficult situation and has experienced a wonderful harvest for the obedience she has sown. Years ago this woman lived with a man who was an alcoholic. Often he came home drunk and dirty, and he acted very ugly. Her heart was broken by his actions and words. She decided to go to church, where she heard the Word of God for the first time in her life, and she gave her heart to Christ.

Not too long afterward, she was filled with the Holy Spirit. This woman knew that because her life belonged to Jesus, she could not continue sleeping with this man. So she moved out of their bedroom into the next room, and she began praying and praying for him.

One day the Holy Spirit said to her, "Dress in your finest dress, fix him the best meal, and when he comes through the door, cup his face in your hands, and say, 'Oh, my love, you've come home to me.'"

She did this, and the man was *shocked*. He saw how peaceful and loving she was — and he stood before her, practically speechless, for nearly two hours!

She sowed this kind of behavior for about two years. My friend testified that it was the hardest thing she had ever done. But in two years' time, this man changed greatly. He began taking responsibility for leadership in the home. He married her, quit drinking, and adopted her daughter. *And he became born again!*

Now, every day — to this very day — whenever she leaves the house, he prays for her and says, "I love you, my princess." Their daughter is now grown, and she's a beautiful, confident young woman who does great in school.

No amount of nagging, complaining, or manipulating could have ever gotten these results. But God has the answer to every situation and circumstance if we'll humble ourselves and obey what He has to say. My friend was obedient, and God blessed her beyond her wildest dreams! Can you imagine hearing your husband say, "I love you, my princess" every time you leave the house? This woman fought a great battle, but she won a great victory. My friend is a real-life Cinderella!

We truly do have the power to build up our home or destroy it.

You may wonder if this husband got saved first and then God helped him make all those miraculous changes. No, that wasn't the order of things at all. This woman was a living example of First Peter 3:1, which says, "Wives, likewise, be submissive to your own husbands, that even if some do not obey the word, they, without a word, may be won by the conduct of their wives." My friend's actions demonstrated the power of the wife who lives like Jesus in front of her unsaved husband. In the words of the apostle Peter, she won her husband "without a word."

For years, this man who had been an alcoholic acted like anything *but* a treasure. Yet my friend treated him like a treasure, and that's what he became. Later when I interviewed her for television, she said with tears, "Without God helping me change and love and accept this man exactly the way he was, I could have lost him."

The next two testimonies are more real-life examples of "Cinderellas and Prince Charmings" finally emerging in their homes when these precious wives gave up their need for control.

◦◜⌒◝◦

Anna

'Okay, God, I Give Up'

I was the head of my family. I didn't recognize my husband's leadership or his authority. I was so used to telling him what to do — I was the boss! He used to stay out late at night, and I felt it was my responsibility to tell him that wasn't right. I felt I needed to call him at midnight at times to say, "You have to come home." I had to go to work, I had to keep up with my house, and I had three children to raise. It was like I was single.

I decided to just do my job and take care of the children, but my husband and I were just living separate lives in the same house. There was no relationship between us. I decided that we should stay married because of the children, but he would have his life and I would have my life. This was not a comfortable, happy way to live.

I felt that even though my husband is intellectual, highly educated, and has an important job, he didn't make enough money. But after I attended the marriage seminars, I received a statement from God: *God will supply.*

Peace came to our home. I began to understand that I did not need to supervise my husband. I made big changes in my heart. Instead of telling him what to do, I just began telling him that he was very handsome, and he would tell me, "I love you."

Our children grew up. We don't have grandchildren. We live alone together again, just me and my husband. It's kind of like a second youth, a new marriage, a sweet relationship again. We can sit together and hug each other.

It's so important to stop saying bad words about your husband. Praise him instead. Even if you think it's too much, just keep praising him, and he will change. I know this to be exactly true — my marriage was a very bad situation. But in addition to beginning to respect my husband as the leader, I spoke good words about him. I said, "You're the best." And he really is!

❦

Veronika

'I Finally Realized
I Was Not the Savior of My Home!'

When I attended the seminars, my husband and I had been married for 25 years. We were every day arguing and discussing divorce. I went to hear these teachings as a last hope for my marriage. My husband had not had a job for eight years, and he had been drowning his sorrows by drinking heavily during those eight years.

I was convinced that my behavior was correct by taking complete charge of our home. In my mind, it was the noble thing to do. I was the organized one. I was the smart one. "I, I, I." My thinking was that I was the "savior" of my home and that he should appreciate how I was trying to straighten him out and change him. I was totally convinced that he should straighten up and listen to me because he was the one who needed correction and instruction.

I came to every class to hear with an open heart how I could save my marriage. I can honestly say I did to the best of my ability all that I was hearing. I repented of judging my husband. I asked him to forgive me for not respecting him. I began to compliment him and serve him and to make him the king of our home. You may say to yourself, *I could never do that.* But all the changes I made as I humbled myself were worth it. Little by little, I began to trust God to help me respect and honor my husband as the provider, protector, and head of my home.

Now my husband, who would hardly even talk to me before, texts me on the phone during the day every day to tell me how much he loves me. He has a great job. He quit drinking, and we are now like two young married people on our honeymoon! There is peace and joy and laughter in our home. Instead of judging him, I am enjoying our differences. Was it worth all the pain and changing that I went through? Yes, it was! I now can truly honor the amazing man God gave me many years ago.

I encourage you to read and study and take this teaching as deeply into your heart as you can. You cannot go wrong by letting Jesus, the Master of good marriages, paint with His graceful strokes of wisdom and grace on the canvas of your heart. He can take any portrait of our bad experiences in marriage and, with our cooperation, bring His masterful touch to add beauty and pleasure to that covenant union — more than we could ever imagine.

When I married my husband, I saw myself living as in a beautiful dream. Then the circumstances of life hit us, and I felt for a long time that we'd lost all that. Later I connected my heart with the teachings contained in this book, and God brought about change, helping us recover our dream. Yes, we are still met by challenges, but through God's Word and His grace, I sometimes feel I'm living in a real-life fairytale. *And not only was my marriage saved, my daughter gave her life to Jesus and her own troubled marriage was saved!*

❦

Is It Important To Say *Thank You*?

Something that causes serious problems in a marriage is a lack of gratitude. For example, a wife who is ungrateful or who constantly complains to her husband is showing disrespect and slowly tearing down her marriage. A lack of thankfulness is a marriage killer! A husband and wife might start out loving each other very deeply, but if she yields to complaining and ungratefulness, she will find the relationship deteriorating and she'll begin wondering, *What happened to our love and to all those tender words he used to say to me?*

All of us as believers must use our mouths for speaking *good* things — words of appreciation, reflecting a thankful heart to God and to others, and especially to our spouse if we're married. (If you feel you've lost your way and don't even know anymore what to be thankful for, ask the Holy Spirit to show you — and He will!)

It's important to think on the good, positive things about your husband and truly value those things. It's vital for the health of your marriage to consider your husband's worth and to be grateful for everything he does for you. It's easy for wives to get caught up in thinking more about their needs, the children's needs, or needs in the workplace. So I encourage you to purposefully make a note of and think about the positive characteristics you see in your husband and to sincerely appreciate those things about him. Then work to *show* your appreciation. An honest demonstration of gratitude toward your husband will do wonders to help bring back some of the tenderness that may be lost from your relationship with him.

If you need help getting started, I've prepared a list of things you can choose from as you make the quality decision to specially focus on your husband's positive traits.

An honest demonstration of gratitude toward your husband will do wonders to help bring back some of the tenderness that may be lost from your relationship with him.

He's honest.

He's hardworking.

He's faithful.

He's generous.

He's thoughtful.

He's intelligent

He's wise.

He's creative.

He's gentle.

He's kind.

APPRECIATE HIM FOR HIS WORK

A man's work is very important to him; therefore, appreciating a man for his work demonstrates respect. We read a description of a man's work in Genesis 3:17-19 when the curse had come after the fall of man in the Garden of Eden: "…Cursed is the ground for your sake; in toil you shall eat of it all the days of your life.

Both thorns and thistles it shall bring forth for you, and you shall eat the herb of the field. In the sweat of your face you shall eat bread till you return to the ground...."

Work is very important to a man because his identity is tied to his work. Since a man's identity is in his work, it would be wise for the woman in his life to appreciate him with words, such as, "Thank you for providing for us. You're doing a great job. You work so hard, and I appreciate the hours you work to make a living for us."

Our husbands want to hear us express our gratitude for how hard they work. They want to hear, "Thank you for the work you do. Thank you for going to work every day to provide for us." Some wives may say, "Well, I work, too, and he has never said 'thank you' to *me*." Usually, husbands look at their work differently than wives do. If a man fails at work, he can feel as if he has failed at life.

Someone asked me, "What if my husband doesn't work?" Then thank him for the strength he gives your family. Thank him for his support of you. Thank him for the father that he is to your children. In other words, *find something about him to be thankful for!* Ask the Holy Spirit to show you what to say to demonstrate your appreciation for him. Simply ask, "Holy Spirit, how can I build up my husband? How can I encourage him?"

Your goal should not be to urge your husband to get up and do something, but rather to encourage his heart. And think about it: In this world of billions of people, *you are the only one who has that place!* It isn't his children or his mother and father who have that place; it's *you*. Out of billions of people, God chose *you* to stand by that man, to honor him as the leader in his home, and to admire and appreciate him for his positive traits and for all the good things he does.

What if your husband said to you, "Thank you for how clean and well-organized you keep the house" or, "Thank you for being so wonderful" or, "You're the best mother — our children love you so much" or, "You are so gracious and kind; I appreciate your patience with me"? Those words would make you feel wonderful. You would want to hear those kinds of comments from your husband. In the same way, you need to say those kinds of things to him. Appreciate him for the things he does that are important to him, such as his work.

I encourage you to esteem your husband as a gift from God and a part of God's good plan for you — and pray for ways to build him up. As you do, you will be building your home to be long-lasting and strong.

Magnify His Strengths

If we have something strong in our character, the other side of that can be weakness if it's not tempered. For example, let's say that your husband is very bold and strong. On the other side of that strength is the likelihood that he can be rude at times.

As a wise woman who builds her house instead of tearing it down, you will benefit from focusing on your husband's strengths. He needs those God-given strengths to do his job or fulfill his position. He may have a job in which he is over other people; he probably has strong opinions about how things should be done and feels the need to convince others about his points of view. A wise woman will emphasize that strength rather than becoming offended if he is rude. She'll say, "Lord, I forgive him because he was rude, and I thank You that he is strong."

Another example of a strength that can have a weak side is the ability to be a visionary and have big dreams and high goals. The other side of that strength is moodiness. A wise woman will pray, "God, encourage him and give me the wisdom to encourage him too. Help him do what You've put in his heart to do."

Other husbands may be very intelligent, but forgetful and even thoughtless. They don't think about the same things their wives do. A wise woman will be patient and merciful and recognize her husband's intelligence and bright mind.

Of course, the same truth applies to women; we can have God-given strengths that can also manifest as weaknesses if we fail to yield ourselves to the Holy Spirit. For example, my strength is that I'm very compassionate. But on the other side of that strength is a weakness I have to guard against. I can get my feelings hurt when it feels like I'm giving so much and not enough is being given back to me in the same way. So I would want my husband — and everyone else, for that matter — to major on my strength of showing mercy and compassion rather emphasizing and judging that weakness.

Just as you would want someone to see and emphasize your strengths, your husband wants you to recognize and magnify *his* strengths, not his weaknesses. And as a wise woman who builds up her home, that's exactly what you should do.

Again, this isn't an easy task by any means. Jesus didn't say the things we need to do would always be easy, but He did say they're possible, and He promised to empower us to do *whatever* He asks us to do. This actually is the key to the greatest effectiveness and fulfillment in marriage and in *life*: to do what is *right* and not just what is *easy*.

A Simple Prayer for Change

There was a time when I've read Ephesians 5:33 and thought, *Oh, yes, of course, I'm a respectful wife.* But the more I've studied this subject of respect over the years, the more I've understood that there were changes I needed to make. The following is a short prayer I've prayed for myself, and I'm praying it for you too. Take it to heart and pray it over yourself often — and expect God to answer!

Father, open my eyes to the truth and help me respect my husband. I want to change and to live my life according to Your Word. Please forgive me for any disrespect I have shown toward my husband. Thank You for helping me. In Jesus' name, amen.

Practical Changes You Can Make To Be More Respectful To Your Husband

(Count the Ways!)

1. If you have taken control of your home, apologize to your husband. Write out James 5:16 (*KJV*) — "Confess your faults one to another, and pray one for another, that ye may be healed…" — and meditate on that verse.

2. Memorize First Corinthians 11:3, which states, "But I want you to know that the head of every man is Christ, the head of woman is man, and the head of Christ is God." Reflect briefly on the order that has been established in your home, and if things are out of order, begin to cast a new vision for your home and family as you purpose in your heart to allow God's divine order to be established. Write out a plan for yourself to begin changing your behavior. It doesn't have to be detailed or long — just start!

3. Get rid of your "Superwoman T-shirt" and discover or *redis-cover* the abilities God has placed in your husband! Write down three of your husband's greatest strengths. Proverbs 3:7,8 states, "Do not be wise in your own eyes; fear the Lord and depart from evil. It will be health to your flesh, and strength to your bones." Don't make excuses for any wrong way you've done things in the past. Be open to God's wisdom, which will always produce peace, joy, and good fruit!

4. On purpose, ask your husband for his opinion and his wisdom and insight about something that's important to you. Thank him for his advice and be sincerely appreciative of him. First Peter 5:5 states, "…All of you be submissive to one another, and be clothed with humility, for 'God resists the proud, but gives grace to the humble.'"

Chapter Four

'HOW CAN I MAKE HIM MORE LIKE ME?'

Have you ever been unpleasantly surprised by your husband's response to you in a way you didn't expect? You may have said something innocently, yet he responded with irritation or even anger.

When something like that happens, it's usually a misunderstanding, but let me help you understand the misunderstanding! *Your husband has feelings.* Even if you didn't intend to hurt him, he probably reacted in anger because his feelings were hurt by something you said or the way you said it. More often than not, the hurt feelings came because he felt put down and unaccepted by you.

Your husband wants to be accepted as he is, just like you do. When he reacts in an angry way, just know that he didn't just start feeling unaccepted *right then*. Usually those feelings have been building up — then the "bomb" suddenly exploded! You just happened to say something at that moment that flipped the switch.

Maybe your husband feels you don't think he can do anything right or that you're trying to change him. If he's thinking that way, he feels in his heart that deep down, you don't think he's good enough.

I know this from personal experience. There was a time in our marriage when I was hurting Rick's feelings regularly and didn't even know it! In fact, I didn't even know he *had* feelings! He was so strong and such a great leader that I thought I was the one with the up-and-down emotions while he was the rock that never moved. But I was wrong.

Let me assure you, your husband has feelings, and they are just as strong as yours. He may express them differently, but he feels things just as deeply as you do.

Don't Violate His Trust in You

A husband looks for a secure, safe place in his wife. Proverbs 31:11 (*KJV*) describes this place: "The heart of her husband doth safely trust in her...." This is not a complaining place on our part, nor a criticizing place. It's not a place he wants to run *from*, but rather a place he wants to run *to*. Your husband needs you to be a friend to him who is supportive and kind — a person he can go to and know that you are on his side.

But when you try to change your husband, he does *not* feel safe and secure. In fact, when you try to change him, he will likely respond with resistance, resentment, and even anger. Why? Because you're presenting an attitude that something he's doing or not doing isn't good enough, and your actions and words are translated to him as, *I don't approve of you.* That lack of approval and affirmation causes him to withdraw from you. It's a vicious cycle if he withdraws and you keep pushing for change, because the more you push, the more closed he will become to you.

Trying to change others is fruitless because we don't have the power to change *anyone*! So why waste our valuable time and energy trying to change others, often damaging precious relationships? Only God can change people, so it would be wise for us as a wife to spend our time talking to Him about our needs and desires — and about how *we* may need to change — instead of trying to change our husband.

Show Respect Through Acceptance

Our responsibility is not to try to control or change our husband, but to be a friend to him. All of this is a part of showing respect and accepting him as he is. In Chapter Three, we looked at three primary aspects of respecting our husband: 1) humbling ourselves and being willing to see our own faults; 2) accepting him just as he is; and 3) appreciating and admiring him as leader of the home. We looked in-depth at appreciating our husbands as leaders in the home. Now I want to address this topic of acceptance because it's such a big part of showing respect.

Accept your husband as he is. It's easy to say those words, but actually doing them on a daily basis is not so easy. For one thing, your husband is very different from you. The two of you probably think very differently. When you look at his faults, they might look very disturbing to you. You might even say to yourself, *How can he do that? I would never do that.* However, accepting your husband as he is will have a very powerful positive effect on your marriage. Accepting your husband just the way he is, without one change, gives him the freedom to hear *God's* voice rather than yours. (We need to hear God's voice above all others; He is the only One who can bring change in our lives.) When you show your husband acceptance, you also give him the freedom to rest in your love for him — and to show more love to you — without concern that you disapprove of him.

What I'm sharing can be hard to see for some women, so let me illustrate this point with an exaggerated, made-up story about how criticism and lack of acceptance makes people feel. As I said, your husband has feelings just like you do — and just like your friends, coworkers, and other family members do. All those other people in your life don't want to feel criticized and unaccepted by you — *and neither does your husband!*

Consider the following scene. You invite a new friend out for lunch, and she accepts your invitation. At lunch, you say to your friend, "I'm so happy we could get together today." As you're sitting there in the restaurant, you notice the "good" and the "bad" of your friend's appearance: her cute blouse, her outdated accessories, her well-manicured nails, her wrong color of lipstick, her perfect shade of blush, her overdone eye makeup, her beautiful hair color, and her hairstyle that hides her face rather than bringing out her natural beauty.

And you've done all that in a matter of seconds!

Then what if you said to your friend, "I'm so glad we could get together today...*hey*, I know a great place where you could get a complete makeover!"

Your new friend looks at you, stunned. Breaking the awkward silence, you quickly add, "I just think if you really saw your potential, you would want to change a few things to maximize that potential and be even more beautiful than you already are. I say this because I *care*."

You already made your checklist of what you like and don't like about your friend's appearance, and now she knows it. Meanwhile, you stand completely ready to help her implement the life changes that you're just certain she needs to make!

The next time you called this person, she would probably not want to get together with you or pursue a friendship with you at all. Why? She'd feel that your acceptance of her is conditional and that you're bent on changing her appearance as a condition of continuing a meaningful relationship with her. And she'd probably be right!

Of course, I'm using this far-fetched scenario to make a point. Most of us would never do something this drastic. Yet many of us do the same *kind* of thing to our husband. We think, *I want him to love me and open his heart to me. I want him to be patient with me. I want him to bring me flowers and say nice things to me.* But in the back of our mind, we're working on our checklist:

- *He doesn't go to church.*

- *He doesn't talk to me right.*

- *He doesn't read his Bible.*

- *I can't stand the way he eats.*

- *He's failing my expectations here and here and here!*

We want a wonderful relationship with our husband, but we're keeping a hidden list of all the things about him we want to change!

Now, please understand — when I talk about accepting your husband, I'm not talking about accepting physical abuse. If your husband is physically abusing you or your children, or if he's looking at pornography, those are the types of deeply rooted, destructive problems that must be handled and not overlooked or ignored. You need to seek help from a pastor or professional counselor.

THE 'CALMING' EFFECT OF CONTROL

So much of the time, we want to change our husband just to meet our preferences or to exert control over him because of our own fears or lack of understanding. Control is a way to bring a false sense of peace or comfort to our lives when we're feeling insecure or when we don't understand something. But it isn't *God's* peace, and it isn't His way. And it will never produce the right kind of change — the kind of change *He* desires.

> *Control is a way to bring a false sense of peace or comfort to our lives when we're feeling insecure or when we don't understand something.*

We may even try to delicately say something, in just the right way, to correct our husband, thinking we'll inspire him to change something that we want to see changed. When he doesn't respond, we think, *He didn't hear me the first time. I'll say it again.* Then when there's no response again, we think, *Maybe I didn't explain myself clearly enough. I'll say it a third time.*

When there's still no response, we think, *He must be tired. I'll say it a fourth time.* Then we say it a fifth, sixth, or seventh time. It's very counterproductive when we do this because, as I said previously, by the time we've repeated ourselves once or twice, our husband has probably closed his ears to us.

The truth is, your husband doesn't need to hear from you for correction; he needs to hear from *God*. If you're the only one he hears, he'll be distracted because he'll have to deal with his heart about you and the way you're treating him. He won't be able to hear God if all he hears is you.

Even if you don't address the items on your "hidden checklist," yet you keep them in the back of your mind, you're not fully cooperating with God and His plan. If you're still thinking and feeling those things on the inside and harboring a hidden agenda to change your husband, it will negatively affect your relationship with him. He will sense your attitude of disapproval.

It's dangerous to keep a list of things you don't like about your husband because in doing that, you might be guilty of desiring to change him into *your* image or ideal instead of allowing Him to be conformed to *God's* image. The task of trying to change your husband is not in your job description! God is the only One who sees the whole picture, and only God can change a person.

Even if we *could* change our husband, we would probably make a lot of mistakes. What if we changed him into someone that God his Creator never intended? We need to leave the work of perfecting our husband to the One who knows him best and loves him most.

When I used to try to change Rick, the Holy Spirit would gently tell me to work on myself and to leave Rick to Him. It has taken years for the Word to develop in my heart and the grace of God to work within me to relinquish control and allow Him to work on my husband. I'm not telling you it's easy to do, but I am telling you that the message I'm writing to you is one I've had to receive and

We need to leave the work of perfecting our husband to the One who knows him best and loves him most.

walk out for myself. As I said, I'm not perfect, but I have improved in this area. Through the years, the Holy Spirit has shown me how to "let go" of trying to control Rick and to accept my husband just the way he is.

Irina's testimony will bless you as she shares about the value of accepting her husband and yielding her will to God and His Word.

◦✑

Irina

'Accepting My Husband Changed Our Marriage'

Our temperaments are different. My husband is a phlegmatic, laid-back person who's never in a hurry. I am a more choleric person — I have to get everything done quickly. He could spend two days thinking over a question or could even forget about it and come back to it later. On the other hand, he doesn't like it when I remind him about something. I would lose my patience so many times and remind him about things again and again. And I wouldn't use the right tone in my voice, and it would cause an argument. My husband became closed toward me, and it took a long time for us to come into agreement deliberately.

I was almost constantly at odds with my husband over everything. Because of my wrong attitudes and actions, our relationship did not improve. There was no peace or joy in any way. I began to understand that I needed to receive him as he was and to quit judging and correcting him. His attitude began to change toward me, but there was still one area where I had greatly wronged my husband: It was our sexual relationship. I knew it was important to him, but I had a wall up. It was four years after our daughter was born, and I was still refusing to have sex with him! I was so wrong. I repented to God and to my husband, and God has restored our relationship. Our marriage is a miracle and a testimony of what God can do if we come to Him with a yielded and repentant heart. Nothing is impossible with God.

To women having marriage problems, I would say there is hope. Everything can be restored. We need God and others who can support us as we walk on our journey.

Also, our thinking is very important. If we have negative thoughts about our husband and about ourselves, we can get caught in an endless loop. I had negative thoughts about myself, and at first I needed help to come out of it. I had rejection in my heart and considered myself in a low position.

It's very important to have personal fellowship with God and to know what He thinks about us. When the Holy Spirit works in us, we can build relationships with others and love them.

It is good to say and confess Scripture verses like this: "For I wrestle not against flesh and blood, but against principalities, against powers, against the rulers of the darkness of this world, against spiritual wickedness in high places. I am more than a conqueror in Jesus Christ. I am seated with Christ in Heavenly places, higher than anything else. God gave me the victory. I am redeemed from any curse, in Jesus' name." (*See* Ephesians 6:12; Romans 8:37; Ephesians 1:17-23; Galatians 3:13,14.)

I took my eyes off my problems and put them on God. I began to accept my husband, and it changed our marriage completely.

HUMILITY AND THE HEART OF GOD

The first step in relinquishing our self-appointed role of "change agent" in our marriage is to throw away our mental list of criticisms and disapprovals. God's Word instructs us to respect our husband, not to try to change or control him. There's only one Holy Spirit, and His name is not "Denise" (or your name, either)! Often I think God could do more if we would stop trying to be the instruments of change we think He wants us to be. The Holy Spirit is able to speak to our husband, deal with him according to God's will, and change him — if we'll just let the Holy Spirit do His perfecting work!

We covered the topics of appreciating our husbands as leader in the home and of accepting him just as he is. In this section, I'll address the subject of humility, because without humility, we will never see change in ourselves, in our husbands, *or* in our marriages. Instead, our "happily ever after" will become a life of endless frustration as we spend our time, our strength, and our energy spinning our wheels, so to speak, and getting nowhere.

It's very humbling to say, "Lord, Your Word is true, and it says that I'm to be respectful of my husband and not to try to change him. He doesn't need me to correct him like I'm his mother. He needs to hear from *You*." But things work so much better when we humble ourselves — when we get a little quieter and softer before the Lord. As we begin entering a place of trust, we can take comfort in the fact that God has all the right answers for our marriage. And it's up to Him, not us, to reveal and unveil those solutions.

Humbling oneself is very close to the heart of God. Jesus is our Example. He had to humble Himself in the Garden of Gethsemane to do the will of God. He prayed to the Father, "...If it be possible, let this cup pass from me" (Matthew 26:39). Although Jesus willingly yielded to the Father's plan to redeem mankind, He didn't relish the idea of being the sacrificial Lamb. Hebrews 12:2 says Jesus "endured the cross, despising the shame." Three times He asked God, "If possible — if there's any other way — please let this cup pass from Me." But then He said, "Not *My* will, but *Your* will be done."

Jesus understands the humility it takes to put ourselves under the direction and leadership of someone else. When we make the decision to humble ourselves to obey the Word of God — to agree with God's Word — He understands how hard it can be. Hebrews 4:15,16 (*KJV*) tells us, "...We have not an high priest which cannot be touched with the feeling of our infirmities; but was in all points tempted like as we are, yet without sin. Let us therefore come boldly unto the throne of grace, that we may obtain mercy, and find grace to help in time of need."

Jesus doesn't stand at a distance in an unapproachable, high place with an austere expression on His face as He looks down on us. If He did that, we wouldn't dare have the confidence to reach out to Him! No, He has told us that He is touched by what we go through. He is touched by the feelings of our infirmities, and it's as if He is saying, "I know how hard it is. I was tempted just like you are. I didn't sin, but I have compassion for you, and I have mercy and help available for you."

This can be difficult to do in the natural. Making the necessary changes to respect our husband — not to say or do things to diminish or control him, but instead to be kind, supportive, and submissive — can be difficult to do in our own ability or willpower. You may be reading this right now, thinking, *In my case, it's not hard — it's impossible!* If you are, you're right. That's why we need a relationship with the Holy Spirit — so He can help us.

God's order for the family — God, Christ, husband, wife — is right. It works, and we must humbly submit to it. In fact, it is the *only* order that works to build successful, fulfilling marriages and produce fruit not only in our lives, but in the lives of those our marriages affect. And we have a God who does the impossible! He can draw near to us and give us the power we need to make changes and adjustments and to live the dream of "happily ever after" in our homes.

Depending on how long you've handled things your own way in your marriage, it might not be easy to make these necessary changes. But it is possible, and it begins with a *decision*. Even after you humble yourself before God and begin turning things around in your heart and mind, you will be tempted many times to pick up the reins of your marriage and go back to your old ways of coping with issues.

> *Change can be scary, especially if God is asking you to do something you've never done before.*

It may even take some time for you to see that your efforts to try to correct, control, manipulate, and change your husband are wrong. Often it's easier to justify old behavior than to admit you need to make a change. Change can be scary, especially if God is asking you to do something you've never done before. But change is necessary if you want to get to the place in your heart God is calling you to — one of respecting and accepting your husband.

Actually, it will often take sheer determination and an act of our will to do what God has instructed us to do in our marriage.

Many times, we'll just have to do what we know is right and trust Him whether or not we completely understand or agree with it. We'll have to obey God in spite of our emotions that might be telling us to do otherwise, and we'll have to persevere without seeing instant results.

Above all, it will take prayer and an intimate, personal relationship with Jesus to obey what He is telling us to do in our marriage. The great news, however, is that Jesus understands every struggle and pain, and He is the One who can and will help us. If we're willing and obedient, and we humbly submit ourselves to His Word, He will develop something inside us by the Spirit of God that's powerful — a gentle and quiet, confident spirit.

Help for the Humble

When God begins working on these issues in our heart, our struggling prayers might sound something like this: "Oh, Father, please help me humble myself in this area. A big part of me does not want to have a good attitude of mercy and understanding toward my husband. The truth is, I want *him* to change, not *me*. I'm tired of changing. And he is so fortunate to have me. He should be more grateful for all the kindness I've already shown him."

But as time goes on, your prayers might begin sounding something like this: "Lord, this is hard, but I'm saying *yes* to You. Your Word is right, and I want to do what Your Word says. Do Your perfecting, refining work in me and help me keep my mouth shut. Quiet my heart before You in love, in Jesus' name."

You may think it sounds elementary, but this kind of humble and heartfelt conversation with God can be gut-wrenching and glorious at the same time. Through your attitude of humility before

God, He can create within you a quiet, gentle spirit that will draw your husband closer. The Holy Spirit will equip and enable you to provide the support your husband needs so that he can be who God wants him to be. Your husband will be strengthened to lead you and your family into the divine plan of God for your lives. And you'll get to enjoy all of it with peace, joy, and confidence. It is a very precious work in God's sight.

MERCY, NOT JUDGMENT

If we secretly think we're a better person than our husband, much of our thought life could be preoccupied with judging him instead of loving and accepting him. But Jesus took upon Himself the judgment we all deserved — He did it for each one of us — so we really have no right to judge anyone.

In Matthew 7:1-5, we read Jesus' words concerning judging others:

> **Judge not, that you be not judged. For with what judgment you judge, you will be judged; and with the measure you use, it will be measured back to you. And why do you look at the speck in your brother's eye, but do not consider the plank in your own eye? Or how can you say to your brother, 'Let me remove the speck from your eye'; and look, a plank is in your own eye? Hypocrite! First remove the plank from your own eye, and then you will see clearly to remove the speck from your brother's eye.**

Sometimes wives can become self-righteous in their attitude toward their husbands, as I have been in times past toward Rick. And in general, we as humans can project the attitude that we're better than other people. We put on our robes of judgment, look down our noses at others, and judge them.

But Jesus said, "Judge *not.*" In other words, He said, *"Don't do it."* And whatever God commands of us, He will help us do.

When we judge others, we open the door for judgment to come back on us. We know the verse: "…Whatever a man sows, that he will also reap" (Galatians 6:7). What we sow is what we're going to reap. If we sow judgmental thoughts or words toward our husband, we will reap back to ourselves what we have sown.

Just look at Matthew 7:2: "For with what judgment you judge, you will be judged; and with the measure you use, it will be measured back to you." If we were to measure judgment in physical units, for example, and we give out 35 thoughts of judgment and criticism — according to this verse, we will get back exactly what we sowed: 35 thoughts of judgment and criticism. *Ouch!* But when we think about our husband, if we accept him just as he is, we're sowing mercy — and we will receive mercy in return, according to the mercy we've sown.

In the natural realm, we might have good reason to judge, to be critical, or to try to control and change our husband. But as Christians, we're called to trust everything about ourselves to Him who judges fairly (*see* 1 Peter 2:23 *AMP*). We can trust the Lord to help us respect our husband as He has commanded. We can trust the Lord enough to offer our husband acceptance and mercy instead of judgment and criticism.

James 2:13 says, "…Mercy triumphs over judgment." So if your husband has some terrible habits that aren't your "cup of tea" or habits that hurt your feelings, give him mercy, acceptance, and respect instead of lashing out at him in criticism and judgment. If you do, you'll open the door wide for God's presence, love, respect, and honor to come into your home.

There is such a great difference between mercy and judgment. If Jesus hadn't died and paid for our sins to restore our relationship with God, we would receive eternal judgment and damnation when we left this earthly life. But because Jesus took our judgment, we received mercy instead when we believed on Him and the great sacrifice He made.

Mercy is very powerful. It is giving to someone more than he or she deserves. We didn't deserve the mercy of God, but we have received it in Jesus Christ. And now we have the opportunity in our marriage to show our husband mercy even at times when he doesn't deserve it. Instead of sowing judgment, offense, unforgiveness, and an angry, critical attitude, we have an opportunity to give him something better than he deserves — *mercy* — just as Jesus did for us.

Luke 6:31(*NLT*) says, "Do to others as you would like them to do to you." If you make a mistake or do something wrong in your marriage, I'm certain you want your husband to have mercy on you. Therefore, you should do the same for him. It would be so powerful for your own heart and for your relationship with your husband if you would show him mercy. And you can do it! As Christians, the love of God has been "shed abroad in our hearts by the Holy Ghost which is given unto us" (Romans 5:5 *KJV*). We have the love of God in us, and the love of God *shows mercy*.

Often when I'm ministering this message to women, I'm asked *how* a wife can show mercy and demonstrate this God-kind of love in the marriage relationship. Mercy might look like this: Instead of saying something that could sound critical, belittling, or disrespectful to your husband, simply choose to be quiet instead! You might say to yourself, *Proverbs 19:11 says it's my glory to overlook an offense. I'm going to forgive him for that and overlook it.*

When you choose mercy over judgment, you're simply agreeing with the love of God that's already in your heart, placed there by the Holy Spirit the moment you became born again.

Mercy for us looks like Jesus on the Cross. Remember, He knows how hard it is for us to change some of the disrespectful ways we've acted in the past. We can say to Him, "Lord, I haven't been respectful. I've been judgmental and critical. Forgive me. Help me. I want to have mercy. I want to receive mercy from You, and I want to show mercy to my husband. I don't want to judge him anymore. I want to accept him and respect him." If we'll do that, we'll open the door for God's power to begin to transform our souls.

Proverbs 3:3 says, "Let not mercy and truth forsake you; bind them around your neck, write them on the tablet of your heart." Solomon instructed us to keep mercy close to us, written on our hearts and minds. How close we keep mercy to our hearts determines the difference between the wife who says, "I can't stand this anymore" and the wife who says, "I'm going to give mercy." If we keep mercy close to our hearts, we open our hearts and our homes to the power of God and the hand of Heaven.

I've known of many women who've become sick in their bodies because they harbored terrible attitudes toward their husbands. If only they understood that showing forgiveness and mercy without judgment is good for their marriages *and* their health. Romans 8:6 says, "For to be carnally minded is death, but

If we keep mercy close to our hearts, we open our hearts and our homes to the power of God and the hand of Heaven.

to be spiritually minded is life and peace." Many specialists say that peace in the heart and soul will produce peace and wholeness in the body. Even medical science has concluded that sickness and disease can be the result of toxic thoughts and attitudes — such as bitterness and resentment — that people have held on to for long periods of time instead of letting those wrong attitudes go.[1]

As we've seen, the wise woman builds her house, but the foolish one tears her house down with her own hands (Proverbs 14:1). Have you ever thought about the fact that it's much harder to build a house than it is to tear a house down? It can take quite a long time to build a house — but with the right explosives, a house can be imploded and practically leveled to the ground in just a short period of time.

Similarly, a foolish woman can tear down her house in just a short time with her temper and her words. But if she'll work with the Holy Spirit, He will help her build her house. From the inside out, He'll work in her life and show her the pathway to a blessed, healthy, and happy life.

BE RESPONSIBLE FOR YOUR OWN WALK WITH THE LORD

Often a wife is tempted to monitor and to try to control her husband's spiritual walk. But if we've learned anything so far in this discussion, it's that we are each responsible for our own life before God, not someone else's life. We can't control another human being, but we *can* control ourselves and submit our own heart to the lordship of Jesus and His Word.

It isn't our responsibility to make sure our husband is doing what the Word of God tells him to do. We're not the

Holy Spirit — we're not our husband's lord *or* his mother! Our responsibility is to allow the Holy Spirit to work change and transformation in our own heart and allow Him to work in our husband's heart *without our help*! It simply pays to obey God and His Word and to trust Him with the order He has established for the marriage relationship — *God, Christ, husband, wife.* That order will work wonders in our lives if we'll yield and submit to it. It will bless us, our husband, our children, and everyone our lives influence.

*O*ur responsibility is to allow the Holy Spirit to work change and transformation in our own heart and allow Him to work in our husband's heart *without our help*!

Our first sphere of influence as wives is our family. We influence our immediate family members with our behavior and lifestyle. When we show respect to our husband in our home, we build something very strong into our marriage and even into the lives of our children.

A few years ago, someone interviewing our sons said to Paul, "Your dad was gone a lot because of the ministry when you were young. Why didn't you resent his being in the ministry and being absent so much?" Paul responded, "I have to say it was because of my mom."

I didn't always model the right attitude to our sons about Rick's absences, but I learned a lot over the years, and the Lord helped me gradually change that area of my life. The change in me helped our sons as well. When they were small, the Lord dealt with me about my attitude toward Rick and the ministry. In fact, He spoke to me that my attitude about Rick being gone so much was wrong. I was resentful, angry, sad, and jealous. I thought to myself, *I married you so we could be together, not apart.* I had a bad attitude.

For example, there were times when Rick would have to leave home for days and sometimes a couple of weeks at a time for the ministry, and I would be in tears as I drove him to the airport so he could catch his flight. Then I would drive home crying. And as I picked him up from the airport when he returned home, I was still upset! I didn't even realize at the time how upset I was, but the truth is, I lived in a constantly frustrated state.

The Holy Spirit didn't tell me at the time that my attitude could have a dramatic effect on our children. He simply showed me that it was wrong, and He gently reminded me that I could choose to have a different attitude. I could choose to be proud of Rick and be happy for him and the work he was doing. I could embrace the call of God on our lives to affect this region of the world with the Gospel. And I could be grateful that God was blessing Rick and our family and that He would always take care of me and the boys when Rick was away.

On the other hand, I could have chosen not to change and to remain frustrated, bitter, and resentful. But had I done that, I would have stayed in my dark prison, and I would have reaped the consequences of what I was allowing to fester and grow in my heart.

By the grace of God, I was able to embrace a better attitude. Of course I didn't always do it perfectly, but little by little, my attitude became better. I'm so thankful to God that He was able to show me that I was wrong and needed to change. He helped me make the decision to agree with Him and His Word and to submit to His dealings. As a result, I was able to make the necessary changes. Years later, I can see the good fruit of my decision in our grown children. Had I kept my bad attitude and not yielded to the change the Holy Spirit desired to work in me, it is very likely my children would have "caught" the same unhappy disposition I was carrying.

I thank God for the Holy Spirit, who leads us into light and truth — far, far away from deceiving, damaging emotions!'

Please let the message in the following testimony minister the truth to your heart that God wants His very best for your life.

～

Kristina

From a Good Marriage to a Better One

When I was attending the seminars, I thought everything was good with my family. I married my husband a second time after we had been divorced for several years, and I thought all our problems remained behind us in the first marriage. But in the seminars, I began realizing that I didn't really respect my husband. The most terrible thing is that I realized I had taught my son by my behavior not to respect his father. Then I realized that I didn't respect my son either!

God showed me how I am — that I am strong and I think I can deal with problems by myself. But that is not a right position. The most powerful message I received in the seminars was that a woman has the power to lift her husband up or to put him down. I began to change some things in my attitude. For example, I began asking my husband for advice. I began shifting some responsibilities to him that he was supposed to have but had not taken. When I started asking him for advice and for permission about certain things — and respecting him as the leader in our home — at first it was kind of strange for him.

Even in our daily life, I began asking him for permission about certain things and I acknowledged his leadership. If I wanted to buy something, I asked him what he thought about it. When my son heard me, he said, "Mom, I do not understand you. You're an adult. Why are you asking him for permission about this?"

Hearing my son's tone, I understood that I was guilty for his attitude toward his father because I hadn't shown respect to my husband. I understood from the seminars that we might have a good family and a good marriage, but we can have a *better* family and a *better* marriage. And I saw that my "good" was not really as good as I thought! These teachings challenged me to go to a more excellent level in my marriage and family.

When I began to look at my husband from another position and began to listen to him, our family changed. My relationship became closer with my husband, and my son also became more respectful.

♾

Make Good Decisions
Throughout the Day *Every Day*

Part of "building our house" is making the right decisions. We make decisions all the time, such as, *What is my attitude going to be at this moment? What am I going to think about this situation that has come to my attention? How am I going to respond to this dilemma?* We may not be thinking those very words, but we choose our own attitudes, reactions, and responses to the situations and crises of life. Our decisions from moment to moment concerning those attitudes and responses are very powerful.

The true test of our character is how we behave ourselves before the Lord in our closest relationships. This is especially true of marriage. So we need to ask ourselves if we're reacting "off the cuff" — without thinking — to the circumstances of life, or if we're purposefully making solid, biblical decisions to maintain godly attitudes and responses in those relationships.

One day we'll each stand before the Lord, and He will know every thought we nurtured and every behavior we engaged in. And if we've shown respect toward our husband in our attitudes and actions, we will be rewarded for that.

A Prayer of Repentance and Beginning Again

Father, right now I come before You and Your throne of grace in the name of Jesus. I know that You hold no judgment against me, but you have great mercy for me. Father, forgive me for being disrespectful, critical, unforgiving, or offended toward my husband. Forgive me for trying to manipulate and change him. I acknowledge right now that I believe Your way is true and right. And by the power of Your

Word and Your Spirit, I turn away from being disrespectful, critical, and judgmental. Forgive me and cleanse me by the precious blood of Jesus.

Holy Spirit, I know You're here to help me, and I receive Your help. You said You would guide me into all truth. You said You would be my Teacher and Comforter and Guide. I recognize and receive Your ministry right now.

Lord, thank You for my marriage. Thank You for my husband. Help me be a better friend to him. Help me not to tear down my house, but to build up my house with my hands, my words, and my wise decisions by Your Word and Your Holy Spirit.

I acknowledge that the way I should choose to go is different from the world's way, and I want to go *Your* way! Help me avoid making the same mistakes and committing the same sins as generations past. I purpose in my heart to completely forgive and release any person in my heritage — whether parent, grandparent, or great-grandparent — who has exerted a wrong influence in my life. And I do it right now, in Jesus' name. Amen.

Exercises To Help You Practice
Accepting and Affirming Your Husband

1. Can you identify some of the things you've said to your husband, even innocently, that have triggered feelings within him of not being accepted by you? Write down two or three of those "trigger points" and meditate on better ways to express yourself in the future. Write down your new approaches to old situations. Ask the Holy Spirit to help you as you write.

2. Think of two ways in which you'd really like your husband to change. Then write a prayer of committal and consecration to the Lord about it — and keep it between just you and Jesus. Every time you think about those characteristics, quietly recite your prayer. Remember and thank God that He is perfecting both you *and* your husband as *He* sees fit. Then leave those thoughts right there at the "altar" as you cast your care upon the Lord.

3. Make it a point to regularly thank your husband for his paycheck and for how hard he works for his family. Emphasize another one of his strengths each time you do this. Do this without bringing up an area he needs to improve in! Use mercy without judgment. (If your husband isn't bringing in income, find work he does around the home, in the yard, or on your vehicle that you can thank and commend him for.)

4. Write a humble affirmation of your acceptance of your husband just as he is *with no changes*. Think about God's love and grace in your own life in spite of your shortcomings. Ask the Father to show you your husband in a tender, new light — the way *He* sees him — and write about what you see in at least one short paragraph.

Chapter Five

'FORGIVE —
I'M SUPPOSED TO DO THAT *TOO?*'

I wish I could say that your husband will never disappoint you and never hurt your feelings again. I wish I could say that after you forgive him for something he did that bothered or hurt you, he will never do anything like that again. I'd like to tell you that *everyone* in your life, including your husband, will behave correctly at all times and never hurt you, disturb your peace, or tempt you to be resentful or angry. But I can't truthfully say that. People aren't perfect, and you know in your own life that you've missed it and sinned at times and have hurt or disappointed others too.

So what is the answer? In this chapter, we'll cover the need for walking in love and forgiveness in marriage. Love and forgiveness is a huge key in all successful relationships, but especially in marriage — and that love includes not insisting that things always have to be done *our way*. In fact, if we really want to be successful in marriage *and in life*, we're going to have to decide to wholly follow God, and that means doing things *His way*. True success means receiving our instructions from God's Word, the Bible, and obeying that instead of just doing what we want all the time.

The Bible isn't just a book of words that have been around for a few thousand years. No, God's words are *Spirit* and *life*

(John 6:63). They are inspired — God-breathed — and profitable to us, containing the power to change our lives if we'll allow them to change us (*see* 2 Timothy 3:16). And God's Word instructs us as Christians to *forgive* (Mark 11:25). That won't always be easy to do, but we can choose to make *God's* way *our* way and refuse to hold our husband or anyone else in unforgiveness.

> *W*e can choose to make *God's* way *our* way and refuse to hold our husband or anyone else in unforgiveness.

In the last chapter, we looked at acceptance of our husband as a way to show him respect. A very big part of accepting our husband is forgiving him when he misses it or when he doesn't measure up to our expectation of him. If we don't forgive, we're not going to be able to accept our husband as he is because the pain or other negative emotions we feel will keep us from accepting and embracing him from our heart.

When we refuse to accept someone as he is, it is a subtle and self-righteous way of judging that other person. And it's important for us to recognize that sometimes we blame someone else when we're not happy or when things aren't going our way while, actually, *we're* the real source of the problem.

WHEN WE THINK WE'RE BETTER

It's such a temptation for us as women to adopt a self-righteous, unaccepting attitude of others. But when we do that, it makes forgiveness difficult. And if we can't forgive, we won't enjoy freedom in our relationships.

Consider the following testimony of a woman who made the choice to stop judging and to start accepting her husband and enjoying their differences.

❧

Lidiya

'I Worked on Changing Me, and My Husband Changed!'

When we were asked at the seminar, "Who thinks she is smarter than her husband?" I was surprised not to see a lot of hands go up! The question could have just as easily been, "Who thinks she is more spiritual than her husband?" I believed I was. I'm a teacher, and I believe I can diagnose anywhere my husband has a problem! When we were dating, I was already correcting him. I corrected how he spoke, and I showed off my teaching ability regularly!

All my marriage, I kept trying to work on myself, being the more spiritual and mature one — or so I thought. Then when I was invited to the marriage seminar, I thought, *Why do I have to be the one to listen? When will my husband start listening to what HE should do?* But after I attended the seminar, I saw changes in myself and then in him. First of all, I saw that always wanting him to change was stealing from my ability to accept him just as he is and to truly enjoy him. I wasn't really respecting him; I was just tolerating him. I repented to God and started making changes in my attitude and actions.

My husband had a hot temper. Of course, he did not beat me, but he could fling a cup across the room or say something very roughly. But I saw a change in him when one night I could see that he had an opportunity to be angry. He was caring for our son and daughter while I was out, and he asked me to come home at 7:00 p.m. to start watching them because he needed to go to work. But I forgot.

On my way home, having finally remembered, I wondered if he would show his temper. I thought, *What should I expect from him? Even if he doesn't throw a tantrum, he at the very least will not talk to me.* But when I arrived home, I asked him to forgive me. He was very calm and said, "Okay." And he treated the situation very calmly and gently. I saw that as a supernatural blessing. Because my attitude is different, he is more patient and forgiving toward me.

⁓

THE FORCE OF FORGIVENESS
TO RESTORE WHAT WAS LOST

The following is a glorious testimony of the power of forgiveness to restore what had been lost and to cause a seemingly hopeless, "barren" situation to bear much fruit.

This testimony came from a woman in Russia whose husband had abandoned her and their four children, one of whom was an invalid. Imagine the pressure this woman faced trying to function every day under that heavy burden! But even before this man abandoned them, life was a constant hardship. He drank a lot and wasn't supportive of her or the children.

The situation was very painful and chaotic for this woman. She no doubt struggled with anger and resentment. Then she heard the message of forgiveness that I'm sharing with you. It touched her so deeply that she forgave her husband and declared, "I want to get my children to forgive him too."

She taught her children what she had learned and exhorted them to forgive and to release their father for what he had done to them. And a miracle happened: Her husband came back to them! But he didn't just come back — he quit drinking, and he is now serving the Lord. This woman is a servant and minister in her local church, and her husband is now a part of the work she does in the ministry.

Of course, not every situation gets turned around so miraculously when a wife forgives her husband. But that doesn't negate the truth that we must forgive, and it doesn't diminish the power of forgiveness — in our own lives and the lives others — when we choose to release those who have sinned against us.

Forgiveness is such a powerful force. When we *don't* forgive, we can put people in an invisible prison, where we can actually help keep them bound to their character flaws and wrong behaviors. Jesus said, "If you forgive the sins of any, they are forgiven them; if you retain the sins of any, they are retained" (John 20:23). But when we forgive, we release those who have wronged us, freeing them from the shackles of unforgiveness. By doing this, we in turn free our own hearts.

So what are we going to do with this verse of Scripture as it applies to our marriage?

Well, just think for a moment about the calling on your husband's life. When you forgive him, you open the way for God to step in, not only to deal with his heart about your marriage but also to free him to pursue his God-given destiny. But if you do *not* forgive him, you're not giving God the opportunity to work in your situation at all.

If you're holding your husband "prisoner" to his offense against you, you could be hindering your own progress and deliverance! There's so much more to your "Prince Charming" than you may be seeing right now. Through your forgiveness of him, you give God an opening to work in your situation, no matter how long it has remained unchanged. You give the Holy Spirit the potential to completely turn your marriage around! Instead of providing no guidance or support for you and your children, your husband could begin yielding to the dealings of the Holy Spirit, treating you with love and honor and exerting a loving, godly influence over the lives of your children.

What a critical truth to understand and apply to our lives as we seek God about a better relationship with our husband!

MAKING *GOD'S* WAY OF FORGIVENESS *OUR* WAY

If we're going to live our lives sold out to God, it is our responsibility to choose to forgive others' offenses and trespasses against us. Our way can no longer be harboring unforgiveness when we are wronged. Forgiveness must become our new way. In fact, there really *is* no other way if we're going to live by the standard of God's Word and bear fruit for Him. We must choose forgiveness every day of our lives. As we set free through forgiveness those who have offended or hurt us, we allow ourselves to be set free as well.

As we set free through forgiveness those who have offended or hurt us, we allow ourselves to be set free as well.

Two Offenses in Comparison

Jesus forgave and released His offenders. On the Cross, He said, "…Father, forgive them; for they know not what they do…" (Luke 23:34 *KJV*). But before that, He taught much about forgiveness. In Matthew 18, for example, Jesus talked about a servant who was forgiven a great debt, but then went out and demanded that someone else — who owed him much less — pay in full the small debt he owed.

That hardly seemed fair, but many of us regularly do things that are similar in nature. For example, we might come out of church feeling grateful for the huge debt Jesus paid for our forgiveness — but then as we're driving down the road, someone pulls out in front of us in traffic, and we become upset.

It's easy to yield to the temptation to "reach our fingers around the throat" of our offenders and say, *"Pay me what you owe!"* Their debt is so small compared to the huge debt of sin that Jesus paid for us all, yet we want to "choke" the payment of debt from those who offend us (*see* Matthew 18:23-35).

Rick and I and our family have lived in the former Soviet Union for multiple decades, and over the years, I've had the privilege of hearing many testimonies of the power of forgiveness in marriage. Years ago when I was in Ukraine, I met a woman who was in the music ministry with her husband. It was their second marriage, and they were very happy. They had a good marriage and a healthy son.

This woman told me about her first marriage. Her first husband was so abusive and overtaken by alcohol that he affected their son's ability to learn. She said, "I divorced him, and after that, I got saved. I was also filled with the Holy Spirit, and it was shortly afterward that I realized that I couldn't keep living with unforgiveness in my heart toward my first husband."

This woman had remarried after her divorce, and God had given her a good husband. But she could see herself starting to put on him the same kind of expectation to disappoint her that she had connected with her first husband. Her second husband wasn't doing those abusive things, but because of her unforgiveness toward her first husband, the woman was being influenced by that wrong expectation and had started projecting that poisonous attitude onto her second husband.

After this woman was saved and filled with the Holy Spirit, she cried out to the Lord. "Lord, I know I need to forgive my first husband, but I need Your help!" One day she was cleaning out a filthy apartment that was filled with things that needed to be thrown away. She had stuffed several bags with trash to throw out and was so pleased with all the work she had done. Then she looked over and saw a tiny piece of paper on the counter and immediately thought, *I'd better get that.*

At that instant, the Holy Spirit spoke to her and said, *"See that big pile of trash that you gathered and you're so proud of?"* She answered, "Yes, Lord, I'm very happy to be finally getting rid of it."

The Holy Spirit continued, *"Now look at that tiny piece of paper on the counter. The debt you owed Me is represented by that enormous pile of trash. You're so happy to have it finally thrown out."*

Then the Holy Spirit said to her: *"The debt of offense and pain that came from your ex-husband is like that very small piece of paper. In comparison to the weight of sin that I removed from you in My death and resurrection, his offense is very small."*

She saw it in a flash! In that moment, she realized, *How can I ever compare the two offenses!* She saw that she had been forgiven such a huge debt, yet she was holding her ex-husband to a small one in comparison. In the perspective of eternity, the abuse her ex-husband put her through was small compared to everything God had forgiven her for. He had wiped her slate clean and had forever thrown out all the many piles of her "trash" — things that were lost in "the sea of forgetfulness," never to be retrieved or remembered. Yet her attention had been focused on one sin, as reflected by that piece of paper lying on the countertop.

When she saw what the Lord was saying to her, she said, "Oh, God, please forgive me! Forgive me for holding my ex-husband to his wrong behavior — the offense he brought to me, the hurt he inflicted on my heart, and the pain he brought to our son. Please forgive me for holding him in that place. I forgive him, and I release him right now."

When she forgave him, this woman set her ex-husband free. As a result, God's blessing was able to begin flowing freely into her second marriage. Now she has a wonderful marriage with her new husband because she's no longer carrying around pain and offense from her previous marriage. She freed her ex-husband, freed herself, and freed God to work grace and mercy into her present situation *and her future.*

Not only that, but God also healed her son! Forgiveness opened the door of Heaven into every area of her life!

It wasn't that this woman's ex-husband hadn't hurt her. He had. He'd committed terrible wrongs against her and her son. She could have held on to that fact and to her "right" to be angry, resentful, bitter, and unforgiving. But did you know you can be right about something and still be wrong? You can hold on to your right to be angry. But if you do, you'll end up acting wrongly in God's eyes, just as the person who hurt you acted wrongly. The Bible says that the wrath of man does not work the righteousness of God (James 1:20). Nothing good, redemptive, or godly is going to come out of holding on to your anger every time someone hurts you. You will never bear peaceable fruits of righteousness (Hebrews 12:11) doing things your own way instead of yielding to *God's* way.

THE DECEPTION OF ALWAYS BEING RIGHT

It's a terrible deception to think we're always right. Just because we've been wounded doesn't mean that everything we think about the situation is right and that everything our offender thinks about the situation is wrong. We might be hurting, but we still need to humble ourselves and follow *God's* way and *His* path that will lead us out of our hurt and pain.

Sometimes we think we're a better person than someone else, or we compile that hidden "checklist" of things we think that person should change. But how can we assume that we're always right and the other person is always wrong? It's a deceived heart that causes us to think that way. And our belief that we have a right to remain in unforgiveness not only limits those we won't forgive, but it limits us as well.

The enemy would love nothing better than to keep us stuck in a place of being offended, where he can gain access to our lives through our bitterness, hurt, and pain. That's the arena where he and his evil work can thrive. But Jesus wants to deliver us out of that place as we open our lives to His forgiveness. It is His highest and best desire that His grace and mercy flow into every area of our life — and certainly that includes our marriage.

Practical Suggestions To Help You Forgive Your Husband or Those Who Have Wronged You

1. Read Matthew 7:1-5 and ask God to show you if you have any judgmental attitudes in your heart.

   Judge not, that you be not judged. For with what judgment you judge, you will be judged; and with the measure you use, it will be measured back to you. And why do you look at the speck in your brother's eye, but do not consider the plank in your own eye? Or how can you say to your brother, 'Let me remove the speck from your eye'; and look, a plank is in your own eye? Hypocrite! First remove the plank from your own eye, and then you will see clearly to remove the speck from your brother's eye.

2. Memorize Ephesians 4:31,32. (I say these verses almost every day of my life.)

   Let all bitterness, wrath, anger, clamor, and evil speaking be put away from you, with all malice. And be kind to one another, tenderhearted, forgiving one another, even as God in Christ forgave you.

3. Ask your husband to forgive you if you've been harboring unforgiveness in your heart against him. If you have unforgiveness toward others, forgive and release them. If a relationship has been strained, ask that other person to forgive you.

Chapter Six

'ADMIRE AND APPRECIATE HIM FOR *WHAT*!'

You might be thinking, *Could you remind me one more time what I should admire and appreciate about my husband?* For one, you could simply admire his masculinity. If there are times when you can think of nothing else to respect him for, you could just appreciate the fact that he's a man with all the natural characteristics of manhood that God has given him.

Being proud to be a man is something God put inside our husband, and that's not something for us to belittle, criticize, or judge. That's why it's so important not to try to teach, correct, or change our husband. It demeans him and wounds his pride as a man. And we *certainly* shouldn't tell him that he should be more humble — or, worse yet, try to humble him ourselves.

AFFIRM YOUR HUSBAND'S STRENGTH AND MASCULINITY

Sometimes a wife tries to humble her husband and "deliver" him from this pride. But the truth is, God made him that way. She needs to enjoy and appreciate her husband's masculine strength.

He likes it when his wife admires him for his masculinity. In fact, most men *need* this kind of admiration.

Women go through the pain of having babies. They are strong in that respect. Probably no man would want to go through the pain of giving birth! But men have a strength that women do not have, and they have a deep need to be affirmed and admired for that strength.

It's dangerous to a man's emotional makeup when someone comes against his masculine strength. Most of us don't fully realize the potential we have as a wife to weaken our husband, whom God made to be strong. But when our words and actions are demeaning and critical, a whittling down of his character takes place.

If a man hears negative words from his wife for years and years, when she is older and needs him to be strong, he won't be able to give her what she'll need from him. She will have torn down her house with her own hands

In fact, if a man hears negative words from his wife for years and years, when she is older and needs him to be strong, he won't be able to give her what she'll need from him. She will have torn down her house with her own hands (*see* Proverbs 14:1), and, sadly, she will have to eat the fruit of her words. Proverbs 18:21 (*KJV*) says, "Death and life are in the power of the tongue: and they that love it shall eat the fruit thereof."

If a wife demeans her husband, she not only has the potential of weakening him and preventing him from being the strong husband she desires, but she also diminishes him in the eyes of their children to their detriment. On the other hand, when she builds him up and affirms him, she releases her husband to become the best he can be in his God-given role as the leader of his family.

For example, I tried the best I could to raise our boys to have godly habits and attitudes. Of course, I nurtured them just like mothers do. I took care of their hurts and pains. I comforted them tenderly when life dealt them a harsh blow. But the strength in our boys didn't come from me. God put that strength in them, but it was developed by the influence of their dad.

NOTICE AND APPRECIATE YOUR HUSBAND'S PHYSICAL AND MENTAL ABILITIES

A wife needs to appreciate and enjoy her husband's physical and mental strengths and capabilities. If affirming her husband doesn't come naturally to her, she may need to simply practice noticing him instead of being preoccupied or ignoring him. A man's need for affirmation is part of his male pride that God built into him. So it's important that a wife use her words to build her husband up instead of tearing him down. In fact, one of her roles as a wife is to affirm her husband.

Even at a very young age, a boy possesses this kind of male pride. Once, our oldest grandchild William showed me with great joy a sword he'd made from paper and tape. It was rather ingenious because there were several components to this "sword." I looked at it carefully and told him again and again, "William, it's amazing the way you put this sword together." He talked to me about his unique creation for about 45 minutes. I made a big deal of it because it was such a big deal to him.

It might be tempting for women to think men are being prideful because of their desire to be admired. But I can't say it enough — this need for affirmation was put in them by God. So be generous with your compliments toward your husband. Tell him often what a wonderful man he is. Compliment his mental, emotional, and spiritual strength. Talk about his perseverance and dedication when times are tough — or his life of honor in a world that is very *dishonorable*. If you feel like you can't do that truthfully, compliment his physical attributes as a man. Your affirmation of your husband strengthens him to dream bigger and go higher. Even when you may feel like giving up, he'll keep going if you'll build him up instead of tearing him down. God placed that kind of drive in him, and it's there for you to notice and affirm.

Another need your husband has is to be appreciated and admired sexually. Just as you shouldn't show indifference to his physical attributes, you should notice him and compliment him in this way too. It might be uncomfortable, but think about how much you love it when your husband talks about the softness of your skin or about other attributes that are unique to you as a woman. In a similar way, you will be meeting one of his deepest needs by affirming his sexuality. If this is difficult for you, I encourage you to pray about it and say to the Lord, "God, You made my husband; please show me how I can encourage him and be a blessing to him."

But even beyond being admired for his masculine attributes and characteristics, your husband has dreams in his heart, placed there by God, and he wants his dreams to be affirmed too. In fact, sharing those dreams and trusting them to you as his wife is very important to him. His dreams are an integral part of who he is as a man, so when he shares them, he is giving you a part of his very self. And perhaps more than anything else, he doesn't want that part of him to be ignored, belittled, or trampled underfoot.

Your husband wants to know that you care very deeply about his dreams and the plan of God for his life — and that you want to stand beside him to see those dreams come to pass. So please don't ever be careless with your husband's dreams and desires. He will stop sharing his heart with you if he perceives that you don't really care.

Remember that when you meet your husband's God-given needs, you're doing it as unto the Lord, and God sees your faithfulness. When you affirm your husband as a man — and *as the man God has given you* — you're also sowing seed for a similar kind of kindness to be returned to you. You're operating in the wisdom of God to build a peaceful, godly home and family as you sow good things into your "happily-ever-after" future.

Your husband wants to know that you care very deeply about his dreams and the plan of God for his life — and that you want to stand beside him to see those dreams come to pass.

AFFIRM YOUR HUSBAND'S INHERENT ABILITY TO LEAD AND GUIDE

Have you ever noticed that when you're talking to your husband about a problem or something that's on your heart, something "strange" often happens? Something's bothering you, and you want to open your heart and talk to him about it — *but he just wants to solve the problem!* That's because he's a guide. You probably didn't want your husband to solve your problem; you just wanted to talk to him about it. But don't automatically ignore his advice. He's simply trying to guide you. He has pride about that because God built it into him. When you say you don't want to hear his advice — that you just want to open your heart to him and talk — that has the potential of wounding him. And if you say it often enough, your husband may lose the desire to guide you. You'll close the door on his guidance. Remember, a woman can *build up* her house or *tear down* her house with her own hands (Proverbs 14:1).

Our husband has a certain pride in being our guide. I used to think it was a matter of control on the husband's part. In my own marriage, I mistakenly used to think that Rick just wanted to control me. I didn't understand what I know now — that he just wanted to help *guide* me. I used to think, *I'll guide myself, thank you very much.* I didn't realize that the desire to help guide was something God placed in him.

I encourage you to be proud of your husband when he guides you, accept the protection he offers, and appreciate the financial provision he supplies. Don't make light of any of these things. Your husband desires to be respected, admired, and appreciated — *valued and affirmed.* It's the way God made him.

Certainly, husbands are not all angels. But we're learning about the way God designed a husband to function so that as a wife, we can conduct ourselves with wisdom and help *build* our marriage instead of tearing it down with our own hands. When we gain knowledge of the way God made our husband, it helps us understand and appreciate him and submit to the gifts God placed in him to bless us.

It's easy for us as a wife to make mistakes in showing respect and appreciation for our husband. So many of our mistakes are due to our lack of understanding. In my own life, I didn't understand for years how to properly respect and appreciate Rick. I had a lot to learn! But thank God, I really wanted to learn and grow, and by His grace, the Holy Spirit was able to teach me so many things I didn't know. As I said, I'm not perfect; I still have further to go. But I'm very thankful for what He has been able to teach me so far.

Affirm His Pride in You and His Desire for Status

Status is very important to men. If your husband wants a better education or a better job — or even if he wants to work more hours at the job he has — be proud of him because God made him that way. He's trying to be a good provider. Providing well for his family is part of his status.

Men have great pride in their status, even the status of having a wife and family who are well-provided for. Have you ever noticed that when a wife dresses up and looks especially nice, most husbands are proud of that? It's as if they're saying everywhere they go, *"This is MY wife. Isn't she beautiful and sweet?"* Having a wife who takes care of herself and displays a godly attitude is part of their status.

Rick honors me in this way in front of others, and I used to get embarrassed when he did it. But now when he says, "This is my beautiful wife!" I smile graciously and take the compliment with the attitude, *Yes, that's me!* I'm doing better today at receiving public compliments from Rick than I did years ago. Now I accept his pride in me because I understand that's the way he's wired, and I don't want to do anything to diminish that characteristic in him.

Years ago before we moved to the former USSR, Rick bought me a very beautiful ring. The wedding ring he'd given me when we were married had broken several times, and I didn't even have a ring for about two years. I was pregnant with Joel at the time and still pushing Philip in a stroller. Rick decided I needed a wedding ring, so he went shopping for one and chose one that was very beautiful. But I was embarrassed about it because it was so beautiful. Somehow I thought I shouldn't have a ring that was so stunning. In fact, I wondered why he would spend money on a ring when we could have used that money for other things, such as for the boys or for us as a family. I knew he was excited about the ring. I simply didn't understand how proud it made him to provide it for me.

Rick would say to people, "Did you see the new wedding ring I gave Denise?" I would giggle bashfully as I held out my hand to show the ring. I'm not sure where the idea came from that I should be embarrassed, but I was. (I think I viewed jewelry as materialistic and believed we shouldn't have things that are fancy or nice.) That thought had somehow been embedded in my character, *and it wasn't a harmless thought* because for a long time, I failed to appreciate properly the nice things Rick did for me.

I should have been the one excitedly saying, "Have you seen the ring Rick gave me!" I just didn't understand that his generous gift to me reflected his pride in me and in his ability to provide for me and to show that he cherished me.

There is another very important reason your husband spends money on you. It's not just because of his status — it's because he wants to show his love to you. Sometimes we as wives make the mistake of thinking we have to be the thrifty, frugal ones. We would rather see money spent on the family than on us, especially if the money spent on us is for things we think are extravagant or not really necessary. But when we fail to receive our husband's gifts with joy and gratitude, we hurt his feelings and diminish his expression of love toward us. Yet according to Ephesians 5:33, love from our husband is one of the biggest needs we have!

I challenge you with this: The next time your husband gives you a gift, just act like you're Cinderella and he's Prince Charming who has just found your glass slipper! Be gracious and appreciative. Affirming his expressions of love like this will go a long way in ensuring a deeper, more affectionate love relationship between you and your husband — and a rich and enduring *happily ever after*!

AFFIRM HIS NEED FOR AFFIRMATION!
(A FISH STORY)

Something else that can diminish your husband's pride is open criticism from you, especially in front of others. For example, he may be talking with someone about a particular event that happened, and you're thinking, *I sure don't remember it that way.* Don't ever do what some wives do, bursting right in and correcting their husband: "No, that's not the story I know" or, "That's not the way it happened at all!"

Don't correct your husband in public because you will really hurt him if you do. It doesn't matter how he tells a story. His way of expressing himself is a reflection of his unique nature and character. If you correct him, he'll resent it. You'll embarrass him, and you'll have to endure the unpleasant effects of it later. Your time together will be ruined — all because you decided to be his personal fact-checker!

Have you ever noticed that at times when we're talking with others, our stories can seem a little bigger than they really are, such as the notorious "fish stories" we joke about so often? Many times we remember a story a little differently than someone else who shared that moment with us.

Here's a question to ask yourself before you speak in a similar situation: *Is it going to matter five years from now if he told the story the way I would have told it? Is what I want to say to correct him worth him losing his dignity — and me losing mine?* I know the answer to those questions will probably be *no*. So I encourage you to be gracious. Smile and be proud of your husband! He needs your affirmation, admiration, and respect, not your criticism.

Name-calling is another thing that can cause so much hurt and damage to your husband. It's important not to put him down in public by saying things like, "My husband simply can't tell the truth!" That is a very judgmental comment. You may have a strong desire to maintain absolute accuracy and integrity in all things, but have you ever stopped to think that maybe *you* could be wrong about the way something happened?

Besides, it's mean-spirited for a wife to call her husband names at any time — but *especially* in front of others. She would cringe with embarrassment if he did that to her, so she should make it a special point never to do it to him.

AFFIRM HIS ABILITY TO PROVIDE
FOR YOU AND HIS FAMILY

In Chapter Three, we looked at respecting our husband's role as leader and provider. A man's ability to provide for his family is very important to him because God made him to be a provider. So it's important that we never belittle anything related to our husband's ability to provide for us.

I realize that many wives have jobs and careers to help provide income and the family's household needs. But it's very hurtful if wives constantly call attention to that fact, especially in front of others.

For example, if you earn a portion of your family's income, you may say something to others about how much you contribute to the family's household income. Maybe it's true that you couldn't even meet your budget without the contribution you make. But that doesn't mean your husband enjoys hearing you talk about it in front of others. You may mention it completely innocently — because you're happy to help your family and be a blessing in this way. But to call attention to this fact in front of others may demean and belittle your husband.

God designed men as providers. Your husband probably doesn't want the spotlight placed on him as someone who needs help to do what God created him to do! Functioning in his role as provider is part of his image and status. When that image is undermined — or even if it's under-affirmed — he feels put down.

I don't want you to feel guilty or condemned if you haven't affirmed your husband's ability to provide for you or if you've hurt him with your words because he's failed in some way in this area. I just want you to see the pain that can result by your belittling him. Calling attention to his failures won't help your circumstances. What it *will* do, however, is hurt him as a man and damage your marriage relationship.

Try putting yourself in a similar position for a moment. Suppose your husband is a better cook than you, or he's a superior housekeeper. What if your children favored him all the time by going to him with every problem or need so he could nurture and care for them? Then imagine being together with friends as your husband announces: "I'll tell you — if it weren't for me, our kids wouldn't know how to tie their shoes, brush their teeth, or do *anything*! And if I didn't cook, they'd never eat healthy food."

I don't know about you, but if Rick had ever said anything like that in public, I would have looked for the nearest hole to crawl into so I could hide!

Women are generally very nurturing. God made them nurturers by nature. And most women take a great deal of pride in their homes, the way their households are run, and how their children are cared for. But what if their husbands started taking over those wives' sphere of responsibility and making belittling comments about how they need help around the house all the time or things would fall apart? It would cause pain in the hearts of those women.

The same is true when a wife interferes with her husband's "provider" role. Generally speaking, a man is not in touch with his feelings as much as a woman is in touch with *her* feelings, so he might not say anything in response to his wife's comments about his ability to provide. But just because he remains silent doesn't mean he won't feel hurt if she criticizes him or fails to affirm him.

It seems that most women can articulate what they feel, why they feel it, and when they first began to feel it! Men don't usually articulate their feelings in great detail, especially their hurt feelings. Instead of talking about their pain, they'll just begin closing their heart. Then before you know it, they'll begin speaking harshly instead of tenderly like they used to.

Of course, a husband can speak in harsh tones when he's overly tired or when he's anxious or worried about something. That goes for wives too. But if a husband's outward behavior changes over time and he loses the tenderness he once demonstrated toward his wife, it could be a sign that he's hurt about something.

Certainly, no husband is flawless in his role as leader in the home. Your husband may show some weaknesses in his masculine role, just as you may show some weaknesses in your feminine role in the marriage. But when you truly understand that your husband simply doesn't think like you, you'll be better able to appreciate your differences and value your husband's uniqueness. And you'll see better the need to affirm and compliment your husband often in his role as leader, protector, and provider.

Affirming your husband can be as simple as understanding his God-given characteristics and design and then genuinely appreciating his uniqueness *and* yours! Your femininity brings out the best of his masculinity. From the way you move and speak to the way you dress — graced with composure and poise — your femininity is attractive to your husband. It enhances his masculinity and helps reveal his potential as the man God created him to be.

Exercises To Help You Build Your House Wisely as You Build Up and Affirm Your Husband

1. When your husband comes home from work, purpose in your heart not to pressure him to talk about his day or to flood his mind with problems you encountered while he was away. Instead, give him time to pause before engaging him in deep conversation. Welcome him home, but give him his space. Recognize that his home really is his haven — the only place where he can truly rest.

2. Does clutter bother your husband and make him feel restless? Make a list of ways you can help make your home a sought-after haven that your husband eagerly anticipates coming home to. I encourage you to work to maintain your home as a place of rest and repose for your husband. He may not always tell you, but he will value and appreciate this gesture of consideration toward him.

3. It's difficult for husbands if their wives excel in something they do well at too. Be sensitive to that. In what ways can you truthfully affirm *his* gifts and talents? Ask yourself the question and answer honestly, *Am I competing with my husband in some area of our lives?*

4. Be sensitive to your husband's dreams. What are they? Can you name a few of both his short-term and long-term goals? Next to his dreams, write down character traits in him that will help him as he moves forward in these areas. Then make it a point to recognize and affirm those traits (his leadership skills, his strength and confidence, his intelligence, his boldness, etc.).

5. Realize that your husband likes to show you his strength and desires to be affirmed. Write down things you appreciate

about his physical strength, including his physical attributes. Communicate those to him as often as you can.

6. When Rick and I travel apart, I'm used to taking care of my own suitcase, but when we travel together, he likes to take care of that for me. In the past, because I didn't want to burden him, I'd resist his help, and I'd unknowingly insult him. But now I say, "Thank you, Honey. I'd be glad if you would take care of that for me."

    Similarly, if your husband carries something heavy for you, opens a door for you, or performs some other act of chivalry in your behalf, be sure to graciously accept his demonstration of kindness and thank him for it!

Conclusion

BECOMING ONE — A LIFELONG PROCESS

I said earlier in this book that in marriage *and in life*, each one of us is on a journey of growth and change. And it's a *personal* journey. Your journey is uniquely yours. Although you entered into a sacred covenant before God in your marriage — and you became "one flesh" with your husband (Ephesians 5:31) — the journey of your walk with the Lord is yours alone to make. It's your own personal adventure of transformation, of discovery of God Himself as your ultimate Husband, and of learning His heart and His ways. It's the adventure of a lifetime — and it's one that *lasts* a lifetime.

In much the same way, when you married your husband, your wedding ceremony was not the ultimate goal for your life. It was only the beginning! Your act of *"I do"* began the lifelong process of becoming one with your husband (*see* Ephesians 5:31). In other words, marriage is not just a single act; it's a *process*. As a married couple, you are two individuals joined in a holy union, the sacred institution of marriage. Now you must learn to flow together and be a blessing to each other and to others as you embark upon a *new* journey.

Our pastor counseled Rick and me just days before our wedding, saying, "It will take you a lifetime to become one." What a precious truth he spoke into our lives on that day!

In a time when people want a "prefabricated" marriage that takes no work of their own to build, these words are especially meaningful. How many times do we see people walk away from their marriage when things get hard or the relationship appears to be stagnant? They do it only to get into another marriage, where they have the same expectation that their "happily ever after" union will somehow be ready-made with little or no effort on their part.

The Maker of marriage knows how to build a beautiful, healthy marriage and cause it to continually grow and thrive. So it stands to reason that we need His help at all times to cooperate with Him in this lifelong process. Yielding to Him — to His Word and His Spirit — may not always be easy, because our flesh doesn't like yielding! Our flesh enjoys taking control, leaning to our own understanding, and having everything our own way — all the things the Bible instructs us *not* to do, especially in our dealings with others. But that is not God's way, and God's way is the *only* way of doing things that He will bless, prosper, and crown with His grace.

My prayer is that the content of this book will add to your tool chest of marital wisdom and help you realize that Cinderella hasn't been stolen after all! The princess and gracious woman of God He created you to be is still inside you. *And Prince Charming is still somewhere in your husband!* Your dreams of a "happily ever after" may have been deferred or even lost for a season. But don't throw your marriage relationship away — and *don't* diminish its importance.

Life brings many challenges to us all, and those challenges have the potential to darken the paths that started out so bright. But in the midst of difficult trials, God's words of truth and light ring true: "Wherefore they are no more twain, but one flesh. What therefore God hath joined together, let not man put asunder" (Matthew 19:6 *KJV*). As you commit to weather life's storms together, the God who commands your commitment will help fortify your union and supply you with wisdom, understanding, and strength "until death do you part."

Of course, your success in life depends on how diligently you navigate your personal spiritual journey before God. As I said previously, my situation was probably different than yours. We can't compare our journey with someone else's because we're each in a different place facing a different set of circumstances.

So don't allow yourself to feel condemned or discouraged with your progress. Yes, progress takes a lot of work — a lot of prayer, patience, and selfless thinking. "Happily ever after" is not just a *dream*; it's an *art*. But you must always remember that because you and your husband are imperfect beings, you must focus on Jesus as your Answer — your Wisdom and your Guide — and on enjoying the journey itself! As you enjoy an ever-deepening relationship with the Lord *and* with your husband, you'll discover your "happily ever after" along the way — with the best of your days together still to come!

My Prayer for You

Lord, I thank You for the woman who has been touched by the teaching in this book. I pray a blessing over her life, her home, and her marriage. What God has joined together, let no man separate or put asunder. I pray that no weapon formed against her shall prosper and that her home will be established in heavenly order — *God, Christ, husband, and wife.*

Thank You for doing a work in this precious woman's heart and bringing her to a place of willing, loving submission to Your Word. Thank You for the power of the Holy Spirit that is already at work in her heart. I acknowledge You, Holy Spirit, that You are her Helper, her Comforter, her Teacher, and her Guide, and You will lead her into the whole, clear, full truth. I pray that she hears Your voice in moments that might be somewhat difficult — Your voice calling her to forgive, to extend mercy, to show respect and appreciation, and to keep quiet and calm at the appropriate times.

Thank You that her marriage will be abundantly blessed by Your hand as she seeks You and opens her heart to Your will and Your ways. Thank You that You're working in this beloved daughter of Yours because she has opened the door of her heart to experience Your wisdom, goodness, guidance, and power in her marriage. We give You all the glory and honor in Jesus' name. Amen.

Endnotes

Preface

[1]Marilyn Murray, "Pain of World War II Is Passed On to Children," *The Moscow Times* 5057 (January 30, 2013). www.themoscowtimes.com/opinion/article/pain-of-world-war-ii-is-passed-on-to-children/474703.html#ixzz2i2Xuia3R.

[2]Helen Andelin, *Fascinating Womanhood* (New York: Bantam Books, 1990).

Chapter 2

[1] www.divorcepad.com/rate/divorce-rate-in-russia.html
Naselenie SSSR 1987 (Population of the USSR 1987). Statistical Yearbook. Moscow, Finansy i Statistika, 1988, p. 190; Demograficheskij Ezhegodnik Rossijskoj Federacii 1993 (The Demographic Yearbook of the Russian Federation 1993). Moscow, Goskomstat of Russia, 1994, p. 97.

[2] http://www.startribune.com/lifestyle/118101934.html

[3] ibid.

Chapter 3

[1] Renner, Denise, *The Gift of Forgiveness* (Tulsa: Harrison House, 2004), pp. 48,52.

Chapter 4

[1] http://www.cnn.com/2011/HEALTH/08/17/bitter.resentful.ep/

PRAYER OF FORGIVENESS

Perhaps you've been wondering why you haven't grown much in your relationship with God lately. If unforgiveness toward your offenders has been holding you back, I urge you to pray this prayer from your heart:

Heavenly Father, please forgive me for holding unforgiveness toward others in my heart. I ask You to cleanse me by the blood of Jesus of all resentment and bitterness and to help me release each of my offenders from the prison I've held them in through my unwillingness to forgive.

God, I ask You to please forgive my offenders and to bless them. Do not charge this sin to their account. I know that Jesus paid for their sin, so I ask You, Lord, to please forgive them. And please, Lord, forgive me for holding anything in my heart against them. Cleanse me right now with Your precious blood.

Father, thank You for the power and responsibility You have given me to remit and release others through forgiveness. Right now by faith in Jesus' name, I set my offenders free. Thank You for forgiving me as I forgive them. From this day forward, I purpose to forgive from my heart all those who trespass against me so that they can be free to change, and I can be free to live in the fullness of Your love, peace, and joy. In Jesus' name. Amen.

ABOUT THE AUTHOR

Denise Renner is an able minister, a mentor to women, an author, and a classically trained vocalist. Alongside her husband Rick Renner, Denise spent years ministering in the U.S. before moving in 1991 with their family to the former Soviet Union, where they began their international ministry. Since that time, Rick and Denise have proclaimed the Gospel throughout the vast region of the former USSR. Their ministry reaches a potential audience of millions in both hemispheres of the world via television, satellite, and the Internet.

Rick and Denise reside in Moscow, where they lead the Moscow Good News Church. Denise directs a large women's ministry in the church that affects women from all over Moscow. Thousands of women have been mentored and trained in her marriage seminars in person or online. Meanwhile, whether in historic concert halls, local churches, or her ministry to women, Denise still regularly ministers in music, using her remarkably gifted voice to bring Christ's burden-destroying anointing to those in need of His touch.

CONTACT RENNER MINISTRIES

For further information
about RENNER Ministries,
please contact the office nearest you,
or visit the ministry website at:
www.renner.org

ALL USA
CORRESPONDENCE:

RENNER Ministries
P. O. Box 702040
Tulsa, OK 74170-2040
(918) 496-3213
Or 1-800-RICK-593
Email: renner@renner.org
Website: www.renner.org

MOSCOW OFFICE:

RENNER Ministries
P. O. Box 789
101000, Moscow, Russia
+7 (495) 727-1470
Email: blagayavestonline@ignc.org
Website: www.ignc.org

RIGA OFFICE:

RENNER Ministries
Unijas 99
Riga LV-1084, Latvia
+371 67802150
Email: info@goodnews.lv

KIEV OFFICE:

RENNER Ministries

P. O. Box 300

01001, Kiev, Ukraine

+38 (044) 451-8315

Email: blagayavestonline@ignc.org

OXFORD OFFICE:

RENNER Ministries

Box 7, 266 Banbury Road

Oxford OX2 7DL, England

+44 1865 521024

Email: europe@renner.org

Brand New!
Free 'Cinderella' Classes

by Denise Renner

For the past several years, Denise has taught marriage classes for the women in the church she pastors with her husband, Rick Renner, in Moscow, Russia. These sessions have yielded amazing testimonies among the families of this thriving church in Russia's capital city.

Denise's book *Who Stole Cinderella?* was written from what she learned in her own life experiences and from her studies as she has led others in seeing their lives and marriages restored and transformed. Her video classes contain expanded information and are ideal for personal study or study with a church group or friends.

"School of Cinderella" lesson titles include the following:

Accept Your Husband as He Is
The Danger of Judging Others
A Life Message More Powerful Than Words
Your Thankfulness Is Powerful
God's Intervention in Forgiveness
How To Open Your Husband's Heart
You Are Free From the Curse
God's Alignment in the Home
Wisdom Is the Principal Thing
Keys To Becoming a Wise Woman
Struggling With Unforgiveness and Bitterness
Submitting Yourself to God Gives You Power
Jesus Is Our Rock!
Be Confident — Jesus Is Still Working on You!
Forgiveness — the Pathway to 'Happily Ever After'

Visit **www.CinderellaVideos.com** to learn more about Denise's teachings on strengthening yourself, your marriage, and your home!

OTHER BOOKS BY DENISE RENNER

*The Gift of Forgiveness**

*Do You Know What Time It Is?**

*Redeemed From Shame**

*Digital version available for Kindle, Nook, iBook,
and other eBook formats. For retail purchases and more information,
visit us online at: **www.renner.org**.

Do You Know What Time It Is?

You may have lost some opportunities in the past because you kept putting off what God told you to do. But it's never too late to stop wasting time! Denise Renner states: "These are crucial times we live in, and how we spend our time is a very serious matter. We must take the opportunities we have available right now to do what God has called us to do, because

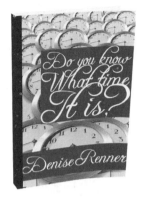

the clock is ticking,

and time is passing us by." Let Denise inspire you to get back on track with God's purposes for your life as you pursue all that He has for you — every minute of every day!

The Gift of Forgiveness

The act of forgiveness is one of the greatest yet most difficult commands that Jesus asks of us. Denise Renner draws both from the Word and from her own life experience to guide the reader from the depths of pain and despair to the ultimate act of love and emotional freedom through the act of forgiving others.

Redeemed From Shame

In this book, Denise Renner demonstrates how the love of Jesus through the power of the Holy Spirit can set anyone free who has been emotionally crippled by shame in his or her life. Let the redeemed of the Lord say, "I am whole!" The message of *Redeemed From Shame* will change your life!

Songs About the Cross (CD & MP3)
Hymns That Herald the Power of the Cross
(CD and MP3 Digital Download)

The awesome power of God's redeeming love for mankind was revealed at Calvary when Jesus became sin and bore its penalty on our behalf.

Denise Renner's "Songs About the Cross" is a collection of nine beloved hymns that herald the transforming power of the Cross. Each hymn extols the marvelous forgiveness and deliverance purchased for us through the blood and death of Jesus Christ on the Cross. With her superb, classically trained soprano voice, Denise magnificently communicates the splendor of divine love through lyrics that remind you of the terrible price Jesus so willingly paid to redeem you back to God. This beautiful collection of timeless hymns, so rich in doctrinal truth, will strengthen and establish your soul as it edifies your spirit and enrich your own personal devotions.

Classical Praise From the Heart
(MP3 Digital Download)
**Experience the Classics
With a Fresh Anointing**

In *Classic Praise From the Heart,* Denise Renner's exquisite soprano voice soars in magnificent beauty and power. The anointing upon her voice and the music will usher you into the presence of God as Denise sings this thrilling collection of standard hymns of the Church.

Order your copy of Denise Renner's *Classical Praise From the Heart* today, and experience the classics in a fresh new way.

To purchase Denise's music in CD or MP3 format, visit:
www.store.renner.org.

BOOKS BY RICK RENNER

Build Your Foundation*
Chosen by God*
Dream Thieves*
Dressed To Kill*
The Holy Spirit and You*
How To Keep Your Head on Straight in a World Gone Crazy*
How To Receive Answers From Heaven!*
Insights to Successful Leadership*
Last-Days Survival Guide
Life in the Combat Zone*
A Life Ablaze*
A Light in Darkness, Volume One,
  Seven Messages to the Seven Churches series
The Love Test*
No Room for Compromise, Volume Two,
  Seven Messages to the Seven Churches series
Paid in Full*
The Point of No Return*
Repentance*
Signs You'll See Just Before Jesus Comes*
Sparkling Gems From the Greek Daily Devotional 1*
Sparkling Gems From the Greek Daily Devotional 2*
Spiritual Weapons To Defeat the Enemy*
Ten Guidelines To Help You Achieve
  Your Long-Awaited Promotion!*
Testing the Supernatural
Turn Your God-Given Dreams Into Reality*
Why We Need the Gifts of the Spirit*
The Will of God — The Key to Your Success*
You Can Get Over It*

*Digital version available for Kindle, Nook, and iBook.
Note: Books by Rick Renner are available for purchase at:

www.renner.org

A LIGHT IN DARKNESS
VOLUME ONE

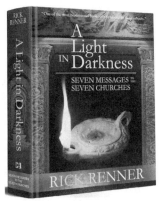

840 pages
(Hardback)

Step into the world of the First Century Church as Rick Renner creates a panoramic experience of unsurpassed detail to transport you into the ancient lands of the seven churches of Asia. Within the context of this fascinating — and, at times, shocking — historical backdrop, Rick outlines the challenges that early believers faced in taking the Gospel to a pagan world. After presenting a riveting account of the apostle John's vision of the exalted Christ, Rick leads you through an in-depth study of Jesus' messages to the churches of Ephesus and Smyrna — profoundly relevant messages that still resonate for His Church today.

Rick's richly detailed historical narrative, enhanced by classic artwork and superb photographs, will make the lands and the message of the Bible come alive to you as never before. Parallels between Roman society of the First Century and the modern world prove the current relevance of Christ's warning and instructions.

In this first volume of the *Seven Messages to the Seven Churches* series, you will discover:

- In-depth scriptural teaching that makes the New Testament come alive.

- A more than 800-page beautifully designed full-color hardback book — filled with photos shot on location, plus photos of classic artwork, artifacts, illustrations, maps, *and much more.*

- A comprehensive, completely indexed reference book.

A Light in Darkness, Volume One, is an extraordinary book that will endure and speak to generations to come. This authoritative first volume is a virtual encyclopedia of knowledge — a definitive go-to resource for any student of the Bible and a classic must-have for Christian families everywhere.

Faced with daunting challenges, the modern Church must give urgent heed to what the Holy Spirit is saying in order to be equipped for the end of this age.

To order, visit us online at: **www.renner.org**

Book Resellers: Contact Harrison House at 800-722-6774
or visit **www.HarrisonHouse.com** for quantity discounts.

SPARKLING GEMS FROM THE GREEK 1

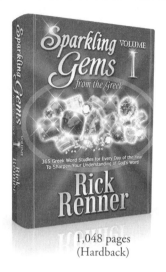

In 2003, Rick Renner's *Sparkling Gems From the Greek 1* quickly gained widespread recognition for its unique illumination of the New Testament through more than 1,000 Greek word studies in a 365-day devotional format. Today *Sparkling Gems 1* remains a beloved resource that has spiritually strengthened believers worldwide. As many have testified, the wealth of truths within its pages never grows old. Year after year, *Sparkling Gems 1* continues to deepen readers' understanding of the Bible.

1,048 pages
(Hardback)

To order, visit us online at: **www.renner.org**

Book Resellers: Contact Harrison House at 800-722-6774 or visit **www.HarrisonHouse.com** for quantity discounts.

SPARKLING GEMS FROM THE GREEK 2

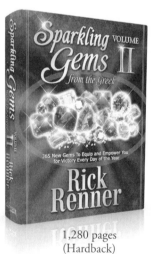

Rick infuses into *Sparkling Gems From the Greek 2* the added strength and richness of many more years of his own personal study and growth in God — expanding this devotional series to impact the reader's heart on a deeper level than ever before. This remarkable study tool helps unlock new hidden treasures from God's Word that will draw readers into an ever more passionate pursuit of Him.

To order, visit us online at: **www.renner.org**

1,280 pages
(Hardback)

Book Resellers: Contact Harrison House at 800-722-6774 or visit **www.HarrisonHouse.com** for quantity discounts.

HOW TO KEEP YOUR HEAD ON STRAIGHT IN A WORLD GONE CRAZY

DEVELOPING DISCERNMENT FOR THESE LAST DAYS

400 pages
(Paperback)

The world is changing. In fact, it's more than changing — it has *gone crazy*.

We are living in a world where faith is questioned and sin is welcomed — where people seem to have lost their minds about what is right and wrong. It seems truth has been turned *upside down*.

In Rick Renner's book ***How To Keep Your Head on Straight in a World Gone Crazy***, he reveals the disastrous consequences of a society in spiritual and moral collapse. In this book, you'll discover what Christians need to be doing to stay out of the chaos and remain anchored to truth. You'll learn how to stay sensitive to the Holy Spirit, how to discern right and wrong teaching, how to be grounded in prayer, and how to be spiritually prepared for living in victory in these last days.

Leading ministers from around the world are calling this book essential for every believer. Topics include:

- Contending for the faith in the last days
- How to pray for leaders who are in error
- How to judge if a teaching is good or bad
- Seducing spirits and doctrines of demons
- How to be a good minister of Jesus Christ

To order, visit us online at: **www.renner.org**

Book Resellers: Contact Harrison House at 800-722-6774 or visit **www.HarrisonHouse.com** for quantity discounts.

LAST-DAYS SURVIVAL GUIDE

A SCRIPTURAL HANDBOOK
TO PREPARE YOU FOR THESE PERILOUS TIMES

472 pages
(Paperback)

In his book *Last-Days Survival Guide*, Rick Renner thoroughly expands on Second Timothy 3 concerning the last-days signs to expect in society as one age draws to a close before another age begins.

Rick also thoroughly explains how not to just *survive* the times, but to *thrive* in their midst. God wants you as a believer to be equipped — *outfitted* — to withstand end-time storms, to navigate wind-tossed seas, and to sail with His grace and power to fulfill your divine destiny on earth!

If you're concerned about what you're witnessing in society today — and even in certain sectors of the Church — the answers you need in order to keep your gaze focused on Christ and maintain your victory are in this book!

To order, visit us online at: **www.renner.org**

Book Resellers: Contact Harrison House at 800-722-6774 or visit **www.HarrisonHouse.com** for quantity discounts.

BUILD YOUR FOUNDATION

Six Must-Have Beliefs for Constructing an Unshakable Christian Life

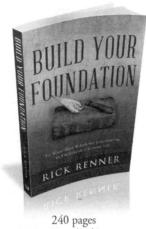

240 pages
(Paperback)

A building contractor has a top priority every time he begins a construction project: *to get the foundation right.* He knows that's the key to the stability and endurance of the structure he is building. If his crew lays the foundation wrong, the rest of the building might ultimately look good — but it will always have problems and will possibly never fulfill its purpose for being constructed in the first place.

That same principle is true as you build your life in Christ. You will never build strong or last long in your quest to fulfill what God has put you on the earth to accomplish unless you first focus on laying your spiritual foundation on the rock-solid truths of His Word.

In this book, author Rick Renner provides the scriptural "mortar and brick" that defines the six fundamental doctrines listed in Hebrews 6:1,2 — precisely the ingredients you need to lay a sound and stable foundation for the structure called your life in Christ.

To order, visit us online at: **www.renner.org**

Book Resellers: Contact Harrison House at 800-722-6774 or visit **www.HarrisonHouse.com** for quantity discounts.

Personal Notes

Personal Notes

_____

_____

_____

_____

_____

_____

_____

_____

_____

_____

_____

_____

_____

_____

_____

_____

_____

_____

_____

Personal Notes

_____

_____

_____

_____

_____

_____

_____

_____

_____

_____

_____

_____

_____

_____

_____

_____

_____

_____

_____

_____

Personal Notes

_____

_____

_____

_____

_____

_____

_____

_____

_____

_____

_____

_____

_____

_____

_____

_____

_____

_____

_____

Personal Notes

Personal Notes

Personal Notes

Personal Notes

Connect with us on

![f] Facebook @ HarrisonHousePublishers

and ![Instagram] Instagram @ HarrisonHousePublishing

so you can stay up to date with news

about our books and our authors.

Visit us at **www.harrisonhouse.com**

for a complete product listing as well as

monthly specials for wholesale distribution.

THE POWER
OF FAITH
WHEN TRAGEDY STRIKES

THE POWER
OF FAITH
WHEN TRAGEDY STRIKES

A FATHER-SON MEMOIR

CHRIS *and* TERRY NORTON
with Christy Hayes

ISBN 978-1-62572-012-2

PRAISE FOR CHRIS NORTON AND
THE POWER OF FAITH WHEN TRAGEDY STRIKES

"Chris Norton has embarked on a journey that few posses the will to endure but many can learn from. I have spent a lifetime working with the worlds extraordinary people and none surpass the drive of Chris. The story of his journey, The Power of Faith When Tragedy Strikes is a book that can illuminate your soul and inspire your life's walk."

~ **MIKE BARWIS**, Founder & CEO, Barwis Methods Companies, First Step Foundation, Athletic Angels, Senior Advisor of Strength & Conditioning, New York Mets, Strength & Conditioning Consultant, Miami Dolphins

"Being a football player, you know you are going to be playing a violent game. It is the lessons that we learn playing the game of football that ultimately help us take on the game of life. When I first got to meet Chris at Yankee Stadium, I knew he was very driven to get back on his feet walking again and also had an amazing support system around him. That support has led him to do amazing things in such a short amount of time. Seeing the video of him walk across stage for graduation brought tears to my eyes and motivated me more than anyone will ever know. Everything happens for reason, and I believe Chris and I were put here on earth not only to motivate each other, but millions of people around the world facing some type of adversity. Just because we have a spinal cord injury does not stop us from living our life, but it has taught us to have a newfound appreciation of life and to live it to the fullest every day."

~ **Eric LeGrand**, Former Rutgers University defensive lineman, author of *BELIEVE: My Faith and the Tackle That Changed My Life*, analyst for Rutgers Football Radio Network, and sought after motivational speaker.

"I witnessed Chris's determination, courage, and work ethic every day for months at Barwis Methods. He inspired me to push myself harder and to never give up in achieving my goals. Chris's journey from injury through recovery and beyond as portrayed in The Power of Faith When Tragedy Strikes will leave you ready to face whatever obstacles life throws your way."

~ **BRANDON GRAHAM**, NFL player

DEDICATION

Chris:

To Emily, Dad, Mom, Alex, Katie, family, friends, and the countless other people who have always believed in me and helped me along the way. I would not be where I am today if it wasn't for their sacrifices and care.

Terry:

To family and friends for renewing my faith in the goodness of people.

FOREWORD

My life's journey has been blessed by wonderful parents and family, my wife and children, and by the people I have met as an athlete and in my chosen profession as a college football coach. Why? Along the way, these people impacted my life and provided me with experiences which reflected great courage, faith, perseverance, and most of all, love. Chris Norton embodies all of that and more.

Football is the consummate team sport for it exposes a person's inner soul. There are no pretenders as it challenges a person on every single play, but it also places a mantle on a person to live up to the sport's challenges off the field. When I first chatted with Chris by phone in 2011, he was facing the ultimate challenge — living. A football player at Luther College, Chris suffered a spinal injury that was so debilitating that the odds were 97 to 3 against Chris even standing let alone walking again. After numerous phone conversations, his friends brought him to Columbus for a visit. I knew then that deep within Chris's soul was the fiber found within all great football players. His courage was ever present as he never backed down from any treatment, and his effort was relentless. His spiritual faith was so strong that even Tim Tebow spoke admiringly about his love of God. Chris also embraced the love of family and friends so strongly that the challenges he faced on his journey were willed aside by the passion he possessed for the love he had for them. The unselfish love that Chris has is what every great football player possesses, it's what causes them to fight with relentless effort for their teammate — the players next to them.

Chris allowed me to be his friend and share his world over the past four years. He helped me reenergize my passion for the great game of football. In my twenty-seven years as a football coach I have met many players and all have had an impact on me — overwhelmingly positive. When you read Chris Norton's book you will come to know him from his journey, and how he walked across the stage at graduation at Luther College fueled by his love of family and friends to receive his degree. A 97 to 3 underdog, Chris was the overwhelming winner in living life and in winning the hand of Emily Summers.

Urban Meyer
National Football Championship
Collegiate Coach

PROLOGUE

What if it was me? What if it was my son or daughter? Where would I get my strength? How is my faith?

~Terry Norton, CaringBridge, October 22, 2010

TERRY

I waved to the car pulling out of the driveway. My youngest daughter, Katie, waved back and the giggles between her and a friend floating out the open windows echoed softly on the cool October night. As a freshman in high school, it wouldn't be long before Katie sat behind the wheel driving to a sleepover instead of her friend's mom. I turned toward the SUV's open hatch, lifted the travel grill into the back in preparation for tomorrow's trip, and slid it between the folding chairs and the collapsible table we found useful for tailgating.

"Save room for the cooler," my wife, Deb, called from the garage on her way back inside the house.

After flashing her a quick smile, I mumbled under my breath, "It's not my first rodeo." We'd perfected the art of tailgating in the few months our son, Chris, had played football

1

for Iowa's Luther College. Saturday's game would be the first time my mom, aunt, and uncle would see him play, and I was anxious for him to do well and for them to see how happy he was in college. He was living every kid's dream, playing more than any other freshman on the division-three team, loving school, and enjoying the many friends he'd made. It did my heart proud to see my kids thrive.

I joined Deb in the house, washing my hands at the kitchen sink before settling in my recliner for pizza and a movie. We usually spent Friday nights out with friends, but with the game the next day and the three-hour drive, we'd elected to stay in.

My wife turned on the TV and slipped a DVD into the player. "I told Alex we'd pick her up at eight and swing by McDonald's for breakfast."

Though our oldest daughter was in her final year of nursing school at Des Moines Area Community College (DMACC), she still showed an interest in her brother's games.

"Did you tell her to be ready when we get there? I don't want to be late."

"Mm-hmmm." Deb nodded, passing me a slice of pepperoni.

After dinner and a comedy I knew Chris would have enjoyed, Deb and I headed for the bedroom. Before shooing our two dogs to the foot of the bed, I drummed my fingers along the ancient Bible on my nightstand. We hadn't made it to church last weekend, and I knew we'd be exhausted after the game and the full day of travel. "We need to go to church on Sunday," I told Deb as she snuggled beneath the covers. Her answering grunt was non-committal.

I lay my head on my pillow that night feeling tired but optimistic. Everything in our lives was going according plan. My kids were happy, Deb and I were happy, and I had no reason to believe things wouldn't continue along that path. Since we'd first met at the University of Iowa, Deb and I had worked hard to create a good life and raise the family we cherished. We went to church, and we believed in God. What I didn't realize as I turned out the light and closed my eyes was the difference between *believing* in God and *trusting* in God. I thought my faith was pretty solid, but my faith hadn't really been challenged.

CHAPTER 1

Have I not commanded you? Be strong and courageous. Do not be frightened, and do not be dismayed, for the Lord your God is with you wherever you go.

~Joshua 1:9 ESV

CHRIS

I grabbed my headphones on the way out of my dorm room in the early hours of October 16, 2010. As I walked to the sports building, my stomach fired with a shot of adrenaline and my pace quickened. I scrolled through my playlist of game day favorites and tried to get lost in the beat as Drake's "Forever" chanted in my ear, channeling my bravado into focused concentration, using the visualization techniques I'd honed in the last four years.

I stared at the hills looming over Luther's campus and saw myself leaping over the line to block a kick. As I pushed open the door and turned into the Rock Room, in my mind I was pivoting on my toes to recover the ball as it slipped from the kick returner's grasp. While I picked up the brown paper sack filled with pregame food, I was dipping my shoulder and taking down the ball carrier with a satisfying grunt. Yeah, it was gonna be a good day.

My focus intensified while watching game film, and the excitement in the air was palpable. Guys in the locker room were getting into the zone by jumping up and down and carting around a deer head with antlers and a red letter "C" painted on it, like they did whenever we played Central College. Some guys thumbed through the playbooks—others watched film or got taped up. Before we did a walk-through and changed into football gear, I wrapped my bad blisters and weak ankles in tape. The locker room smelled of musk and sweat, and the steam from the showers hung like a thick fog in the air.

Five minutes before game time, we hustled through the tunnel with music echoing in our ears and thumping in our chests. Almost as soon as we hit the field, we stood at attention for the national anthem. It felt comforting, being with my teammates—my friends. We'd practiced together, lived together, and hung out together for the last eight weeks. We had a good relationship, like family, and it was a blast to spend Saturdays facing the competitor—the enemy—as a band of brothers.

Standing shoulder to shoulder with my teammates, I felt great, I felt ready, I felt healthy. Nerves skittered under my skin, and I bounced on the balls of my feet in anticipation. Even though I didn't have a very big role because I wasn't a starter on offense or defense, I was ready to do my job on special teams and get more reps at safety. Central was a formidable foe, and I peered across the field at the coaching staff and some players I recognized from when they'd recruited me to play for their program.

After a slow start to the game, Luther had picked up momentum by the end of the second quarter and was mounting a comeback midway through the third. Our sideline was buzzing, and the cheering crowd had me pumped and ready to roll.

I ran onto the field for the kickoff. As the player positioned on the far right side of the field, my job was to contain the outside and not let the ball carrier find an opening. The kick was short, and my fingers

"If Coach Boyd liked you, you ended up with a nickname. Boyd came up with a name: "Rookie". He called him that because Chris was that first year player that just kept showing up!"

Dan Marlow, Former Defensive Coordinator for Luther College Football

twitched as the ball drifted to my side of the field. I was going to make the play. I needed it. Sprinting downfield as hard as I could, holding the ball carrier on the inside, I angled over to make the tackle.

One of my teammates hit one of their blockers hard, and the sharp crack of helmets colliding echoed in my ears. Where was the ball carrier? Pure instinct drove me to the hole he planned to break through. The guy with the ball was maybe six foot two,

two-hundred thirty pounds, so he had three inches and fifty pounds on me. I had to take him out below the knees. Some guys tackled headfirst, but I knew better than to lead with my head. I was respected for tackling hard, but I wasn't reckless.

Even though I lost the carrier for a split second, and it was hard to gauge how fast he was coming, I made an educated guess and dove low like I'd done a million times before.

The kick returner's knee careened into my neck, a direct shot from the side. Before I could blink, I lay face down, the pungent odor of muddy grass filling my nostrils. The clap, pop, and thud of other collisions sounded over the top of me while I waited for the pile to clear. My head didn't feel rattled, so I tried to move. Stuck. I stared at the thick carpet of grass. *Oh, crap!*

The sound of teammates disentangling and retreating to the sidelines became obvious, but I didn't join them. I couldn't feel anything. Oddly calm, completely motionless, I stared at divots of grass. *Do not draw attention. Get up so the trainers don't come running out. Come on, get up! This is embarrassing.* It didn't matter how long I lay there berating myself, I physically didn't feel a thing, or make my body move.

The tackle felt like any other hit. There wasn't anything wrong. My head felt fine, even though it was weird that I couldn't move.

While playing a rival school during my junior year of high school, I lowered my shoulder to tackle their enormous quarterback and he hit me around the collarbone, rocking me backwards and making three-quarters of my body go numb. I couldn't get up, and the same thoughts went through my head. *Get up, this is embarrassing!* I didn't want to give the quarterback the satisfaction of running me over, but I couldn't move. That time it'd taken a couple of minutes before feeling returned to my arms and my leg, and I was eventually able to sit up and walk off the field.

The same thing must have happened with this play. Why wasn't any feeling coming back?

"Come on, Norty," one of my teammates on special teams said. "Come on, man. Get over here. Let's go. What's wrong?"

Luther's head athletic trainer, Chris Kamm, sprinted onto the field. "Get back. Get away," he told my teammate. "Don't touch him."

Out of the corner of my eye, I noticed the offensive team huddled on the field ready for the transition. Mortification settled over me when a hush spread over the field, and I heard players talking in low voices.

"Oh, he's really hurt," someone said.

"Something's going on."

"He's not moving."

Kamm knelt down on my side and put his head next to mine. "What are you feeling?"

"Nothing," I said.

"Is your head okay?"

"It feels fine." That was the truth.

"Do you feel any ringing in your ears?"

"No."

"Are you breathing okay?"

"Yeah," I said. "I'm breathing fine. Everything's fine. I just can't move right now. I don't know why."

Kamm took a deep breath. "Don't move your head, but tell me, can you move anything else?"

"Not currently."

"All right," he said in a firm but compassionate tone that helped convince me nothing serious was wrong. "I'm going to grab your hand. Let me know if you can feel it. Can you feel this?"

"No." As he called for the other trainers and a doctor who was present at the field, the tiniest twinge of unease skimmed along the edge of my subconscious, but I ignored it.

The doctor knelt in the grass out of my line of vision. "Can you move your right fingers? Can you move your left fingers? Now try making a fist."

I kept trying, but I couldn't do any of it.

"We need to stabilize him and roll him onto his back," Kamm said. Kamm placed his knees on either side of my helmet, making sure my head didn't move. The doctor knelt at the main part of my body, and the student trainers held my legs. They turned me over on time sequence. *One-two-three.* Now I was face up, and they continued to poke and touch me.

"Can you feel this?"

"Can you feel that?"

"What are your thoughts?"

"Is your head ringing?"

Face up, I saw a cluster of bugged-eyed student trainers standing around me in a semi-circle. They had a decent understanding of what was going on, having gone through some training themselves, and I could tell they were kind of tense by the way they gaped with furrowed brows. I disregarded their open-mouthed stares and focused on Kamm and the physician.

"I'm fine," I told them. "Everything's good, but I can't feel anything right now. I can't move anything."

The sun's rays came in at an angle, but the people standing over me and the trainers and doctor testing my sensations and movements, blocked me from the glare. I lay there completely calm, embarrassed by the scene I'd caused, waiting patiently for my sensations to return. At eighteen years old and in the best shape of my life, I felt invincible, like nothing serious could ever happen to me. This would pass; I'd jog off the field and have a great story to tell when the game was over. But after about ten minutes of answering questions and following instructions, I started inhaling a bit harder.

The questions didn't stop. "Are you breathing okay? Are you comfortable?"

I was fine, and I wasn't out of breath, but I wasn't able to take in as much air as I wanted. I couldn't speak a full sentence without taking a breath. I'd breathe in, say a couple of words, and then repeat the breathing-speaking-breathing pattern all over again. The sensation was really weird, and it chipped away at my composure.

My voice had always been kind of low and monotone, but it started getting softer. I wasn't able to speak as loud as I wanted. I wasn't struggling, but I really had to work at inhaling because the air was just not getting through. That, more than anything, sent my panic meter rising.

A couple of my coaches came over, as well as Central's head coach, Jeff McMartin, and leaned between my trainers and the physician. "You're all right," they said before easing back. "No worries, Norty. You'll be fine. Just stay there. Just be calm."

Yeah, I'm good. I'm calm. It was only a stinger, so I sure didn't want to make a scene on the football field. I just wanted to get to the sidelines, rest up for my next play, and get back to the game. I wasn't scared, but the whole experience was really odd. The whole time, I believed my feeling had to come back sooner or later.

Silence permeated the space around us. The only people talking were trainers or coaches, and beyond that, I could have heard a penny drop in the stadium. Ten minutes went by as questions continued. "Can you feel us grabbing your foot? Can you feel this on your leg? Do you feel this prick on your arm?" I kept saying, "No, no, no, no!"

I had no idea what position my legs or arms were in, but they felt like they were sticking up, almost as if they were suspended in the air. "Are my legs straight?" I asked Kamm. "Are they down?"

"Yeah," the trainer responded, "they're straight, and they're down."

Despite the time I'd been on the field unable to feel my body, I tried to remain calm, even as they called for the ambulance. Having been a lifeguard, I knew it was important to call an ambulance right away if there was ever any sort of head, neck, or back injury.

> "As the trainers worked to assess the severity of Rookie's injuries, and his parents and sibling made their way to the field, time stood still. No one in a stadium of 5000+ people uttered a word, the wind stopped blowing, the birds stoped chirping, and the clouds stopped moving. It was a moment in time I will never forget."
>
> Benny Boyd, Former Assistant Coach, Luther College

"We need to take him to Mayo or La Crosse, and we're going to need a helicopter," someone said within earshot.

Panic threatened to choke the rest of the air from my lungs. *Okay, this is for real. This is serious. Holy cow, this is a big deal.*

My dad poked his head in between the trainers. "Chris, it's going to be all right, buddy, it'll be all right. Just stay calm."

Even before I saw my dad and the strained look on his face, the seriousness of the situation had hit home. I'd been at football games where an ambulance had been called for someone who'd concussed or was knocked out, but never for me. Now I was scared. I closed my eyes to block out what was happening and the concerned looks on everyone's faces. That must have worried the trainers and EMTs, because they started questioning me again to see if I was okay.

I assured them I was fine—I just didn't want to look. It was a beautiful October day, my family had made the trek to see me play, and I had plans after the game with my roommate, Richie. I didn't want to see or think about the nightmare that was playing out around me, so I squeezed my eyes closed. This wasn't real—it wasn't happening. I prayed for God to help me through it. I didn't know what was going on, but I knew everything happened for a reason. I prayed that all feeling in my body would return.

"All right, we need to remove his helmet." The sound of the trainer's voice broke my concentration, and I opened my eyes.

First, they had to remove the face mask. My Luther trainer was so even-keeled, so composed, that it helped me rein in my fear even as the seriousness of the situation began to register. He used a small precision saw to cut off my helmet. The other trainers stabilized my head while breaking pieces off my helmet to make it as loose and open as possible. With someone holding my neck and head up so my head didn't drop, they pulled the helmet off, slipping on a neck brace to stabilize my neck.

I didn't go into hysteria. I didn't freak out. I tried to stay as calm and just take things as they came, concentrating on breathing, and praying. I kept my eyes closed most of the time, blocking everything out. I wanted to wake up from the crazy nightmare. Sure, I'd heard and read about stuff like this in the news, but it couldn't be happening to me.

As the EMTs, the doctor, and the trainers loaded me onto the stretcher and began wheeling me across the field, I heard soft clapping from the stadium. Growing up, I watched a lot of sports, and whenever a player was wheeled off the field on a stretcher, he usually threw a thumbs-up to the crowd. I wished I could give a thumbs-up or a wave to assure people I was okay, but I couldn't even do that.

No longer in denial, fear blazed into an inferno inside my head as I was pushed across the field, put into the ambulance, and sped through the quiet streets of Decorah to Winneshiek Hospital.

CHAPTER 2

Saturday night when things were at their darkest, I sat there with my eyes closed and thought about every wasted night, every wasted minute I had spent worrying about things that didn't matter. Stress at work, drama with friends or a youth sport, you name it, I thought, what a waste. When you finally face a real "challenge" you realize how much time we spend worrying about insignificant things.

~Terry Norton, CaringBridge, October 18, 2010

TERRY

Saturday, October 16, 2010, was a beautiful fall day. The rising sun felt warm on my back as I scrambled to get our cooler and everything packed in the SUV. Deb and I left our hometown of Bondurant, picked up Alex in Ames, and made our promised stop at McDonald's for breakfast. The rich colors of the leaves on the trees bordering the highway, and the anticipation of a Saturday college football game, made our drive one of the fastest and most enjoyable we'd ever made to Luther College.

Deb, Alex, and I spent the ride reminiscing about family trips and dreaming of what our future would look like in retirement. My wife and I agreed we'd like to spend the winters somewhere warm, with visions of the kids coming to visit. Alex

15

said she'd definitely become a frequent guest if we moved to a warmer part of the country. All three of us were riding high on life, feeling the kind of joy that, if it were possible to bottle and sell, my retirement plans would have included a Caribbean island.

We got to Decorah and drove to the spot where we normally tailgated with other players' families. We set up our table and chairs, and I tossed brats, hamburgers, and hot dogs onto the grill while Deb opened containers of side dishes she'd made the day before, placing them on the table as we chatted with our new friends. The aroma of sizzling meat, the cool but not cold breeze, and the sea of Luther's royal blue and white colors added to the ambiance.

We appreciated the friendly atmosphere at Luther's tailgate. Most of our adult life was spent socializing with parents of our kids' teammates. The camaraderie helped make youth sports fun; thus, our kids' sports teams dictated a lot of our social life. As loyal fans and Chris's parents, (and myself an admitted extrovert), we hoped to duplicate that fellowship at college.

Our fears evaporated as quickly as the smoke rising from the grill. We had already met and bonded with Pat Vickers and his wife, Buzzy. Their son Rich was Chris's freshman roommate and one of his best friends, and we really enjoyed their company. With each game, we got to know more parents and soon realized everyone was really friendly. That was the culture at Luther. They totally embraced the freshmen, and parents were accepted the same way. The players and their parents made us feel like we'd been there for four years.

My mom, aunt, and uncle showed up, and they joined us at the tailgate. I introduced them around while they piled their plates with food. When the game started, we left the grill and everything set up, as was customary, and made our way inside the stadium. At halftime, after a slow start to the game, we came back out to the tailgate and snacked, drank, and rehashed the first half with friends before going back in for the remainder of the game. We sat around centerfield, probably about fifteen or twenty rows up.

In the third quarter, after slashing Central's lead, Luther kicked off from the south end zone to the north end zone. Chris had the sideline coverage right on our side of the field, and the ball got kicked to a guy on his side. Chris could go through the whole game and might never get the ball kicked to his side of the field. My pulse quickened. He was going to have a shot at the play.

As Chris cut his opponent off on the outside, the kid turned back to the middle. Chris pivoted and made the tackle at his legs, causing the ball carrier to flip over. I saw the collision and heard the familiar smack of helmets and exhalation of grunts. Multiple players lay piled on top of each other, their legs and arms entwined. The ball carrier extracted himself from the pile and limped around holding his thigh. I looked back to where other players were pulling each other from the heap. Someone was still down. One of the Luther players raced over to the bench signaling the problem, and the trainers ran onto the field.

Parents have a sixth sense about their kids, and right away I felt in my bones the downed player was Chris. I'd spent years looking for him from the stands—I knew his build and every nuance of his stance, his walk, and his run. So even though I didn't see number sixteen, Chris's number, I knew from instinct that he wasn't standing around the

> *"As the play was nearing completion, I turned to talk with our QB [Chris Reynolds] about our thoughts for the next offensive series. Suddenly, Chris said, 'Norty [Chris Norton] is down.' Reynolds quickly repeated it and added, 'It doesn't look good!'"*
>
> Mike Durnin, Former Head Football Coach at Luther College

field with the other players. My heart lodged in my throat as the breath jammed in my lungs. Chris was down.

In all of Chris's years playing sports, his nose had been broken playing basketball, and his ribs were broken and his shoulder partially torn playing football, but Deb and I had never gone onto the field to check on him. Chris wasn't very big or imposing; he was just super tough. And when he got hurt, he never wanted any attention. If Chris ever stayed down, I knew he was really hurt.

After I'd scoured every jersey on the field and sidelines looking for number sixteen, realization hit like a thunderbolt.

18

He'd been down a long time. I looked at Deb, and the color drained from her face. I had to be strong for her. I squeezed her hand. "He's going to be okay."

She nodded, but her eyes exposed her fear. We were both desperate to smother the ugly truth that every parent fears—some kids get seriously hurt playing the game they love. *He's tough, he's strong, he's a fighter*, I reminded myself and then called on God. *Oh, please let him be okay; please let him just have the wind knocked out of him. Please God.*

"Should we go down there?" Deb sat at the edge of her seat. "Do you think he's all right?"

He'd been down too long. I swallowed my fear, and we made our way down to the bottom of the bleachers. We stopped at the railing as everyone gathered around him. One trainer had knelt onto his hands and knees, and leaning close to Chris's face, was talking to him. We hadn't seen Chris move. My heart and stomach dueled with hope and nausea as we walked through the gate and headed onto the field. All the players on both teams had taken a knee.

Deb and I inched forward, our gazes locked to the prone body of our son. Usually, when somebody was hurt, they rolled around a bit or slapped the ground in pain. Chris was immobile; he didn't move at all. It would have calmed my rapid-fire pulse if he were slapping the ground with a bad knee injury, or a broken ankle, or whatever. Warning bells sounded in my head. Chris hadn't moved since the moment we first saw him on the ground.

19

Coach McMartin from Central jogged across the field, and he and Coach Benny Boyd, Luther's defensive backs coach, the man most responsible for Chris attending Luther, and Luther's Head Coach Mike Durnin, tried their best to comfort Deb and me. They seemed confident and very supportive, but we could tell Chris had suffered a serious injury. They didn't offer any of those, "Hey, he's going to be okay; he's going to be all right," pep talks. They were guarded with their remarks, like they didn't want to offer false hope. They knew it was serious.

> *"I remember Chris's parents coming down out of the stands and asking Chris if he would move his feet or hands. The look they had as their child was being worked on will always stick in my head. I had become a father eight months earlier that year and I couldn't imagine what I would be like if that was my daughter being worked on."*
>
> Chris Kamm, ATC, CSCS, Former Head Certified Athletic Trainer, Luther College

While we still didn't have any details about what was going on, I let go of Deb's vice grip and stuck my head between the trainers. I was Chris's biggest fan, his oldest coach, and his long-ago hero. Despite my mind-numbing fear, it was time to live up to that billing. "You're doing good, son. Your mom and I are right here."

The professionals worked on him, touching different parts of his body. The whole scene just seemed surreal. As they brought the stretcher over from the ambulance, I knelt close to Chris's head. "You're going to be okay," I uttered in my most reassuring voice, the same voice I'd used on him as his coach growing up. "You're going to be all right."

It seemed like everything went in slow motion. They couldn't get his helmet off, so they had to use special equipment. They literally cut the face mask off and then peeled the helmet off piece by piece. The paramedics worked together with the trainers to move him safely onto the ambulance stretcher. They did everything slowly with the utmost care and precision.

The part I remember most, the part that burned like a knife in my gut, was that as they stabilized him, he didn't move at all. Not one part of his body had moved.

CHAPTER 3

fear not, for I am with you; be not dismayed, for I am your God; I will strengthen you, I will help you, I will uphold you with my righteous right hand.

~Isaiah 41:10 ESV

CHRIS

Two EMTs sat in the back of the ambulance next to me, their expressions sober. "We're en route to medical center with an injured football player with no feeling or movement below the neck," another said into a walkie-talkie. "Need to prepare ER for X-ray and wait upon further directions from a doctor."

I'd left behind the field and everything familiar — my family, my coaches, my teammates — with no idea where I was going or what to expect. I lay in a stable position, only able to move my eyes, the sanitized smell of the ambulance adding to the unreality of the situation. Within twenty minutes, a helicopter would arrive at Winneshiek, the local hospital in Decorah, but as we rushed through the streets of my new hometown to the unfamiliar hospital, I felt groundless. My mind refused to accept what was happening.

"You need to decide where you want to go," one of the EMTs said. "La Crosse or Mayo in Rochester."

Since I'd never been to or heard of Mayo or La Crosse, I had no idea. "What's the difference? What do you guys think is the best place?"

"It's up to you," he answered with a shrug, looking at the other EMT, "but I'd probably go to Mayo in Rochester."

With that, my decision was made. If the EMTs thought Mayo was best, who was I to argue?

Our arrival at the hospital almost felt like a scene from *ER*. A doctor and a group of nurses surrounded me and began asking questions as they hustled me through the hallway. They sawed off my shoulder pads and immediately removed the other equipment. They cut my jersey all the way down and ripped off my wristband—a reminder of one of my friends who'd passed away in a car accident that summer. I always wore it, and it annoyed me that they so callously cut it away.

The hospital staff communicated back and forth with Mayo, pretty much repeating the same questions asked on the field.

"Can you try squeezing, or making a fist with your hand?"

"Can you try curling, or wiggling your toe?"

"Can you feel me grab your finger; can you feel me pulling on your finger?"

"Which foot am I touching?"

All the same questions. I was tired of them. I wanted someone to do something that would help me regain the feeling in my body. I wanted answers. I kept saying, "I have no idea, I don't know, I don't know, I don't know."

My eyes were closed during most of the questioning. *This isn't happening. How in the world can this be happening?* When the doctor asked me a question, I'd open my eyes just enough to let him know I was fine; other than that, I kept them closed.

My dad, mom, sister, and grandmother arrived at the hospital not long after I did. They talked to me and encouraged me. "We're here, Chris. You're going to be okay. They're going to take good care of you."

They assumed I had some sort of head injury because I kept closing my eyes. "I'm fine," I told them. "If I keep my eyes closed, I can pretend this isn't happening."

My grandma stood on one side of the gurney, holding and rubbing my hand. "Can you feel this?" she asked in a calm and soothing voice.

"No, Grandma."

She kept massaging my hand and arm, as if trying to will the feeling or movement back into me. Grandma's brows bunched, and she held her lips tightly together. She was scared for me.

My dad and mom were listening and taking everything in. They attempted to stay out of the way, yet be there for me as usual. I could tell they were trying to be strong as the medical staff asked questions, set up the steroid drip, and prepared for the X-rays, but my mom appeared close to tears.

I heard a lot of hustle and bustle around me. The overhead lights shone brightly in my face, even with my eyes closed. *Stay calm and relaxed. It'll work its way out. This is happening for a reason. Just ride it out. Don't overreact. They don't know anything yet.*

My voice was getting softer, so they asked if I needed any assistance breathing.

"I'm okay," I said. The last thing I wanted was an invasive procedure.

"If your breathing gets more difficult, and you don't think you're getting enough air, let us know right away," the doctor said. "We can insert a tube down your throat to help you breathe, but we don't want to do that unless it's absolutely necessary. We're not sure about the extent of your injury yet, and we don't want to risk any further damage to your neck."

"I'm good," I said, because I sure as heck didn't want a breathing tube or to cause any further damage.

An X-ray showed significant damage to my neck. There wasn't anything more they could do for me at Winneshiek, so they wheeled me up the elevator to a top floor to wait for the helicopter.

As I lay there trying to process what was happening while still hoping it was all a bad dream, I craved normality. Like my dad, I was an avid Iowa Hawkeye fan, and the team was on my mind every Saturday during football season. Iowa was playing

Michigan that day, so I asked if anyone knew the game's score.

Not only did I want to keep track of the game, but focusing on something ordinary helped to tamp down the fear that gnawed at my subconscious. I had a broken neck and was waiting on a helicopter to transport me to a Minnesota hospital I'd never heard of or wanted to visit. I was supposed to be on the football field, helping my team win, planning for a night out with my friends, not parked on a hospital gurney with my family's worried faces hovering above me. When I heard Iowa won, I considered it a hopeful sign.

> *"I remember hearing the helicopter flying in and I knew that he was going to be sent to Rochester, MN to the Mayo Clinic. Our team physician returned toward the end of the game and told me what Chris's injury was and my heart sank."*
>
> Chris Kamm, ATC, CSCS, Former Head Certified Athletic Trainer, Luther College

As they ushered me onto the helicopter and strapped the gurney to the floor, the surrounding sights and sounds were overwhelming. Supplies and a first aid kit sat tucked inside netting along a dark gray ceiling, and the helicopter smelled like a new car after a fill-up at the gas station. The speed and *whop-whop-whop-whop* of the propellers made it difficult to hear and communicate.

The pilot and the two EMTs wore helmets with earpieces and a microphone through which they conversed by radio. The helicopter EMT reiterated what the doctor had said inside the hospital. "If you're losing your breath, let us know, and we'll put in the trach tube. We don't want to have to mess with your neck, so it would be a last resort, but let us know."

A last resort? Fantastic. I tucked that little grenade away and tried my best not to freak out.

As we were taking off, I kept my eyes closed, again searching for a way to quell my deepest fears. Not five minutes into the ride, my panic spiked, forcing my eyes open. I couldn't breathe! I was strapped to the stretcher with the neck stabilizer belt over my head. When I frantically looked over, neither EMT was paying attention.

"Help," I said. "Can you help me? I can't breathe." I could barely project my voice over the clamor of the helicopter. My voice was too soft to get their attention.

This was it. I was at the point of no return—the last resort was necessary—and the EMTs weren't responding! It was so loud in the helicopter I couldn't hear myself breathe, and because of my neck injury, I couldn't feel any air going in or out of my lungs. I tried to keep calm, but I didn't feel like I was getting enough air. Fear shot through me. I needed oxygen down my throat. I couldn't take it anymore!

I closed my eyes and started counting every single breath just to be sure I was breathing. Every time I inhaled, I counted. One breath, two breaths, three. I kept going.

Don't panic. You're breathing, or you'd be unconscious. Just count. I stopped trying to get the EMTs' attention and focused on counting. Finally, after about a minute of timing my breaths, I started to relax. It was terrifying for the few minutes I wasn't sure I was getting enough air in my lungs and the EMTs couldn't hear me. Maybe it was a good thing I wasn't able to get their attention. What if, in the process of trying to insert the tube in the helicopter, they'd moved my head or done more damage to my neck?

The helicopter ride lasted between twenty and thirty minutes, and I spent most of that time counting my breaths and praying for the ride to end. When we landed at Mayo, the EMTs removed me from the helicopter and released me to Mayo's transporter, who had the job of pushing patients to and from the helicopter. Once I was out of the helicopter, my anxiety subsided because I was more comfortable with my level of breathing and my surroundings were a lot quieter.

However, the action was just beginning.

The transporter handed me off to a physician and a nurse who then rushed me to an elevator. After a short ride, the elevator opened and I was wheeled into a big, sterile room full of people wearing white coats and masks. They were all waiting there for me, as if my entrance injected them all with a dose of adrenaline, setting them into motion. To say it was weird to see that many people attending only to me would be an understatement.

People began taking off my socks and pants. Others began setting up an IV drip. Someone took a blood sample. There was so much going on at once, I felt dazed. Again, they started asking questions.

"Can you make a fist?"

"Move your toes?"

"Can you try moving your arm?"

"Can you compress your stomach?"

"Can you squeeze your butt or push out?" That was a new one.

They were poking me and touching me as they peppered their questions, but I still couldn't feel anything until someone jabbed me in the butt. "Oh!" I said. "I felt that." They didn't respond, but it was encouraging to feel something below my neck.

My head, neck, chest, and waist were X-rayed to make sure I hadn't sustained other injuries. Once it was clear the rest of my body was okay, the doctor told me I had a grade IV dislocation requiring surgery. He wanted to get an MRI of my neck and body, but first they needed to realign my neck using traction. I didn't know what that was or what it entailed, and I'd never been very good about seeing blood or hearing bones crack, so I wasn't too keen on the whole alignment process. I did everything I could to stay calm despite envisioning a boot on my head, a rope around my neck, and a leather strap between my teeth.

They placed my head within a device that had screws on each end, rattling any composure I'd mustered.

"This is probably going to hurt," the doctor said.

Awesome.

He shot some numbing medication into the side of my head to reduce the level of pain. Then he began spinning something, perhaps the screws that were pressing into my head, and excruciating pain exploded in my brain.

"Did you actually numb my head?" I asked in all seriousness. "I don't know if this is numb yet." It literally felt like someone was slowly driving a nail into my head, going deeper and deeper and deeper. I kept saying, "This isn't numb at all. I feel everything. Do you have any more of that numbing stuff?" They injected more of the numbing medication in each side of my head, but I could still feel pain and warm blood trickling down my face.

Once my head was secured and locked into place, weight was added by using a pulley system to push my neck back into alignment. The doctor explained he wanted the subtlest force to push the bone over, so he kept adding more weight in five-pound increments. Forty pounds, forty-five, fifty, fifty-five. He said they didn't want to go any higher than seventy pounds. I heaved a sigh of relief when, at sixty-five pounds, I heard a crack, and my neck snapped back into place. That sound — like a bite into a celery stalk — would haunt me for the rest of my life.

I was so thankful to finish with traction, as it was one of the most agonizing experiences of my life. After traction, they removed the head stabilizer and put me in a neck collar that was more secure and made transport easier and safer, but the new collar was terribly uncomfortable. It wrapped around my neck and chin, came up to the middle of the back of my head, and its lip dug into my scalp.

The doctor explained that since my neck was now in line, they'd take pictures with an MRI. The procedure would take approximately an hour, and from there we'd go into surgery. The neck collar continued to bite into my head. It was so uncomfortable, I finally asked if there was any way we could readjust the collar or if there was something more comfortable. The doctor told me to fight through the pain because it was important not to move my head or neck.

They used a lift system to pull me into a tight-quartered, enclosed MRI cylinder. The MRI machine made a rattling noise that was super loud, almost like an air conditioner or furnace working double time. My neck brace made the experience extremely uncomfortable.

Oh, God, this is going to be the longest hour of my life. I'm miserable. God, I need an escape. Please, if you could just let me have some sleep, some peace of mind, that's all I want. Can I just sleep to get through this?

As evidence of God's hands resting on me that night, before

I knew what had happened, I was lowered from the MRI. By the grace of God, even with the noise level duking it out with my anxiety and the shooting pain in my neck, somehow my prayers were answered and I was able to go to sleep, sparing me an agonizing hour in the MRI machine.

After the MRI, my family and I had a quick exchange. My mom and dad assured me everything would be all right—we'd get through whatever we were facing. But their demeanor had changed. There was no hiding the concern on their faces and in their body language. They looked sad, as if they were in shock. And so was I.

"We'll be here when you wake up," they said, blinking rapidly. "We'll be out in the lobby. We're here with you, Chris." My dad glanced at the medical staff standing around. "The doctors are going to take great care of you. Don't worry." Then they had to leave the room.

> *"I wish I somehow could've known what I know now… that no matter what we as a family can get through anything that is thrown our way."*
>
> Alex Norton, Chris's sister

Seeing my family upset didn't make me feel better, but it didn't make me feel worse. I knew we were on the same level emotionally, feeling drained and numb. I knew we were all wondering the same thing: was this really happening?

An optimistic person, I tried to see the positive side of things and tried to stay calm under most circumstances. I understood that before they ran their tests and knew the extent of the injury, the doctors couldn't tell me anything. I respected that, and I knew they didn't want to give me false hope, so I avoided asking any questions or demanding answers. I kind of maintained a wait-and-see attitude. But before they wheeled me into surgery, the doctor asked if I had any questions. There was only one on my mind.

"Am I ever going to walk again?"

I couldn't find the words to explain the doctor's expression. He avoided my eyes, bowed his head, and said in a very soft voice, "I don't know."

The gentleness of his tone didn't diffuse the sting. I felt fragile, as if he'd cracked open my chest, ripped out my beating heart, and threw it on the ground, stomping out all my dreams. I slammed my eyes closed and fought back the tears that wanted to flow, because that's when it really hit me. *Holy cow, this is my life, this is really happening. This shouldn't be happening.* I kept my eyes closed, praying and pleading for help.

God, I don't care if I ever play football again. I don't care if I ever play any sport again. Just let me walk, and I'll call it quits from athletics for the rest of my life. Screw sports, screw activities, just let me do the basics. I don't need to run again, just please let me walk.

Inside the OR, organized chaos ensued. The doctors and nurses prepped for surgery, starting me on fluids and setting up the gas mask. The surgeons donned gloves and masks, and carefully arranged their tools. They slid me across a giant platform with an opening at my neck in case they had to operate from both the front and back, and tied me down with straps.

At that point, I understood the situation's gravity. I could no longer keep my eyes shut and pretend I was having a nightmare. As the preparation continued, I lay there looking up at the nurses and doctors who stood over me with masked faces. These men and women held my fate in their hands. Some of the nurses seemed upset about having a young adult on the table.

"Please help me," I said. "Please fix me. I really want to walk again."

"We'll take care of you, son," the surgeon said. "We'll do the best job we can. Don't worry." The doctor's concerned but confident answer gave me comfort as the gas mask enveloped my face. Then it was lights out.

CHAPTER 4

Chris is a fighter and I am so proud of his determination. He has his "game face" on.

~Terry Norton, CaringBridge, October 18, 2010

TERRY

Chris was born March 20, 1992, in Des Moines, Iowa, three years after his sister, Alex, and four years before his sister, Katie. When we were in the hospital and Deb was in labor, we didn't know the baby's gender. When his head and shoulders were out, the doctor told us he was a boy. *Wow,* I thought, *this guy was really good.* Later, when I asked how he knew Chris was a boy, he explained he'd never seen a girl with shoulders that broad.

Like a typical man, I was excited to have a son. I couldn't wait to share my love of sports and the outdoors with him. I envisioned all the things we'd do together as he grew up — shooting baskets, playing catch, hiking through national parks, kayaking down rivers, and riding horses through our family's pastures. Plus, after Chris was born, we had one of each—Deb had a shopper, and I had playmate.

Chris was a very good baby. We were fortunate he didn't have any health issues, and he was a good sleeper. We'd take him places, and he'd always nestle underneath a bunch of covers and go to sleep. As a toddler, he went through a challenging phase; if things weren't perfect, he'd have a meltdown. For example, if I was feeding him a Pop Tart for breakfast and a corner broke off distorting the shape, he'd throw a fit. If Deb was feeding him a banana and a piece broke off, he'd have a tantrum. Fortunately, that phase didn't last long, but it foreshadowed the intensity he'd bring to every part of his life.

I was coaching high school basketball when Chris was a toddler, and he loved going to practice with me. He'd stand on the side of the court dribbling a ball while I ran the kids through drills. He used to wear a little team jersey and ride the bus after some of the games. The town rallied around the team, and Chris's little eyes lit up when we'd attend pep rallies along our quest to win the state championship. Chris always had a ball with him. It didn't matter if it was a football, a basketball, or a soccer ball, he was always moving and playing with a ball.

When Deb took him to the pediatrician, she told the doctor, "He's not potty trained, but he can dribble the length of the floor with the basketball."

Chris used to climb on everything. I'd come into the kitchen and find him up on the counter, searching the cupboards for something to eat. When he was a toddler, we had an above ground pool with a privacy fence around the perimeter. Of course we watched our kids, but Chris was so active and athletic that if I looked away for a second, he could get into trouble.

One spring, I was out working in the yard, and on three occasions when I turned my back to do something, he had climbed up onto the filter and was hanging halfway over the pool. That night in bed as I lay staring at the ceiling, I said to Deb, "It's got to come down." The next day, I cut the liner open, drained the water out, pulled the sides down, and removed the whole thing within two hours. We just couldn't live with the risk.

Chris started playing sports before kindergarten and fortunately, his friends did too. Deb and I were excited to see him channel all that energy into something constructive. By elementary school, Chris was a good little athlete. He worked hard, and he liked to practice. He was a bit of a perfectionist, but not in a bad or unhealthy way; he wanted to do well in both school and sports. Whether he was kicking a ball, hitting a baseball, or practicing his spelling words, he wanted me to work with him every day. Our daughters were different.

"You can go outside and shoot baskets for an hour a day and you'll average four points more over the season." I thought that possibility would encourage my children to practice.

Alex had other ideas. "I think I'd rather go shopping with Mom."

On the other hand, Chris accepted the challenge. "If that's how much I can improve in *one* hour, what if I shoot for *two* hours?"

Katie put in more time than Alex, but sports weren't an obsession for either of them.

By sixth grade, Chris and a few of his friends wanted to play tackle football. We didn't have a program in our area, so we signed him up to play in Carlisle, about thirty minutes south of our hometown. Each week, the parents took turns driving the boys to Carlisle for practice.

As I sat in the stands at the first game, I questioned our decision to let him play in an out-of-town league. The rest of the players were all Carlisle kids except Chris and his three friends. The two coaches were parents, and I feared they wouldn't give Chris a chance. I'd forgotten that youth coaches liked to win too. Chris, with his little glasses and big helmet, was small but shifty. He played hard, and he wasn't afraid to tackle. Despite my worries, he got a lot of playing time, and his team ended up winning the championship.

Chris continued his quest for perfection. One year during grade school basketball, he was unsatisfied with his left-handed layups. He was getting frustrated so I told him, "Chris, a left-handed layup is hard when you're right handed."

"Dad," Chris said with an all-too-familiar determined look in his eye, "I've got to do better. I'm going to get better at this."

The next night, we went to the YMCA to practice, and Chris announced he wasn't leaving until he could make ten in a row. I tried to quell his frustration by pointing out that as the varsity basketball coach, I had varsity guys who couldn't make ten in a row with their off hand, but he refused to leave. We stayed, and it took him a while, but he made ten left-handed layups in a row. That's how stubborn and committed he was. When I'd take him to shoot and rebound for him, he wouldn't leave if he felt he wasn't shooting well. He'd just keep shooting and shooting.

His basketball coach used to tell a story demonstrating Chris's never-say-quit attitude. Chris always wanted to stay after practice and shoot, but the coach had to get home to his family. So, the coach took the balls and locked them in the storage closet. Chris refused to be deterred and started bringing his own ball to practice. The coach decided the best thing to do was turn off the gym lights, forcing Chris to go home.

"Chris was always and I mean always the last kid out of the gym. It used to drive me crazy."

Chad Carlson, Principal and Former Boys' Basketball Coach, Bondurant-Farrar Community Schools

As his dad, I had to watch Chris because he would push himself harder than anybody I'd ever seen. If a coach asked him if he was tired or if he needed to come out of the game, he'd never admit he needed a break, even when I knew he did. There were many nights I'd lecture him on the ride home about not pushing himself to the breaking point.

Parents of Chris's teammates used to ask me if I would talk to their kids about sports because they wouldn't listen to their own parents. I'd happily talk to other kids while appreciating that Chris was just the opposite. On my championship basketball team, a lot of the older kids were excellent role models and really took Chris under their wings. He saw those kids look up to me, so I had to be careful, because when it came to sports, he hung on my every word. He attributed that team's success to my coaching ability and knowledge of sports.

Through the years, I coached Chris in flag football, tackle football, baseball, basketball, and soccer. He wanted me to coach his teams, whereas some kids didn't want their dads involved. I enjoyed the time with him and his buddies, and it was a great opportunity for us to be together, as well as a bonding experience with the parents. Even though I didn't know much about soccer or baseball, I knew how to organize a practice, and I knew how to keep the game in perspective. I saw too many coaches volunteering for the wrong reasons. As a coach, I was intense, organized, competitive, and I'd get after the players who weren't playing hard, but we always had fun. With the exception of tournament basketball, I stopped coaching Chris when he was in high school.

There were several reasons for Chris's success. Not only did he put in a lot of practice time, watch a lot of sports, and understand the games he played, but he always had better form than most of his teammates. My dad was a PE teacher and a coach, and I always had better form in sports because of his background, which helped when I wasn't as naturally gifted. Chris had better form for the same reason, and he used that exceptional form to his advantage when he was younger and people tended to underestimate his ability. He worked extremely hard to overcome his physical limitations.

Whenever Chris was recognized for his athletic achievements, like when he was selected for All-Conference or All-District in sports, he took the accolades in stride. In fact, praise seemed to motivate him to play harder. For example, in a basketball game when the other team focused on him as if he were the guy they had to stop, he typically had his best game. He fed off the pressure and rose to the occasion.

He was always very humble, and he was a good teammate. On more than one occasion, a former coach or those I coached against would contact me and say, "I respect your son because he has a great attitude and he's never cocky." He was well liked and respected, and that made me proud, and not just from a sports standpoint. I long believed being a good teammate made a person a good coworker and a good family member. I knew those things carried over into every aspect of life.

Chris had a variety of nicknames in high school. A particular favorite came from one of his high school basketball coaches who dubbed him "The Silent Assassin" during football season.

In the hallways at school, the coach explained, Chris never came across as aggressive, but when the football pads went on, he put a licking on opposing players. He'd get tangled up with another player during a play, and somebody would shove him or talk smack, and he'd just walk away. He was always calm, cool, and collected. His quiet competitiveness earned him the distinctive moniker.

As a high school athlete, he scored over a thousand points in basketball, making him sixth on the all-time scoring list at Bondurant-Farrar High School. In one game, he scored a personal high of thirty-four points. In football, he still holds the record for the longest touchdown return on a kickoff, and the most yards in a game for a return. Despite his small build, Chris was voted hardest hitter during his junior and senior seasons of high school football. He served as captain of both the football and basketball teams.

Deb and I took a lot of pride when Chris did well in sports because it was a reflection of his efforts. His basketball coaches would always tell others, "You guys see Chris's success? What you don't see is that I have to chase him out of the gym after practice every night because he doesn't want to leave. He's always up here shooting."

Because he was a good kid and a compassionate teammate, we felt he served as a good role model. He proved to kids that they didn't have to act like jerks or be cocky in order to be successful.

One day, not long after he'd left for college, Deb and I were getting ready for work. As I dragged a razor over my face and studied myself in the mirror, I kept thinking about times when I might have pushed Chris too hard toward excellence. I'd always told him to work hard and that he couldn't

> *"The Chris Norton we saw on the football field, basketball court, or track refused to quit and refused to let his teammates quit. That is persistence."*
>
> Adam W. Busch, Former head football coach at Bondurant-Farrar Community Schools

take a day off. But in my zeal to channel his passion for sports, had I gone too far?

Swallowing my pride, I glanced over at Deb. "Do you think I pushed Chris too hard?"

Without hesitation, without even blinking, she looked me in the eye and said, "No, you've made him who he is."

Still unconvinced and feeling guilty as only a parent can, I sent him a text message asking the same question. *Hey bud, did I push you too hard growing up? I asked Mom and she said that made you who you are.*

He responded right away. *Mom is right.*

I think part of the reason I pushed him was because he'd shared with me his goal of being an all-state player and playing sports in college. In my mind, I wasn't doing him any favors if I didn't say, "Okay, if that's what you want, you need to remember you're competing against everybody in the state and all the states around Iowa. When you're talking about college ball, you're competing on a much broader spectrum. You can't just be good for Bondurant, or good for our area, you've got to be really good. You've got to be one of the best. And you can't be one of the best without putting in the time."

Deb and I knew Chris was going to be successful in whatever he chose to do because of his innate drive. Nothing came easy for him—not in sports and not in school—but he wasn't afraid of hard work. When Chris had problems with reading in elementary school, we got him extra help. He graduated with a 3.86 grade point average and was in the top 13 percent of his class. When he was younger, he had speech therapy to correct a lisp. He overcame his lisp, took speech in high school, and now does presentations around the Midwest. As an athlete, he was small but he pushed himself to be the best. We knew he was going to be successful because nothing had ever been handed to him, and he was willing to do whatever it took to achieve his goals.

Little did we know he'd been training his whole life for the biggest challenge of all.

CHAPTER 5

Commit your work to the LORD, and your plans will be established.

~Proverbs 16:3 ESV

CHRIS

I grew up the middle son of Deb and Terry Norton in Bondurant, Iowa, a residential town not far from Des Moines. Bondurant was a close-knit community where everybody knew everybody, and our social life revolved around school. My mom was very nurturing; she took care of the day-to-day chores while working full time. She was easy to talk to, but she wasn't afraid to lay down the law. My dad was fun loving, outgoing, and very serious about athletics considering his coaching background. He worked in education, coached all sports, and tried to help me develop into the best athlete possible.

As the oldest sibling, Alex was kind of a second mom to my little sister and me. She was mature at a young age and very responsible. We got along well throughout grade school and high school. As the baby of the family, Katie was a feisty little pistol. We used to fight a lot because I was stubborn, she was stubborn, and we were both really competitive. Sometimes the girls ganged up on me when I teased or picked on them, but both sisters have always been very supportive. We had our little fights, but we were close. We took family vacations, and we loved hanging out together after church on Sundays, our family day.

> *"With Chris being the middle child, and only boy, my sister Katie and I provided him lots and lots of love."*
>
> Alex Norton, Chris's sister

I always had an easygoing nature and never really stressed about much, usually preferring to go with the flow. I was kind of a teaser, just to be annoying or fun, but there were certain things I knew not to tease my sisters about. Growing up between two females, I knew how to read girls better than a lot of guys. As the only boy, my dad and I enjoyed our guy stuff while my mom and sisters did their girl stuff. My dad was very adventurous, and he loved the outdoors and sports. He helped me develop an appreciation for both. My parents encouraged me to work out, practice, and stay away from distractions like video games because they knew I'd get really frustrated if I didn't perform well in a game. They pushed me harder than my sisters because they knew I was more passionate about sports.

I was a Minnesota Vikings fan, and their Hall of Fame wide receiver, Cris Carter, was my idol. I also liked Michael Jordan for both his story and his success. My dad was always my hero and a great role model. He taught me so much about life through his experience as a player, a coach, a teacher, through his work with at-risk kids, and through life lessons he learned from his dad. We did everything together; we'd go to the movies or to the gym and shoot baskets. He'd always rebound for me and help me with my shot. Some kids hated when their dads coached, but I liked it. He was great with my friends, and they really liked and respected him. I did too.

My parents always encouraged us to be involved in activities. My sisters and I were constantly on the go. We were a very social family. When I was young, I played peewee basketball, baseball, football, and soccer. I quit soccer in fifth grade and decided to focus on running. My friends and I played tackle football in another town because we didn't have a tackle football league in Bondurant until junior high and we wanted to get an early start. Ironically, the same kids who went to Carlisle to play tackle football were the four senior captains of our varsity football team. Photos of the four of us when we were young and as senior team captains commemorate our dedication to the sport.

In elementary, middle, and high school, my life revolved around sports. I never minded, and neither did my parents, because there were so many values that carried over between sports and life in general. I learned to be a team player, I worked hard, and was taught the value of competition. As a young boy with sports on the brain, there was nothing better than playing weekend tournaments with my friends.

My dad knew how competitive I was and how much I wanted to win, so he pushed me to be a better athlete and a better person. The only thing we ever had to work on between us was *how* he pushed me. There were times when I was younger that I hated him being my coach because he would be tougher on me than anyone else. Sometimes, after a basketball game when I hadn't played my best, we'd end up mad at each other. He'd get caught up in the moment and yell, "What were you doing? What were you thinking?" and I'd feel even worse for messing up. He wasn't trying to make me feel bad, but he was passionate about sports, and he knew I wanted to do my best.

By the end of middle school, I'd worked up the courage to talk to him. "Dad," I said, "please don't make faces during the game. I know you're trying to help, but you're hurting my confidence." Like all kids, I responded better to constructive encouragement.

He'd say, "Okay, okay," and try his best not to express his emotions. By high school, he'd learned to chill out and be supportive, and that really helped my game.

Growing up, I dealt with disappointment internally, never expressing frustration through body language or with words. I remained calm and collected on the outside, even though my stomach would burn after a game where I played poorly. In games or at practice when things weren't going my way, my dad would get frustrated because I'd never show any emotion.

"You act like you don't care," he'd say.

"I *do* care," I would tell him, and then pound up the stairs to my room. I expected the best from myself and was consumed with achieving my goals.

Once I went home frustrated and pouting after not playing well in a basketball tournament. I crashed on the couch and played video games, trying to forget the whole weekend.

My dad walked right up to me and said, "If you don't like where you're at, if you're not meeting your goals, don't pout. Do something about it. If you really do care, if you don't want to perform as poorly as you did, let's work on it. Let's go to the gym. Let's practice more."

What he said, and how he said it, his words just clicked with me. *Yeah, let's do something. Let's practice ball handling. Let's practice shooting. Let's run drills.* It was a turning point for me, the moment when my mentality shifted. Why should I feel sorry for myself when I was the one in control of my destiny? I finally understood that all outcomes were a direct reflection of my input. I had to change what I was doing in order to accomplish my goals.

Once my head was in the right place, I became a better athlete and a better player simply by working harder and not feeling sorry for myself. From that point on, I began to think about where I wanted to be physically — with my muscle mass, with my weight, and about my goals. In basketball and football, I wanted to win a district championship, and I knew that the little things I did would add up and help me achieve those goals.

By the time I was in ninth grade, I played on the freshman, junior varsity, and varsity baseball teams. As a freshman, I was the youngest on the team, and thinking back, I laugh at how nervous and uncomfortable I was on the field because I didn't want to let the team down and look like an idiot. Everything I loved about the sport seemed so much harder because I was in the spotlight and thrown into a position where I didn't feel confident.

In Iowa, baseball was played over the summer. Because I had baseball games every day, I couldn't participate in football or basketball camps, lift weights, or go to the pool and relax. I got burned out and ended up quitting the team halfway through my freshmen year. I regretted that decision when the team ended up going to state. After I quit, I focused on track, football, and basketball.

I loved the atmosphere of our high school gym. It was compact and old, filled to the brim with people, and the band played right behind the visitor's bench drowning out their fans. I started playing freshmen basketball, moved up to JV, and eventually got called up to varsity. Playing varsity basketball for Bondurant was a dream come true because I idolized the program.

I started on varsity my sophomore year and scored eighteen points the first game, but I was more excited about the second one—our first home game. I'd waited forever to be a varsity starter for Bondurant at home. We had pictures that day and after the pictures, I left my jersey in my locker so I'd be ready for the game.

As we changed into our uniforms, my friends said, "Chris, you've got the wrong color jersey. Where's your white home-game jersey?"

My stomach dropped as I looked down at my blue shorts. I grabbed my keys and took off running to my car. I didn't want to disappoint the coach, and I was embarrassed about making a rookie mistake on our first home game of the season. I sped recklessly to my house, raced inside, grabbed my white jersey, and ran outside only to stop dead in my tracks. A cop stood in my driveway next to his car, blue lights flashing.

"Put your hands up," he said, pushing me against the car and spreading my legs. "Do you know the owner of this house?" he asked, frisking me for weapons.

"Yeah," I said, nearly drowning with embarrassment and guilt. "It's mine."

"Do you own this car?"

"It's mine too."

"Let me see some identification," he demanded, depositing me in the back of the cop car. "This car is registered to a Debra Norton. Did you steal this car?"

"No! She's my mom. My parents gave me the car." I kept thinking about my parents and my whole family — everyone on my mom's side and my dad's side — waiting for me at school, wondering where I was when the team came out for warm-ups.

The cop called my dad. "I've got your son in custody. I clocked him going ninety-four in a fifty-five mile-per-hour zone. I'm taking him in and impounding the car unless you come get him." They had to pick me up, and I didn't make it back to the game until the second quarter. I couldn't believe I'd missed the start of my first varsity home game.

I felt even worse when my coach explained that they kept extra jerseys at school or that my parents could have gone home and gotten it, eliminating the need to speed. In my panic, I'd made a poor choice. Not only did I lose my school permit and my driver's license until I was seventeen, but I learned a valuable lesson that day. I became much more responsible. Instead of forgetting things at home like my football gloves or basketball shoes and expecting my family to bail me out, I began packing my bag the night before with everything I needed.

After that rocky start, I ended my sophomore year as the team's leading scorer, and despite our barely winning record, I received an All Conference honorable mention. My junior year, I averaged sixteen points per game, was chosen first team All Conference, led the conference in steals, and came in second in assists and points scored. Senior year, I was unanimously voted first team All Conference, with a second place finish in points scored in the conference and first in steals and assists. We had a really good team, but lost the district championship game.

Basketball was always my favorite sport, except during football season. While I loved basketball, I also found it frustrating. I could never just show up and play consistently, so I put in a ton of time perfecting my shot. If I slacked off even a little, my shooting suffered. Despite working hard all year long, my shots were really streaky. I put in ten times the work, but was never ten times the player. Looking back, I know I maxed out my ability, and for that I was really proud. By my junior year, I knew I'd never play division one ball. Stuck at five foot eleven and a decent athlete at best, I could enter college and play football, whereas basketball would take a couple of years to see the court, so I decided to try and play football in college and play basketball on the side just for fun.

There was a ton of pressure to run track in high school because most of the track coaches were football coaches. I knew running was good for me, so I always did it, but by the end of junior high I was tired of running track. My friends were growing taller and running faster than me, so I tried hurdles and fell in love with the event. I didn't have to be the fastest guy on the hurdle team; flexibility and technique were my keys to success. We went to state two out of my four years at Bondurant, and we won districts—a first in school history—my senior year. I even qualified for state in the distance medley.

Football was the biggest sport during high school, and all

my friends were involved, either on the field or in the stands. As a freshman, I caught a lot of passes as a wide receiver, played corner and linebacker, was voted offensive MVP, and even played some junior varsity. My freshman coaches started calling me "The X Factor" because I would make a big play for the team whenever our butt was on the line. I started on varsity my sophomore year as a cornerback and wide receiver. I was nervous, but also excited to help the team succeed. We went five and five, and I was selected first team All District that year as a corner.

By junior year, our team was really starting to gel. I had a great season as a corner and was voted hardest hitter. We placed third in our district, making it to the playoffs for the first time in school history, and I made second team All District. As a senior, I moved to safety for our "season of firsts." We won the district championship for the first time ever, won the first post-season game in school history, and were close to making it to the final eight when we lost. I was again voted hardest hitter and selected first team All District.

My senior year homecoming game, we played our rival school, Collins-Maxwell Baxter (CMB). Tied for third in the state, the winner would most likely be crowned district champs. We scored with a minute left in the game to take the lead, but CMB marched the ball down to our twenty-yard line. With only seconds left on the clock, I intercepted CMB's pass in the back of the end zone and ran the ball back twenty yards until time expired. I slid into the grass, ending the game. The thrill of the interception, the joy of watching my teammates run onto the field in my direction, and the sound of the fans walloping cheers exploding into the night helped create an unforgettable memory.

Our football games drew the whole community; people filled the bleachers to capacity and stood along the fence, watching intently. As a player, the atmosphere was intense, loud, and indescribably fun. Even college ball didn't compare to the feeling of making big plays in front of sellout, hometown crowds.

> "He played with such intensity and focus that I knew that I wanted this guy to be part of our football program."
>
> Dan Marlow, Former Defensive Coordinator for Luther College Football

I loved every part of the game, from training to practice to game time. I had the physical strength, athletic prowess, and mental fortitude to succeed, and I wasn't afraid of anyone. When I put on a football helmet and pads, something clicked inside of me, ratcheting my intensity into a whole different gear. I loved that I could be mean and rough people up during a game without getting in trouble.

I dreamt of playing college football for the University of Iowa; I had the toughness and tenacity to play there, but no matter how hard I worked, I lacked the strength, height, and speed. The division three programs that recruited me pretty much guaranteed I'd play right away on special teams, and they said I'd have the chance to compete for the safety position. With my competitive nature, I thrilled at the chance to make a difference as a freshman and be an impact player like I was in high school.

I'd always been athletic, but as a sports technician, my dad really gave me an edge. His whole side of the family was really involved in sports, and he'd been around sports all his life. I grew up listening to stories about my grandfather as a coach and athlete, and my uncle as a division one basketball star and professional baseball player. I also considered myself a student of sports, watching games on TV and in person, and really studying techniques of the best players.

With my ambitions in mind, I prepared for the future by doing what I could each and every day. The football season started in the spring with track and weight lifting. I had to think of football as a yearlong sport. The same was true with basketball. I couldn't sleep at night if I felt I hadn't worked hard enough during the day or put in the extra time to work on ball handling, shooting, or lifting. I'd get really upset with myself and then commit to working harder and doing more because I didn't want to feel edgy at night. Knowing I wouldn't be able to sleep if I didn't push myself kept me motivated.

There were times I felt annoyed when my dad pushed me to work harder. It felt as if he was saying I wasn't good enough, but in fact he was being a good coach and trainer. I had to get over myself and view him as my coach and not my father. He saw more in me than I could, and he expected more out of me than I thought I could give. He understood that sometimes even highly motivated athletes needed pushing in order to make the leap from a good player to a great player.

My dad made me into a great player. He helped me become a better athlete, a better student, and a better person. I was lucky to have him because sometimes, as self-motivated as I was, I still needed someone to push me further and to believe in me more than I believed in myself.

Now, injured, I needed him more than ever.

CHAPTER 6

I am not going to pull punches. We are in a battle. We are in a battle for Chris to regain function of his arms and legs. Through our faith, support of family and friends, skilled medical staff, and the determination of our son, he will walk again. We believe this.

~Terry Norton, CaringBridge, October 18, 2010

TERRY

I knew Chris's injury was severe even before the EMTs said they were taking him to Winneshiek Hospital. Deb and I just looked at each other in stunned silence because we didn't know the town of Decorah, and we had no idea how to get to the hospital. It seemed easier to focus on the logistics than on our son being driven away in an ambulance.

We stumbled toward the car while the other players' parents tried to tell us how to get to the hospital, but my mind wouldn't focus. Everyone was staring at us. We felt like we were under a microscope as we got into the SUV while people packed our stuff and told us not to worry about anything we left behind. My mom, Alex, Deb, and I were in the car trying not to freak out and let our imaginations run wild.

We arrived at the hospital in Decorah, and a nurse led us

back to where Chris lay on a stretcher, his uniform in tatters and his neck in a collar. We attempted to pump him up with meaningless phrases like *we're here,* and *everything's going to be okay,* even though we didn't have a clue if that was true.

We were asked if we wanted Chris to go to Mayo in Rochester, Minnesota, or to La Crosse, another Mayo hospital in Wisconsin. We'd never been to either and didn't know what to do. Winneshiek had called the neurological team at Mayo in Rochester as soon as they heard from the EMTs that they had a severe neck injury patient en route. Mayo instructed them to start a steroid drip to reduce the swelling and said he'd need surgery as soon as possible. Mayo didn't have any helicopters available, so they called La Crosse, and one was en route even before we got there. Distance wise, Mayo and La Crosse were about the same, and the doctors at Winneshiek told us that the main facilities for Mayo were in Rochester. Armed with that information and little else, we chose Rochester.

The doctors and nurses at Winneshiek continued with sensation tests to see what feeling Chris had below the injury site, and prepared him for transport. He needed to get into surgery as soon as possible. They started a steroid drip and continued testing to make sure his breathing and vitals were okay.

With his head in a collar, tubes running into him for the IV steroid drip, and his uniform shredded, Chris opened his eyes and asked who won the Iowa-Michigan game.

Like his dad, Chris was a die-hard Hawkeye fan, and his seemingly routine question and our discussion of the game eased the tension as we waited for the helicopter to arrive.

Then he looked at me with tears in his eyes. "Will I ever walk again?"

With a slab of granite sitting squarely on my chest, I muttered something inane like, "You're in good hands," or "Let the doctors do their job."

I had to hold myself together, not only for my son, but also for the rest of the family who kept watching me for signs of a crack. If I lost faith, the whole family would take a turn down a very dark road. I wasn't willing to go that route, even though every cell of my body screamed to let my worst fears take over.

Chris kept closing his eyes.

"You don't have to sleep," Alex said.

His eyelids fluttered open before closing once again. "I don't want to know what's going on."

The defeated sound of his voice nearly crumbled my resolve. I never thought anything could happen to my kids, or me, or my family. The idea of a spinal cord injury never crossed my mind. I'd always imagined a career-ending football injury as something like a badly torn ACL or a broken bone, but a spinal cord injury never even blipped on my radar.

If Chris had suffered a career-ending torn ACL, I'd have thought that was a big deal. Or if Chris had broken his leg, I could hear myself say, "Oh my gosh, he's only a freshman and he broke his leg! He's going to miss half the season." My perspective had suddenly changed.

Deb was kind of shutting down at that point. Her eyes were glazed with shock and glittered with unshed tears. The whole experience—from the ambulance, to the frantic drive to the hospital, to the antiseptic smell of the facility—was very upsetting. I could tell she tried not to think about what happened, and she tried not to focus on what it might mean for our son's future. We attempted to encourage each other with a touch here or a reassuring nod there, but to be honest, we were both faking it for each other and for Chris. We teetered on the edge of something ugly, and we knew if one of us fell down the dark pit of despair, the other would surely follow. We tried to stay positive, but the sight of Chris on the table, hooked up to machines with his uniform cut off was almost too much to bear.

It was a relief to have Alex there. In the midst of her nursing program, she was concerned about her brother, but her rational, even-keel approach to the situation helped to steady us all. My mom was probably one of the strongest Christian women I'd ever known. She'd experienced a ton of adversity in her life, and yet was always full of joy. Her presence was another steadying force, a rock to lean on when things seemed so bleak.

They wouldn't let any of us ride in the helicopter. There was just room for Chris, the pilot, and the EMTs. After Chris was loaded onto the chopper and we watched it rise into the air, I attempted to drive to Mayo. Word of Chris's injury had spread.

The game had been podcast over the computer, and some Bondurant parents had seen it and knew what had happened. Once people knew that Chris was injured and had been taken by ambulance to the hospital, people began calling each other, and our phones started blowing up.

Katie hadn't come to the game with us; she was at a birthday party, and we couldn't get hold of her. We also had dogs and a cat at home, and we weren't going to be there to care for any of them after the game. I was scared and concerned, and

> *"The news of Chris's injury is one of those moments that people from Bondurant and Central Iowa will never forget."*
>
> Chad Carlson, Principal and Former Boys' Basketball Coach, Bondurant-Farrar Community Schools

in between incoming calls, I contacted individuals with the news. I told them Chris had a severe neck injury, that we were on our way to Rochester for surgery, and that we needed their prayers. That was all we knew at the time. Spreading the word and asking for prayers was my way of doing something.

Chris's fate was in God's hands and that of his doctors. But I knew the power of prayer, I believed in the power of prayer, and I set to work. I was upset, on the verge of tears, and I couldn't drive. The more I talked about Chris's injury and expressed the uncertainty of our plans, the less I was able to concentrate on our route.

I finally pulled over. It was best for Alex to drive the car so

Deb and I could notify people and deal with the phone calls. We frantically tried to track Katie down because she wasn't answering her phone, and we were worried about how she was going to find out about her brother. Was she going to hear about his injury from someone else and feel scared to death? Her whole family was headed to Rochester, Minnesota, and she was in Bondurant. She was going to feel isolated, and she'd want to be with us. Deb got a hold of our minister, and he and one of our really close friends, Tina Hargis, went to the birthday party and got Katie. They arrived at the hospital hours later.

The drive seemed to take forever. I just kept wondering if it was real and hoping when we got to Mayo the doctors would tell us his injury wasn't as bad as they thought. I kept imagining the doctor telling us he'd regained movement on the helicopter ride and that he'd be released very soon. We were still in that dreamy shock-like state.

We'd never set foot in Rochester and didn't realize there were three Mayo hospitals. Winneshiek had given us directions, but when we got to Rochester, the highway signs confused us. Our instructions would have led to the hospital, but we saw a Mayo exit and panicked. We followed the signs and ended up driving around downtown, stressed and taking it out on each other. We finally found St. Mary's Hospital, pulled into the parking area, and tried to find the emergency entrance. A tall man with a bright blue Luther sweatshirt waved through a window.

Was he waving at us? We went from the football field, to the hospital in Decorah, and directly on to Rochester. How in the world was someone from Luther waving at us and pointing to a door? We parked the SUV and hustled inside. The man with the Luther sweatshirt came up to us and introduced himself as Keith. He'd already inquired about Chris's status, knew the room Chris was in, the floor he was on, and showed us how to find him. Deb and I stood in the lobby dumbfounded. Who was this guy, and how did he get here?

Keith, a Luther alumnus from Rochester, Minnesota, had recently lost his wife to cancer, and the Luther/Central game was the first game he'd attended in three or four years. Keith had a feeling Chris was going to end up at Mayo, so he went straight to the hospital so he'd be available to help. We were simply stunned. He led us through the hospital maze to the right set of elevators and walked us to the neurological trauma ICU and directly to Chris. Meeting Keith was like encountering an angel.

We visited briefly with Chris, then the surgeon pulled the four of us—Deb, Alex, my mom, and me—into a small conference room where we all sat. The metallic taste of terror

"I saw them coming through the door. A man and woman wearing Luther apparel each with that look of a thousand years of burden on their face."

Keith Northway, Luther College Alumni

coated my throat and pooled in my belly. We were going to get answers to questions I'd been too afraid to ask.

The doctor looked at us with cool, expressionless eyes and told us our son suffered a severe spinal cord injury between the C3 and C4 vertebrae. Based on the field assessment, the X-rays, and his lack of sensation below the injury site, Chris most likely severed his spinal cord causing a complete injury. As the doctor droned on explaining the difference between a complete and incomplete injury in a monotone voice, as if explaining the difference between synthetic and regular motor oil, my mind seemed to freeze, rejecting the absorption of incoming data. Only broken bits of phrases played on a loop in my brain: broken neck, severed spinal cord, no recovery below the injury site.

Just when my brain began to reengage at the mention of an incomplete injury and the possibility of an un-severed cord and nerve damage from swelling around the injury site, I heard the one thing I never wanted to hear. When considering the extent of his injury, the doctor estimated Chris had less than a 3 percent chance of ever having movement below the neck.

The doctor couldn't have pained me more if he'd pulled out his scalpel, cut the skin along my torso, cracked my ribs wide open, and ripped the beating heart from my chest. Without thought, without even a glance at my family, I fell forward onto my knees and started sobbing. Whimpers tore from my lips as my body shook with grief. *Three percent chance? Three percent chance?* How could that be? How could the doctor be talking about my son? About Chris? Hours ago he had everything going for him, and now he only had a 3 percent chance of ever moving?

Livid with the doctor for sucking all the wind out of my sails, I somehow reined in the anger that threatened to explode at his blunt and meticulous prognosis. I'd rather Chris have a great surgeon who didn't have the best bedside manner than a doctor with a great bedside manner and lesser skills as a surgeon. And, really, how could he have couched his diagnosis or phrased it in a way that made it palatable?

The news flattened Deb; she began to weep, unable to hold her emotions in check. Everything we'd feared from the instant Chris went down hit us like a shot blast to the gut. And my mom, the strongest woman I knew, had tears streaming down her face. That moment was a big turning point in my faith. I could almost hear God whisper, *Do you trust me?*

I always believed God existed. I believed Jesus Christ walked the earth. I believed everything I'd ever learned from the Bible. But did I really trust? Could I put all of my faith in Jesus Christ knowing I had no control over the outcome? It was easy to say I believed all those things, but I'd never been put in a position where I had to trust that he was with me at all times regardless of the circumstances. It was easy to trust when nothing in my life had ever gone so terribly wrong. I knelt in front of my family and the man who'd given me the worst news of my life because I had to decide right then. Did I trust God or not?

I'm going to trust God, I'm going to trust there will be a positive outcome. Suddenly, I went from feeling like somebody had hit me with a baseball bat to being wrapped in a blanket of calm. I'd given everything over to God, and he had my back.

I got up, dried my tears, and with Jesus and my family by my side, faced the future head on.

CHAPTER 7

So be strong and courageous! Do not be afraid and do not panic before them. For the LORD your God will personally go ahead of you. He will neither fail you nor abandon you.

~Deuteronomy 31:6 NLT

CHRIS

I pried my eyes open and everything appeared blurry. My muddled mind attempted to fire as I tried to get my bearings. *Where am I?* Noises beeped in my ears. My eyes fluttered, adjusting to the light, as reality surfaced like a submarine emerging from the darkest depths of the ocean. Everything that had happened flashed before me in an instant. I was injured on the football field, taken by helicopter to Minnesota, and rushed into emergency surgery.

I lay flat on my back in a hospital bed. A TV hung in the corner of the room, a chair sat to the side of the bed, and a bunch of medical boxes and IV stands perched on each side of the bed feeding liquids through the assortment of tubes and wires attached to my body. The curtain in front of the bed was closed. I was alone in the room except for a nurse looking at the monitors, checking my heart rate, and noting the stats the noisy machines recorded.

A giant tube down my throat helped me breathe. I could feel it in my throat where physical sense remained. I didn't like it. I moved my head around, trying to spit it up; I put my tongue on the tube and tried to move it. But I moved my head too much, and a painful shockwave reverberated throughout my body from my surgery site.

The nurse came up to my face. "No, no, no. You have to keep that in. Don't move the tube around."

I knew I could bring air into my lungs on my own and push it back out without the tube in my mouth, so I ignored her and kept moving it around with my tongue.

"No, don't touch it," the nurse said. "It's helping you. Don't do that."

I dozed off and woke up maybe thirty minutes later, and my mom and dad were there with me. They looked tired, upset, and very concerned. They asked if I was feeling okay, but I couldn't answer because of the tube down my throat.

I still felt confused. I had no idea what the surgery accomplished and what to expect next. I didn't ask for answers or demand to know what was going on because of the breathing tube, and I figured they'd eventually tell us.

The surgeon came in for a consultation with my family. I didn't doubt their support or their commitment to my health and recovery, so whatever happened, whatever lay ahead, I knew I wouldn't face it alone. But that also meant everything I faced moving forward would also affect them. The surgeon, directing his attention to both me and my parents, explained that the operation went well. He started off with some encouraging facts: he thought it would take between five and six hours to complete the surgery, but it only took three; they thought they'd have to operate from the back and the front of my neck, but they only had to go in from the back; and they removed a piece of my hip bone and put it in my neck to replace a bone, and to help fuse my C2, C3, and C4 vertebrae. Screws and the bone piece now fused my C2-4 vertebrae.

As loopy as I felt, the specifics amounted to information overload. The only part that registered was "removing a piece of my hipbone." Why had they taken a piece of my hipbone

> *"It is hard to put into words what I felt walking into the room and seeing Chris for the first time. He was lying on the bed with a breathing tube in his mouth not looking like my brother at all."*
>
> Katie Norton, Chris's sister

and put it in my neck? The children's song about bones echoed in my brain. *The thighbone connected to the hipbone. The hipbone connected to the backbone. The backbone connected to the neck bone...*

The surgeon continued giving me the lowdown on how I'd suffered a grade four dislocation. I had a fractured break of my C3 and C4 vertebrae indicating an American Spinal Cord Injury

Association (ASIA) classification of A, which meant a complete injury, or no feeling or movement below the injury site.

After the surgeon explained all the technical aspects of the procedure, he looked me straight in the eye and explained in his serious, measured tone that the X-rays showed extensive damage to my C3 and C4 vertebrae. Due to the lack of sensation and movement below the site of the injury, he initially ruled my injury complete. Some of my responses elevated my injury to incomplete, or ASIA B, but considering my current lack of motion and feeling, he'd still give me an approximate 3 percent chance of recovery below the injury site.

I must have heard him wrong. He couldn't have said three, as in one-two-*three*. But the look on my family's faces told me there wasn't anything wrong with my hearing. My vision went white, my ears began to ring, and if I'd had any feeling in my stomach, it would have felt like a sucker punch. A 3 percent chance? I squeezed my eyes shut as the room began to spin. When I opened them, I was still there, still flat on my back in a room I didn't recognize, unable to move my body.

No. Just no.

The thunderbolt I felt when I moved my head, that's the same kind of shock I felt when I heard the doctor's prediction. As soon as I heard his prognosis, as soon as I realized he wasn't kidding, I knew right away I couldn't accept that as my fate. The news went in one ear, jolted my system, and went right back out the other. As long as I had breath in my body and blood pumping through my veins, I wasn't going to let that happen. I would beat the odds.

All the questions they'd asked before surgery started up again: How do you feel overall? Can you squeeze your hand? Make a fist? Wiggle your toes? Not much registered beyond the doctor's horrific prediction. My brain was too foggy and full of disbelief, and I didn't want to hear anything that couldn't help me get better. I tried to feel what I could feel, and move what I could move. I was both excited and mad when all I could manage was a little shoulder shrug.

"That's awesome," the doctor said. "That's huge." He seemed really impressed by the movement.

By shrugging my shoulder, I immediately defied the 3 percent odds. That was great and all, but that little sliver of good was overridden by the surreal nature of the experience. I was still struggling to believe I was really in the hospital, unable to move my body, and not simply stuck in a nightmare that wouldn't end. I had to keep repeating to myself *this is my life, this is really happening, this is my life,* because my mind kept screaming *No! No! No!*

What would my future look like? What would recovery entail? I had so many questions. There weren't enough answers, and no one seemed to know anything. The doctors and nurses weren't keeping anything from me—they were up front and honest about everything, and they answered every question my parents or I asked to the best of their abilities — but unfortunately they just didn't know. My first reaction was anger. How could they not know? They were doctors — professionals — and they should've known when or if I'd ever be able to move again.

I quickly learned that recovering from a spinal cord injury was basically a waiting game. I naïvely assumed that doctors had all the answers, but the moment they admitted they didn't, it threw me. The outcome for my kind of spinal cord injury was very inconsistent. Doctors couldn't predict how my body would react once the swelling went down and the healing began. No one knew, and the vague answers were difficult to stomach; the more nebulous the answers, the more I became distraught. How was this happening? Why me? Why did this happen to me? And how could I possibly spend the next four weeks in the hospital? I had school, and a life...

"[Chris] is a man of great faith, trusting in a greater plan for us all and making the most of the new journey he has begun."

Brian Solberg M.A. L.A.T., Assoc. Professor of Health and Physical Education, Program Director of Athletic Training

It soon became crystal clear the best thing I could do, the only thing I could do, was turn to God. I reverted back to my faith. Just like when I prayed and asked God for help when I was first injured, after receiving the devastating news from the doctor, rejecting it, and then nearly suffocating from worry, there was nothing left to do but pray.

I prayed for God to give everyone—my family, the doctors, and the medical staff—the confidence, strength, and focus they needed to help me. I had to put my trust in everyone who worked on me, because at that time, I had no control over my future. I didn't have a clear understanding of what the doctors and nurses were doing, so I just had to pray they did the right thing.

No matter what people told me, or how they tried to comfort me, the only thing that brought comfort was asking God for help, strength, and direction.

"It's all going to be okay," my parents and family told me. "We're here for you."

"We're going to do the best we can," the doctor said.

None of those statements gave me comfort. Putting my faith in God and knowing that his strength and will would see me through was the only thing that helped keep me together. The injury happened for a reason; I believed that. It was planned. I didn't know the reason or the plan, but I knew I had to trust God.

Both before and after the surgery, I wondered about the purpose of the accident. I wanted to know why it had happened, because I couldn't simply accept that it had. I trusted God, and I did have faith, but I wanted to know the reason immediately in order to ease the pain and the sadness of being so disappointed.

I asked God to please fill me in on what he had in mind for my life going forward, and for the answer to why this was happening. I didn't doubt my faith, but I wanted to fast forward to the point where the meaning behind my situation was clear. Somehow, I thought knowing the purpose behind the accident would make swallowing my fate easier, because at that moment, I felt like every choice I had for the rest of my life was gone.

CHAPTER 8

I truly believe the saying that life is about 10 percent of what happens to us, and 90 percent how we deal with it. We are not going to let the 10 percent determine our 90 percent.

~Terry Norton, CaringBridge, October 20, 2010

TERRY

Even with my faith, the 3 percent chance almost broke me physically and emotionally. It hit me so hard that I just went off into my own little world for a second, just God and me. I mentally returned to the hospital and glanced at my mom — my rock. It killed me to see her crying. Deb was sobbing, her body wracked with grief; Alex was teary-eyed and trying to absorb the news.

The surgeon got up, said he'd give us some time, and left. We sat in our seats, shattered and uncertain, but there wasn't time to break down. Chris was headed into surgery and we had to be strong for him. I gave the family a little pep talk about how young people were killed in car accidents all the time, and how thankful we should feel that Chris was still with us. No matter what happened to him physically, he was the same kid we knew and loved.

Before Chris went into surgery, we kissed his head, told him we were there, and that we'd see him when it was over. As he was wheeled away, the doctor told us to expect the wait to last anywhere from five to six hours, depending on whether they had to operate from both the front and back of his neck. We had a long night ahead. Drained, exhausted, and ever fearful, we made our way to the waiting room.

> *"We then were able to see him right before surgery, trying to remain as strong and positive as possible, pretending we hadn't just been told some of the worse news that nearly broke us."*
>
> Alex Norton, Chris's sister

Before long, parents, players, and friends of Chris's and ours started arriving at the hospital. People were streaming in, people were praying. It was a mob scene. Everybody — teammates, parents, and our family friends — surrounded us with love. Katie finally made it to the hospital with Tina Hargis and our minister, Peter Mitchell. Katie sat on my lap in the waiting room, hugging me. My teenage daughter was somewhat affectionate, but it wasn't exactly normal for her to plop in my lap. The shock of her big brother's injury hit her hard.

The president of Luther College, Rick Torgerson, and his wife were there, along with the football coach, Mike Durnin, and his wife, Karen. Mike and Karen were very thoughtful; they went to a drug store and bought us toothbrushes, deodorant, and some necessities because they understood we weren't prepared to stay at the hospital.

The waiting room was mayhem. Luther recruited a lot of Minnesota students, so many people stopped by on their way home after the game. Our good friends from home like Bob and Kate Burrows started arriving at that time. To be honest, hearing the grim diagnosis from the surgeon was the lowest point for us; we'd hit rock bottom. Everything that came after felt like little positive baby steps, and the most meaningful to Deb and me was the support of friends, family, and near strangers.

I told Pat Vickers, Chris's roommate's dad, that they didn't need to stay.

Pat turned to me with a look of steel in his eyes. "Terry, if you want me to leave, I'll give you some privacy and move away from you. But we're not leaving the hospital until Chris is out of surgery."

That kind of loyalty and friendship felt like the arms of Jesus reaching out to hold me. I was grateful Pat stayed, and I asked him to help me find a hotel room. We were back before Chris was out of surgery.

I told Mike Durnin, Luther's head football coach, that he could head home.

"He's my family too," Mike said. "I'm not leaving."

To this very day, those words and the sentiment behind them bring a smile to my face. Deb and I greeted and updated people as they came in. All the love and support they offered felt overwhelming.

I didn't know anyone who'd ever had spinal cord damage, so we had no idea what Chris's injury really meant for our day-to-day lives. Even after hearing the grim prognosis, it kind of bounced off of us because we were convinced the doctor wasn't talking about our son. His condition just refused to penetrate, even after we told his story over and over again.

Deb and I didn't have time to go off and process everything that had happened and what it meant for the future. Even if we'd had the time, I'm not sure we would have because saying it out loud, and making plans beyond the then and there, would have validated the reality of the situation. I think subconsciously we didn't want to face what was happening.

While Chris was in surgery, I tried to picture him living from the neck up. What would his life be like? Would he get married? Would he have kids? Would he have to live at home forever? Not that we would mind, but I just couldn't wrap my mind around a young, vibrant person like Chris having to live with his parents for the rest of his life. There were so many unanswered questions. Would he finish college? How could he ever work? What could he do for a job? All those things started flashing through my mind.

Whenever I thought of a person in a wheelchair, I thought of someone with legs that didn't function. I imagined someone in a wheelchair participating in wheelchair basketball or wheeling themselves around with the use of their arms, like a student I once knew. He wheeled himself up to his car, transferred himself into the vehicle, grabbed his chair, folded it up, put it in the back seat, and drove away. When the doctor talked about Chris not moving from the neck down, it was both horrifying and overwhelming.

Deb looked shattered, like a shell of her happy self held together by sheer force of her will. Her eyes laser-focused on me; I had to portray confidence and be a rock because my reactions affected her. Deb was a strong woman, but she was crushed emotionally after losing her dad — I knew she needed my strength and encouragement now.

Alex embraced the medical aspect of the situation, so she didn't appear to be emotionally distraught, even though she was concerned and upset because she loved her brother. Her composure was a comfort to me, because if I had to explain what happened to one more person, or if I had to worry about her emotionally, I may have broken. Alex's nurses training and demeanor allowed her to explain the circumstances to people so Deb and I didn't have to do all the talking. Plus, I think Alex didn't want to add to our concerns by breaking down herself.

Our oldest daughter was pretty reasonable. She was always able to look at the big picture, analyze the situation, and not get emotional. I didn't know if she was like that because of her medical training or because her relationship with Chris as a sister was different from our relationship with him as his parents, but either way it helped a great deal.

My mom's presence was very comforting. She could always come into any situation, blend in, and help ease the tension. That night in the waiting room, my mom encouraged Deb, the kids, and me with her words. I knew she was praying for Chris and praying over us. Her presence was a calm in the storm.

It was a blessing to have so many people around while Chris was in surgery. If it had just been our family in the waiting room, I think the gravity of his condition would have sunk in, and we would have gone to a very bad place. With all the people there, it prevented us from having private talks amongst ourselves and from becoming overwhelmed with what we faced. Even though most visitors were very close friends, we couldn't completely let our guard down, and that kept reality at bay.

At around two in the morning, after only three hours in surgery, the doctor came out to speak to Deb and me. He said in his professional, non-emotional manner that the surgery went very well. They didn't have to go in through the front side, and they were able to stabilize Chris's C3 and C4 vertebrae through the back. The surgeon explained that they put a screw in on one side of Chris's neck. On the other side, they removed a bone from his hip to support that side, so Chris also had a surgery site on his hip. Overall, the doctor felt very positive about the procedures.

The doctor mentioned numerous times that Chris being an athlete had given him an advantage because his body was in tiptop shape. Because Chris was right in the middle of football season and he didn't have an ounce of fat on him, his lung capacity and his body was physically capable of withstanding a trauma better than most, even in terms of recovery. He told us that Chris was one of the fastest cases they'd ever had from the time he was injured to being completely through with surgery.

I took everything he said as positive. I was worried about complications during such a long surgery, so I felt it was good news that it only took three hours. The difference between recovering from a three-hour surgery and recovering from a six-hour surgery, including the trauma to his body, seemed huge. I had to remind myself not to think too far ahead and to slow down and take each day, each moment, as it came. That was hard for me, especially when I was so used to looking twelve steps down the road and preparing for what came next.

Deb seemed to feel good about the news. Her shoulders settled into a more natural position after we met with the surgeon. She mentioned being relieved they didn't have to operate from the front. We were both worried about his breathing and other complications that might arise during surgery, so hearing Chris was doing well made us both feel better.

We were in the hallway just off the waiting room, and everybody was looking at us through the glass. They waited until the surgeon left and then came out to the hallway for an update. By that time, the initial rush of people were on their way back home, and it was down to just a core group of people including Pat and Buzzy Vickers, Tina Hargis, Peter Mitchell, our family, my mom, Mike and Karen Durnin, and Bob and Kate Burrows.

After relaying what the surgeon had told us, Alex tried to reinforce the medical positives and make us feel comfortable about Chris's status. She was upbeat after hearing what the doctor had to say. Chris had made it through surgery, his neck was aligned and fused, and his vitals were good. We heaved a collective sigh of relief while still holding our breath about how tomorrow and the days ahead would unfold.

Chris was just coming out of surgery and would be out for a while. The surgeon suggested we leave and get some rest since we weren't going to be able to see Chris anytime soon, and he wouldn't be awake anyway. That was the only night he stayed in the hospital alone.

Those of us left in the waiting room were emotionally and physically exhausted. The surgeon's report ushered in a sense of relief and gave us what we needed in order to go to the hotel and get a couple hours of much-needed sleep.

The hotel we stayed at the first night was small and hot, but it was close to the hospital. My mom, Katie, Alex, Deb, and I all stayed in one room. The five of us were packed into this little hotel room that smelled of cigarettes and stale air. It was a miserable night on top of a miserable night. I dozed off for a little bit into a restless, fitful sleep that only knocked the sharpest edges off my exhaustion.

The next morning, we got up, showered, and simply prayed for the best before leaving for the hospital. The family never talked about what to expect when we arrived there or how we would get through the day or the next few weeks. Our silence boiled down to ignorance. We knew nothing about the road that lay ahead.

At the hospital, Deb

"I remember that fall Saturday afternoon of Chris's injury very well, but one moment that I have thought about and relived many times since is the expression on the face of Terry Norton in the ER at the hospital. As he exited the doors of the ER, I remember looking at him as he explained what was happening and thinking there is a father who is uncertain of the future, shaken by what was happening to his son, and doing all he can to keep himself composed. Little did I know that his expression that afternoon was more than uncertainty and concern for his son, but the expression of a new beginning. A journey that challenges your faith and reminds you what it really means to live in community. An even greater surprise is that Chris would be the leader, the strength, and the vision for where they were going."

Brian Solberg M.A. L.A.T., Assoc. Professor of Health and Physical Education, Program Director of Athletic Training

84

and I took a deep breath, linked hands, and walked into the ICU to see our son for the first time since his surgery and to meet with the surgeon. My mouth went dry seeing Chris with the breathing tube down his throat and no less than six tubes hooked up to his body. I could tell Chris wanted the breathing tube out right away by the way he moved his tongue around his mouth.

As the surgeon told Deb and me that Chris had a good night and seemed to be recovering and breathing well, I looked at Chris. As soon as we made eye contact, he began shrugging his shoulder and winking at me because he couldn't talk with the tube down his throat. By showing us he could move his left arm, it was as if he were saying, *Dad, I can move. I beat the 3 percent odds!*

I'm not usually a crier, but my emotions were so close to the surface that Deb and I both began weeping. When we'd left the hospital the night before, we had so little hope. The morning sun had done nothing to brighten our outlook. Seeing the determined look on Chris's face and a spark of optimism in his eyes flung open a door we thought had been barred shut. The doctor still couldn't predict the extent of Chris's recovery, but the shoulder shrug was a positive sign.

With tears in our eyes, Deb and I went out to update the others in the waiting room. We didn't stop to think how our appearance would seem to those waiting for word of Chris's fate; we were just so happy to have a sliver of good news. We heard a collective intake of breath and realized my mom, Alex, and Katie assumed the worst.

But our tears came from joy at God's blessing. It felt as if a huge cloud had broken open and allowed the sun to shine through. We had a long road ahead, but we couldn't have cared less. Chris had shown a sign of life below the injury site, and I'd seen the determination to fight in his eyes. There wasn't anything he couldn't accomplish when he set his mind to a task, and regaining as much use of his body as possible meant more to him and his family than words could express.

CHAPTER 9

Faith is the confidence that what we hope for will actually happen; it gives us assurance about things we cannot see.

~Hebrews 11:1 NLT

CHRIS

I couldn't wrap my mind around not being able to move my body at will. I was in phenomenal physical shape at the time of the injury. Because of football, I worked out four hours a day, every day. In the blink of an eye, I felt tied down to the bed, as if my body were completely wrapped and unable to move. Perhaps it would have been easier to accept if I'd slowly lost movement, one limb or inch at a time. But the abrupt manner in which I lost feeling in my body left my mind and my emotions grappling to catch up.

The doctor explained I would be in the Intensive Care Unit until I was medically stable and strong enough to be transferred to the rehabilitation floor. My stay in ICU could last anywhere from five days to five weeks, depending on how my condition improved from that point forward. I'd be looked after attentively in ICU for any serious medical issues, and my eventual transfer to the rehab floor would be a positive step and a sign of regaining health and recovery.

My family was with me constantly while I was in ICU — Grandma, my sisters, Mom, and Dad. My Luther coaches came by, along with friends, and a lot of extended family. An uncle from Missouri drove all the way up to see me just for the night and then drove back. Another uncle, an aunt, and some cousins drove from Iowa City to Omaha, then up to Rochester, and then back again. I was humbled by the amount of driving they all did just to see me for one day. I knew they wanted to lend support to my family and tell me they were praying for my recovery. It meant a lot that they all came. Alex helped Mom and Dad set up a CaringBridge site so they could keep family and friends updated on my condition. The comments and prayers started pouring in from everywhere, and hearing from so many people really helped me not feel so alone.

The Sunday immediately following the accident, while watching Sports Center on ESPN, I heard the announcers talk about head and neck injuries in football. They mentioned the Rutgers University player, Eric LeGrand, and how he broke his neck making a tackle on a kickoff return, replaying his injury over and over again. I thought it was crazy ironic how I got hurt on the same day, the same quarter, the same play, the same everything. I'd never read or heard about anything like that happening in college football, and I wanted the announcers to know Eric LeGrand wasn't the only one who suffered a life-altering neck injury that day.

The irony continued when, during the NFL games, an unusually high number of players suffered concussions. The whole weekend there was a huge concentration of head and neck injuries, drawing a lot of attention to the risk of head injuries for football players, and the topic pretty much dominated conversation on ESPN. The concussions and spinal cord injuries that happened that weekend caused the sports world to spend the next week discussing ways to make football safer.

We watched a lot of movies and TV while I was in ICU. That first Sunday night, our whole family watched the movie *Tarzan* together. Films were a great escape because I could simply indulge my mind and focus on the entertainment. It felt normal, and *anything* normal at that point felt great. Nights were by far the most difficult hours of the day. I was fine throughout the day; I didn't get emotional or angry when people were around. It was upsetting coming to grips with what happened and accepting what I faced ahead, but there was too much going on to feel overwhelmed during the day.

Nighttime was different. I had so much time to think and wonder and get angry. *Why is this happening? I don't want to live like this. When will this be over? When can I just be done with this and move on?*

I wanted to fast-forward two years and get past the first

stages of grief. I tried to bargain with God. *Just let me get through the next couple of years in the next couple of days.* In a couple of years I would be a lot better, but how much better, I didn't know. I just wanted out of the helpless phase that felt like a living a nightmare. It *was* a nightmare.

When I was by myself and it was quiet, thoughts started running through my head like when I was a kid. I still felt strong in my faith and relied upon God to get me through. I continued to pray for something good to come out of my situation, and for God to use me as a tool.

My family would read the very moving CaringBridge responses to me when I was awake. It was difficult to comprehend the magnitude of the effect my injury was having on others while still searching for meaning and a purpose behind what had happened. My optimistic dad and I talked about the impact my injury had on so many people, not only in our small community, but also around the country. We discussed the opportunity I had to show the true nature of my character and faith through adversity.

CaringBridge allowed us to really absorb the outpouring of support from so many others. Countless people were praying for me and keeping track of my progress, so many that it became impossible to ignore the influence I could have on others. I *had* to stay positive, not just for my own mental health, but for those who expressed how my situation had affected their own lives. Through CaringBridge, we realized we had an opportunity to encourage, motivate, and inspire others. It was a welcome, yet compelling distraction.

Most days in ICU passed with a lot of doctors coming in and out of my room, and nurses checking on me, asking questions about how I felt, and examining me. Even in ICU, I spent thirty minutes to an hour every day with a physical therapist. The physical therapist (PT) stretched my body and talked to me, getting to know me a little better. I also saw an occupational therapist (OT) who stretched my arms and had me concentrate on trying to move different parts of my body.

> *"I knew the next day in ICU when the PT Lori came in and started working with Chris that he would walk one day."*
>
> Connie Norton, Chris's Grandma

One of the first things I did in PT while in the ICU was to move my head. Because of the surgery, my neck was really stiff, and moving my head was excruciatingly painful. My surgery site was super sensitive. Whenever I adjusted my head or anyone moved my limbs, a shockwave, like a thunderbolt or waves of lightning, shot down my body. What I could feel, when touched, felt like a searing rain of fire from the top of my head to the tips of my toes.

Every day I worked on nodding my head *yes* and shaking my head *no*. Both the PT and the OT told me to do as much as I could. One of my PT sessions was spent transferring me to a tilt table and having me sit up because my body was having trouble regulating my blood pressure. I felt lightheaded and nauseated whenever I sat up even slightly. The PT wanted to push my blood pressure a little higher and try to get my internal controls working better, so I used the tilt table every day as often as possible.

At first, flat on my back, I couldn't see my whole body. Even when my head was raised, most of the time, blankets covered my arms and legs.

Then, nurses came into my room in ICU to give me a sponge bath, and I got a good look at my body for the first time since the accident. It was surreal watching them move my legs around and scrub them up and down, and not be able to feel them. A tight ball of emotion lodged in my throat. I felt completely disconnected from my body.

I'd spent my whole life working hard to make the most of myself physically. Baseball, basketball, football—all the sports I loved required physical dexterity and control that came from endless hours of practice. I'd always physically pushed my body to the limit, and now I couldn't even feel my arms and legs or make them move. It was simply too much to comprehend.

Besides having no connection with my body, I felt completely drained and exhausted, while suffering with pain from the surgery site. It was frustrating that I couldn't adjust my arm, or fix something, or scratch an itch, or drink and eat on my own. I was eighteen years old, and I couldn't even feed myself.

Another troubling consequence of the accident was the effect on my voice and breathing. I couldn't laugh. I couldn't cough. I couldn't take a deep breath. I had to speak one word at a time because my breathing was so shallow. It was hard to finish a sentence. Because I was so soft-spoken, people had to move really close to me in order to hear what I was saying. All I wanted was to have a normal conversation, and laugh, and cough, and not have to be so dependent on other people. I was used to doing everything on my own, and having privacy. Before I could even absorb what had happened, every shred of privacy was completely stripped away.

During my time in ICU, I met a physician named Georgia who changed the course of my recovery because of something she said to me in the middle of the night. I'd get really restless at night, wanting to do something, wanting to get better, like when I was a kid and wished I could jump out of bed and go to the gym right then.

Georgia came into my room while I was restless. She turned to me and said, "Do you know who I am?"

"No," I said. "I don't know."

"I'm Georgia. I'm from Wyoming. Do you know anyone from Wyoming?"

"No." I couldn't even guess where she was going with the conversation.

"People from Wyoming don't tell lies." She was so serious and intense. The way she stared at me with her eyes completely sober, it felt as if she was looking into my soul. "You're going to beat this," she said. "You *will* get through this. I have no doubt about that. You'll do this. I believe in you."

Having her show so much hope and confidence in my recovery at that moment in my life, especially as a physician, meant the world to me. The way she looked me right in the eyes and said what she said without pretense was just what I needed to hear, and something I'll never forget. She was the first medical professional who talked to me like a person, in a really intimate way, and I drew strength from her conviction.

I was anxious to move to the rehabilitation floor where I could actively participate in my recovery. Once I transferred to the rehab floor, I'd continue to recover, learn how to participate in everyday life, and transition out of the hospital. That's the part that stung—one minute I was an honor student playing football at a prestigious college, the next I had to relearn the most basic skills in order to function. The doctor said the sooner I started rehab, the better, as often the most significant recovery took place in the early months after an injury. I was eager to get started.

I thought I'd be out of the hospital in a couple of weeks, and at that point, weeks in the hospital felt like an eternity. I'd never spent a couple weeks doing anything other than going to school and playing sports. How could I miss that much school? It was tough not to look ahead and get scared and depressed. I wondered if where I was at that moment—unable to move and do anything on my own—was where I would be for the rest of my life. That scared me to death.

Would I always need help? Would I ever improve? There were so many questions. The future looked discouraging, but if I concentrated only on what was directly in front of me, I could feel happy and proud about my progress. I'd be in a better position to take control of my recovery in a month or two, so until then, I had to focus on one day at a time.

For the first couple of weeks, my family never left my side. It was comforting to know I wasn't alone, and I didn't have to worry about anything slipping between the cracks because my family stayed on top of my care. They wanted to be there for me, and they were happy to be there, so I never felt like a burden to them. Being with me wasn't an obligation, and it wasn't work for them; they had no other choice. I counted on their positive, upbeat, and constant presence.

While in ICU, little bits of sensation started to come back in my body. I began to feel tiny sensations in my feet and in my upper body, prompting my sisters and my grandma to do their own kind of therapy with me. My sisters either covered my legs and hands, or they asked me to close my eyes. Then they wiggled a toe, rubbed my foot, or massaged different parts of my legs.

"Which toe am I touching right now?" one would ask.

"Which part of your leg am I touching right now?"

Their game helped me stay in tune with my body. My

grandma rubbed lotion into my hands and feet every day. She rubbed them for twenty minutes trying to rub the life back into them. I always liked when she did that. Even my dad, in his own goofy way, would tell my feet to move as a way of talking to them.

It was so weird to see how flaccid my arms and legs were. Even though it was sad and emotional, I watched whenever the doctors or nurses moved my body or when the head of the bed was elevated so I could see myself. It got a little easier, or maybe I was getting used to it, but it was still hard seeing my legs manipulated and not be able to feel them or make them move. Despite the threat of a lengthy stay in ICU, I was released to the rehab floor after only five days.

My naturally upbeat personality and outlook on life helped keep me focused and positive during those first few weeks in the hospital. I was an optimistic person and not the type to dwell on bad things or to complain. There were things in life I had to do in order to succeed, and I felt there was no sense in complaining. After the initial shock of the accident passed, it was tempting to feel sorry for myself. People would understand, but it wouldn't do any good. I simply needed to do whatever I could to get better and be happy with the outcome.

Yes, the odds were bad, but I'd beaten bad odds before. Feeling sorry for myself was stupid and unproductive. I adjusted my mind and tried to stay focused on each day and getting a little bit better that day. Although when night came, the distraction of therapy and guests was gone and the hopelessness of the situation crept back in, making sleep difficult.

Throughout my injury and hospitalization, I was very fortunate that my prognosis kept improving. There was always a little bit of momentum and forward progress, so it was easier to stay upbeat and positive when I didn't suffer a medical setback where I got really sick or something happened that derailed my progress. The steady but small increments of improvement helped to liven up a pretty horrible situation. My journey, for better or worse, had just begun.

"I went up to see Chris while he was in hospital pretty early after he had surgery and he was already talking about starting rehab, and I couldn't believe his attitude. He was already thinking positively. I can't imagine the strength that took to not feel sorry for himself like so many might."

Chris Kamm, ATC, CSCS, Former Head Certified Athletic Trainer, Luther College

CHAPTER 10

Everyone would be so proud to see the determination on the road to recovery that [Chris] has demonstrated so far; just as he has demonstrated in all of the sports he has done throughout high school.

~Terry Norton, CaringBridge, October 17, 2010

TERRY

The first time we saw Chris after the accident, the doctor gave us an update on his condition and told us what they were going to do for him medically, but he left out a lot of details about what came next. When we went out to tell the family and everybody came back to the ICU, that's when the surgeon said Chris was going to be in ICU until he didn't need acute care and was strong enough to transfer, and we'd have to start thinking about where we wanted him to go to rehab.

Our heads were spinning. We'd barely taken a breath between the time he was ushered off the playing field, flown to Minnesota, underwent major surgery, and woke up in ICU. Now we had an ill-defined timetable for ICU and plans to make for the future? Whenever I tried to think big picture, it made my stomach churn. We were three steps behind from every direction. But then I looked at Chris and tossed my unease to the side. I had to be strong for my son and my family. The worry could wait, as we had nothing but time.

The first day in ICU, there were six or seven IVs in him and the room felt crowded with all the equipment and our family inside. The surgeon took the breathing tube out and hooked him up to oxygen. The first thing Chris said once the tube came out regarded his left arm.

"I can move my left arm," he whispered. His throat was sore from the tube, and his lung capacity was compromised. "I can feel my arm. I think I can feel my right arm too."

Everything he said was positive. He was already doing self-checks, assessing his body and figuring out what he could feel. He was chomping at the bit to start working toward recovery, and his attitude helped to lighten our load.

The surgeon was basically our point person, checking on Chris, bringing his X-rays, talking with us about his condition, examining the surgical site, and overseeing his medical care. The folks in ICU took care of his day-to-day needs, like monitoring his blood pressure and making sure he wasn't getting skin sores. The ICU staff were unbelievably on top of this, turning Chris every two hours, and keeping an eye on the common sore areas like the heels of his feet, his elbows, and any place on his body that would rub. If any area ever got even a little red, they tried different techniques such as elbow pads to address the spot.

Right away he had visits from PTs and OTs who were specifically assigned to the ICU floor to get him started on therapy, even before he was released to rehab. I tried not to become overwhelmed by the medical implications of his injury in addition to his lack of movement. Except for Alex, we felt woefully unprepared for the crash course in medical schooling.

From day one Chris started asking us to touch his toe and let him try to guess which one we were touching. His sisters did that constantly. Somebody told us that the more stimulation we gave him, the more it would help. Alex and Katie would each take a foot and they'd move his toes, rub his arches, and massage his calves. We were constantly stretching his fingers and hands, trying to get things moving and regain sensation.

As the planner of the family, I shouldn't have been surprised when Chris asked in his quiet, monotone voice, "Dad, what's the plan for today?" on his first day in ICU.

Deb called me the family "salesman" because I always tried to take something ordinary or routine and make it sound fun. I would sell the plan. I couldn't believe Chris wanted me to tell him what we were going to do while he was in ICU. As if I had a clue. From that point forward, we spent time getting to know the hospital and available restaurants so I could put together "fun" activities.

The girls did a great job of keeping things upbeat on our first day in the hospital. They went to the library and checked out DVD equipment and a bunch of movies and brought them back to his room. We were all desperately trying to keep the depression that stalked us at bay, so we gratefully watched movies and did anything we could to keep Chris happy.

"I could tell from the start that he came from a very supportive family structure, and in physical therapy outcomes, that can mean the difference between success and failure for the patient!!"

Lisa Krieg, PT Euro-Team in Decorah

But I was feeling pressure to be all things to every member of my family. During a low moment, I sent a text to my friend Steve Pinkley to ask some of the men in our community to pray for me to have strength as a father so I could be everything I needed to be for my son and family through this challenge. I needed strength from other dads who might understand my concerns.

Steve, never to take a request lightly, called me from the high school that night where he'd assembled over twenty-five of my friends in a classroom. They passed the phone around and each person gave me words of strength and encouragement after I shared my story. It was an amazing show of friendship and gave me the strength I desperately needed to see us through.

Deb and I were trapped inside our heads; too afraid to stare reality in the face, we clung instead to the comfort of denial. Initially, we thought Chris could try to finish the college semester. We had no idea what we were facing. We actually spent time brainstorming ideas on how he'd get an extension on his assignments and how we'd run his homework back and forth to school. We thought about silly things like how his car was still on campus, and we questioned how we'd get it home.

We did our best to portray strength and encouragement, but I wondered if he'd ever walk again and lead a normal life, as though one led to the other, even though in reality the two were not at all related. Many people led extraordinary lives and never walked.

The Mayo psychiatrist explained that able-bodied people equate happiness and joy with being able to participate in physical things like running, jumping, skipping, and climbing. They wonder why people in wheelchairs aren't depressed or discouraged, because it's assumed if they can't walk, their life must not have meaning. People in chairs put more stock in character, personality, making a difference, and finding a deeper meaning in life rather than focusing on the physical.

That was a hard lesson to grasp, but we needed to change our mindsets. After all, I had life all planned out. I'd spend every fall Saturday going to college football games, taking my son out to eat, and mixing in some trout fishing in Northeast Iowa. He'd graduate from college, get a business degree, hopefully meet a nice girl during college, and have a successful life. I'd hoped they'd live fairly close to us so we could play with our grandkids.

From the stands where I'd planned to spend the next four years, I watched my dreams dissolve in an instant. Coming to terms with how drastically life had changed was no easy feat, but it started by taking stock of what was important. Chris playing college sports, for example, was no big deal because in four years, regardless of what happened, it was over and done. A lot of things I thought were important were in fact meaningless. The accident brought everything into focus.

For some reason, the rules of how many visitors were allowed in ICU never applied to us. We stayed in his room way past visiting hours, and Deb, Alex, or I spent the night sleeping on the foldout chair. A stiff neck and a sore back were a small price to pay for the peace of mind that Chris wasn't alone.

Sleeping in the room with Chris did more for me than him because it gave me a purpose. He'd call out to me so I could scratch his head, face, and arms when they itched. Not being able to move his arms was frustrating, but he kept a good attitude.

Chris was eighteen, so we ran into the Health Insurance Portability and Accountability Act (HIPAA) restrictions. The doctors and nurses always looked at Chris for permission, and he'd assure them they could tell Deb and me anything and keep us updated. Despite having to ask if it was okay to share information, most of the medical staff directed their information to the three of us—Chris, Deb, and me. They didn't just talk to him and let us overhear; they knew we wanted to be included in any decisions that needed to be made about his care.

During the first few days in ICU, the doctor told us Chris

103

would most likely be in the hospital for four weeks, including rehab. Four weeks quickly changed to eight, and that sounded like forever to all of us, but especially to Chris. He gave an *are you kidding?* look when the doctors shared the news.

"Chris," I said without hesitation, "we're not going to leave you alone. We're going to be here through it all. It's going to be fine. Let's do this, get your rehab done, and get you taken care of."

He nodded and took me at my word. I fleetingly wondered how I'd manage to be away from work and our home for that long, but the thought disappeared as soon as I looked at Chris, lying in a hospital bed, unable to move. No job or responsibility meant more than being with my son.

On his second or third night in ICU, Chris was having a rough night. Katie and Alex were staying with him, and Deb and I were at the hotel. The girls called at four-thirty in the morning and said Chris needed me, so I threw on some clothes and went over to talk to him.

Chris shared that he was struggling emotionally, and it highlighted his need for me at that point in time. Deb and I had different rolls in Chris's life. Deb was the nurturer and the caregiver, while I was the coach and motivator. He needed my strength, my motivation, and my encouragement to face the incredible challenges that lay before him. I prayed every day that I was strong enough to help him through.

Deb and I talked a lot about not projecting our fears onto

Chris. The physical side was hard enough, but we had to take our emotional cues from him. We always put everything in our own point of reference, but that wasn't fair to Chris. Fortunately, he had a great attitude and his lows were few and far between.

There was no rest for the weary. Within a day, the therapist's stated goal was to get him upright. They brought a table into his room that looked like a bed/table, slid him onto another mattress, and put him onto the table to slowly tilt him upright. They kept close tabs on his blood pressure, and if it got too low, they backed the table down. They worked every day toward getting him upright, and they monitored how long he could sit up before his blood pressure dropped to an unhealthy level.

The PT, Lori Eaton, started therapy right away. Chris's first therapy was to nod his head *yes* and shake his head *no*. Even though most of his neck wasn't damaged and he could move his head, he'd still had major surgery on his neck and was very sore. She told Chris to repeat the action a few times, and she'd come back and check on him. Chris being Chris, he worked for an hour straight until she came back and told him to stop. Lori couldn't believe he'd been doing that exercise the whole time she was gone, but that summed up Chris's attitude and work ethic. In many ways, he was still like a little kid in that he'd do whatever anyone wanted, no questions asked. That was how he was hardwired. If he thought it would make him better, he'd do it, and he brought that same determination to rehab.

Chris blew into a breathing tube called a spirometer to try

and increase his lung capacity because he couldn't talk very loud. He'd try to lift the ball inside the plastic column up to a certain level. He kept blowing and blowing, again and again and again, and he instructed us to write down how he did each time. From day one, he said, "I've got work to do."

His second day in ICU, the team of rehab doctors gave Chris some good news. He no longer required oxygen, and sensitivity continued to spread throughout his body, indicating that the spinal cord was functioning and what feeling would come back would do so as the healing process continued.

My pride swelled as Chris donned his game face, fighting to stay on the tilt table as long as possible and working on his exercises over and over. When he said he was getting tired, I told him he could lay down and sleep, but he wanted to keep working on his exercises. He was so determined, and within that first hour of doing his neck exercises, he showed great improvement.

Even though we were used to Chris's never-give-up attitude, we were concerned about him overdoing it. He'd suffered a severe spinal cord injury and just had major surgery, so we asked the therapists if he could hurt himself by working too hard, or if he'd simply wear down. They loved his work ethic and enthusiasm, but would cautiously tell Chris that at some point, rest helps with recovery. We then tried to find a balance, and what worked best with Chris was to admit that *we* needed a break. I'd tell him that he was wearing us all down, and he'd finally agree to take a break.

It broke my heart and simultaneously made me angry whenever the doctor and therapists talked about Chris using a wheelchair as if it were a foregone conclusion. It was clinical and prudent advice, but none of us were ready to accept his fate and run out and install a ramp at our house.

"Never once did I hear Chris complain about his situation or refuse therapy. NEVER."

Megan Gill, PT, DPT, Clinical Lead Physical Therapist for Spinal Cord Injury, Mayo Clinic

"They're basing it off the worst case scenario," I told Chris. "You're going to beat this. They don't know you. They don't know what your outcome will be."

I tried to walk the fine line between reality and optimism, not to feed him false hope, but to keep him positive, uplifted, and encouraged. It was a delicate balance, and to be honest, I probably learned best how to keep things in perspective from watching Chris.

I seriously couldn't imagine being in his situation and staying focused on one day at a time the way he did. The way he always had. When he went to sleep at night, he knew he'd done everything he could that day, and he didn't face tomorrow until it arrived. We learned to model our behavior on his and the way he instinctively did what was necessary and then moved on. As the dad of the family and the man in charge, it wasn't an easy lesson to learn. Many nights, the only reason I fell asleep was sheer exhaustion. But of all the people I knew, Chris seemed uniquely prepared. In some ways, he'd trained his whole life to handle this kind of adversity. He took things as they came, found joy in every experience, and never complained.

Everyone involved in his hospital stay provided information about his care and were very helpful, but some made a lasting impression. Dr. Georgia, a feisty woman from Wyoming, was probably the single biggest inspiration to Chris because she was the first medical professional to tell him he was going to beat this. Deb told him that, his sisters told him, we were all telling him he could get better, but it wasn't until a medical professional said it that he truly believed. Her interaction with Chris proved that the personal aspect of medicine was as important to his recovery as the medical aspect.

The hospital's social worker set up an appointment for Deb and me to tour the rehabilitation therapy floor at Mayo, and we were very impressed. He also gave us information on other rehabilitation facilities to consider and offered to help us make contact. While his assistance was helpful, it also felt as if he'd placed a live grenade in my hands. Chris's entire future depended on us making the right decision about his care, as we knew rehab was where he'd improve the most. We all took turns doing research using the computers in the waiting room, but the ultimate decision rested on my shoulders. I had to choose wisely, and there were many factors to take into account.

The only facilities we really considered other than Mayo were the Rehabilitation Institute of Chicago (RIC) and Denver's Craig Hospital. There were other excellent facilities we investigated, including Kessler Institute of Rehabilitation in New Jersey and Shepherd Center in Atlanta, but they weren't in the Midwest. We had to look at the big picture, and we all felt the best therapy Chris could get had to include the support of family and friends. If he got great treatment but felt discouraged, depressed, and isolated from those who loved him, it wouldn't matter how good the rehabilitation was because he wouldn't thrive. We had to consider both his physical and social needs.

Searching for the right rehab facility for Chris was probably the most difficult decision I have ever made in my life, especially as I had to sift through the "noise" of everyone trying to be helpful. Every friend, family member, and colleague had a suggestion, story, or recommendation. What if I picked wrong and changed my son's life forever?

Then a person at Craig Hospital told me exactly what I needed to hear. She said that what was going to come back in Chris's body would come back, no matter where Chris did his rehab. No facility had a magic wand or a silver bullet that would make a significant difference in what function actually returned. The difference between the facilities came down to which was better suited for strengthening and maximizing his recovery.

Knowing there wasn't a wrong choice lifted that huge burden off my shoulders, but I continued to research. I didn't want to stay at Mayo simply because it was convenient when another facility could help Chris walk again or regain movement in his hands. From day one, we were working with the physical and occupational therapists from Mayo's rehab floor, so that gave them a leg up. We knew they were knowledgeable, professional, and caring, but they weren't just talking about what they would do, they were already working with him.

We talked to Chris about his options. Luther's proximity to Mayo was a very strong factor for him, because as an eighteen-year-old college freshman, he didn't want to be cut off from his friends. After much research on Mayo, RIC, and Craig, and considering Mayo was an hour and a half from Luther, Mayo seemed like the best choice for Chris. Not only could Mayo provide world-class care, but his friends and fellow students could come up on the weekends or even come up for dinner and then head back. It was a win for everyone.

With the decision made as to where he would rehab, the financial burden of living out of a hotel could no longer be ignored. We spent the first night in an awful place, but we were too mentally and physically exhausted to find another. Besides, two weeks in a decent hotel would have wiped out our savings at a time when we needed money more than ever. But while Chris was in ICU, some friends of ours got together and paid for two weeks at the Courtyard Marriott near the hospital, paying the hotel directly and without asking our permission. Our wonderful friends also brought clothes from our house and helped us move in because we still had the grill, chairs, and cooler in the back of our vehicle.

However, the family planner didn't have a plan for what to do after those two weeks were up. All we knew was that Chris would be in the hospital for eight weeks, we couldn't leave him three hours away from home all alone, and he needed his dad by his side. We looked at Chris and knew we'd do whatever it took to be with him. Sell the house, empty our savings account, dip into our 401-K. Nothing was off the table.

We had less than five thousand dollars in savings and that wouldn't last long. I'd been in my position with DMACC for just under two years, and I'd quickly fly through my vacation and sick time and have to go without pay. None of that gave us a moment's pause in our decision for me to stay, but facts were facts: we needed both of our incomes to make ends meet.

CHAPTER 11

Always be joyful. Never stop praying. Be thankful in all circumstances,
for this is God's will for you who belong to Christ Jesus.

~1 Thessalonians 5:16-18 NLT

CHRIS

My family was very close and we'd always been there for each other, but going through my injury and recovery together brought our family to a whole new level of closeness. Everything we shared was more emotional and intimate than anything we'd ever experienced before. Seeing how much my family and my sisters in particular wanted to be there for me, and how much they looked forward to being with me on the weekends made me realize how blessed I was to have them in my life. My injury and lengthy hospital stay after the death of a high school friend and during a time when I lost my maternal grandmother helped me recognize the value of all the relationships in my life.

But like a typical eighteen-year-old, I initially took my family's support for granted, not realizing how vital they were to my recovery and how important it was to have them by my side. I spent most of my non-therapy hours in my room for the first couple of weeks. During that time, the nurses, therapists, and doctors all commented on how great my family was, and what a huge support they were for me because they didn't see that kind of devotion very often. I'd kind of shrug off their comments because that was just my family acting like my family. If I had a game or a part in a play growing up, they'd be there. If my sisters had an event, we'd go, no questions asked.

Even when I went to college, my parents came to all the home games and the away games if they weren't too far. I wouldn't have blamed them for staying home—I wasn't a starter and I wasn't on the field very much, but I loved having them there. After home games, they'd take me out to eat in Decorah.

I was so busy at school that I didn't do a great job of communicating with my family, but that didn't stop them from driving three hours to see me stand on the sidelines and get into the game for a handful of plays. It wasn't until further along in the rehab process when I began to see other people—even people around my age—going through therapy with no one there to help or support them that I truly realized how blessed I was to have my family by my side.

For the first two weeks I was in the hospital, having my whole family around meant I never felt alone. I could ask them for anything. I had a nurse, of course, but she wouldn't sit in the room right next to me like my parents did. If I needed a drink, wanted to watch something on TV, needed food, or anything at all, they were right there. They came to every PT session, helped me get into my chair, and were a fantastic support. They wanted to make my time in the hospital as comfortable and easy on me as possible.

There were some awkward times when I felt uncomfortable having my family around because I was more exposed, like when I had to go to the bathroom or take a shower, but I would have been uncomfortable with anyone at that point. By far, the most awkward part of my hospital stay was being washed by a stranger. The alternative involved transferring to a shower chair, but that process included the uncomfortable and painful lift system. I still had a lot of neck pain, and I didn't like water touching the surgery site or having my head scrubbed because it was so sensitive, so a sponge bath in bed and all its embarrassment was the best choice.

But that didn't make it easy to accept. It was just so weird being washed by someone I didn't know, a strange woman, or worse—a guy. The hospital tried to set me up with guy nurses because they thought that would make me feel more comfortable, but that was *not* the case. I'd rather have a woman any day of the week. The truth was, I hated every part of personal care. Every. Single. Part. Having a stranger see me naked, wash me down, and touch every part of me caused all of the anger, fear, and disgust over my situation to pool under a heavy blanket of shame. Every time I needed to use the bathroom, shower, or brush my teeth, I was reminded of just how low I'd fallen. And it hurt.

The nurses did the best they could to ease my discomfort. They'd tell me beforehand what they were going to do, and they encouraged me to tell them if they ever did anything wrong or did something that made me feel uncomfortable. In fact, they preached about how important it was to be an advocate for my care. Once I knew the routine, it was easy to speak up for myself, and their attitude and professionalism lessened my anxiety. The level of care and attention I received only reinforced that I was where I needed to be, doing everything I could to get better. The rest was in God's hands.

After two weeks, my mom and sisters left, which was hard on both my dad and me. I loved having my mom around because I felt so comfortable with her loving support, and my sisters were a great source of entertainment. They'd run to my room and hug me, and their love and the joy they seemed to feel at being with me lifted my spirits. I fed off their energy. We'd laugh together and they'd constantly poke me and rub me, so it was livelier with them around. I wished they could have stayed, but I understood my mom had to go to work, and my sisters needed to get back to class.

One night, maybe a month or two after my injury, it was just Katie who stayed. After the usual where-am-I-touching-you games and talk, she very seriously asked how I was feeling and how things were going. She got really quiet for a minute after I answered, staring down at her hands before she lifted her eyes to mine. It hit me like a punch in the face when I saw the tears glistening in her eyes.

"I wish it was me," she said, as her chin quivered. "I wish it was me going through this. I would trade places with you in a heartbeat."

The depth of her feelings, and the sincerity of her words, left me speechless.

"You're so motivated and so driven," she continued. "You had so much going for you. I just hate that you're going through this. I wish it was me."

I got emotional hearing how much she looked up to me and how much she loved me. She meant every word. She would have traded places with me without hesitation. I was totally blown away by her unselfish display of love, and her admission reaffirmed that despite my circumstances, I was very blessed.

> *"He is the one person I know that can get through something like this and never lose hope or give up."*
>
> Katie Norton, Chris's sister

Having my dad around was an incredible comfort to me, particularly when the rest of my family left to go home. He and Mom had talked and he wanted to stay, go through rehab with me, and make sure I wasn't alone. He said we'd beat this—*we*—because it would never be me on my own. I loved him for that and for his confidence in the outcome. It was awesome that his job allowed him to stay with me so I could just focus on getting better.

My hero and coach never left my side. He gave great advice, and if I ever felt bad about something, he knew the right thing to say to get me back on track. He always pushed me to make the best of myself growing up, and he was able to do the same during therapy. He helped motivate me, he got along really well with my therapists, and he was fun to be around too.

He kept telling me how proud he was of me, and while it felt good to hear him say that, I was still the same person inside. I didn't feel any different, or think my attitude ever changed. I was just as determined to get better and improve myself after the injury as I was growing up in regards to school and athletics, but this time the goal wasn't a good grade or a state championship. The outcome meant so much more to my life. With my back against the wall, there was only one way to go— move ahead and get better. I had no other choice. I think a lot of people in my situation would have done the same, but from the outside looking in, it probably seemed like an overwhelming task.

My dad slept over every night. I felt reassured having him right next to me if I ever needed anything or wanted to talk. We really didn't have much downtime, but at night if we weren't reading CaringBridge, we'd watch TV, or I'd Skype, or talk with friends. Sometimes, he'd wheel me down to the cafeteria, or up to the top floor of St. Mary's and hang out, or just explore and get us both out of the room.

My dad and I learned a lot about each other that we never would have known otherwise. For example, he likes to repeat things a lot. I called him Captain Repeat. He'd tell the same story over and over again about something that happened the other day or the conversation he had with someone.

My dependence created some awkward situations and a good dose of frustration for both of us. I wanted to have normal privacy to chat with friends and catch up, and I didn't want to do that with a parent there. It was weird having my dad text my friends for me, and he wasn't very good with technology or the computer. He was a really slow typist, which made him a really slow texter.

Whenever he wanted to open up a new tab on the Internet, he couldn't figure out how to do it, no matter how many times I told him. I swear, I showed him how to open up a separate tab twenty times and he instantly forgot. And don't get me started on his social media skills. He was just completely oblivious to a lot of technology and social media. It was hard to be patient when I had to explain using words because I couldn't point. I tried to use my eyes, but that never worked.

It didn't take much to please me, and it took a lot to make me unhappy, but when I needed other people to help with everything, I realized that everyone had their own routine and their own way of doing things. When I was in control and doing everything for myself, the way I like things done went completely unnoticed. Like brushing my teeth, for example. I brush my teeth really hard, and I brush them for a long time, especially in certain spots. When I tried to explain how to brush my teeth and those helping me didn't understand, I got annoyed. I just wanted to do it myself so it was done right.

Eating was another challenge. I wanted to eat at my own pace, but because anyone feeding me had a meal at the same time, I had to go with their flow. Sometimes I'd get a bite, and then they'd take a bite, and if they weren't paying attention, they might get a drink and take another bite before feeding me again. I sat there, trying to be patient. *Hello? Is it my turn yet?*

I soon realized that my dad was a big sauce person. He loved to drown his chips in salsa or drench his french fries in ketchup. I liked a moderate to a minimal amount of sauce. I kept having to say, "No, too much ketchup." He eventually learned to ask how much I wanted before dipping anything in sauce. The little picky things I liked doing my own way made me seem very particular and high maintenance.

Frustration at my dad when eating, brushing my teeth, and communicating with friends was a small price to pay for his twenty-four-hour devotion to my care. I love my dad and loved hanging out with him, but it was nice when my family and friends came up on the weekends. It was good to see some new faces and mix things up a bit. He needed a break from me, and I enjoyed spending time with my mom, sisters, and friends.

It was never a distraction having family and friends around. On the weekends, I had an abbreviated therapy schedule, and other people came at night when I didn't have therapy and they were done with school or work. In the beginning of my rehab, I needed to sleep a lot when I wasn't in therapy, and sometimes people came during therapy hours and I couldn't take time to visit. Sometimes my family had to explain that it wasn't a good time and why. It was a bit of a balancing act where we really appreciated the people who came, but at the same time I needed to do the work. My family did a great job of helping me focus on therapy by handling unscheduled visitors.

My mom and sisters got super excited whenever I accomplished something new, and although I never got really excited, I liked that everyone else did. My mom was fun to tease and prank because she was so gullible and emotional, so if I got a movement or a feeling back during the week while she was gone, I'd find a way to surprise her when she arrived on the weekends. When I got movement back in my arm, I told her there was something off with my heartbeat and it was making a weird sound. When she leaned all the way over my chest,

"The tragedy of Chris's initial injury followed by the miraculous surgery that gave him the chance to work towards recovery was only the beginning. The real story began the next day when Chris started down his path to recovery."

Rich Vickers, Chris's college roommate and close friend

I pulled my arm up and put her in a chokehold. She started crying and laughing and got super emotional.

When I wasn't in therapy, eating, or watching movies, Dad and I had a lot of deep conversations about faith and grit that came out of our talks about game planning. We brainstormed things that would help me get better, and then we discussed the importance of following through. We talked about what it takes to get better, what I had to work on, and the plan to get better. It was an emotional time, so it was natural to rely on God and faith and my own determination. It was a very stressful experience, and talking it out helped to release some anxiety and work things out in my mind.

My injury aimed a spotlight on how close my family was in the same way my work ethic and determination was exposed publically following the injury. We were always close, and I was always resolute in achieving my goals, although CaringBridge and the media's reporting of my accident and recovery made it seem unusual. Our family's bond remained as strong as ever, and the only thing that changed was my appreciation for my family's love and unconditional support.

I did worry about the sacrifices my family was making. I worried about my sisters. Alex came up and visited a lot, and I didn't want to get in the way of her studies and derail her from becoming a nurse. I worried about Katie giving up basketball in order to be with me on the weekends. My mom and dad assured me that their employers understood and wanted them to be with me, so I never worried about their jobs. Family and friends pitching in and making it as easy as possible for them to be away from home so much took a lot of the stress off my parents, allowing us all to focus on my recovery. Every day brought a new blessing, be it a card from a stranger with words of encouragement, a particularly moving CaringBridge post, or a new sensation in my body.

Despite the uphill battle, I felt surrounded by God's love.

CHAPTER 12

I have witnessed one small miracle after another, whether it is an unknown person stepping forward and offering their home, or family and friends helping us with taking care of our pets at home, chores around the house, and fund raising. We have had people call or send cards at times we have really needed it. I believe there are good days ahead.

~Terry Norton, CaringBridge, October 31, 2010

TERRY

I called my boss's cell phone the day of Chris's injury and told her Chris had been injured, we didn't know the extent of his injury, and it didn't look like I'd be at work on Monday. Little did we know that by Monday I wasn't going to give much thought to work. I was fortunate that my boss couldn't have been more supportive. She told me to take care of my family, and they'd make it work in my absence. Deb's boss gave the same magnanimous response. We were very, very blessed that the people in the companies we worked for understood. But that was a short-term solution.

When we looked at what was best for Chris, Deb and I agreed I needed to be the one to stay. With the challenges we'd already faced and so many more looming in the distance, Deb feared she'd become overwhelmed and wanted me there to handle things. She was struggling to keep her emotions in check, and she understood that Chris needed my strength. I was physically stronger and better equipped to help Chris in therapy, and my planning skills helped organize the appointments, meetings, and decisions we tried to anticipate. It was immensely difficult for her to leave him, but she knew we'd made the best decision for what he needed at the time.

With his rehab beginning at Mayo and the decision made for me to stay, we needed to process the logistics. I took the Family and Medical Leave Act from work, which protected my job, but I didn't get paid. I used all my sick time and vacation first, but I didn't have a lot of either because I hadn't been in my job very long. I'd spent most of my life as a teacher, and when the kids were little, Deb job shared and stayed home, so we never had a ton of money. What little we had was going fast. Too fast.

Like angels sent from God, friends came to our rescue. They told me to stay with my son, and they would take care of the rest. I didn't have the words to express what a huge relief that was, and how grateful Deb and I were to them and the many, many others who stepped up to help during our time of need. It was the beginning of a string of blessings where people from the community came together and took care of us in ways too numerous to list. Our hearts, while suffering for Chris, swelled with love and gratitude.

When our friends told us they had our backs, the community started organizing. We began receiving gift cards, and they put together fundraisers back home. Our friends organized a prayer vigil at Bondurant-Farrar High School through the Fellowship of Christian Athletes. A bunch of football players from Central College came, as well as some area high school football teams. I called in and delivered the welcome and opening prayer.

I gave an update on Chris and talked a bit during the prayer vigil about some things I'd learned since his injury. I explained that we never asked *why* because why didn't matter. I gave thanks for the opportunity Chris had to use his faith to have an impact on people. I went on to say that many people had asked what they could do for us, and how we wanted people to use Chris's injury as a wake-up call. I asked those in attendance to honor the battle Chris faced by living each day to the fullest, giving thanks for the little things in life, and facing the future with courage to take on the challenges and obstacles life presents. Finally, I asked people to examine their faith.

All the little dramas and petty arguments in my life just went *poof* when Chris got injured. Everything I said at the prayer vigil seemed Holy Spirit driven. I found a quiet place in the hospital lobby to write some notes, and it felt like I went into a zone—the words just flowed. One of the big things I wanted to express was that although Chris's body was currently broken, his spirit was not.

Someone showed me a picture taken at the prayer vigil, and

while there were an incredible number of people there, I had to ask about the scoreboard. Chris's high school football number was five, and his college number was sixteen. The organizers put those numbers all over the scoreboard: on the clock, in the score, and other slots. The attention to detail was truly amazing.

With the help of our friends, we finally had a plan. Deb would come up every Thursday after work, and Katie would miss school every Friday and stay until Sunday. Katie quit the basketball team. She talked to the coach, and he was willing to work with her, but she said it was more important for her to be in Rochester with her family. Everybody had to make sacrifices, and I think that really drew our family together. It was tough at the end of the two weeks when they left. We shed some tears and seemed to repeat the same torturous routine every weekend.

Alex came with Deb and Katie if she didn't have class on Friday. They were so excited to see Chris, they'd get to the hospital and

"Every day, every minute I spent with Chris and his family, then and now the words that come to me are: a young man and a family who would not allow a tragic event to become a tragedy. A young man and a family who believed and lived their lives knowing that with faith, family & friends you will overcome all obstacles and make a difference in the world. A young man and a family who would forever be in my heart & soul."

Mike Durnin, Former Head Football Coach at Luther College

literally run through the halls to get to him. His sisters would put a cot on each side of his bed, and they'd massage his hands and tickle him.

Typically, the girls stayed with him on Thursday nights so Deb and I could be together. Occasionally Alex and Katie stayed two nights, and Deb sometimes covered a night to give me a break. Chris was waking me up every couple of hours to scratch his head or his nose. Sometimes he'd want me to turn on the radio or do something else to help him sleep, so by Thursday, I was pretty exhausted. When the rest of the family was there, I got a good night's sleep so I could be refreshed enough to handle the upcoming week.

Sundays were very difficult for both Chris and me. Weekends in general were tough. During the week, we had a full schedule. Occupational therapy might run from eight to ten, and physical therapy would run from ten to twelve, and he'd get some additional therapy afterwards. Then, he'd rest or have appointments with different doctors. The weekdays flew by, and we felt productive and proactive working toward his recovery. On the weekends, Chris had an hour or an hour-and-a-half of therapy or forty-five minutes of each. There was a lot of down time, so if we didn't have many visitors, the weekends sometimes felt long for me.

Saturdays and Sundays were hard on Chris too. During the week, he was too busy to notice he wasn't in college anymore. The weekends brought his isolation into focus. Of all times,

Rochester had one of the worst winters they'd had in years, and the snow totals were staggering. There were a lot of weekends when his friends had planned to come to the hospital but couldn't because of the weather. That was tough because an eighteen-year-old doesn't mind hanging out with his dad and mom during the week when he's doing therapy, but hanging out with Mom and Dad on Friday or Saturday night isn't normal. Weekends could be fun with everyone around, but they were challenging too.

Chris's friends from home and school would come, watch a movie, keep Chris entertained, and help him stay connected. It was a testament to Chris's personality that he formed such a close bond with his friends and teammates at Luther in such a short amount of time. He was a funny guy, but he didn't dominate a conversation. He was a good listener who liked to talk and have fun. People just genuinely liked him.

Deb and I worried about some of Chris's friends falling away because they wouldn't be able to handle what he was going through. Would his friends see him as too much of a challenge? Would they look at him and think they had to take care of him? But we never had anyone say, "I can't deal with it." In fact, we were pleasantly surprised, and we wondered if they realized how important it was for Chris to have friends around and how vital they were to his recovery.

With much attention devoted to Chris, Deb and I realized early on that we also needed to make time for the girls. So, when

Chris's friends came for visits, we took those opportunities to get Alex and Katie out of the hospital. They still had an identity, and they still had needs. One of the things Deb and I consciously talked about was that we didn't want Katie's high school years remembered as Chris's injury years, and we didn't want Alex's end of college years remembered only as the time when Chris was injured. We didn't do a perfect job of that, but we made a conscious effort to preserve their identities separate from their brother's challenges.

By Sunday, when the family was all together, it was loud and festive; we had stuff going on, we were watching movies, picking up food. People were coming to play cards and hang out. Our friends came up a lot, which was a great help. By four o'clock on Sunday, only Chris and I remained in the quiet hospital with lots of time to think. Sunday nights were really, really hard on both of us. But the generosity and prayers of others helped see us through.

Whenever Chris was sleeping or I was alone, I'd update the CaringBridge site and think about all the things I'd left at home. Winter was coming, and I hadn't fixed the garage door. I'd been opening it manually with the intention to fix it before the weather turned cold. The gas gauge on our car didn't work. Our kitchen needed painting. Before I even had time to stress, a group of friends got together and paid to put in a new garage door, a guy took the car in and had it repaired, and they painted our kitchen. And that was just the beginning.

Friends visiting would stay overnight at the hotel, and they'd hand us money. I tried protesting, but our friends insisted. They knew we had to eat out. They knew we had gas expenses. They wouldn't take no for an answer. We went back and forth. It was really uncomfortable at first, but turning down their gifts would have hurt their feelings, and in all honestly, we needed their help to survive.

Deb and I went to the University of Iowa where there were thirty thousand students, so we'd never experienced the small college networking system and the sense of community around a smaller school. Because of the Luther alumni network, all of a sudden, we had six families offer their homes for us to live in so we didn't need to stay at the hotel anymore. One of them was Joyce Carlson, a widow whose husband had been a doctor at Mayo Hospital. She generously offered us her home to use, and we took her up on it and used her place when necessary. We kept some of our stuff at her home, and whenever my mom came up to see Chris, she stayed with Joyce. They shared coffee in the mornings and quickly became friends.

The Rochester newspaper ran a big article on Chris, and shortly afterward we were in Chris's room when a guy showed up at the door. He introduced himself and said he was a Christian man, a local retired superintendent of schools, and he'd read about Chris in the newspaper and felt compelled to come over. He and his wife lived in a two-bedroom condo less than five minutes from the hospital, and he explained that they went to Florida for six months out of the year. He read the article, sympathized with what our family was going through, and insisted we accept his offer. We were blown away and a little taken aback. We didn't know what to think. That weekend, Deb and one of her girlfriends went over to the condo and met his wife, checked out the place, and within a week we were using their condo as home base.

When it was just Chris and me in Rochester, I kept my clothes at the condo and showered there every day. When our family was in town, we stayed at the condo. We used Joyce's house when a larger group was in town. One of us stayed in Chris's hospital room every single night.

As the gifts poured in, Deb and I had to have a serious talk, because although we weren't arrogant, we did have a fair amount of pride. We'd always been the ones who'd rally around somebody else in their time of need, but we'd never been in a situation where we needed others to rally around us. Deb and her group of friends started Bondurant Fundraising Friends (BFF) for a friend in the community who had cancer. They raised almost thirty thousand dollars with one event, so they turned it into an annual thing for families and individuals to apply. They'd pick a recipient, the BFFs would organize an event, and the guys all got recruited to help. With our history in mind, Deb and I discussed how we needed to swallow our pride and accept the help others offered. We knew from our own experience how good it felt to help someone, and we couldn't take that joy away from those who so generously wanted to give. Truth be told, we wouldn't have made it on our own.

There were so many examples of people's goodness and the kindness of strangers. A guy Chris barely knew who lived on his floor at Luther, Rich Holton, made bracelets and sold them, sending us cash periodically. Chris hardly remembered Rich, yet he sold bracelets to raise money for Chris. Later, Rich became one of Chris's college roommates and closest friends.

A girl that Chris went to high school with made T-shirts and sold them as a fundraiser. She made twenty-five hundred dollars in profits and sent the money to Chris.

I received a letter from a high school football team that had played at Bondurant. They heard Chris's story, and on the way home, they passed a hat around the bus and collected money. They sent a wad of beat-up one-dollar bills. I pictured those kids who were just like my son, pulling worn dollar bills

"In retrospect, ordering those bracelets was something of an act of desperation. It was the only immediate thing I could think of to do which would maybe be of some sort of help. I couldn't do anything to really help Chris, to fix his life. That was up to him, his family, and those doctors at Mayo. But this was what I could do, and my thinking was that if everyone just did what they could do, however seemingly small and simple, then perhaps we could come out of this thing okay in the end."

Rich Holton, Luther classmate and friend

132

out of their pockets and giving all their change from the heart to a kid they didn't even know.

There were so many little stories that brought us closer to God and his glory. An autistic kid worked at a place where they provided jobs, and he made a pillowcase for Chris and put a twenty-dollar bill inside the pillowcase. So many heartwarming stories of people wanting to help, people we didn't know, people just like us, and even some who had less. The benevolence we received was awe-inspiring and a treasured gift from God.

At one point, I thought I should probably take the gift cards we'd received back to the hotel, but before doing so, I went through and counted them. We had over three thousand dollars in different kinds of gas and gift cards. They were streaming in, and the help they provided was immeasurable. Alex had gone back to college, so she was driving back and forth between school and the hospital. We were eating out all the time and just burning through our money. Then, this outpouring of support from our friends and community slowly started coming in and kept us from going under.

So many blessings in the midst of so much uncertainty only reinforced that a higher power was in control.

CHAPTER 13

Not only that, but we rejoice in our sufferings, knowing that suffering produces endurance, and endurance produces character, and character produces hope, and hope does not put us to shame, because God's love has been poured into our hearts through the Holy Spirit who has been given to us.

~Romans 5:3-5 ESV

CHRIS

After five days in ICU, I was moved to the rehab floor of the hospital to begin the next phase of recovery. I could already activate the muscle in my left arm, bicep, and shoulder, and was eager to get started on regaining function. The two things I needed in order to improve were time and effort; I had nothing but time to focus in rehab, and I had the tenacity to work as hard as they'd allow. It felt great to have already proven the doctors wrong and beat the horrendous odds they'd presented, but I was a long way from being satisfied.

There was so much time to think, and I used that time to put my mind in the right place for recovery. The doctors said it was common to experience improvement for up to two years, but the most significant improvement would occur within the first six to nine months. Hearing that definitely gave me a sense of urgency that reinforced the need to stay focused and commit to doing whatever it took to get better. I wanted to get better, I *needed* to get better, and I knew I didn't have much time. In rehab, I went to bed knowing I'd worked hard that day, so hard I couldn't even keep my eyes open because I was so tired. With the clock ticking, it really helped knowing that I'd maxed out my day, and that allowed me to relax and have peace of mind.

I'd always been a big believer that if I put in the work, the results would follow. My whole life was a testament to that theory. I also believed that God had a plan for me, but in order for that plan to work, I had to do my part—I couldn't just wait and let things happen on their own. I knew God would present me with opportunities, even as I lay on my back in my bed unable to move more than ninety-five percent of my body. I had to take advantage of the opportunities, however small, and be willing to do whatever I could to get better.

The prayer vigils at home and at Luther, as well as fundraising efforts, provided a great deal of comfort and encouragement. Knowing so many people were praying and willing to support my family and me reinforced the goodness in humanity during the worst tragedy of my life. I felt fortunate to be a part of the Bondurant and Luther College communities and appreciative of the many relationships I'd made. We never asked for help, but the fact that people offered and were willing to do so was very moving.

The first day in rehab, I met my main PT, Megan Gill, and

together with help from my dad, I got dressed in my own clothes. It was excruciating. Lifting my head and slipping on a shirt was difficult and painful. My range of motion was limited, and my arms and shoulders were stiff. Having no control over my body made it nearly impossible to get into the correct position. It sounded so simple, but it was a tedious process getting my arms into the armholes, and extremely discouraging that I needed assistance getting dressed. It was a stark and painful reminder of the independence I'd lost.

"Chris's true test would not take place in the spotlight of a college stadium filled with the excitement of five thousand onlookers, but instead would play out in the therapy room day in and day out in a relentless test of devotion, with no one there to cheer him on but his family and friends."

Rich Vickers, Chris's college roommate and close friend

In the beginning, rehab consisted of a lot of stretching and range-of-motion exercises intended to keep my muscles loose and my joints flexible so that as my strength increased, I wasn't so stiff. For example, the nodding I did during my time in ICU strengthened my neck and increased my range of motion. OT worked with my upper body—my arms and fingers, while physical therapy concentrated more on my lower body and core strength. During recreation therapy, the RT asked me what I liked to do for fun, and then tried to adapt those activities so I could still enjoy the things I loved. We worked on random activities that made my stay in the hospital as pleasant as possible.

Every day, my family and I learned something new about my medical condition. It was like learning a whole new language, since none of us were in the medical field besides my sister Alex. They gave us a book that explained the functions of the body, talked about a spinal cord injury, and what to expect during recovery. Then they strongly suggested that we learn as much as we could before we left the hospital so we'd know what to expect.

Honestly, it was hard to read because it was impossible to accept that the topics discussed in the book applied to me. I never accepted that I was going to be in a chair for the rest of my life, and I remained convinced I'd walk out of Mayo within a few months. Although I felt pressured to read the book and be aware of the changes in my body, I felt I could gain a decent understanding just by living it and talking to and asking questions of the therapists, doctors, and nurses in charge of my care. It made more sense to ask the professionals we were working with day in and day out rather than read a book I felt didn't apply to me anyway.

Right away in physical therapy, Megan wanted me to somehow get from the bed into a power wheelchair. Just like my time spent on the tilt table in ICU, the goal of sitting upright in the chair was to help my body better regulate my blood pressure. Her suggestion sounded crazy considering the difficulty I had just getting dressed, and I wavered between not wanting to try and wondering how the heck we were going to do it.

Megan calmly explained that they'd use a ceiling lift system and slide what looked like a big net underneath me by rolling me onto one side, and then over onto the other side. First, they had to wrap my legs with elastic bandages as tightly as possible to keep the blood from pooling in my legs, which would reduce dizziness. They'd also put on a chest binder that would squeeze my ribcage and keep my blood pressure elevated. Once the net was underneath me, they'd hook it to a lift and hoist me into the chair.

Submitting to the lift was the scariest thing I'd ever done in my life, and I was a thrill seeker who loved roller coasters. I'd never felt more vulnerable than when I lost the use of my body and had to count on others for help with everything. The pain in my neck made me hesitant to try new things, as I was paranoid about damaging my neck even further. The staff members were professionals, but my life was literally in their hands, and it didn't sit well knowing how much power a stranger held over me. I accepted help from my family easier, but trusting people I'd just met with my safety felt beyond impossible. What if they dropped me? What if they weren't sure what they were doing? I reminded myself that we'd all agreed Mayo was the best facility for my recovery. Then, while enduring excruciating pain in my head and neck, I swallowed my fear at having no control over my body.

A handful of strangers stood at my feet by the chair and next to and behind my head, positioning the net just right according to Megan's direction. Because I couldn't hold my head up, someone had to support my head so it didn't drop, and the smallest of head movements shot a jolting pain through my body. I swallowed the ache in the back of my throat, and trusted strangers and an odd-looking lift system to move me a couple of feet to a big chair while suffering through immense pain. I was completely terrified, and my family was too, standing wide-eyed and fidgety as they watched from the periphery.

It took close to thirty minutes to get out of bed because of all the bandaging and wrapping and getting the lift system and chair into place. Once in the chair, my blood pressure bottomed out leaving me nauseated, lightheaded, and with white, spotty vision. They leaned me back as far as the chair could go to help regulate my blood pressure, but it was difficult to control. Megan wanted me to sit up a little longer if I could tolerate it, so I fought back my fear and nausea. I wanted my condition to improve, and this was an opportunity where I had to do my part. Once I felt slightly better and the nausea had marginally subsided, Megan used the power chair's joystick and drove me around the hospital.

After fifteen or twenty minutes, with every drop of energy expelled, I needed to go back to my room. They had to perform the ceiling lift maneuvers again in order to get me back into bed, and it was just as terrifying the second time around. Once in bed, the therapists stretched my limbs, effectively ending my first therapy session. It was a good start, and Megan and her team felt encouraged by my progress, but I was exhausted.

I gave it my all during therapy and tried to feel happy for all of the twitches and sensations that were firing below the injury site despite the slow recovery pace. I felt a sense of relief being in rehab because I was able to work out my frustration in a way I couldn't while in ICU. There wasn't a whole lot of therapy I could do in ICU, and being on the rehab floor helped ease the anxiousness and restlessness that I sometimes felt.

When I heard I'd be in the hospital for four weeks, and then eight, it sounded like a long time. Who stayed in the hospital for eight weeks? While I definitely didn't want to stay that long, I soon realized the only way to get better was through therapy. I was getting better, they had nice equipment, and I wanted as much time in therapy as possible because I was making progress. I still believed beyond a shadow of a doubt I'd walk out of the hospital at the end of rehab.

Once a week, as a requirement of the program, I had to see a psychiatrist even though I didn't think I needed his help. When asked to rank my spirits on a scale of one to ten, with one meaning devastated and ten meaning full of hope and in great spirits, I said "ten" without hesitation. I felt good about where my recovery was going, the support I had from family and friends, and my faith was strong. Things were going as well as they could, and I knew it could have been worse. Time with the psychiatrist was beneficial—I was able to talk to him about things I was uncomfortable discussing with my family. For example, I didn't know if I'd be able to have a family of my own, and that was a topic the psychiatrist talked about a lot because he knew that was something I'd worry about, considering my age.

Outside of therapy, I'd literally pass out from exhaustion. I could barely keep my eyes open while in bed, and I didn't fight the urge to sleep during the day because I remembered my ICU PT, Lori, saying that rest was an important part of recovery. All day and of recovery. All day and

"I often joke around with Chris about how I don't think he is human because of how positive he is all of the time. When I first met him I didn't believe that he could be so happy and positive everyday when he was dealing with some very challenging things, but I've realized he is always like that."

Emily Summers,
Chris's girlfriend

night, the nurses came into my room every two hours to check on me, or to roll me and adjust my body because they didn't want me to get bedsores. A good night's sleep, or even a decent nap, became impossible because of all the poking, checks, and rolling. At first, I was really polite and didn't like to voice what I needed.

"You don't want to be uncomfortable," the nurses would say. "Just be assertive about what you need."

Their advice really helped, and hearing it made asking for help easier.

I definitely felt I was in the right place in order to maximize my recovery. I felt good about all the people I was working with, as I got great care and was happy with the staff. The doctors and nurses were all very informative, and they communicated well. Since I had no medical background, they explained the million different medical terms flying at me all the time in a way that made sense.

I enjoyed my time with the PT and OT. I was never uncomfortable around them, and I looked forward to being with them and working hard toward recovery. Megan Gill was really good at striking the right balance between being nice and focusing on the business at hand. She liked to make things fun, but she knew I wanted to work hard. We worked well together because she understood when to relax and ease the intensity, and when to really push me hard to focus. Every step forward was the result of teamwork, and if there was one thing I understood from my years of playing sports, it was the value of teammates. Through good days and bad, my therapists at Mayo had my back.

My first Saturday in rehab, while trying to adjust to sitting upright in the power chair, I watched *College GameDay* on ESPN and tried to keep my mind off of everything that had happened within the span of one week. My ears began to tingle when I heard the announcers discuss Eric LeGrand and give an update on his condition. I sat in my chair, trying to make sense of our twin injuries, and was caught completely off guard when I heard my name mentioned as another college athlete who was hurt on the same day and on the same play. My spirits were instantly lifted knowing the sports world not only knew about my injury, but also acknowledged it on TV. I hadn't been forgotten after all.

Despite the accident, I never blamed football for my injury. I played the game and accepted the risks, even though I had no idea how truly devastating a football injury could be. Even after the accident, I never discouraged anyone from playing football. People who crash their bicycles or get into car accidents don't stop riding a bike or driving. Football taught me valuable life lessons such as teamwork, hard work, leadership, and was especially effective at toughening me up both mentally and physically. I never wanted to be out in the scorching sun for two-a-days doing sprints and conditioning, but it helped me develop the grit and determination I needed to battle back from my injury. I loved the sport, and even though I could no longer play, I enjoyed watching my teams and my favorite athletes, and it helped doing something normal on the weekends.

If I'd been at school, my days would have been filled with classes, workouts, and practice in preparation for the upcoming game. The goal of each week was to win, and every day was spent training to achieve that goal. My days in rehab were similar, although my goals had changed. I wanted to walk out of the hospital. I wanted my independence back. I wanted to spend every day doing everything possible to achieve those goals. With my family by my side in one of the best rehabilitation hospitals in the country, I knew I had a fighting chance—not against an opposing team, but my very own body.

CHAPTER 14

I told him I am more proud of him now than I have ever been in his life. His attitude is good, and he is ready to stay the course.

~Terry Norton, CaringBridge, October 19, 2010

TERRY

Our eighteen-year-old son had to be dressed by somebody else. During his first therapy session, the PT dressed Chris in his own clothes. The whole experience was more emotionally painful than physically painful—for Chris and all of us watching. Chris confessed it freaked him out internally to watch the hospital staff stretch and move his legs and not feel it. As an eighteen-year-old, being dressed by someone else was another emotional slap, and it was an in-his-face reminder of how drastically his life had changed. That was how we all felt watching him struggle to get into his clothes with an uncooperative body and a very sore neck.

We were on an emotional roller coaster where something positive would happen, like moving to rehab at Mayo and feeling good about our decision, and then something negative, like watching him struggle with the most basic task. We were scared because we saw how completely vulnerable he was and how very far he had to go. For parents, the worst thing in the world is for something bad to happen to their child. If something bad had happened to me, or Deb, or one of our parents, it would have been awful, but not as devastating as it happening to a child—even a grown child. I relied almost completely on my faith during those first two weeks because my worst nightmare—other than the death of one of my kids— had come true.

Chris got down to the rehab floor, and within a few days, they told us he would most likely be there for eight weeks. While that sounded tremendously long, by that point we knew the longer he stayed, the better they thought he'd improve. The hospital staff said he was making a good recovery, and they thought he'd benefit from more intense therapy.

As an organized, list-making person, I liked to be in charge and plan things out. Not knowing an exact timeframe was really hard for me. When his stay in rehab went from four weeks to eight weeks, and later seemed open-ended, we couldn't make plans, and I had to adjust my mindset. The goal became survival while trying to anticipate the next step in our journey.

Right away the hospital gave us a three-ring binder and some DVDs they wanted us to work through. The material was to prepare us for the changes that were going to take place in his body and what we were going to have to do differently. It was a kind of a "weekly cares and concerns" checklist to get us prepared for life going forward.

At the time, we fought the doctor about reading the binder and watching the DVDs because we refused to accept the worst. Chris was a fighter, and we were trying to stay positive. To be honest, we were in denial. I thought by reading the book and watching the DVDs, it would somehow seal his fate. I'd ask questions, and the doctors would ask if I'd read the manual or watched the DVDs, but I stubbornly refused. I got into a little bit of a tiff with a doctor who kept pressing me to review the material.

"Terry," he said, "you need to read that stuff."

They wanted us to start mentally preparing for what we would face once we left the hospital, but I felt they should've waited and let us get adjusted. But they knew what we'd go through, and there wasn't time to wait. As a way to put an end to the badgering, I acted like I'd looked at the material, but I only gave it a cursory glance. For better or worse, we just figured things out on our own.

The nurses came into Chris's room all the time to catheterize him, check on him, or turn him to make sure he was positioned so he didn't get bedsores. Initially, Chris would get me up in the middle of the night to help him with little things, like scratching his head, or moving his pillow, but he soon realized he needed to let his dad sleep. He eventually started using the call button and asking the nurses for assistance. The longer he was there and the healthier he got, the nurses didn't have to come and check on him as often.

Chris needed help with everything. He needed to be fed, he needed help brushing his teeth, washing his face, putting his contacts in, getting him setup on his computer, scratching his itches when he was uncomfortable, getting dressed, and getting undressed. The most challenging task was helping Chris with his contacts. I wore contacts, but putting them on someone else's eyes was so much different and so much harder than doing it to myself.

Right away, the staff wanted to teach us how to take care of him, and I mistakenly thought they were being premature. I resisted, thinking they were trying to shorten their list of responsibilities. In reality, they were trying to teach us because we needed to know how when he was eventually released. There was also a disconnect in terms of personal care, mainly due to our insurance.

When a person was discharged from the hospital under normal insurance plans, a family member was expected to handle shower and bathroom care. The National Collegiate Athletic Association (NCAA) insurance that we were fortunate enough to have because Chris was playing a college sport at the time of his injury, paid up to a certain amount per year for nurses, so we didn't have to perform some of the nursing functions they wanted to teach us. I kept trying to explain to the nurses that we had insurance, and that an eighteen-year-old didn't want his mom or dad performing his bathroom care. We *could* do it, but it was more comfortable for him to have a nurse execute the task. It didn't help that we were also in the denial stage and didn't want to accept daily bathroom care as something Chris would have to deal with once he was released from the hospital.

I wore my denial like a badge of honor. From day one, they kept telling us we needed to put a ramp in our house. I didn't want to hear about a ramp, and every day when the PTs brought it up, I gritted my teeth and ignored them. I wanted to scream every time somebody asked about a ramp, but they were simply doing their jobs. The professionals at Mayo had seen enough people go home unprepared because they couldn't accept reality. I tried to turn my resentment around and be a positive influence in Chris's life, but navigating the line between optimism and reality was like balancing on a tightrope.

Deb and I talked about how we needed to put on a strong, solid, positive face because Chris would look to us to see how we were responding. Were we down? Were we devastated? Were we discouraged? How did we respond to other people in front of him? We made a conscious effort to put aside whatever concerns and fears we had so that Chris never saw us upset. We didn't try to keep anything from him, but we always focused on the positive.

From my experience as a coach, teacher, and supervisor, I knew that people tended to rise to the expectations placed upon them. I likened it to shooting a three-pointer in basketball. If a shooter expected the ball to go in the hoop, the likelihood of success increased. We believed that expecting Chris to recover, both mentally and physically, increased the likelihood of him recovering. It helped that Chris told the psychiatrist that his attitude on a scale from one to ten was a ten, meaning the most optimistic. To say the psychiatrist, and Deb and I were surprised by his answer would be an understatement. Chris credited his faith, family, and friends—a phrase that became our family's mantra during rehab's most difficult times.

The mental part of his recovery included surrounding him in an uplifting environment. His room was like a shrine. The girls basically took everything out of his bedroom at home and put it up in his rehab room. Plus, professional sports

> *"From the moment I walked into room 68 on the inpatient rehab unit, I immediately felt the embrace from not only the Norton family, but also the community. The room was packed with letters, cards, pictures, and signed momentous from college and professional athletes. With this embrace brought nerves about the expectations of my role as a provider."*
>
> Megan Gill, PT, DPT, Clinical Lead Physical Therapist for Spinal Cord Injury, Mayo Clinic

teams and colleges sent signed footballs, hats, and autographed pictures. Visitors and staff loved to look at his collection. His room played a big role in his positive outlook.

One of the first things the PTs did in rehab was put Chris in the power chair so he could begin to tolerate sitting for longer than twenty minutes at a time. We felt helpless watching Chris struggle with trusting the rehab staff and the lift system they used to get him into the chair. I could tell he struggled with accepting his condition almost as much as I did. He'd gone from being an athlete in his prime to fighting to sit upright in a wheelchair. The disappointment, pain, and frustration were evident on his face as he fought the sudden and dramatic drops in his blood pressure that left him nauseated and dizzy in addition to the debilitating pain in his neck. The first outing in the wheelchair left him exhausted and all of us fighting not to show our concern about the steepness of the battle we faced.

Because Chris was naturally optimistic, his attitude rarely slipped, but we tried our best to keep his baseline up by surrounding him with positive and uplifting messages. I read him a lot of different passages at night before he went to bed — cards that people sent, CaringBridge posts, Bible verses — and I knew in advance what I was going to read in order to keep him uplifted. Whenever I read the posts from CaringBridge, Chris literally got tears in his eyes knowing so many people were praying for him. Realizing that thousands of people were pulling for him gave him a little extra *oomph* in everything he did. He felt like he was running a marathon, and all those people were lined up clapping for him as he ran along the route.

It made staying positive for the folks reading the CaringBridge posts that much more important. We had conversations about how he could talk the talk, but he also needed to walk the walk. We discussed overcoming adversity, meeting challenges, working hard, and rising above his circumstances, but through CaringBridge, he had a real opportunity to demonstrate those traits on a larger scale than the average person. Neither of us took that responsibility lightly.

Despite his positive attitude and all my hard work, deep down I worried. I kept thinking about all of the things he wouldn't get to experience, like the outdoors and athletics — all the things he was so passionate about before his injury. Would he ever be able to go back to school? Would he have a job? Where would he live? Would somebody look at him and see the person and not the wheelchair? Would he get married and have kids? My single biggest fear was that Chris would at some point feel disappointed with his life. I never wanted him to ask, "Why me? Why did I get dealt this hand? Why does my life suck?"

I worried that people -- friends and potential girlfriends — would judge him based on the wheelchair and on the amount of work he'd require and the inconvenience of taking care of him. When I shared this fear with others, friends reminded me that if Deb were in a car accident, I'd be there for her. But that wasn't an adequate comparison. I already loved Deb; we'd been married for almost thirty years. If I didn't already know and love her, dealing with the kind of limitations Chris faced would be a tough hill to climb. But like everything else with his injury, there was little I could do but pray and give my worries to God.

I tried my best not to read or research spinal cord injuries because I couldn't handle the truth. With only a fleeting search, I discovered that people with spinal cord injuries faced a myriad of related health issues. Part of the reason I didn't want to get too deep into spinal cord research was because there was so much misinformation on the Internet. People were constantly telling me about some article they'd read about a procedure in India or stem cell trials in Russia or China. I could have driven myself insane chasing the Holy Grail of a miracle cure, and I couldn't afford to get distracted.

After Deb and the girls left, my typical day started at seven in the morning. I'd go down to the lobby and get a cup of coffee, look out the windows, read uplifting Christian books friends had sent, and basically use that hour to get my game face on for the day.

At eight, the nurses dressed Chris and got him ready, and then I'd spend the whole day with him in rehab. Getting Chris equipped for the day was like preparing for "battle." They wrapped his legs in elastic bandages from his toes clear up to his groin, and then they suited him in an elastic chest compression device, elbow pads, and wrist braces.

I went to every rehab session, and so did Deb when she was in Rochester. We observed, stepped in to help if they needed an extra set of hands, and talked to the therapists to get their input about what things Chris should be doing on his own. Our days in rehab meant being there with him all the time. If it was close to lunchtime, I might run across the street and grab him something to eat and bring it back, but otherwise I was right by his side. Rehab continued all afternoon. Afterwards, he usually liked to take a little nap before we did his exercises.

For a college-aged kid, eleven at night was still early. When Chris was in rehab, he was working, and he was focused. That was what he normally did at college—lift weights, work out, and go to class. But if we finished rehab at four, we had seven hours to fill. That block of time was the toughest part of the day—the biggest challenge—because that was when it hit home that Chris wasn't in college anymore.

I had to figure out a plan for those seven hours, and sometimes it was daunting. Chris didn't like me asking him what he wanted to do, so it was better if I came up with a plan, laid it out, and sold it. We played a lot of cards. We pulled in this kid from the room next door—or my mom when she was up—and usually played rummy or euchre.

Chris rarely got upset about his injury, but when he did, it ripped my heart out. I didn't know if I could deal with him feeling emotionally upset all the time now that he and I would mostly be on our own. We talked to some other kids who were there in rehab, who went through really dark times where they didn't want to leave their room because they were so depressed. They just wanted to give up. If dealing with his injury sent Chris spiraling into a tailspin, my single biggest fear was that I wouldn't be strong enough to handle it alone.

For Chris, hearing from other young men and women in rehab actually helped him appreciate how fortunate he was that we were able to stay with him. It broke my heart to see the eighteen, nineteen, and twenty-year-olds who didn't have anyone with them. I think that made Chris appreciate the support system he had and helped to stave off depression.

I was more proud of Chris during those first few weeks after his injury

"While going to Rochester was never about me, those trips helped me just as much as Chris. They helped me see purpose in my life, grow in my faith, and I would leave inspired knowing that Chris would walk again."

Joe Gilson, Lifelong friend

than I'd ever been of him in his life. I'd watched him score a lot of points in sports, do well in school, get different awards, make all-conference, and achieve many accomplishments, but my pride had nothing to do with his accomplishments and everything to do with his character. His determination, attitude, and effort were laser focused on doing whatever he could to get better. Especially in the first couple of weeks, friends and acquaintances said they'd come by to lift Chris's spirits, but they left his room uplifted.

We had a long road ahead, and staying upbeat was our highest priority. We could handle what we had to deal with physically, but I never wanted him to feel alone. Despite the sacrifices and the hardship on our family, staying with Chris while keeping our heads above water had become the focus of our lives.

CHAPTER 15

For the Spirit God gave us does not make us timid, but gives us power, love and self-discipline.

~2 Timothy 1:7 NIV

CHRIS

Eventually during PT, I was able to stay in the chair for longer periods of time, and we'd go outside to the courtyard where the fresh air eased the nausea and afforded me my first real look at Rochester and the Mayo complex. Breathing fresh air and looking around outside helped me feel normal, so we'd go outside as much as possible.

As my body tolerated longer bouts in the wheelchair, Megan and her team wanted me to try transitioning from riding in the chair to driving it on my own. Even though I desperately wanted to drive, I didn't feel very confident. The machine was pretty fast, and I worried that if I couldn't direct it, or if my hand dropped off the joystick, the chair would spin out of control. Fortunately, my longing for independence far outweighed my fear.

After experimenting with an array of joysticks, we finally settled on one that looked like a field goal and held my hand in place. Megan was right there with me, and it was definitely nerve-wracking for both of us the first time I tried to drive, but we gave it a whirl. The first few tries were epic failures because my arm wasn't very strong. Disappointment fueled my determination to work hard with the OT on my left arm and wrist, and to practice with the chair every night after rehab until my arm screamed from fatigue.

My frustration showed, but when Megan suggested using a sip and puff wheelchair driving system that used a straw and head movements to control the chair, I adamantly refused. I knew the sip and puff chair was used for patients who needed the most extreme assistance, and I was stubborn enough and determined enough to fight for a joystick-controlled chair that I could drive on my own. After much pleading, Megan relented, and I made it work the following day. Learning to drive the power chair was more difficult than I ever expected, and it took patience and hard work, but I was ready for the challenge.

As I started to adjust to being in my chair and we drove around the rehab floor and through the PT gym full of mat tables, I looked forward to the day when I would be strong enough to use the mat table for stretching, exercises, and working on chair-to-table transfers. At that time in my recovery, my neck wasn't strong enough to support itself, and I'd get lightheaded in my chair. Even when we began to use the mat table, my body had little to no strength, and I had to count on at least two people to move me to the mat, using a sliding board that acted as a bridge under my legs.

Once on the table, I had absolutely no core strength, so my body would just fold over. Megan had to coddle me like a baby to keep me upright, sitting directly behind me with her legs on the outside of mine, as if we were riding a four-wheeler together. With little core strength, I easily folded to one side, or hunched forward over my legs, fatiguing my neck and forcing me to lay back against Megan. Although embarrassing, I had no choice but to lean back on her when my neck screamed from muscle pain. With time and practice, my neck began to fatigue less and my core muscles started to activate.

Within a couple of weeks, I was able to sit without the support of a person. A defining, yet nerve-wracking, moment came when Megan wanted to walk across the room to grab a weight band, and she asked if I could hold my balance without falling. My heart began to race at the thought of not having someone right there to catch me. I could hardly move, let alone break my fall. I nodded with fearful confidence because I knew I needed to push myself out of my comfort zone. I felt like I was balancing on the edge of a cliff. Falling could set my recovery back. I sat extremely still, barely breathing as Megan slowly stepped backward while watching me closely. With intense concentration, I was able to remain balanced, prompting a forward progression in my recovery. Over time my strength and confidence grew, so when no one sat right next to me I wouldn't freak out knowing I could sit and not worry about falling.

There was a reason behind everything we did in therapy, and the therapists always explained the goal. For example, when they placed electrodes on different muscles in PT, they said it was to help wake up the nerves and keep the muscle strong, firing, and to keep it from atrophying. The therapists were good about keeping things objective. They didn't set specific goals because everyone had their own pace of recovery, and they couldn't predict the speed at which I'd recover.

I probably enjoyed PT the most because that was where I was most active, so I felt more like myself. I'd started using an electrical stimulation bicycle, the RT300, where, while seated in the wheelchair, the PTs connected my feet to stationary bike pedals. The RT300 used a motor to drive the pedals until my legs, aided by the electrodes, took over. It felt great to do something familiar as well as productive. Everything in PT worked toward getting my body used to being in the upright position so I'd eventually be able to use a walking treadmill system called a Lokomat. In OT, I worked on feeding myself with the aid of an anti-gravity machine, and dressing myself—important skills involving my fingers and increasing my dexterity—but I enjoyed the more active PT.

Throughout my stay in rehab, I had twice-weekly visits with the medical staff. Each professional gave an update on their part of my recovery and talked about how they planned to move forward with my care so that everyone was on the same page. My family called those meetings the "State of the Union" because they included my doctors, the floor nurse, my nurse for the day, my lead physical therapist, my lead occupational therapist along with an OT student, the social worker assigned to my case, and any residential doctors or nurses on rotation.

I dreaded the "State of the Union" meetings because they'd talk about areas where they weren't seeing any progress and what kind of assistance I would need once at home, such as a home lift system and a medical bed. I didn't want to talk about what I'd go home with when every day was an opportunity to get better. Their talk became like white noise as I tried my best to block out their negativity and not get discouraged by the slow pace and their low expectations for my recovery.

To counteract the effects of the "State of the Union" meetings, my dad and I talked about things we'd done in the past and made plans for the future in order to stay positive and provide a sense of normalcy. Looking forward to the future and knowing things would get better helped me stay optimistic because my life wasn't over. I needed something to look forward to and something to strive for when everything seemed so uncertain.

One of the most difficult things about being in the hospital was when the weekends rolled around because I only had one hour of rehab on Saturday and one hour on Sunday. During the regular week, Monday through Friday, I stayed completely focused on working hard and getting better during my therapy hours. On the weekends, however, after about a month of adjusting to my schedule, it was tough accepting that all my friends were having fun without me while I was motionless in the hospital with my family. I was a very social person, I had lots of friends, and I loved constantly being on the go, so the weekend downtime was challenging. My friends visited whenever they could, and having them around helped a ton, but sometimes other activities and the weather kept them away.

At first, when my friends came to visit, they were cautious around me. It was tough for them because they didn't want to upset or offend me in any way. They wanted to be there for me, but they didn't know how to absorb the reality of my situation. They didn't know much about my injury or what took place in the hospital, so being around me was definitely something they had to get used to. They wanted to help; they just don't know how. It was uncomfortable for most people at first, wondering about my condition and if I'd changed emotionally.

Being a prankster, I couldn't help but play a sick joke on my friends one of the first times they came to visit. Not even three weeks into rehab, I was able to leave the hospital for four hours at a time and go over to the Marriott across the street. My friends came in two vehicles; one carful parked right away and came into the restaurant. They planned to stay and eat, and we began talking normally. For some reason, I thought it would be funny to cross my eyes and stick my tongue out when my other group of friends entered the restaurant.

Their chins dropped comically, and the look on their faces revealed their shock. As soon as I realized how upset they were, I stopped and told them I was kidding. As mean as it was, the prank ended up lowering the tension level for everyone and eased my friends' discomfort. They realized my spirits were high, I could still joke around, and despite my injury, I was still the same goofy guy I was before the accident.

My Luther coaches, Mike Durnin and Benny Boyd, came to visit a lot. We went outside whenever possible to visit and read Bible verses. Their presence kept me connected to the team when it was hard not being with them. I had to take care of business at the hospital, and they had to get through their football season, but they always took time to see me. It helped a lot when many of my guests, both friends and strangers, took the time to tell me how my

"As we continued to visit and did what would become customary, to share bible verses and discuss the meanings we found in them, it became increasingly clear to me how special this young man truly was, and that there was a purpose for his life that was much greater than anything he would be able to accomplish as an athlete in an athletic arena."

Benny Boyd,
Former Assistant Coach,
Luther College

attitude helped them cope with the struggles in their own lives.

Most of my life, and most of the time going through rehab, I stayed positive. Obviously, I had weak moments when I felt vulnerable, scared, and uncertain about my future, but we never announced the hard times on CaringBridge because it was a very small part of what was happening and totally against my nature. I felt some responsibility not to share my weak moments because I didn't want people to think I was being negative or pessimistic. I think everyone expected my situation to be really hard on me — and it was — but it was mostly at night when the negative thoughts crept in.

I dreaded the end of therapy and being done for the night because that was when my thoughts ran wild with uncertainty, especially as my body adjusted to the pace of rehab and I wasn't exhausted all the time. Sometimes, I'd jiggle my arm or shoulder just to see and feel it move because I despised the claustrophobic feeling of being strapped down to the bed. I frantically tried to move anything I could in order to feel a small sense of freedom, but the effort left me with a racing heart and a million frustrating thoughts pinging through my head.

I wondered what would happen next, and I wanted to work as hard as possible to get better, but my emotions seemed so close to the surface. Sometimes I wanted to move a body part I'd been able to move during the day, but at night I was too fatigued and it wouldn't budge. Sleep seemed impossible, so much so that I had to take sleeping medication to reduce the restlessness that kept me awake.

Talking about my thoughts and feeling with whoever stayed with me at night helped a lot, as did reading the positive comments from those following my journey on CaringBridge. I'd been trying to better myself by working hard my whole life, but this time, through CaringBridge, I had a platform. Knowing people found hope and inspiration from my story helped motivate me, especially during the emotional moments of my recovery when I felt down, but I'd have worked just as hard to recover with or without an audience. CaringBridge highlighted the goodness in people and helped ease my mind knowing my family and I were in so many people's thoughts and prayers.

I prayed every night. I thanked God for my family, my friends, and the progress I was making. I asked God for a full recovery, to get stronger, and to walk again. When I was younger and during the early years of high school, I only prayed every once in a while, and most of the time my prayers referenced something specific.

During my senior basketball season, I went through a rough patch that shook my confidence as a player when I went from having one of the best streaks of games in my life to one of the worst. My coach gave me a sports Bible, and I found a verse that really stuck with me. Joshua 1:9 helped me believe in myself, and it told me that no matter what I did or what I went through,

God was with me. I wrote the Bible verse on my basketball shoes in high school, and I continued to rely upon those same words to see me through each day in rehab. Throughout my recovery, my prayers were full of thanks and appreciation for my support system, the medical staff, the people helping me, and the feeling I regained every day.

After about a week, I was sick of the hospital food, and it didn't help that I'd lost my appetite. I refused to eat the hospital food. Between the loss of appetite and my muscles atrophying, I began losing a lot of weight.

Finally, my family asked, "If you could eat anything you wanted, what would it be?"

"Steak and shrimp from Applebee's," I said, simply because I'd seen it on a commercial and it looked good. The next day I'd say, "Enchiladas," for the same reason.

I lost thirty pounds within a few weeks because I never felt hungry and the smell of hospital food made me sick to my stomach. I knew it was important to eat, and when I got down to 151 pounds and I could tell my family was worried, I made a real effort to start eating.

By early November, I could tell my body was healing. My energy returned, and I was able to stay in my chair for longer bouts without feeling fatigued. The fewer transfers they had to make getting me in and out of bed meant I had more time to practice skills like driving and feeding myself.

I also began feeling as if my legs were in a cast, like having a leg inside my leg that couldn't break free. I could feel my legs, but I couldn't move them. My whole body felt that way; I could visualize and feel signals traveling to every part of me, but it was as if they'd hit a hard casing and couldn't budge.

Because I was getting feeling back, but no movement, I asked people to touch my legs and feet so I could guess what leg or foot they were touching. The exercise helped me re-establish the communication between my brain and my body by forcing me to concentrate and figure out which limb or foot was being touched. It also helped me understand where my body was in space.

I also experienced leg spasms. My legs would start shaking or my knee would pull up uncontrollably. The nurse explained that the movement was a normal byproduct of the injury, but it freaked me out to see my leg move when I didn't have any control over it. Everything in my lower body felt dull, as if my legs had fallen asleep and were waking up. I had a little bit of feeling whenever something touched my legs, like a little tingling sensation, but not enough to tell the size, shape, or texture of the object. I also couldn't tell the temperature around me.

Calls and gifts from sports teams kept coming. Ryan Clark of the Pittsburg Steelers called and encouraged me not to give up hope, and he continued to reach out through calls and texts. Adrian Peterson of the Vikings sent an autographed football, and I received calls from Tim Tebow, Colt McCoy, and Drew

Brees. I never expected to hear from people I didn't know—famous or otherwise—who wanted to help just because they'd heard my story. A student from Luther who'd been hurt three years before me came to visit with the Luther pastor. I enjoyed talking to him about how I was feeling because he was a student, and we were almost the same age. He mentioned he got some leg movement back around the five-week mark.

Talking to people who'd been through my situation and could relate to what I was going through was huge, because even the doctors, nurses, and therapists didn't really know what it felt like not to be able to move their bodies. Even though I loved hearing from people who'd suffered spinal cord injuries, learning about their home life, and asking questions about what I was experiencing, I definitely thought I was different. I was going to walk out of the hospital, and I wasn't going to have to face their daily struggles. I never said that out loud, but in my head I was convinced my outcome would be better.

Former Penn State player Adam Taliaferro, who suffered a similar injury a decade prior, called during my first full week in rehab. I asked him a lot of questions about how long it took him to do certain things, how long he was in the hospital, how much movement he currently had, and if he was using a chair or walking on his own. I felt encouraged when he said he was able to walk, thanks to continued rehab and stretching. He was a successful lawyer, so that gave me hope for the future too. I think he said it took him six weeks to get movement back in his legs, and that gave me some peace of mind knowing there was still time to recover. While I'd come a long way in a few short weeks, regaining movement in my legs and walking was constantly in the back of my mind.

The five to six week range for leg movement seemed consistent with those I'd spoken to who'd suffered similar injuries and had similar prognoses, so that deadline loomed large in my head. I felt optimistic since I was getting feeling back in my lower body, but I worried that if I didn't get movement by the five to six week point, I'd probably never walk again. Despite my worries, I never told anyone about my internal deadline, even though it seemed like a giant elephant in my hospital room.

One of the doctors told my mom and me that I was one of the hardest workers he'd ever seen come through rehab. I wasn't shooting to be the most industrious worker, or working diligently for the acknowledgment or respect of others. I was simply hardwired to do my best and give it my all. I was happy with my efforts, but when he sat me down and told me I was the hardest worker he'd ever seen, I felt proud. That pride fed my belief that I wouldn't need the chairs and ramps they kept saying I'd need when I left the hospital.

I set goals for myself to use the Xbox by Christmas and to walk out of the hospital, so every time I experienced something new or felt better, I was excited for that moment, but quickly moved on to the next task because the clock was ticking. But

I couldn't deny reality. I was making progress, I was getting better, but it wasn't going at the rate I wanted in order to achieve my ultimate goals. While frustrating, facing the truth helped me refocus my goals and thoughts.

I still felt optimistic about everything, and I was still appreciative of my progress, but I had to change my mindset, and that was a real challenge. I clung tightly to my belief that I'd walk out of the hospital, but I also began setting my own internal goals for therapy knowing all I could control was how hard I worked, and not the outcome. Daily goals were much easier to set and achieve because it was really hard to predict where I would be in my recovery in a week or a month. I set a goal every day to do whatever I could to improve, and I never cut myself any slack because I'd achieved a goal. I had so much work to do.

Now that I was physically strong enough to stay in my chair for longer amounts of time, and I wasn't fatiguing as much, or sleeping as often as when I first arrived in rehab, I needed more time than the three hours allotted me to work each day. There

"He knows he can't give up. He makes a plan, he implements it, and he moves forward until he gets to the finally *of one small goal, and then he moves to the next goal..."*

Lisa Krieg, PT Euro-Team in Decorah

were so many things to work on. As a college athlete, I had a list of exercises that helped me improve leg and arm strength.

With a spinal cord injury, my whole body needed work. My fingers, my toes, my lung capacity — literally every single body part needed help, and we only had three hours per day to work on everything. After a meeting with the doctor and the rehab staff, they agreed to increase my rehab from three hours to four.

I also wanted to do more when I wasn't in therapy, and thankfully my parents wanted me to do as much as possible too. They knew how much I wanted to get better and stronger, and they knew I'd want to spend some time outside of therapy working toward that goal. They were very involved with my therapy, and by doing so, they observed and talked to the therapists about what they could do to help. We were all on the same page and that made it feel as if we were one team focused solely on my recovery. With every day that passed, the clock was ticking, and Team Norton had a lot of work to do.

Chris, Alex, Katie, and Terry, 1996.

High School Homecoming, 2009. Chris with his sisters Katie (left) and Alex (right).

Fall, 2010. Freshman Shawn Burrows #19 and Chris Norton #16, Luther College Head Football Coach Mike Durnin (center). Photo by Luther College.

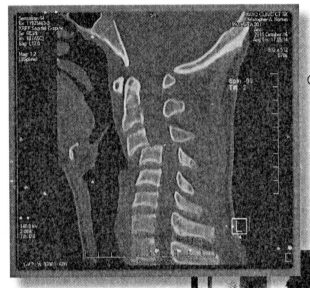

X-ray of Chris's
neck taken
October 16, 2010.

Christmas at Mayo, 2010.
(L-R) Aunt Ginger Palmer,
Uncle Gary Palmer, Alex,
Chris, Katie, Grandma
Virginia, Terry, Deb.

Mayo clinic with
friends, 2010. (L-R)
Shawn Burrows,
Tanner Douglas,
Rich Vickers, Eric
Essendrup.

Chris's Mayo therapists fall 2011. Lori Eaton PT, Kathy Johnson OT, Amy Sikkink PT Tech, Megan Gill PT.

Chris on Lokomat December 2010

Terry & Chris at Mayo, 2010.

Flying to NYC for the first time since the injury, 2011.

Norton family on CBS, The Early Show, after Chris won the Courage in Sports Award, 2011.

The Norton family at the first SCI CAN Foundation event, The Decorah Tour, September 2012. The funds raised were used to purchase RT300 bike for Winneshiek Medical Center. Photo by Winneshiek Medical Center.

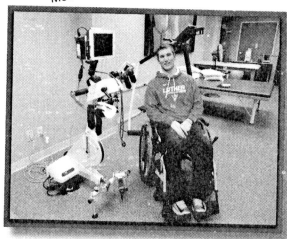

Chris with the RT300 bike SCI CAN fundraised for Winneshiek Medical Center, 2012. Photo by Winneshiek Medical Center.

San Diego Vacation – Deb, Katie, Chris, Alex, Terry.

Spring Break, 2013.

Senior day for football November 2013. Deb, Terry, and Chris. Photo by Jeff Nelson.

With Coach Meyer at The Ohio State, 2013.

Chris walking on the indoor track at Luther College with Emily in the fall of 2014. This was the first time Emily didn't have to hold onto the walker while he walked.

Decorah therapists. Bottom left Jennessa Luzum OT, top left Amanda Stockdale PTA, Allison Herman OT, Lisa Krieg PT, top right Alex Johnson PT. 2014

Chris and Luann Smith, his "Decorah grandma." She spoiled him like a grandson, wrote to him, gave him care packages with food, and took him out to eat while Chris attended Luther College.

Emily and Chris kayaked at the 2014 National Wheelchair Sports Camp in Rochester, MN.

Working on walking at Barwis Methods with strength coach Mike Rhoades in February of 2015.

Chris getting stretched and worked out by Mike Barwis during his evaluation in August of 2014.

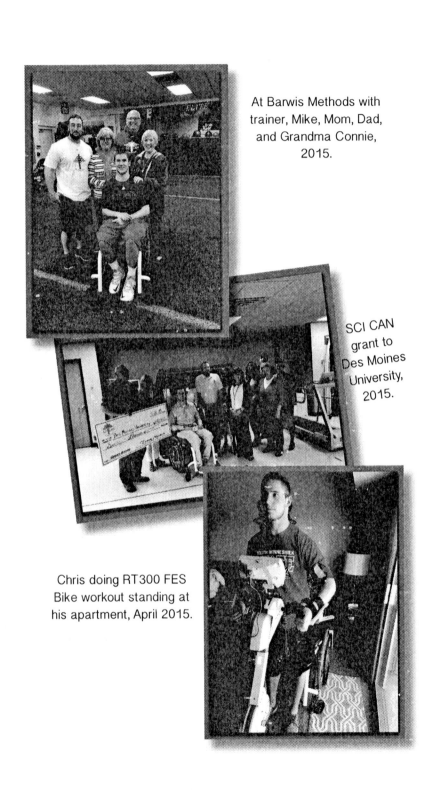

At Barwis Methods with trainer, Mike, Mom, Dad, and Grandma Connie, 2015.

SCI CAN grant to Des Moines University, 2015.

Chris doing RT300 FES Bike workout standing at his apartment, April 2015.

Emily and Chris simulating the graduation walk two weeks before graduation, 2015. Chris had Emily's brother's gown on and she wore a dress to practice.

Proposing to Emily on May 23, 2015. She was crying. Photo by Tyler Rinken.

Chris and his friends after Chris proposed to Emily May 2015. Rich Vickers, Alex Peterson, Rich Holton, Zac Pearson, and Tanner Douglas. Photo by Tyler Rinken.

At the end of the graduation walk, Chris shook hands with Luther College's president, Paula Carlson. 2015. Photo by Luther College.

Emily and Chris in the green room of a studio in Johnston, Iowa, before they streamed live on FOX & Friends, May, 2015

Graduation, 2015. Photo by Luther College.

The Norton family on the Good Morning America set after interview with Robin Roberts, 2015.

CHAPTER 16

My world right now is a ten-foot by ten-foot hospital room in a city I have never been before. I am usually "Mr. Directions," and right now I feel like I have no idea where we are other than this room. I ask multiple times a day what day of the week it is, as I have nothing to identify one day from the next.

~Terry Norton, CaringBridge, October 22, 2010

TERRY

The day after his surgery when Chris was able to move his left arm but couldn't wiggle his fingers, the doctor told us that moving anything below the injury site was a good sign because that meant everything wasn't damaged. He told us that his fine motor skills, like moving his fingers, would come last because spinal cord injury patients recover the bigger muscles ranges first and then recovery spreads to the extremities. It was a good sign, and we were so incredibly thankful for any movement, but in my mind, I thought if he could move anything at all, he was on his way back to 100 percent. The slow pace of rehab did little to extinguish that hope.

By the time Chris was transferred to rehab, everyone in the family had moved into a role pretty quickly. I became the face and strength of our family. I dealt with people who wanted to visit and talk to Chris. He received a lot of media attention, probably because he was a college football player, and Deb insisted I represent the family. She was concerned she wouldn't be able to control her emotions during the various newspaper and phone-in radio interviews the media requested on a pretty regular basis. I was also the one who'd work with the hospital in terms of his care.

In addition to working full time, Deb continued to be the nurturer, the giver of emotional support, and the food coordinator—all the things that felt like home. Having her around meant I had my partner back, and we always made time to reconnect with each other. She told me what was going on at home, and I filled her in on Chris's progress in rehab. She also made sure the girls were on track with school and friends and basically tried to keep their lives as normal as possible.

Alex and Katie both provided a lot of encouragement for Chris. They came on the weekends, planned his activities, and made his days fun. They were always working on his room, rearranging things, cleaning it up, and redecorating. It was important to them that Chris remained positive and happy in his environment.

Our short and long-term plans were to keep Chris as positive as possible and to keep our family together. One of the things Deb and I talked about was not letting his injury and the months we'd spend separated tear us apart. We were already close, but the whole experience really drew us together because we needed that emotional support from each other. It definitely made us more considerate of the other, and even though we'd always had a very loving marriage, we realized how much we needed each other.

We'd never gone through a personal challenge, a crisis as a couple, or a family tragedy before. We'd heard stories about people who'd lost a child or something else terrible had happened in their family, and it ended up destroying their marriage. We knew how easy it would be to start channeling our anger and emotions into something ugly that we took out on each other. We were determined to stay together throughout his recovery, and equally determined that Chris would have a wonderful life regardless.

> *"Chris started wiggling his left shoulder and I knew right then and there that our family was going to be on a long journey, but we would make it through."*
>
> Katie Norton, Chris's sister

We started accepting that things were going to be okay no matter the outcome. What Deb and I didn't care for, however, was people telling us to get used to our "new normal." For some reason, it felt like they'd stuck a knife in our backs. It really hurt. It felt as if people expected us to simply accept Chris's situation immediately. We were really resistant to the phrase *new normal* because *nothing* in our lives felt normal.

Chris continued to work hard in therapy, especially PT

where the immediate goal was for him to drive his wheelchair with his left arm. Megan was phenomenal. I compared her to a really good coach because she had an eye for detail, she always had a plan, she was professional, and the perfectionist in her made sure everything was done correctly. She was one of many at Mayo who made us feel that Chris was right where he needed to be.

Watching our son drive a wheelchair was another one of those emotional slaps to the face. Despite the effort it took for him to drive on his own, we continued to consider the wheelchair as something temporary. One of the doctors did a really good job of helping our frame of mind by explaining that Chris would be given all of the services and adaptations he needed at the time, and as he no longer needed the devices, the staff would peel them away. I compared his situation to having knee surgery and starting off on crutches, and then progressing to a cane or a knee brace. When we thought of the wheelchair as a recovery tool and a step in the right direction, it helped to view it as an accomplishment and not as surrendering to a new way of life.

Chris got a lot of calls and even some visits from people who'd suffered spinal cord injuries in the past. He asked them questions, but I wasn't ready to hear from people who'd learned to live with their injuries—I didn't want to plant that seed. I held tight to hope and still believed that Chris wasn't going to end up in a wheelchair.

In the midst of all the pain, there were a lot of blessings because of the opportunity to be at one of the best facilities in the world. The professionals at Mayo were so kind to Chris and our family. They couldn't have treated him any better. We spoke to the doctors frequently, sometimes daily.

Once Chris moved to rehab, we saw the surgeons less and less. They did stop in periodically just to see how he was progressing or to take an X-ray. Every so many weeks, Chris was rotated to one of three doctors. We saw the doctor in his rotation almost daily, even if just in the hallway; they were always around.

His doctors were all very different. One of them was matter of fact, one was optimistic, and one was in-between the two.

The matter-of-fact doctor said in terms of personal care, "Let's learn to adapt with where you are now because you may not get any more recovery than this. You don't want to do bathroom care every day and give up two hours of your life, so you need to do it every other day."

The optimistic doctor talked to us like he was a friend who just happened to know a lot about medicine. He approached the same topic in a different manner. "If Chris continues to need bathroom care, then you may want to consider going every other day if his body can withstand it so you're not having to take time out of your schedule."

Just by saying, "If he continues to need it," he left the door open for a chance Chris wouldn't, whether through medical advancements, his own recovery, or some breakthrough. We really appreciated the thoughtful way he phrased his words, not selling us false hope, but giving us hope.

Deb and I used to say that when mothers and fathers had a severely hurt child, the parents became like teenagers all over again. We were just hanging by a thin thread onto everything the doctors, nurses, and therapists said and the way they said it. Our day could be crushed because we were so vulnerable to both the words and tone of the doctors.

So when one doctor said, "You don't want to have to do bathroom care every day," in our minds, with our teenager mentalities, he was telling us, "You're going to be doing bathroom care for the rest of his life. He's never going to recover from this." That wasn't what he meant, but that's how it came across.

Whenever one of the doctors said, "You need to have a power chair," the other said, "Start out with the most adaptive devices you need, and then pare back as recovery continues." Leaving the door open for recovery was huge when we were so thin-skinned. I connected better with one of the doctors because he always said, "There's so much going on in medical research right now, and for these young guys, we just don't know." We needed to hear there was hope and an opportunity for future recovery.

Twice a week, the doctor, nurse, physical therapist, occupational therapist, recreational therapist, and psychiatrist met in his room to give a "State of the Union" update. I dreaded the rounds because we tried to put a positive spin on everything, and those meetings didn't leave much room for the possibility of hope. I didn't begrudge the doctors, the nurses, and so forth for coming across as pessimistic because they were just doing their jobs, but no one truly knew what tomorrow, the next week, or the next month held.

During rounds, they addressed Chris's current abilities or lack thereof. The whole experience was just discouraging. They talked about needing a ramp and Chris getting fitted for a wheelchair — things we weren't ready to hear. We held out for the possibility that he was going to walk out of the hospital, or that he would walk at some point, and everything they said came across as very negative.

They were simply being realistic, but I personally didn't think they needed to talk about home care so soon. Maybe they found from experience that they had to keep bringing it up in order to push people to the point of acceptance. But I couldn't bring myself to tell my eighteen-year-old son, an outstanding athlete I'd always seen as invincible, that he was going to be in a wheelchair when we left the hospital. I just couldn't spin that in any way that would come across positively, so I absolutely dreaded the rounds.

I tried to go numb and just nod my head and get through them. There were times when I pushed back. For example, one of the things I felt they wanted to do too early was talk about making adaptations, like teaching us to dress Chris and teaching us to help Chris get himself dressed. At that point in time, I wanted to focus on strength and recovery and then focus on what adaptations he'd need.

It used to be that when someone had a spinal cord injury, that patient stayed in the hospital for a year before being sent home. At the time of Chris's injury, patients stayed for four weeks or eight weeks before getting discharged. For better or worse, medical professionals wanted patients to start integrating back into the community quicker, even while the patient's body was still recovering. Instead of teaching us to dress him two weeks into rehab, I wanted to focus on getting him as strong as possible first, and then in a few months' time, reassess and make changes.

Some of the old-school doctors and therapists worked toward prepping Chris for his departure home, while I and the more progressive doctors and therapists tried to focus on getting him stronger. I knew they had their checkpoints, or things they had to be sure we knew before he was discharged, and they knew I wanted to spend every day on recovery before worrying about the checklist. We had a philosophical difference with some of the team where we basically looked at Chris's injury and recovery from two different angles, but we managed to find a happy medium.

One of the issues that came up during rounds was when Chris wanted more therapy. Spinal cord injuries cut across all bounds, so therapy was designed for a cross-section of people. If a fifty-year-old man suffered a spinal cord injury after falling off his roof, or a thirty-five-year-old woman fell down some stairs and suffered a spinal cord injury, the standard therapy was three hours a day because that was what most people could physically stand.

Chris was a college athlete at the time of his injury, and he was used to working out all the time. Some patients were runners or swimmers and able to withstand a more rigorous pace of therapy. Despite the average, everyone was different. Frustrated with the slow rate of progression and physically able to do more, Chris asked why he was only getting three hours of therapy. He was told it was the average number given.

Chris countered with a very profound statement. "I'm not average," he said. Some people fell into the average range, but he didn't, and many others didn't either. He wanted more time to work with the therapists, he could handle

> "*Experiencing this journey with Chris has given me the tools and confidence to challenge those who criticize SCI recovery.*"
>
> Megan Gill, PT, DPT, Clinical Lead Physical Therapist for Spinal Cord Injury, Mayo Clinic

more work, and to their credit, they bumped his therapy to four hours a day.

Even after he went from three hours of rehab per day to four hours, that still wasn't enough to satisfy Chris. He was beyond focused on getting better and wanted to maximize every second of every day. Once, in the middle of the night, while sleeping in his room after a hard day of rehab, I heard him say, "Dad?"

"Yeah?" I responded, worried something was wrong.

"You know, the extra things I do are what's going to make a difference in my life. I'm going to be successful because of all the little things I do."

"That's right," I said. "It's all the little things that make anyone successful."

"I'm going to focus on today and do the best I can," he said.

Goal setting was similar to planning, and they didn't call me the salesman for nothing. "Do you want to put a list of goals together? We can post them on the wall."

"Yes," he said, "but I want my goals to be on what I'm going to do, not the outcome. You need to help me write a list of all the things I can work on."

"That's a great idea," I grumbled, relieved he wasn't hurting, "but can we wait three hours to get started? It's four in the morning!"

Even in the middle of the night, that made so much sense. In other words, he didn't want to put on the wall that his goal was to move all of his index fingers or to walk by a certain date. We based his goals on whatever he was working toward at the time—for example, to complete ten sets of head nods every day, or to have the therapists stand him up for five minutes.

Sometimes the goals didn't change. If they did, we updated the list or changed it altogether. His goals focused on the process instead of the end result. Very early on, Chris understood that he could only control his end of things. He even coached me through setting achievable goals because I kept thinking too big. He understood well before I did that the outcome would take care of itself. Chris was constantly thinking about ways to improve. We put that list up on the wall, and then we spent time doing those things in addition to therapy. He was just go, go, go all the time.

The whole time Chris was at Mayo, I don't think he ever ate a hospital meal. At the time of his injury, he played the safety position at 185 pounds. He was lean, wiry, and strong, and there wasn't an ounce of fat on him. Within a few weeks after his injury, he was down to a 151 pounds and we were very concerned. We expressed our unease about his weight loss to the doctors and nurses. Part of the answer was muscle atrophy and a decreased appetite, but we knew that couldn't possibly account for the sheer bulk of weight he'd lost.

We kept bringing up his weight loss until a nutritionist got involved, agreeing he'd lost too much weight and starting him on protein shakes and smoothies. That experience taught us early on in his battle that even though the professionals were doing the best job they could, we still had to look out for his care. Our family, along with Chris himself, was his single best advocate. There were times when I had to move outside my comfort zone and push for what I knew was right by asking myself, *If you don't do this for your son, who's going to?*

In addition to pushing to get a nutritionist involved with his weight loss, we were very vocal about how many people were necessary for helping him transition to the chair using the overhead lift system. We insisted they put in their notes that three people were needed. I quickly learned how to help, so it was typically myself and two other nurses, but whenever they started to transfer him without three people, we intervened and insisted they get more help. His neck was extremely sensitive, and he couldn't protect himself during the transfer.

Chris told me he felt like he was strapped to the bed in a full-body cast that gradually moved down. The doctor said he would improve for up to two years, with the bulk being in the first six to nine months. For an eighteen-year-old trying hard to focus on one day at a time, six months sounded staggeringly long. The mantra I started using with Chris was "six months for sixty years." I don't know where I came up with it, but I told him he had to give up six months of his life to gain sixty years of living. In other words, six months sounded like a long time right then, but he'd get to six months, and he'd recover to where he was going to recover, and he'd have sixty years of life after that to be at that point. He had to give up six months for sixty years.

In talking to people who'd suffered spinal cord injuries, we discovered most regained feeling in their legs around the six-week mark. Some said four weeks, some said five, but by six weeks most had gotten some life back in their legs. I lay in bed at night as we closed in on that six-week mark and wondered how we'd keep his spirits up if that marker came and went without movement. Chris stayed positive, even after a month of not being able to move his legs, but we were using that six-week timeframe to fight off some of the demons. That was easy to do during the first two days, or the first two weeks, but as we inched closer to the six-week mark and he still hadn't moved his legs, I prayed and prayed for progress.

CHAPTER 17

I can do all things through Christ who strengthens me.

~ Philippians 4:13 NKJV

CHRIS

At the beginning of November, therapy really picked up steam. They were helping me get used to standing up so I could use the Lokomat, an advanced walking machine. We worked on feeding myself in OT, and we'd just started working with the electrical stimulation bike (RT300) in PT. It felt as if my body were coming out of that post-surgery drowsiness, and the fatigue that kept pulling me under.

As my recovery sped up and I was able to handle more in therapy, I enjoyed staying busy because it helped keep my mind off the future. I'd get caught up in the present and what I could do now, so the constant activity kept me focused. When it was just my dad and me, one of my favorite things was to hear stories about his childhood. My grandpa, his dad, was very tough and determined, and I drew strength from knowing his blood ran through my veins.

At the very beginning, I didn't really trust my nurses, PT, or OT with my body. With every day and through every session, I became more comfortable with what we did, and I developed an essential comfort level with them. It didn't happen overnight—it took closer to a month—but they definitely earned and upheld that trust. Eventually, whenever they wanted to do something different, I set my nervousness aside and did whatever they recommended because they knew what was best for me and I trusted them completely.

One of the things I enjoyed the most was being able to do the arm bike portion of the RT300 when my shoulders weren't really stable enough to support themselves. The first couple of weeks I spent using the arm bike, I was belted into my chair around my stomach with my shoulders pinned to the backrest of my chair because my core was so unstable I would fall to the side. The electrical stimulation increased the range of motion in my arms and really helped keep my muscles strong. I hated how my muscles shrank and I went from having a toned, muscular body to losing a lot of weight because of muscle atrophy. Being able to work my muscles and fight the atrophy felt fantastic and made me feel normal.

I wanted to be in top physical shape for the RT300 bike and eventually the Lokomat, which would help retrain my nervous system and simulate walking. Due to the long setup time for the Lokomat, I needed to be able to stand for at least fifteen minutes. It took forever to get my body used to not feeling nauseated whenever I'd go from a sitting to a standing position. We used a standing frame to hoist me from sitting to standing. I'd go up, and then my blood pressure would drop so I'd have to go back down. I'd go up again, and I'd have to go back down. We just kept repeating the process until my body got used to being upright.

Whenever they raised me up and I passed out, it was almost as if a light switch went off. On a few occasions, I passed out on the standing machine because the drop in pressure was too sudden. I woke up back in my chair with my legs propped up and my dad, the PT, and the gym tech hovering over me with worried faces, asking if I was okay. It took a few seconds before I knew where I was or what had happened. One time they cranked me to the upright position, and I immediately went down. I passed out another time while being raised up into the Lokomat. My grandma was present, and she nearly fainted because she was so upset about me losing consciousness.

Controlling my blood pressure was the first step in getting me ready to stand or walk. The therapists

> *"I had no idea how strong mentally Chris was, how courageous Chris was, and how determined Chris was."*
>
> Connie Norton,
> Chris's Grandma

continued to put Ace bandages around my legs and chest to help me tolerate being upright. I was never able to withstand being in the upright position for extended periods of time, but the Lokomat's harness helped keep my blood pressure up long enough to save me from passing out. I had to fight the nausea that lingered whenever I was upright, but it felt wonderfully normal to stand and move my legs in the walking pattern. Using the Lokomat was an important step in my recovery and fueled my desire to walk, but it wasn't the only device that drained me both physically and mentally.

I got sick a couple of times while using the leg bike, so I had the PT set a garbage can beside the bike. I needed to work hard in order to get better, and pushing myself to the limit was what I'd always done. I'd spit up into the garbage can and just keep going. I'd gotten sick maybe once or twice from football conditioning, but I was never a big puker.

During my senior year, while doing two-a-days, our drills included running across the field and back a bunch of times. It was exhausting. One day, I'd stupidly eaten at a Chinese buffet earlier, but that didn't stop me from pushing myself hard. I was the first one done every time, but at the end, my lunch made a return appearance. I caught some serious flack, but I just drank some water and moved on to the next drill.

In rehab, whenever I passed out or got sick, I did the same. I got some water and then tried again. Getting sick or passing out never made me want to quit. We'd figure out a better or slower way to get me upright, I'd take a minute, and then we'd get right back to work. I couldn't afford to miss a whole PT session because I'd gotten sick or passed out. I had work to do.

The nurses, therapists, and doctors seemed very impressed by how hard I worked and how much better I got based on where they thought I should have been, considering my injury. The way they cared for patients seemed pretty back and white, so I think my attitude changed their outlook on the possibilities of recovery being based on the patient's work ethic, attitude, and determination.

Perhaps watching me work so hard while maintaining an upbeat attitude gave them a sense of encouragement and a feeling of satisfaction in their work. When they saw miracles happen as my strength returned and I got better, it gave everyone a sense of hope that spread to other patients. Hope was a determining factor in the recovery of all patients, myself included.

When I first got movement back in my arm, I didn't think much about which hand I could use because I just wanted to do something on my own. My coordination was off, but I was happy I could move something. Despite having more movement and control in my left arm, it felt foreign as a right-handed person to have to rely mostly on my left hand.

One of the bigger milestones I reached in therapy was being able to use my arm to scratch my cheek. That was huge because trying to describe to someone where I had an itch without using my arms was quite difficult. "My right cheek," I'd say. "To the left a little bit. No, more to the right." Having people touch my face was annoying, so being able to do it myself felt wonderful.

Lifting and curling a half-pound weight seemed laughable, but everyone, including me, got excited the first time I accomplished it. I was thankful and happy, but after thinking about how much I used to curl when I was in top shape, feeling excited about curling half a pound seemed ridiculous. I fought the urge to compare my prior life to my current state, because curling any amount of weight was a big step and I tried not to feel discouraged.

We worked in OT on using adaptive computer equipment. We tried the Dragon dictation system where the computer learned my voice commands. While frustrating, it did help me become a little more independent. I could direct the mouse to open programs, but because I didn't speak very clearly or well enough for the computer to recognize all of my commands, the system didn't always do as I instructed. I yelled at it a lot. We tried other adaptations with a little sensor I put on my head where a light controlled the mouse. It all helped, but the learning curve was steep. In RT, we eventually figured out how to play video games on the computer, and we later took a field trip, or what was commonly referred to as an "outing," to the movies.

I made good friends in rehab. I met a guy from Iowa who got hurt three weeks after I did, and we became good friends with him and his family. We could relate to each other, and I really appreciated talking to someone who was going through the same kind of situation. I also met another guy a year older than me who didn't have much family support. My family and I tried to visit him and have him hang out with us as much as possible.

Another patient had already been at Mayo for eight months. He was injured in a car accident that messed up a bunch of internal organs and broke his neck in a way so he couldn't swallow. His situation made me realize things could always be worse. It was humbling for a lot of people to see me, but it was also the other way around when I realized there were others who had it worse than me. Going through therapy with him and reading about other people's hardships on CaringBridge definitely made me appreciative and thankful for what I had.

My friends in rehab and I developed a brotherhood because we were there at the same time, going through the same things, and we could relate to each other by facing similar hardships. I felt comfortable and normal around them, but outside of the hospital, I felt uncomfortable because people stared and I felt different from everyone else. When I was with them, I just felt normal and accepted.

In order to stay positive and not get frustrated with the pace of recovery, I thought about all the good things I had to be thankful for and focused on the good parts of my recovery. I watched a lot of TV shows and movies when I needed a distraction, and I trusted God and relied on my faith by believing that God would someday reveal the purpose and reason for the accident.

I never had any regrets about how I lived my life before my injury and that brought me a lot of peace. I had experienced a lot, and I was pleased with the effort I put forth during those experiences. Eighteen years with a fully functioning body was not that long, but I felt I'd maxed those years out the best I could.

I really wanted to have success at the college level, so not being able to see how far I could go as an athlete was disappointing. Being an athlete was a part of my identity because I'd always participated in sports, was very competitive, and loved playing sports for fun, but I never felt I lost my identity after my injury. My circumstances had changed, and even though I never thought I could live without being active, I still knew who I was, where I came from, and what was important in life.

I tried to take one day at a time. I thought about what I could do on that day in order to get better and just stay goal oriented. I wrote out actual workouts that my PT and OT put together and asked my parents, my family, or my dad to do extra workouts with me.

My therapists encouraged me to work on my own time because there was so much work to do, and I only had so much time in therapy. The doctors made sure I understood the difference between my nerves and my muscles, and that nerve fatigue was different from muscle fatigue. If I worked out hard and burned out a muscle, there wouldn't be any harm, but burning out a nerve might stop the signal for a while and I couldn't afford to have that happen. Rest was key.

Their guidance was essential because I was willing to do anything I could and maximize every opportunity. A clock in my head was gunning for that six to nine month range, and I didn't think I'd get any movement back after that time frame had come and gone. My dad told me over and over again that I was being tried by fire and that I'd come out as steel. I definitely felt like I was tried by fire, but God knew I could handle it. I *did* handle it, and I felt stronger because of it. Having something completely alter my life helped me keep things in perspective and made me numb to some stresses. Life's little dramas and occasional ups and downs didn't bother me anymore. I was able to take a step back and look at the big picture in order to determine what was important and what I should let go.

At about five weeks in, an unfamiliar sensation occurred in my left big toe. My legs felt like they were in an invisible cast, and I could sense the cast everywhere but my left big toe. It was as though it had broken free from the cast. Something was happening; I didn't know what, but it felt different. My dad got excited, my family was thrilled, and I was eager to tell my doctor.

Something good was happening. I didn't know if what I

was experiencing was normal or if it was something he could explain, but either way I was excited to tell the doctor. He responded that often times people with an injury as serious as mine believed and hoped in something so much that they tricked their mind into thinking it was real. He called it a "phantom feeling." The whole time he was talking, I kept thinking, *Are you serious?*

"Can you just check it?" I asked him. "I can feel it. I think it might be a muscle firing."

He explained the whole phantom syndrome, adamant that it was all in my head. I was devastated, and it must have shown on my face, because when I looked at my dad, he had tears in his eyes. The strongest man I'd ever known had his teeth clenched and was fighting back tears. That really threw me back as that was the first time I'd ever seen him cry.

As soon as the doctor left, my dad turned to me. "Do not let anyone tell you what you can and can't do. You're going to beat this. I don't care what they say. You're going to beat this, and we're going to do it together. I'll be here with you, and we're going to prove them wrong."

Hearing the conviction in his voice and seeing the tears in his eyes made mine water up, but that was exactly what I needed to hear and see. *Exactly.* I vowed to never back down, and never let anyone tell me what I could or couldn't do. I responded to the doctor's answer with even more determination and hope.

When he told me I couldn't move my toe, and my dad said not to let anyone — even a doctor — tell me what I could or couldn't do, it made me want to do it even more.

On Thanksgiving morning, just a few days later, I felt an even stronger connection with that big toe. I concentrated really hard on moving it and jerked back in surprise when I saw the sheets move.

My sisters had spent the night in my room, so I called for them. "Alex! Katie! Pull my sheet back and watch my big toe." I moved it again.

They both started screaming. "Do it again! Do it again!"

> *"It was one of the greatest things I have witnessed, yes something as simple as a toe wiggle is by far the greatest thing I've seen- it was a sign of hope, answered prayers, and of a positive upcoming future."*
>
> Alex Norton, Chris's sister

I kept moving it, watching in disbelief. I'd proven the doctor wrong and flung the door wide open for hope. It was an unforgettable moment.

We wanted to surprise my mom and dad, and we thought of the perfect way to make it happen. My dad did this quirky thing where he'd pull my sheets back over my legs and yell at my feet, "Move, feet! Talk to me! Come to life!" So when my parents got to my room, Katie and Alex encouraged my dad to try talking to my feet again.

He pulled the sheet back. "Talk to me!"

I wiggled my toe, and he stood upright, looking shocked. "Did you just do that?"

"Yeah." I did it again and again.

He was stunned speechless, and my mom immediately started bawling.

"Why didn't you tell us sooner?" she cried. She was happy *and* mad that we didn't tell them right away. "Why did you wait?"

My nurses came in and I did it for them, to their surprise and amazement. Megan happened to be working that day in PT, so I asked the nurses to get her. She was thrilled at seeing the movement, and she felt happy for my family and me. I wanted the nurses to get the doctor who'd told me I couldn't move my toe, but he wasn't on call that day and was home with his family for Thanksgiving. I'd never experienced so much exhilaration before in my life. It was one of those moments where I felt on top of the world, like I'd just scored a game-winning touchdown. I felt like the Hulk; I wanted to rip open my shirt and have "Dr. Phantom" come into my room so I could tell him, "Phantom this." It was an awesome moment and a great start to a special day. My whole family on my mom's side moved Thanksgiving to the hospital, and we had a huge Thanksgiving feast in a big conference room with all my cousins, aunts, and uncles.

That unbelieving doctor rotated off the floor, and the next time I saw him was two months later when he came in to watch a physical therapy session. At that time, I'd gained even more movement and strength in both legs. After my therapy session, he congratulated me on my progress. He said he was wrong, and that he was very glad that he was.

Defying the odds by moving my legs brought even more attention to my recovery. As word of my injury spread, I received a lot of requests for interviews from newspapers and local television stations. My first time around a TV camera was kind of uncomfortable. I didn't know how to act, so they told me to pretend they weren't there. I tried to go about my normal business, but it still felt different. I actually liked it when the media came around because I tended to have my best therapy days whenever I was in front of the camera.

Even though I didn't find my story that newsworthy, after the stories aired, people reached out and sent letters. I didn't mind being public about what was going on when people seemed to find inspiration and hope from my story. I worried I was showboating or coming across as arrogant, but my dad said it wasn't showboating when people were inspired and it was something they wanted to hear. My dad thought it was best to be as vocal and outspoken about it as possible, and that helped me turn a corner and take the interviews in stride.

I never wanted or asked for the media's attention. I never read the articles or watched the videos. I never liked the sound of my voice, and I already knew the story. I did get irritated whenever the media only mentioned the facts of the story and neglected the intangibles like my family, friends, faith, determination, and my work ethic that was in place before my injury. In fact, when I got hurt, it was just a repeat of everything I'd already done, but just on a different level and with a bigger audience.

I didn't recover alone, and working hard was only a small part of my recovery. If I didn't have faith, family, and friends, I don't think my hard work would have paid off or I'd have recovered as much. The story wasn't about my injury, but about how and why I was able to keep going and the strength of my spirit.

CHAPTER 18

I have been involved in sports all of my life and have watched people who talk the talk, but don't walk the walk. They use words like "heart," "competitor," and "winner," but what I have found is that we all look good and sound believable when things are going well. It is easy to talk about these things when things are going our way, and we are "front runners." But where these words really have meaning is when things don't follow our plan, when things don't go like we want them to, or when we are truly faced with adversity and the wheels are falling off.

~Terry Norton, CaringBridge, November 17, 2010

TERRY

My life began to feel like the movie *Groundhog Day*. I'd get up, have coffee downstairs, read my book, go up to get Chris ready, go to therapy, get lunch, go back to therapy, and plan the evening. Our routine became a real pattern that played out over and over again. Thursday couldn't come fast enough for Chris and me to have Deb and the girls around to break up the monotony.

The days went by fast for me, and it helped that the PTs (Megan and Lori), and the gym tech (Amy), were great people. Chris called Amy, "Big Cat," because she made the whole PT room so lively, he wanted to go to the gym. They did an excellent job of taking a difficult situation and making rehab fun. The therapists were also excellent communicators. They explained what they were doing and why, how everything tied together, and what kind of reaction they expected from certain activities and exercises. They told us we couldn't predict where he'd be in a week, a month, a year, or even five years, and they educated us on the depth and breadth of spinal cord injuries. We learned a ton, and it was interesting too.

By early to mid-November, while working on getting and staying upright, Chris often became lightheaded. PT had a machine called a standing frame. The therapists wheeled him up in the chair, put straps on his legs and a harness around his butt, and then basically winched him into a standing position.

"I can honestly say, the experience and privilege of working with Chris and the 'Norton Nation' has molded me into the therapist I am today. After meeting Chris, I feel a better understanding of what my clients/patients desire and strive for."

Megan Gill, PT, DPT, Clinical Lead Physical Therapist for Spinal Cord Injury, Mayo Clinic

They also had a table that operated in a similar fashion that they used to position him at certain angles.

Chris got frustrated whenever his blood pressure dropped and he became lightheaded, sometimes to the point of losing consciousness, but it was completely out of his control. We were both discouraged by the setbacks because he desperately wanted to be upright. Medication helped, but too much made him drowsy. Everything had a downside, and the only thing that worked was to keep trying.

As the one who set him up on Skype and responded to his texts, I knew just how important Chris's friendships were. Deb and I were concerned that over time, everyone would go back to their normal lives and forget about Chris. Thankfully, he usually had visitors. The toughest weekends were when his friends couldn't come for one reason or another, whether the football team had an away game or there was bad weather. A college kid didn't mind hanging out with his mom and dad during the day, but he needed his own social time.

We experienced one of our most enjoyable weekends when two visiting college girls planned to go home after their quick trip to see Chris. A blizzard hit, so they bought some essentials at the gas station, and we took them to a hotel room across the street at the Courtyard Marriott. Deb assured their parents they wouldn't leave and try to drive home in the blizzard. We made the most of their misfortune, and they spent the whole weekend playing games with us and hanging out.

It was a huge deal for Chris whenever people were around and he'd close his eyes and guess which leg they were touching. The further along he got in rehab, the more accurate he became. At times I wondered if he really could tell which leg was being touched. Personally, I didn't like him performing this drill because if he got it wrong, I didn't want him to get discouraged. Thank heavens he got it right most of the time.

On weekend nights when Alex and Katie stayed with Chris, Deb and I might have dinner together, read a book together, or go down and sit in the bar area at the hotel and just talk. We really didn't go out, but it was nice to spend time together, just the two of us, and be able to visit and catch up.

Both of our roles had challenges. When Chris and I were alone, there was no way to escape the severity of what we were dealing with. On the flip side, I didn't have to pick up the mail, pay the bills, or take out the dog and the garbage. At home, Deb didn't have to face the reality of what we encountered every day, but she definitely had more chores to do.

During the seven months while Chris was in the hospital, Deb and I only spent one night together in our home. We were either in opposite places or together in Rochester. Our one night at home happened when friends put together a big fundraiser for Chris. It was important to attend together, and they wanted me to speak, so the girls stayed in Rochester with Chris.

Deb stayed with Chris while I made a quick trip home before Thanksgiving, and I realized it was harder to be away than it was to be with him every day. When I was with him, I got to witness the strength of his faith, as well as the miracles God granted as Chris continued to heal. At home, I started to look past one day at a time and get discouraged.

We were both busy, but Deb and I handled the time apart by texting and talking daily. We didn't like being apart because we'd never been separated that much, but we both learned that we could handle more than we thought we could. If I'd known I was going to be away from home for months at a time, I'd have said it was impossible. When it was thrust upon us, we didn't have time to think, so we just did what was necessary.

When everybody went home on a typical Sunday afternoon, especially on a weekend when a big group of Chris's friends were there, I watched him closely. I'd try to do something fun, or we'd watch a movie, because I anticipated his spirits plummeting. Mine did.

The two or three times Chris got upset were the most trying for me. We could deal with physical challenges, but emotional struggles were so painful. I could tell he was having a rough day if he got a little quiet or just stared off into space and wouldn't make much eye contact. The rounds, in particular, were really hard on Chris.

Once after rounds, the doctor kept going on and on about how Chris would always be in a wheelchair; therefore, he'd need a ramp at home. Chris asked him to check his toe because he thought he could feel it. The doctor brushed it off as a "phantom feeling." Afterwards, it hit Chris so hard, he had tears in his eyes.

I'd always been able to hide my emotions from him, but when I saw him upset, I couldn't control it and I choked up too. "Don't ever let anyone define you," I said. "Don't ever let anybody else tell you what you can or can't do."

"I never will," he said.

214

That seemed to calm him down, so I excused myself and went into the bathroom to pray for strength so I could hold it together. Normally, I could anticipate the setbacks and head them off, but we couldn't avoid the rounds, and I certainly couldn't control what was said. I tried to go numb and not really listen, but when I saw him upset after they left, it was just like a punch to the stomach. I couldn't hide it from him, and I instantly started crying.

It led to a good moment for us, but getting there was torturous. I credit both my years of coaching and my reliance on God for help in getting through the difficult times. On several occasions, I felt the Holy Spirit's presence lifting me up, because I didn't know where I came up with the words to say, or how I came up with them so quickly.

But it wasn't hard to stay positive because Chris rarely got down. He figured out quickly that he had it better than a lot of people, and he had it worse than other people. He didn't go down the road of comparing his situation to anyone else. If I started thinking about what his life was going to be like a year out, or wonder how he was going to go back to college, I'd quickly avert my mind. I'd turn to Scripture and pull out the verses that were really helpful, or I'd lean on close friends, my brother, or my uncle to lift me up. Sometimes, when it was nice outside, I'd go for a walk or get coffee across the street.

On Thanksgiving Day, a few days after the doctor upset Chris, to our great relief and astonishment, Chris moved his big toe. He couldn't wipe the smile from his face or hide the pride he felt at proving the doctor wrong. Deb and I were ecstatic. Watching him move his toe was in-your-face progress, proof positive that we were heading in the right direction and his body was healing. It might have been painstakingly slow improvement compared to what we wanted, but it gave us all hope.

We believed he had between six to nine months to regain anything he could. Moving his toe meant more recovery was possible. Within a day of moving his toe, Chris demonstrated firing in his glutes, quads, hamstrings, and calves, and he moved toes on both feet.

Because of his progress and positive attitude, Chris never focused on things he wouldn't be able to do, and I gave him so much credit for that. For him, it was just a matter of refocusing his mind on what he could do, but with modifications. Instead of asking if he'd ever be able to walk again, he quickly became focused on what he needed to do to be able to walk.

One of his biggest fears was not being able to go back to college and reconnect with his friends. Chris didn't want to be isolated or cut off from a normal social life experienced by young college students, but it wasn't something he talked about because we purposely avoided anything negative. Deb and I made a plan of what we needed to do in order to get him back in school, and we asked ourselves what support systems needed to be in place. We bounced our ideas off of the therapists at

Mayo who had experience with transitioning patients to college environments.

Knowing Chris's goals helped them tailor his therapy. For example, a lot of the doors at Luther had keycard access, so Chris had a school ID card that snapped right below his wheelchair seat. The therapists put a metal ring on the ID card so he could hook his thumb through it and practice pulling it out. They also put a water bottle where he could hook it with his thumb. They were great at looking at the chair's setup and the school's accessibility, and then practicing whatever he would need on a day-to-day basis.

Making practical decisions for his return to college didn't squelch my hope that he'd be able to walk, as I figured once he was able to move his leg, he was well on his way. What I didn't understand was that even though he looked strong, he didn't have the body strength necessary to support himself. Also, his sensation wasn't nearly as good in his legs as it was higher up on his body. The learning curve with spinal cord injuries was huge, and my inclination was to expect the most optimistic outcome. I had the hardest time grasping that with spinal cord injuries, sensation, movement, and strength weren't necessarily connected with the central nervous system.

I learned the most by watching Chris in action. Whenever he was in rehab with the occupational, physical, and recreation therapists, I observed and also assisted if needed. I didn't miss a session, and I learned a lot about the process. The PT had aggressive plans for him to walk using the Lokomat treadmill three days a week, and on other days, he worked on the bike. In OT, he continued to work with the arm bike.

Chris was up for the challenge, and within only a few days, they were able to lower the guidance on the Lokomat and increase the weight bearing on his body. By mid-December, he was able to stay upright in the standing machine for forty-five minutes and work on flexing different leg muscles and on upper body alignment. When he first started, he could barely manage forty-five seconds before his eyes would start to roll back and he had to be lowered down.

Watching my son relearn the most basic functions every day in rehab was really hard at times. I had to battle my feelings of dismay by celebrating his accomplishments and realizing how far he'd come. We went from ground zero—only seeing him in a prone position—to sitting upright, either in a wheelchair or sitting up in bed. We felt such a sense of relief just seeing him upright in bed. The first time we took him in the car and he was sitting up, we looked like just another father and son going to a ballgame. Instead of feeling bad about it, it felt really good. He was coming back and making progress.

Every new movement was a positive sign. Moving his arm after surgery, for example, led to him being able to feed himself, brush his teeth, wash his face, and scratch his head. Those were probably the most instrumental leaps that took place since he'd been hurt. Those movements also led to him using his computer, an iPad, and a cell phone. Even though his fingers weren't nimble, that left arm movement was the first step in regaining some independence.

Watching Chris work on feeding himself in OT, as well as using the standing machine, the Lokomat, and the RT300 in PT was really uplifting. It was all progress toward him getting strong enough so he could feed himself, stand, and walk without the aid of machines. The bike's electrodes made his muscles fire, so even though we knew the electrodes were doing most of the work, watching his legs move after they'd been lifeless was a beautiful thing to see.

We experienced the same excitement while he worked toward feeding himself with the aid of a special anti-gravity machine that came up behind his chair. The machine reduced gravity, while the weight helped to offset the reduction, so he was able to work with what movement he actually had. Going from having somebody feed him to the ability to feed himself using the anti-gravity equipment was progress toward his ultimate goal.

Chris wasn't the only one learning new things. We had to learn how to help him with the most basic tasks, and at first we were timid because we really didn't know how to help. When we took him on an outing, people from the hospital put his sweatshirt and coat on because we were scared we would hurt him. We eventually learned little tricks, like if he was going to put a sweatshirt or a coat on, we put it on his weaker arm first because it was easier to get his better arm through the armhole. Putting his sweatshirt over his head before threading his arms through worked best, and if we were going to put him into bed, it was easier to take his shirt and sweatshirt off before we laid him down because once he was down, it was that much harder to get them off. We basically got comfortable helping him and quickly learned we weren't going to break him.

We also learned to look out for and interpret signs that something with him was not quite right. Whenever part of his body was stressed, a different part of his body exhibited a problem as an alert. For example, one time we put his foot into a new shoe not realizing the toe area was blocked and his foot was scrunched. His leg began to spasm as a signal that something was wrong. He might get a headache because his toes were caught underneath his foot, or a spasm when a wrap was left on too tight. We learned to watch for any signals and to seek out possible causes.

From a pride standpoint, Chris didn't like that he couldn't dress and feed himself, but he wasn't offended at having others help him. Whenever I talked to other people with spinal cord injuries, they often told me they absolutely hated being dressed and fed. Chris wanted to do those things himself, but I don't think it bugged him as much as other people more set in their ways. I think he saw it as assistance, and it drove him to want to feed and dress himself. It gave him something to work toward, and he took pride in working hard.

We focused on the little improvements he made and celebrated each one to keep the slow progress from frustrating us both. For his own mental stability, Chris had to approach rehab as a marathon and not a sprint. If he waited to celebrate when he could feed himself on his own, for example, and not celebrate being able to use the anti-gravity machine, he was going to have a tough time staying motivated.

Chris understood that the effort he put in each and every day would determine his eventual outcome; he couldn't skip any steps. From my coaching background and his athletic background, we both knew that was the recipe for success. We acknowledged his incremental progress, set achievable goals, and faced each day as it came because with spinal cord injuries and recovery, the pace was torturously slow.

I turned fifty in December, and the difference in our ages was never more apparent than when we were forced to cohabitate. I hated when he went away to college, and I used to joke that I wanted to be his roommate. During our time in the hospital I got to be his roommate; we were living together, and there were challenges. When I read on another CaringBridge site about the difference between the schedules of a teenager versus an adult, I felt validated.

The schedule of a teenager (or upper teen like Chris) and my schedule as a middle-aged adult were vastly different. Chris napped during the day, either over his lunch break or after therapy. Around eleven o'clock at night, he'd want to start a movie or have me set him up on Skype. Typically, by ten o'clock on a work night, I'd start getting ready for bed. From a purely physical standpoint, I was ready to sleep when he was just getting started. Plus, I'd always wake up early, whether I wanted to or not, but he'd sleep another hour and a half. Our schedules never meshed.

During our downtime, Chris enjoyed hearing stories of my childhood, and in particular stories about my dad, which was ironic because Chris reminded me so much of his grandfather. My dad graduated from a very small high school in Iowa, so small they didn't have a football team. He attended the University of Iowa, a perennial powerhouse in many sports, bound and determined to be a three-sport letter winner at the Division I level. My dad walked onto the football team his freshman year despite never having played. The first time they padded up, he didn't know how to put his pads on and went through most of the practice with his shoulder pads on backwards because he was too proud to ask for help.

My dad made the freshmen team (a retired practice at D-1 schools) and proved to be a hardnosed wide receiver, but suffered a career ending shoulder injury late in the season. He then attempted to walk-on in basketball and baseball every year for four years. He got cut every year and always met with the coach, upset he hadn't made the team. My dad and his indomitable spirit just refused to give up.

Growing up, I loved Louis L'Amour books. He described

a hero in his westerns as *not having any backup*. That was my dad to a *T*. He never complained, enjoyed life, took what was thrown at him, and always worked hard.

My dad had two favorite sayings. One was, *stay in the Word*, meaning the Bible, and, *sometimes you have to arch your back*, meaning when life gets tough, dig in and give it your all. I saw my dad's look on Chris's face every day in rehab. He would set his jaw and make a face, and I could tell he was giving his all and not quitting until the task was done. Unfortunately, my dad and Chris never got to meet, as Dad died of liver cancer at age fifty-six.

A lot of people asked us after his injury how Chris felt about football and if we'd ever question someone playing the game. Neither Chris nor anyone in our family blamed football, because his was such a freak accident. There was a patient at Mayo who rolled out of bed, hit his head on the nightstand, and broke his neck. Another guy broke his neck at a tailgate party. There were just so many ways to get hurt or injured, it seemed ridiculous to steer people away from an organized sport.

Several media people asked if Chris still watched football. I had to laugh because he loved watching the sport. I had a hard time watching games at Bondurant-Farrar High School and Luther College only because Chris played for both of those teams and it was emotional, but watching a good college football game on television was one of our favorite pastimes.

We were so engrossed in working hard during rehab that

we sometimes forgot how Chris's story affected others. A friend told me that reading our CaringBridge site had changed his opinion and renewed his faith in the goodness of people. It did the same for me whenever similar stories came in about how the site was encouraging other people who had suffered spinal cord injuries, or had lost their faith, or were battling depression. Stories were also shared of how Chris was impacting people we didn't even know. Every card and e-mail we received motivated me to keep posting about Chris's progress and to keep the posts positive. Certainly there were times when we felt discouraged or he suffered a setback, but we decided not to air that on CaringBridge because it wasn't just about us.

Some teachers were using Chris's story to inspire kids in school. A middle school class in Carroll, Iowa, watched all of Chris's YouTube videos and wrote Chris letters telling him about the impression he'd made. Often classes would take Chris on as a project. A

"Many people would hear that grave news 'you have a 3 percent chance of ever regaining any feeling below the neck' as validation to resign to a fate we had no control over. But Chris made the choice to hear those words as a challenge. He made the choice to be a living example to people with spinal chord injuries and to those without, proving that one is never out of the daily fight to be the best possible version of yourself until you choose to be."

Rich Holton, Luther
classmate and friend

grade school class from northeast Iowa collected pennies and spare change for Chris, and sometimes he received packages of cards from elementary schools.

To me, what was amazing about Chris was that he wasn't amazing, and I don't mean that in a bad way. Chris wasn't a professional athlete, he wasn't a superstar, or a rock star—he was a regular guy from Nowhere, Iowa—and that's what made his story amazing. He worked hard, had faith, had to overcome, and had the determination to succeed. He wasn't perfect, and I'd never put him on a pedestal because he had faults like all of us, but to me, the special part of the story was watching people focus on what a regular guy could accomplish when his mind and heart were in the right place.

CHAPTER 19

Jesus looked at them and said, "With man this is impossible, but with God all things are possible."

~Matthew 19:26 NIV

CHRIS

My therapists seemed to amp up the intensity of rehab after Thanksgiving, probably because I wiggled my toe for the first time. Sensations in my legs and my upper body were firing and feelings were coming back slowly. I had more energy and was thrilled by the changes I saw happening. Everything seemed to be coming together.

The therapists had a plan for my therapy and did a good job explaining why they did certain things and the expected outcome. The more time I spent in therapy, the more information I learned about spinal cord injuries, and the more comfortable I became suggesting things to work on or things I wanted to try. For example, if I said I wanted to work on my core strength and balance, and asked what kinds of exercises they'd recommend, they'd give me some ideas and we'd run with it. By that point in rehab, I felt like a layman therapist.

At the very beginning of rehab, the idea of plateauing after nine months wasn't even on my radar. I was convinced I was going to walk out of the hospital, and I had so much to work on that I fought the urge to look too far down the road. I couldn't think negatively and make it through the often-grueling therapy sessions. As the months wore on and improvement seemed painstakingly slow, I did start to worry about reaching a point where I no longer progressed. Fortunately, Megan kept up with the latest research that indicated patients didn't plateau. Nine months became the focus when insurance companies discontinued paying for intense therapy after that length of time. Armed with this knowledge, I stopped looking at the calendar and worked full steam ahead.

Once I'd regained feeling in my legs and began working hard in therapy on walking, each day felt gratifying, but I began to get frustrated with the slow return of feeling and control in my wrists, hands, fingers

"To continuously challenge Chris and provide him with cutting edge evidence based therapy principles, I found myself researching article after article to provide myself with answers of what we were experiencing together. His recovery was indescribable and he was responding to the program."

Megan Gill, PT, DPT, Clinical Lead Physical Therapist for Spinal Cord Injury, Mayo Clinic and triceps. My triceps were so tight I couldn't straighten my arms and reach out to grab things. Even if I could, I needed my hands, and they just weren't coming back as fast as I wanted. My biceps were stronger than my triceps, but they'd get so tight that my hands would come up and get stuck on my chest, under my chin, and by my face, especially when I slept. I couldn't stand the claustrophobic feeling and needed help to straighten my arms.

By mid-December, with a lot of work in OT, I was able to brush my teeth and feed myself using my left hand. I could fork food with a wrist cuff on my left hand and hold things in my left arm, but my right arm and hand weren't strong enough. Even though I wasn't using my dominant side, it felt wonderful to do something on my own and regain some independence. I wanted my life back, and being able to brush my teeth and feed myself without the assistance of another person and doing it the way I wanted it done felt awesome.

It didn't take long to realize how important my hands were. No matter how much movement I regained in my arms, my fingers and hands controlled what I wanted to do, and the dexterity wasn't coming back quickly. By January, I was feeding myself two times a day plus snacks, and I eventually made a giant leap by regaining the ability to hold a sandwich in my hand. Each incremental step led me further along the road to independence.

Alex stayed with Dad and me over her Christmas break

from school, and she really worked me hard during non-therapy hours. We worked a lot on strengthening my core and on shifting my weight from one foot to another in order to mimic the walking motion. As the therapists introduced the standing walker into my PT routine, along with the Lokomat and some assisted manual walking, I came to appreciate how complicated the walking motion was and how much coordination it required from so many muscle groups. I needed my newfound energy and appreciated the exhausting workouts that continued to garner daily improvements.

Alex wasn't my only overnight guest during the holidays; several lifelong friends visited. Dustin and Andrew stayed one weekend with me, and we were up late into the night watching movies, talking, and laughing like it was a junior high sleepover. I loved having them around—it meant the world to me. My friends, Shawn and Nick, spent the night with me in rehab and followed me through my sessions over their winter break. It meant a lot to me because I was at the point in my hospital stay where I was with my family constantly. I appreciated my family's support and I loved being around them, but I was an eighteen-year-old kid, and I just wanted some time with my friends in order to feel normal again.

Growing up, Shawn, Nick, and I were like the Three Musketeers. We rotated houses every weekend, and we knew everything about each other. Nick was a student at West Point, and I knew it was hard for him being so far away in New York.

It was nice for us to visit in person because when we'd Skype, I could tell he was pretty beat up about what had happened to me and the fact that he wasn't there. Shawn was just an hour and fifteen minutes south at Luther College, and he and my roommate, Richie, and my really good friends from Luther came to see me a lot on the weekends. I couldn't imagine going through rehab without those visits.

We had fun together during Shawn and Nick's winter break visit, goofing off and talking about things I didn't feel comfortable talking about with my family. Being with them also helped me reconnect with what other people were doing on the weekends while I was at the hospital and helped me feel a part of that social life.

After a long day of therapy, I liked to blow off steam and have a little fun, especially when my partners in crime were in town. Richie, Tanner, and my temporary roommate, Shay, all got in wheelchairs—I had my power chair, one of the guys got into my power-assist chair, we found a manual chair, and Shay used his chair—and we decided to explore Mayo Hospital. I took them to the basement and the tunnels underneath, but the security guards caught us and told us to go back to our room. As if we'd gotten caught by the college dorm resident assistant, we found the experience amusing.

My therapists put my friends to work as helpers, as having extra hands and bodies during PT helped a lot. They were fun loving, outgoing, goofy guys, and it was fun to laugh and talk with them throughout the day. Having them there was also helpful because to those who weren't familiar with the types of therapy I received, everything was foreign and no one really understood the equipment and the names of all the accessories. For them to actually see where I was and what we were working on gave them a better understanding of what I was going through, and when we talked and I told them what I did in therapy and how my recovery had progressed, I didn't have to explain.

At the end of December, with a bit of pushing, Mayo extended my stay from January into February. I was really happy about the additional time because I felt I was making a lot of progress, and I needed the Mayo equipment and the therapists assigned to my case. I had a nice routine, I was comfortable with the intensity of therapy, and I felt like I made great strides under their care, so I didn't want to break that pattern.

A lot of changes happened after the first of the year. By New Year's Eve, I was able to hold my own glass of sparkling grape juice and make a toast. My dad had asked everyone to pray specifically for improvement in my fingers, hands, and wrists, and it seemed to be working, because my hands kept improving. As my dexterity increased, I was able to use the computer and my phone by myself. Having the ability to text someone, post on Facebook, or Skype with someone privately felt empowering.

With every taste of freedom, I longed for more. Transitioning from the big power chair with the joystick to a power-assist chair that I'd be able to wheel around using the force of my own arms became a priority. At the time, my core strength was too weak, so the therapists had to transfer me into the power-assist chair and put straps around my chest so I was anchored. My arms weren't strong enough, and I could barely make it move on my first attempt.

Undeterred, my dad (or whoever was with me at night) would strap me into the wheelchair and time how long it took for me to go from one end of a fifteen-foot long strip of tile to the other. On my first attempt, it took me twenty seconds to go fifteen feet. I continued to practice every night until my arms and core got stronger and I was able to sit up without falling over or folding in half like Gumby.

I craved competition, so turning therapy and my power-assist workouts into contests seemed natural. During therapy, I didn't compare myself to anyone else because everyone had their own problems and their own recovery. I kept track of my times, my distances, and my metrics in order to push myself.

Ironically, a couple of weeks into January, I felt I was ready to move out of the hospital. I was tired of some of the rules and the constant checkups, so when a room at Mayo's Ronald McDonald House became available, I thought it would be a nice change of pace and offer us a little bit more freedom. I was glad to continue with rehab, but equally glad to get away from the hospital's daily grind. All it took was that one extra month to be ready to transition to outpatient therapy, and nothing really changed other than where we slept at night. I still had the same amount of time with all my therapists, and I still did everything I normally did. So, it wasn't too big of a transition other than our struggle to find a competent nurse to get me ready in the morning and at night.

When we moved to outpatient therapy and into the Ronald McDonald House, my dad took on a lot more responsibility. We soon realized how well the inpatient nurses did their jobs, happily doing what needed to be done so I could get on with my day. Suddenly, my dad had to help more than he was used to, and the nurses from the agencies needed time to adjust to my needs and my schedule, so in a way it felt like starting over. Despite the transition pains, I was happy to be out of the hospital.

The worst part of living in the Ronald McDonald House was that the rooms were really small, and traveling from there to St Mary's in the dead of winter wasn't fun. The best part was the community atmosphere and just being out of the hospital. There always seemed to be something going on, whether groups came in and cooked our meals, or we hung out in the lounge areas and played cards, it was nice to stay at a place so close to Mayo that wasn't the hospital or a hotel.

I still saw my doctors for checkups and progress updates every couple of weeks. They wanted to chart my recovery, check me out medically, answer my questions, and make sure I had a plan for the future. My lead surgeon took another job out of state, and when I met my new surgeon, he pulled my X-ray and asked me to explain how the injury happened. He'd never seen a break like mine before.

According to my new doctor, when the spine breaks, typically the bones splinter and shatter, or compress against one another creating a lot of fragments that cause even more damage. My break was unusual because it was a severe dislocation but nothing splintered, cracked, or compressed. I didn't know how to take his news at first, but I started to think maybe that was why I recovered as much as I did because it was such a "clean" break.

Shortly after the move to the Ronald McDonald House, my dad had to get back to work, so my parents started rotating weeks. Switching helped alleviate repetitiveness and had no bearing on my day-to-day therapy, so it was a good change of pace for all of us.

As a part of recreation therapy, Shay and I got to check out Rochester's bus system. Having grown up in the country, I didn't know how the bus system worked. It was nice to know that public transportation was available to people in wheelchairs. While needing public transportation was another reminder of the independence I'd lost, it also felt as if the public was looking out for us and that we hadn't been forgotten.

My friends from Luther came up after my first full week in the Ronald McDonald House, and we took the bus to the mall using the public bus stop right across the street. It felt good to get away from the family for a while and hang out with my friends outside of the hospital. We had a great time at the mall purchasing matching sunglasses from the kiosks and goofing off together. It was great to be one of the guys again, and even away at rehab, I made a new friend from Luther. Tanner was a freshman football player who was friends with Richie and Shawn, and he visited frequently.

Other than moving out of the hospital and my visit to the mall, I hadn't been on an outing in a while, so my family and I attended the Rascal Flatts concert featuring Chris Young and Luke Bryan. It felt great to do something outside my normal routine. The concert was awesome, and thanks to one of Mayo's resident doctors, we got backstage passes. Unfortunately, the event happened to be on one of the coldest winter days, with temperatures hovering just below zero.

We didn't have an accessible vehicle to get to the concert, so we had to take a regular car, and I wasn't strong enough to get into a vehicle without needing a lot of help. Fortunately, two of my PTs, Megan and Lori, got tickets and came with us. Getting in and out of the car was a challenge, especially because it was so cold. Despite the chill, it felt wonderfully normal to sit in the front seat.

During the concert, my body began shaking and spasming because of the cold temperature. When we got back to the hospital, my hands were cold—something I hadn't been able to feel for months. Because of my injury, my body didn't adjust to changes in temperature very well. The cold forced my body to work harder to keep me warm, but it also caused me to shake. Once I got cold, it took forever to warm up again.

I discovered that heat had the opposite effect; it relaxed me and made me feel as if I were melting. I had a harder time in the heat because it made me feel very weak, and because I no longer perspire, I couldn't keep myself cool. My feet and parts of my legs got a little sweaty, and my forehead would get a little moist, but nowhere near how much I used to sweat before my injury. Because of my body's inability to regulate its temperature, I preferred to be in the shade, and I had to drink a ton of water whenever it was hot. I learned different ways to cope with temperature extremes.

Whenever I went out in public, to a restaurant, the mall, or a concert, I attracted a lot of unwanted stares, which stunk because I just wanted to blend in. I didn't want to draw attention because I was different, although I assumed some of the gazes I received were because of my age. Having to sit in a specified area at a movie, concert, or ballgame felt very isolating, although sometimes I got the best seat in the house.

By late January, my sensations continued to slowly return. I could tell, for example, when my sweatpants weren't on just right, or I'd feel uncomfortable when my shirt wasn't pulled all the way down. I knew if my shoes weren't on right or if my sock had rolled down. I began to realize I was hungry and could tell when I was full—something I hadn't experienced in months. I felt grateful to recognize those feelings and be able to respond.

Returning to Luther in the fall was my ultimate goal, but my first time back on campus after my injury was to attend the football banquet in February 2011. It was interesting to drive back and look at my surroundings because I didn't have a good sense of where Rochester was in respect to Luther, and I had no concept of the route my friends took going between the school and the hospital.

I never thought about attending college anywhere else, and I was excited to be back on Luther's campus for that event, but my life began to feel like it had two stages, pre-injury and post injury. Viewing the campus through the post-injury lens felt disorienting and made me wonder about the logistics of my return. I didn't feel sentimental or emotional about being back, but it was good to see everyone again and be a part of the banquet.

By early March, I began going home to Bondurant on the weekends. It had been over six months since I'd been home, and I was beyond excited to be back at my house, see my dogs, and see all my friends from home again. Fortunately, a number of my friends either worked right after high school, took a break before going to college, or went to school really close by and were around for the weekends. On my first weekend home, my friends had a little get together for me at my buddy's house.

As soon as I got home, I wanted some freedom, so I asked

my family to teach my friends how to transfer me in and out of the car. My friends wanted to help, were strong enough to help, and the only way to learn was by trying. I was kind of nervous and uncomfortable about asking, but I longed for alone time with them. Besides, if my parents and my family could transfer me, my friends could too. There was a learning curve, but we got it worked out, and the more they did it, the more comfortable we all became. When I had to leave to go back to Rochester on Sunday, I didn't want to go.

I celebrated my nineteenth birthday with family and friends on a weekend home from the Ronald McDonald House. The night before my birthday, I went to my friend's house and hung with my buddies from high school. On my actual birthday, Richie came down from Luther and a group of us went out to eat for a birthday dinner.

When leaving to go to the restaurant, Shawn transferred me into the passenger seat and his butt hit the lock button. His keys were inside the car, so when he shut the door, I was locked inside the car. As I attempted to unlock the door, they cheered me on, but I couldn't reach the unlock button, and he didn't have a spare key with him. Embarrassed by my predicament, I got frustrated with my situation because I couldn't unlock the door. We were already running late for the reservation and a friend at the restaurant was waiting for us to arrive.

I couldn't stay aggravated long when Richie made a joke out of it by looking through the window, bugging his eyes, and saying, "Conserve your oxygen. You only have five minutes to live. Slow your breathing."

> *"Here we all were trying to navigate the first stages of adulthood and independence with our bodies fully intact, and he now had to do that with a 3 percent chance of ever regaining any feeling below the neck."*
>
> Rich Holton, Luther classmate and friend

We made the most of a bad situation, and I realized it was useless to get upset. Friends took another car to get the spare key, and forty minutes later, we were on the road.

My family and I made sure to celebrate each improvement, no matter how small. It was too easy to look ahead and become impatient with my progress. During my time in Rochester, whenever I'd get frustrated, I'd remember my initial prognosis and how much progress I'd made. Taking stock and realizing it could be worse—that it had been worse—helped the bad days not seem so bad. Not only did looking back lessen my frustration, but it definitely made me feel good about where I was and how far I'd come.

As the weeks passed and I got mentally prepared to move home for good, my biggest concern was getting new therapists and going to a new rehab facility. I had such a close relationship with the people around me day in and day out. The PT, OT, Gym Tech, and nurses were like family, and I couldn't imagine not seeing them every day, but I was ready to go home. I wanted to be near my friends and family, I wanted a permanent spot, and I felt physically ready to leave. I didn't necessarily need Mayo's specialized equipment, and that made the transition easier to stomach.

I was nervous about leaving, and I didn't know what to expect, but the rehab facilities we talked to in Des Moines seemed like good replacements. I'd still get the care I needed. The transition would be hard at first, and I knew it would take time for my new therapists and me to figure each other out, but like my move to outpatient, the timing just felt right.

But going home was only a temporary stop, as my ultimate goal was to get back to college. My parents and I talked about how I'd go back to school, but I couldn't imagine making that happen when I still needed so much help. Alex was about to graduate with her RN degree, and she was ready to move on to the next chapter of her life, but she didn't know where she was going or where she wanted to live.

As we discussed the future, one day she said, "I can help you go back to school. I can live in Decorah, get a job there, and continue with some school and help you out." She was ready to do something different, she didn't want to live at home, and she knew it would make me — and our parents — feel more comfortable about me returning to school.

I was totally blown away by her offer, and it released the pressure valve of anxiety that tightened whenever I thought about or we discussed me going back to college. Suddenly, going back to school didn't seem like such a dilemma with her by my side. The best part was that it was *her* idea; she wouldn't have volunteered if she wasn't willing, and I don't think going back would have worked if she hadn't. Finally we had a plan, now all we had to do was put it into place.

CHAPTER 20

I have learned many things through all of this, but two I want to share right now. 1. God is great. Through Him all things are possible. 2. People are good. Do not let what you see on TV, read in the papers, hear on the radio, etc. bias you. We have received love, support, prayers, help, kindness, and caring from literally thousands of people.

~Terry Norton, CaringBridge, January 3, 2011

TERRY

The holiday season brought many blessings and ushered in a flurry of new experiences. In December of 2010, we took a big step forward when two of Chris's close friends stayed with him overnight. Alex and Katie had stayed with him, and we all knew the routine—the nurses coming in and out of the room and the multitude of things Chris needed help with—but no one outside the family had ever stayed with him before. It was like watching him go off to school for the first time and being forced to let go of the reigns, but it also helped us realize he could survive under someone else's supervision.

I was petrified of him returning to school. I took care of him constantly, opening doors, fetching water and ice, getting him snacks, turning on the TV, and a million other things during the day and night. I thought there was no way he could go to college when I couldn't be there with him. I just stewed about it all the time, but when his friends stayed with him overnight, it proved that he could go back to college and a normal life. His friends *did* want to help, and it wasn't a burden. People felt good about helping, especially when that friendship was already in place. He didn't have to have his family around all the time; we could eventually pass the torch to others.

After only three months of inpatient therapy, Mayo planned to move Chris to outpatient, so I pushed hard to get his stay extended from January into February. I wanted him to get as strong as possible and have as much recovery as possible before we went outpatient. I felt relieved when they agreed to the extra four weeks because I knew another month would mean greater gains for him and an easier transition for us. For example, transferring Chris into a vehicle was easier as his legs got stronger because he could use those muscles to help. Fortunately, Mayo cooperated with us and really helped meet our needs.

Four weeks went by fast, but before Chris was ready for outpatient, we had to find an accessible place to live. Fortunately, Chris was still eighteen when the accessible room at the Ronald McDonald House opened up. I loved it there. The people were phenomenal, and the concept of the Ronald McDonald House and the benefits they provided to families in need were innumerable.

Although Chris was more than ready to get out of the

hospital, I was nervous about transitioning to outpatient care. It felt similar to when we took Alex home from the hospital after she was born, and we realized we were all alone. With Chris living in the hospital, we had support services, and then all of a sudden, there was no call button. If we needed some help, we were on our own. I was scared and wondered if I knew everything I needed to know to be his sole caretaker.

While grateful to be out of the hospital and continue with outpatient care, there were a number of challenges, some unforeseen, when we moved into the Ronald McDonald House. His room was tiny, even with a laundry area, a kitchen, and a small den. It felt claustrophobic for us because it was essentially a place to sleep. When we were at the hospital, if we got bored, we went down to the gift shop, the chapel, the cafeteria, or the sixth floor lobby where we had a great view of Rochester. Mayo was huge and there were many different places to visit, including some common areas with ice cream machines. We never felt penned in or trapped because all areas of the hospital were accessible.

At the Ronald McDonald House, we only had our room. We couldn't just go down the hallway and talk to other patients because the other families were coming and going at different times, dealing with different issues, and a lot of them had younger kids. That, and the fact that Chris was the only eighteen-year-old patient at the Ronald McDonald House (he was grandfathered in when he turned nineteen), was why we never really made any connections with the people living there. We missed the nurses who'd pop in on a regular basis and the doctors we'd see in the hallways.

My biggest challenge when we transitioned to outpatient was the additional responsibilities that fell on my shoulders. Without the nursing staff at the hospital, we had to use home healthcare. The initial home healthcare worker wasn't qualified, and Chris didn't trust him not to unintentionally hurt him, so we called the company and asked for a new worker.

I organized Chris's medications for each day and made sure his prescriptions were filled. In the morning, I woke him up, got him out of bed, and moved him into his chair. If he had nursing care that day, I got him ready before the nurse arrived. After she left, I'd finish getting him dressed and brush his teeth, and then off we'd go to get breakfast. In the afternoon, if he was worn out and wanted to take a nap, I transferred him to the bed and later back into the chair. I had to make dinner and then get him ready for bed, which was a long and laborious process.

At that point in his recovery, Chris's arms would get locked around his face when he slept, and they'd be really tight in the morning. He wore braces at night on his arms and feet, and loading him up with all the gear was like getting him ready for combat. The arm braces held his arms and fingers straight during the night while he slept, while the foot braces kept him from getting what's known as "foot drop" by keeping his heels prone.

If I had any type of issue during the night, I had to deal with it on my own, unlike when we'd been on the rehab floor. There, we'd hit the call button and a couple of nurses would quickly appear ready and willing to help. When we first moved into the Ronald McDonald House, Chris fell to the floor and no matter how hard I tried, I couldn't get him up because his legs weren't strong enough to assist, and I didn't know the proper technique. I had to use the Hoyer lift. With extra time in rehab, his leg strength increased, and I learned how to position him so he could help. I wouldn't have learned any of this if we'd been in the hospital because I'd have pushed a button and the nurses would have taken care of everything. Needless to say, the adjustment from hospital care to outpatient made for a tough few weeks, but it was an essential step in preparing us for life at home.

When Chris's friends from Luther visited, Deb suggested they go to the mall after looking at the bus routes. The recreation therapists encouraged using public transportation, and the boys really wanted to get out and have some fun, but we were nervous. I'm sure his friends thought we were crazy for talking them through everything, including having the right change for the bus and making sure they were on the right side of the street. The outing provided a good view into the future for him in using public transportation and another cutting of the apron strings for us.

I peeked out the window because the bus stop wasn't far,

looking down the street to make sure everything went okay.

The trip was a pivotal step forward for his friends to use public transportation, and it was good for them to understand the whole accessibility issue. Every

"Every chance I had, I traveled to Rochester so he knew we were now on the same team."

Joe Gilson, Lifelong friend

outing Chris and I took opened my eyes to the many challenges people in wheelchairs faced on a day-to-day basis.

Once we'd settled at the Ronald McDonald House, I started back to work every other week. I'd been gone from my job for a long time, and we'd reached a point where it made more sense for Deb and me to alternate weeks. Deb was able to work remotely from Rochester with a laptop and Internet access, and my job required more face-to-face interaction. I started earning a much-needed partial paycheck and got back into a work routine, while Deb took a more active role in Chris's rehab. Chris and I had spent a lot of father-son time together, and we'd reached a point where we'd discussed every subject, rehashed every story, and relived every sports memory, so having his mom around seemed to lift his spirits.

While ready to earn a paycheck and spend more time with Katie, I underestimated how hard it was to leave Chris behind. I ridiculously assumed nobody could take care of him as well as I did, worrying that Deb would get too tired to scratch his itches, make his food, and make him comfortable. I went overboard telling her everything he liked, and she indulged me because she knew how hard it was for me to leave. Of course everything got done, and she and Chris did great, but I still had trouble letting go.

Once home, I thought I'd regroup and catch up on some sleep, but I felt guilty for not being there to help. I also let my guard down and started thinking about the future and all the ways life had changed. My emotions bounced from anger that Chris wasn't able to use his upstairs bedroom to fear over the challenges we faced ahead. I finally understood what it was like for Deb when she was at home alone.

Deb used to get upset with me because in Chris's hospital room and in the rehab rooms where he had PT and OT every day, we got terrible phone reception and my texts wouldn't go through. In the midst of getting through the day, I was too busy to call and text frequently. I finally understood her frustration with being left in the dark when I wanted constant updates but they hardly ever came.

Working every other week presented a unique set of challenges, and the hardest part was not giving 100 percent to either job. I felt partially present in both worlds, but not immersed in either one. Each week it took time to refocus my mind and get back into the swing of things. Toward the end of the workweek, I'd return a call or ask somebody to call me back knowing I wasn't going to be around the next week. Both at work and in Rochester, I was left wondering who was going to be responsible to make sure things got done when I was gone, forgetting that I'd been gone from work for months and that Deb could handle things in my absence.

I was grateful for the weeks at home alone with Katie. It was nice being together and having time to reconnect away from the hospital. Because I found it hard to come home from work and cook, we ate out quite a bit. I gained a lot of respect for Deb and felt blessed to have a spouse with whom to share my burdens.

One of the reasons we stayed so long in outpatient rehab in Rochester, even though the living conditions and being away from home was difficult, was because I was worried about what life would be like once Chris was out and we were on our own. Even though it wasn't convenient being away from home for an additional three months, I wanted to make sure he had the best equipment, the best therapy, and the best therapists working with him for as long as possible. Mayo's rehab facility and staff were the best available, so as long as he was improving and we were able to make it work, we stayed.

It wasn't easy. I started reaching out to friends and asking if they could come and help. We had another bed in the room for friends to stay and help me get Chris ready for bed, or run out and get us food, or more importantly, help me get him in and out of a regular vehicle so we could go somewhere. We didn't have a handicap vehicle, and I couldn't get him into a regular vehicle by myself. We needed two people in order to transfer him so we could go to a movie or go out to eat. When friends were around, we didn't feel so trapped and bored. I had to push Deb because she wasn't comfortable asking for help, yet I knew how critical it was to have support. I started contacting her friends and asking them to go up and stay with her and Chris.

During that time I learned the true meaning of friendship. It was easy to tell people I had their backs and I'd be there for them if they ever needed me, but that typically never happened. My friends came to Rochester when we were closing in on seven months away from home, we were tired, it was a lot of work, and we were worn down from the whole experience. They came when I asked, and they had our backs. I'm sure they had things going on at work and with their own families, but they dropped everything to be there for my family and me. Through the hardest times, our friends were there and saw us through.

Despite the monotony, I felt blessed for the time Chris and I got to spend together, time I wouldn't have had otherwise. He was right in the heart of what would have been the best years of his life where so many of his independent views were shaped. If not for his injury, I wouldn't have had his attention or the time to talk to him about faith, goal setting, character, and things I'd read that held meaning for both of us. Those definitely weren't the circumstances either one of us would have chosen, but I did the best I could to be there for him, support him, and use that time to reinforce our values.

We attended the Luther football banquet—Chris, Deb

and I—in February 2011. Chris wanted to go, but I had mixed emotions about attending. On the car ride down, I felt better than I'd felt since his injury because he was riding in the front seat with me and sitting upright as if the accident hadn't happened.

We arrived at the football banquet, and my emotions took over. Chris received a tremendous reception, and then I got up and said a quick thank-you to everyone for all of their support. Despite the warm welcome, the event was emotionally taxing.

One hundred young men. Every college in the nation has one hundred young men. Why, out of this one hundred, did our son have to be the one who got hurt?

Chris's football career was short-lived whether he got hurt or not, as he only had four years of college left to play regardless. The other guys at the banquet would be done after four years also, but they'd go on and live the rest of their lives no worse for the wear. Our son came into Luther just like everybody else—to have fun, make new friends, play more sports, and experience a little competition—but everybody else was going to walk away with their lives intact. Chris's college football experience was going to impact him—and us—for the rest of our lives.

The beautiful part was that Chris never looked at it the way I did. His perspective was completely different from ours in that it didn't seem to bother him. He liked going to the banquet, seeing his friends, and being around the guys. If it didn't bother him, I shouldn't have let it bother me, but I couldn't control my reaction. Face-to-face with what was taken away, my emotions were raw, and all I felt was the hurt.

We returned to Rochester, life got back to "normal," and I was able to focus on the bigger picture. If Chris hadn't gotten hurt, he wouldn't have had the opportunity to make an impact on people we didn't even know.

While Chris was doing outpatient therapy and living in the Ronald McDonald House, we started bringing him home on the weekends before he officially moved home. He was so excited to see our golden retriever, get back in his own house, and see his friends, but once again my emotions took over. In the hospital, I came to accept his injury because that was all we'd known there, but reality hit when we brought him home to a place where I had memories of the past. I'd clung so tightly to the idea he'd walk out of the hospital, that coming home with him in a chair felt like a blow. For his sake, I curbed my unease, let his excitement take over, and looked forward to the day when our family was back together under one roof.

Never one to sit home for long, Chris immediately asked us to teach his friends how to transfer him in and out of a car so they could go to the movies. My nerves went into overdrive thinking of all the things that could go wrong because they didn't know how to handle him safely. So much of it was technique that involved using the legs and the correct positioning of the body.

His PT, Megan, was a little bitty thing, but she moved Chris around like he weighed nothing, proving a transfer required more than brute strength. Transferring correctly was like a finely choreographed dance where one misstep ruined the whole performance. Deb reminded me that we were in our fifties, but his friends were young and strong, so lifting him up and getting him in and out of a car was no big deal for them, especially after I'd spent a long time showing them how to do it correctly. If the transfer didn't go quite right, they'd all think it was funny, Chris would think it was funny, and no one would suffer.

> *"As Chris neared his dismissal from the rehab unit and then ultimately back to the Des Moines region, I did worry that he wasn't going to cope with being in real life very well. Not because he showed signs of struggle, but mostly because that is a common occurrence for those who have suffered such a severe injury."*
>
> Megan Gill, PT, DPT, Clinical Lead Physical Therapist for Spinal Cord Injury, Mayo Clinic

Getting him out the door was only the beginning. Chris and his friends would go out late and stay out even later because they were young and that was normal, but Deb and I were struggling. We went to bed knowing that at two or three in the morning we'd get a call and have to get up and get him ready for bed. We didn't sleep well before the call, and then once we were up, it was hard to get back to sleep. Exhausted by the weekend routine, we finally decided to teach his friends how to get him ready for bed and then have them stay with him until morning. It was a workable solution that helped his parents and eased his eventual transfer home.

I wasn't able to post every day on CaringBridge while staying at the Ronald McDonald House, mostly because we were so busy and our access to a computer was limited, but also because I started to feel ambivalent about CaringBridge and what I termed the "CaringBridge Syndrome." While I thought it was important keep our posts positive, as time went by, I started feeling as if it masked reality. Everything with Chris wasn't always wonderful, and his day-to-day challenges were daunting for all of us. There was a fine line between appreciating how far we'd come and facing the reality of what he had to deal with for the rest of his life.

I don't know why it started to bother me, probably because I was so worn down. Without the support of the hospital staff, providing most meals on my own, feeling confined to our small room, and going back and forth on the weekends, my energy lagged. Writing things out on CaringBridge had always been good for me because it allowed me to process everything that had happened, step back and look at the big picture, and share some life lessons along the way, but I'd lost my zeal to post. I never wanted to focus on what Chris couldn't do because that diminished the miracles that had taken place since his injury, but never discussing our daily struggles felt a little disingenuous. Posting less frequently helped lessen my anxiety over the "syndrome."

Throughout Chris's recovery, Deb and I couldn't have been more proud of our girls. I think part of why Alex and Katie rallied around their brother so much had to do with how I was raised and how we chose to raise our kids. My older brother, Randy, was a tremendous athlete, and growing up, he was always one of the "captains" for any of our neighborhood or school sports teams. It was telling to get picked on a team and just as telling to get picked last.

One day I came home from a neighborhood game in tears because my brother hadn't picked me on his team. My dad pulled Randy aside and bent down so they were eye to eye.

"Your brother will be by your side for the rest of your life," my dad said. "He'll always have your back, and you need to always have his. Other people will come and go, but family's always there. You pick him first."

My brother picked me on his team from that day forward all the way through college.

Deb and I raised our kids using the same philosophy, and the girls really stepped up their game when Chris got injured. We were proud parents watching how they cared for and nurtured their brother, and by how much they sacrificed, even though they didn't look at it as a sacrifice. Katie gave up basketball and left every Thursday, missing time with her friends to be with

Chris over the weekend. Alex's breaks were no longer spent at home but in the hospital. I think Chris saw his sisters in a different way because they became partial caregivers.

Growing up, Alex wanted to go into nursing. I always pictured her doing something where she gave back or did something for others, so I shouldn't have been surprised when she brought up the idea of moving to Decorah with Chris to help him go back to school. She'd been thinking about it for a while, and when she first floated the idea I wasn't sure it was necessary. Although I was scared about him leaving us, I really hadn't thought through the logistics.

Her suggestion totally blew us away, and as we talked it through, it really was a brilliant idea. She'd soon graduate from college and didn't yet have a job. She could use her medical training, she was good at helping him, and she'd been around him enough that she knew what to do. Chris was very independent, but I think he really liked the idea of having Alex as a safety net. He didn't want to burden his friends, not that they'd see him as a burden, but he liked that she'd be there to take him to appointments and to therapy. We didn't know what initially prompted her to volunteer, but it turned out to be a crucial step for him to go back to school and another example of how his injury brought our family closer.

CHAPTER 21

Cast your cares on the LORD and he will sustain you; he will never let the righteous be shaken.

~Psalm 55:22 NIV

CHRIS

Eventually, I reached a point in my therapy at Mayo where I thought, *All right, I feel satisfied with what I've done here. I feel comfortable transitioning outside of their care. I'm ready now.*

Pulling out of Rochester for the last time was kind of sad. I was comfortable receiving therapy there, and I was nervous about transitioning to a new place. I was ready to move on and it was time to go home, but as I mentioned, my life felt like it was divided into two stages, pre- and post injury. All I'd known post injury was the Mayo Clinic in Rochester, so leaving to go home was like starting a whole new adventure. We thought we had everything lined up ahead of time, but we couldn't predict every situation.

Throughout my injury and recovery, pride was a big stumbling block. I had no choice but to let go of my old life where

257

I was a very independent person, made my own decisions, and did my own thing, and accept that I needed help with almost everything. Having to ask people for help was really hard because I didn't want to be a burden. I also had to swallow my pride after thinking I was going to walk out of the hospital, no matter what everyone tried to tell me.

I left Mayo with a power-assist chair, but pride tried to stop me from ordering the joystick controlled power chair for home. Megan and I went round and round about her ordering the power chair because I was adamant I'd only need the power-assist chair. She said we should order a power chair "just in case," because it was her job to make sure I was prepared when I left Mayo. Even if I didn't use it, she said it was smart to have one on hand.

She guilted me by saying she wouldn't have been doing her job if she sent me home without something I might need, and after all the trust we'd built between us, I couldn't say no. I understood her argument, but at the time I felt she didn't think I would walk again. Megan also reminded me of the importance of timing. If I didn't order the chair when I left Mayo and later discovered I needed it, I'd have trouble with insurance covering the cost.

Before I came home, and before the end-of-spring semester, I made a trip to Luther to register for classes and tour where I'd live in the fall. We met with Luther's disability coordinator, the academic support office, the residence center, and my academic advisor to devise a plan so I'd be ready for class. It was cool to see all my friends again, and I was excited to see where I'd live on campus with my future roommates. The student who lived in my new room was the same boy who came to visit me a couple of times with the pastor from Luther. He was a great resource for campus logistics.

On that same trip, I attended Luther's end of spring football meeting. It felt great to be included, but as they talked about summer workouts and their expectations for fall, I let my guard down and got emotional. I loved working out in the summer and bettering myself as an athlete. The meeting made me think about what the future would have been and how I'd miss out on being a starter the next season. I was living proof that wishing didn't change a thing, so I tucked the hurt aside and tried to focus on my goals for the summer.

The best thing about being home was just being back in a familiar place, eating home-cooked meals, going to watch my sister's softball games, and being around my friends. It provided a sense of normalcy, and I'd really missed our pets. The hardest thing about being home was working with new people and getting used to living life in a wheelchair. Our older home wasn't wheelchair accessible, and it was hard to get around the small rooms when I'd grown accustomed to maneuvering around the spacious hospital. Being stuck in our family room because I couldn't get through to the kitchen felt very isolating. It was weird not being able to go up to my room, but we made a new bedroom for me in the dining room and we made it work.

We had to find a new nursing agency, and the nurse had to figure out my routine under my direction. As we learned in our move to the Ronald McDonald House, the adjustment period was challenging. I was at the mercy of someone else's schedule. If the nurse didn't want to work on the weekends, for example, but I still needed care, accommodating my needs took time to coordinate.

I got so used to asking my family for help that I took them for granted and often forgot to say please and thank you. My parents and siblings wanted to help and they knew the severity of my situation, so in the beginning, they didn't give me grief for not asking nicely. But now at home, when I got too comfortable with them and forgot to use manners, they brought it to my attention.

They also began to recognize that I could do more things on my own if I tried. So, when I asked for help, they encouraged me to attempt it first. That was good for me because I discovered that I didn't always need their help. It was another learning period, because as I got stronger, I was able to do things I hadn't been able to do before. I was living the cliché, "You never know until you try."

While my friends were off for summer break, my parents and sister still had to work. I needed them to help me get ready for bed and put me to bed, but they wanted to end their night by ten. If my friends called and invited me to an eleven o'clock movie, even though I wanted to go, my parents didn't want to stay up until I got home. They needed their rest, but living by their schedule kept me isolated from my friends. If I did go out, they had to wake up when I got home and get me ready for bed, but that was exhausting for them. I hadn't thought about our nightlife patterns and how that would affect the family and me when I came home.

We'd taught my friends how to put me into bed and get me ready when I was coming home on the weekends, but I still needed someone to sleep by me or sleep in the room every night because I needed help with my legs and arms. I'd get muscle spasms at night where my legs would randomly kick up and swing over, and my arms would push against my face. Trying to sleep when my leg was back and to the side, and with my arms right on my face was awkward, uncomfortable, and claustrophobic. I couldn't straighten my arms and legs without help. Even if I went to bed at ten with my parents, they didn't get much sleep because I still needed help. Some nights, I woke them every hour, which was tough no matter what time they went to bed. I really struggled sleeping, and it was a job in itself just to care for me at night.

Alex volunteered to have me as her summer job, take me to therapy, be with me during therapy, and do anything else I needed. We were with each other for long stretches of time and we got sick of each other and got on each other's nerves.

If I didn't want to be on other people's schedules, I had to find someone to stay over who could go to bed when I wanted to go to bed.

The biggest blessing was having my cousin Nolan move in with me and become my personal care assistant for the summer. Nolan and I grew up together, were the same age, and had a really good relationship, so when his family came up to visit and he said he didn't have a job, he seemed like the perfect solution. At the time, we were trying to find someone to take part of the load off my sister and my parents. I was trying to use some of my friends who weren't working, but then I suggested Nolan. My parents thought it was a great idea, so we talked to him and his family, and they agreed. Nolan was a lifesaver and a great friend to have around. We were already close, but when he relocated from Iowa City to put up with me for a whole summer, we became like brothers.

We had an accessible van with a ramp at that time so Nolan could drive me where I wanted to go. When my friends wanted to go to a movie or out to eat, they didn't have to drive to my house, pick up my van, and go to the theater. Nolan living with me eliminated that time-consuming step, and he and I just met my friends at the restaurant or theater. It was great having him along because I loved hanging out with him and so did my friends.

Asking for help from my friends was definitely uncomfortable because I didn't want to be a burden. I had buddies who understood, and I think they knew I didn't want to ask. I'm not certain, but I think my family may have communicated with them about helping, because my friends were so good about jumping up to help and asking if I needed anything. The more I asked, the easier it got, and I could tell when someone didn't mind. They stopped what they were doing and did whatever I needed with a smile on their face.

My goal for that summer was to increase my independence, walk, and regain as much function and control as possible. During that time, I wore wrist cuffs from my forearm to my hand to prevent my wrists from dropping. I used the small slot in the cuff to slide silverware inside so I could eat independently, and I wanted to increase my hand strength so I could grip silverware on my own. I also worked to increase my arm strength to better use the power-assist chair and my leg and trunk strength so I could stand longer. I was basically trying to improve everything and get stronger overall.

I came home with a loaner chair to use until the custom chair I ordered was delivered. I tended to slouch, and Megan constantly reminded me to sit upright because it would help my core strength and comfort if I used correct posture. Throughout the day, my butt slowly slipped forward to the point where I'd eventually have to push myself back several times a day by leaning all the way over my legs and pushing on my feet to get myself slipped back into place.

The angle of the loaner chair was unfamiliar, so on my first day at rehab in Des Moines when I went forward to lean and push myself back, the chair was like a slide and I slipped out. I'd spent seven months at Mayo and never fell out of my chair, but on my first day in a new place I hit the ground. They got me up, I wasn't hurt, and I reminded myself to be patient because we were in a transition period.

The therapists were constantly telling me to keep moving, shift my weight around, and lean forward because staying seated in the same position for a long time put a lot of pressure on the tailbone and could cause a sore. Within a few days of falling out of my chair at rehab, at the Iowa state track meet with my friend Logan watching his girlfriend run, I leaned forward to adjust my position in the chair and felt myself slowly slipping out headfirst. *Oh, no!* The only thing between a six-foot drop and me was a railing. I tried yelling to get Logan's attention, but my voice was too soft to be heard over the crowd at Drake Stadium. My face smacked the bar of the rail, stopping my momentum and keeping me from falling off the bleachers.

I called for help. Thankfully, Logan and a couple of strangers grabbed me and hoisted me back into the chair. Logan's faced looked as if he'd seen a ghost, while my face probably looked as if I'd been in a fight. I learned the hard way to be extra careful whenever I leaned forward, but mostly I couldn't wait to get rid of the loaner chair.

My therapy hours decreased to ten hours per week, and we had to fight with the insurance company to get more. I was desperate to see improvement, and thankfully we were able to return to twenty hours a week. Even with the increased hours, the transition from Mayo was hard. The dark, cellar-like atmosphere of my PT in Des Moines was so different from Mayo's PT room with lots of windows and natural light. Des Moines also didn't have a gym tech like Amy ("Big Cat") to brighten the room with her energy.

The first couple of weeks, I wasn't doing as well as I thought I should, but I tried to be patient. Unfortunately, Des Moines didn't have equipment that was assistive enough for me to work on standing and walking. I knew from my research that the more I replicated normal gate walking, the more likely it was that the spinal cord would reprogram itself and help the nerves reconnect. We tried countless ways to replicate standing and stimulate walking, but Des Moines just didn't have a good setup, and my progress came to a screeching halt. Profoundly discouraged, I was a mess—on edge and more frustrated than I'd been throughout my entire time in rehab. My last day at Mayo had been the best therapy I'd ever had, and I was pumped about going home, only to backslide.

I was so frustrated, that my parents arranged for Alex and Nolan to do drive me to Mayo three days a week, stay in a hotel for a couple of nights, and then drive back. I was relieved to go back to Mayo and work with the therapists and Big Cat again. I was once again able to work on balance, bear weight on my feet, and perform the walking motion. After only two weeks of back and forth, I was back to where I wanted to be and making progress.

I used the RT300 therapeutic bike every day while at Mayo to help coordinate my movements, keep my muscles from atrophying, and help stimulate my arms and legs. We went through the NCAA insurance to order my own RT300, but it took a month to arrive and there wasn't another bike available near Des Moines at that time. Before we decided to spend three days a week at Mayo, we contemplated driving two hours to use the bike because I felt restless, I wanted more therapy, and things weren't going well in Des Moines.

In addition to rehab, we spent the summer at home making plans for my return to Luther. As the end of summer approached, my parents wanted me to wait one more semester before returning to college. Sending me off to college the first time was hard enough, but by the end of my senior year of high school, I was barely around due to my jam-packed schedule. The second time was much more difficult because they knew how much help I still needed. They were a part of my everyday life, and I was very dependent on them.

Alex had the most influence on their decision to let me go. Not only was she going with me, but as a recent graduate, she convinced them I needed to have the full college experience. She knew it would be good for me to get away and that I'd be fine once we established a routine. It also helped that my parents knew my Luther friends were responsible. They'd been around enough both at Mayo and at home in the summer that they understood my needs, and my parents trusted them.

My parents weren't the only ones with doubts. I needed lots of help, and it was reassuring that Alex wanted to live nearby. I'd only spent ten weeks at school my freshman year before the accident, and fortunately I'd developed really meaningful relationships with my friends in a very short time. I needed help with a lot of personal matters, so being comfortable with my friends and roommates was important.

Luther only had one dorm on campus that was accessible, and my friends agreed to live with me in that dorm. The school also allowed four guys to live in the cluster so one could stay with me overnight if I needed help with straightening my legs, bending my arms, adjusting the covers, or whatever came up. I had a lot of anxiety wondering what would happen if my friends weren't able to stay with me, help me into bed, take me to

"After months of intensive rehab and physical therapy at the Mayo Clinic, Chris was able to return the following year as a full time student. When he was in the process of finalizing the roommates who would make up the twelve-person handicap accessible dorm in Farwell Hall, he extended to me the last spot in the small single room. I took him up on his offer, not knowing that I was entering a period in my life where I would develop some of the most important friendships of my life."

Rich Holton, Luther
classmate and friend

class, and do all the things my family had been doing since my injury.

With my living arrangements and class schedule already in place, I was able to move in two weeks before classes when the rest of the football team arrived. It was good to get there early, get adjusted, and have both Nolan and Alex to help with the transition. We used that time to prepare for life on my own in the dorm and to teach my friends how to help me before Nolan had to leave and Alex moved into her own place.

When I transitioned to school, I didn't feel comfortable asking people I didn't know well to help because I felt like a burden. If someone sighed and asked, "What do you need now?" their half-sarcastic, half-true reaction rubbed me the wrong way.

Early on, when I felt a sense of grief, I wanted to say, "You know what? I can't do this. I'm sorry I can't do it on my own. I wish I could."

Over the course of my injury, as I became more comfortable asking for help, I slowly stopped saying please and thank you again. While grateful for help, saying please and thank you seemed redundant because everyone—including me—knew I needed help. The assistance I needed to function day in and day out with tasks like putting on a coat or transferring me to bed didn't feel like favors because it was just my life. I always asked nicely, but I didn't show as much appreciation as I should have. I took for granted that my family and friends would help because I was used to being cared for and helped. Fortunately, during my first year back at college, I learned that showing appreciation helped ease my guilt, and that family, friends, and acquaintances didn't mind helping when I was grateful.

My friends made my time at college possible because they took the time to drive me places, push me places, help me get food, or brush my teeth, and assist with a thousand other things. They went out of their way to make me feel comfortable by sacrificing some of their freedom in order to make sure I was included. My friends were the reason I was able to have a regular college experience, and I didn't have the words to express the depth of my gratitude.

Considering my experience in Des Moines, I was also nervous about the therapy options in the small town of Decorah. Mayo was closer—an hour and fifteen minutes away as opposed to three hours from home—so we made arrangements to travel to Mayo twice a week. I had class on Monday, Wednesday, and Friday, and I spent Tuesday and Thursday at Mayo. Most of my therapy took place in Decorah, which meant finding the right facility.

After a tough summer back home and falling to the ground during the first training session there, I had serious doubts about locating adequate therapy in Decorah. I prepared for the worst when I visited Euro-Team and PT Lisa Krieg. My biggest concern about going back to college was my recovery, so therapy during school would essentially make or break my college experience. When Lisa said she wanted to stand me up right away, I thought she was kidding. PTs err on the side of caution, and it took weeks before someone was comfortable enough to stand me up by themselves at Mayo. I knew I could do it, but I was taken aback by her fearlessness. She was short but strong and pulled me right up to standing without a problem. I grinned inside and out because I knew God had planted me in the right place to maximize my recovery.

Lisa reminded me of Megan in that she was very proactive, she wanted our time together to be intense, she wanted to push me, she wanted to try new things, and she was willing to do whatever it took to reach my goals. Since both Megan and Lisa were my therapists,

> *"I will always remember when Chris and his family came to Euro-Team that first day, willing to trust a PT in a small, rural clinic to keep him going toward his bigger picture of moving, walking, and living!"*
>
> Lisa Krieg,
> PT Euro-Team in Decorah

they communicated about what was working well for team Norton.

Having my own therapeutic bike at the Luther training area was a huge benefit because I used it all the time to maintain my muscles and get stronger. I worked out on the bike as often as possible for extra therapy. One of my friends would come along and set me up, and the head trainer always made himself available because he also knew how to set me up on the machine.

I was happy with my role on the football team as a source of motivation. I didn't want or need special attention, I just wanted to be treated like a player. Coach Durnin was great about letting me choose whatever role I wanted. He said I could be a coach and come to the coaching meetings, or be on the sidelines as a player, or do both. But it turned out that I had a very small role with the team because I was busy with school, and my therapy was always during practice.

Coach Durnin told me I'd be the honorary captain at Luther's first home game. I was thrilled, and I knew right away I wanted to stand on the field with the help of the other captains. I was strong enough that the guys could position themselves on each side of me and help me stand. I was nervous about the logistics, but it was a good way to celebrate how far I'd come with my family, friends, and some of the Mayo staff who were a big part of my recovery.

I was really worried about physically standing because I was so inconsistent in my attempts at therapy. On a bad day, or even just an okay day, I might not be able to stand. I prayed to God, practiced, and communicated with the captains who'd push me out to the center of the field and stand me up so they'd be prepared for anything. We rehearsed by simulating the whole process a couple times with Alex there telling them what to look for to make sure I didn't get lightheaded. While the captains were friends, they were also juniors and seniors who were unfamiliar with my routine. Thankfully, it went off without a hitch, and it was great to have so many friends—old and new—in attendance.

Around my return to Luther, I realized how lucky we were to have the NCAA insurance. My parents appreciated it once they understood that along with the medical bills, the expense of commuting back and forth between Rochester and Des Moines was eligible for reimbursement from the NCAA. Until that time, they were flying through their resources, paying for everything on their own and with the help of friends. NCAA insurance lifted some of the financial pressure, and I could tell it helped ease their tension.

Once we realized the full extent of the policy's coverage, we began paying people by the hour for assistance. At first, the insurance company said a family member couldn't claim the assistance funds, so when my sister was taking me to therapy in the summer as part of her job, my parents were funding her the best they could. Then they decided to fight the insurance company. We believed Alex should get paid because she was sacrificing her nursing career to help me. The insurance company relented, and she got paid for helping me every day with my therapy.

The same applied to Nolan when his job was to take care of me for the summer—and my friends at college when they'd get me to bed, stay with me overnight, and help me travel. Being able to pay my friends took the pressure and attention off of the time it took for them to help. Knowing my friends were getting paid and not just doing favors for me relieved some of my stress. Sometimes they didn't feel good about accepting money because they were my friends, and while I understood, I wanted them to get paid so they'd never feel put out. Occasionally, I wanted them to assist with extra work outside my therapy and paying them eased my guilt at asking.

There was a huge learning curve doing my schoolwork on an iPad, and it was really hard to figure out how to write papers and type with my arms. Sometimes I could only use my left arm to type because my right arm was still really weak. I had to take frequent breaks from schoolwork due to muscle fatigue. I tried to use my right arm when my left needed a break, and over time both arms got much stronger and the breaks were less frequent. No matter what arm I used, I was terribly slow because I had to type one letter at a time with the side of my knuckle. Sometimes I used the voice recognition software, but it was far from perfect. I tried dictating papers to my sister, but I'd lose my train of thought. Writing papers, getting my schoolwork done, and figuring out programs that allowed me to turn in my work and complete worksheets were some of my biggest challenges.

Despite my busy schedule, I didn't want to give up any therapy time just because I was in school. I was still doing six hours of therapy a day on top of school and the two-and-a-half hour round-trip commute to Rochester. At first, my life was nothing more than school and therapy, sixteen hours a day. After the first couple of weeks on that schedule I got sick because I was completely worn down. I eventually acclimated to the intense schedule, and it turned into a strict routine I refused to break.

Alex often said she didn't know how I fit everything in, being a full-time student, a full-time therapy patient, and making time for friends, but it wasn't a choice. I didn't complain even though it was a ton of work because I did what I had to do to get by. On the weekends, I always made time for fun, as it was the only way I could make it through the week, and that was enough to keep me sane.

By late October, I needed Alex less and less. Going back to school was definitely a transition that turned into a progression. For example, in the beginning I had Alex push me to my classes and meet me at different places on campus. After establishing a routine, I realized I had friends whose paths I crossed along my route who were more than happy to help me get from place to place, so I needed her less frequently. Once back at school, I made even more friends, and my pool of helpers was larger too. Within a few months, I was living on my own terms, pursuing a college degree, working hard to physically improve, and enjoying every bit of fun along the way.

CHAPTER 22

I give thanks that I had the benefit of growing up in a coaching family. I believe coaching and parenting have so much in common. These last eight months have been my toughest assignment for both. Through them I learned the difference between "punishment" and "teaching," the difference between "building up" and "tearing down," and the difference between "encouraging" and "discouraging." As a parent and a coach, our children/players need us the most when things are not going well. That is when the true character of a parent/coach comes through.

~Terry Norton, CaringBridge, June 28, 2011

TERRY

The technology and adaptive equipment we needed to purchase for Chris once he was out of rehab was overwhelming, and it didn't help that I was really resistant to even discussing it when he was still at Mayo. I wanted him to have everything he needed, but I remained convinced he was going to walk out of the hospital. We'd make it happen whatever it took, but in the back of my mind I thought we weren't going to need much, and what we did need, we wouldn't need for long.

For example, even after seven months in rehab, we chose to have our insurance company rent a van instead of buying one ourselves. I thought for sure we'd only need the vehicle for a month or two, so it made more sense to rent it a month at a time. When Chris went back to school, we came to our senses and bought a van, thanks to the NCAA insurance policy.

We didn't fully understand how blessed we were to have the NCAA's catastrophic policy until about three or four months into our hospital stay when we realized all the extra things they paid for that our primary insurance didn't cover. Unfortunately, at the beginning, we had to fight for every benefit.

Despite the bumpy start, the catastrophic policy proved instrumental in Chris's continued recovery and our ability to maintain a normal life. Primary insurance, for example, typically didn't cover home healthcare. They only covered up through a certain point, and then you were on your own, if not for the catastrophic policy. Most often, families had a family member take over once insurance ran out, or they hired a service, but home healthcare was very expensive.

In deciding what needed to be done to the house, I tried to balance the belief that Chris was going to walk again with the reality that it might not happen within the timeframe we wanted. Deb helped me realize that installing a ramp didn't mean we'd given up on him walking, and putting in a roll-in shower didn't mean he'd never be able to take a standing shower. I had to come to that gradually, because initially it felt like waving a white flag and giving up on everything we'd fought, prayed, and hoped for. Deb said that making life easier for Chris didn't diminish our hopes and prayers for improvement, but would make our lives easier in the meantime, and she was right.

Luckily, we lived in a wonderful community, and a local contractor stepped up and offered to help. Our original plan was to have the company oversee the project while our friends volunteered their time to do the labor. Knowing better, the contractor brought his crew in and had the work completed in one day free of charge. We only paid for the materials. They raised the main floor where there'd been a stair, knocked an opening between the den and the kitchen, installed a ramp, replaced our shower with a tile roll in, and widened the entrance to our kitchen. Other than those accommodations, we didn't do more because we wanted Chris to live in the house to really know what we needed changed. We also had the insurance company to deal with, which slowed the process.

As the weeks passed and we mentally prepared to move home for good, one of our biggest priorities was to make sure Chris stayed connected with Mayo. On our own, it was nearly impossible to keep abreast of the latest technology and equipment, while Mayo stayed on top of the most current research and passed along information about any big breakthroughs or new pieces of equipment. I had mixed feelings about leaving Mayo because we'd met a lot of great people, but we were there for such a tough reason. Mayo was great, they were professional, and a lot of people really came through for us, but at the same time we wished he'd never been a patient.

I couldn't wait to be together again as a family. I missed

having family time, sleeping under the same roof, having our network of friends close by, the normalcy of working during the week, and getting together to play cards with others or go out for dinner on the weekends. Coming home on the weekends while we stayed in the Ronald McDonald House had given us a taste of what we craved and helped us ease into the challenges we'd face once home for good.

Probably one of the worst things I had to do was clean out Chris's dorm room. Luther College really worked with us because I started getting calls pretty quickly after his injury about getting his stuff out of the room. His roommate was upset because they wanted to move another person in, and with everything we had to deal with, cleaning out his stuff was the last thing on my mind. I told the football coach, who got a hold of someone in administration, and we didn't have to move his stuff out right away. Problem solved.

When I finally had a chance to clean out his room, I drug a friend along with me because I knew it would be emotionally taxing. We'd moved him into college with lots of hopes and dreams for the next phase of his life, and all the little things we'd packed for him were there having hardly been used. Cleaning it out felt like getting a beat down, and I was grateful to have a friend along for encouragement.

Deb and I knew there was no way to repay the friends, family members, and strangers who'd been so generous since Chris's accident. We paid it forward whenever we could, and followed up with folks who hit hard times, even when it wasn't convenient. The one thing we learned was that we needed to be more deliberate in helping other people when they were hurting by not asking how we could help, but finding something to do and getting it done.

The first few weeks at home were pretty frustrating. The biggest challenge was trying to match our schedules and finding reliable home healthcare. God continued to grant miracles when we needed them most. My nephew, Nolan, needed a job at the exact time we desperately needed help. The same age as Chris, Nolan was the perfect nighttime until morning companion. He stayed the summer, helped us move Chris back into college, and even stayed in Chris's dorm room those first few days to help show his buddies what needed to be done.

Chris's feelings were hurt on more than one occasion when he wasn't invited out because his friends didn't know how to include him, and there was nothing worse than watching him struggle emotionally. Getting from where he wasn't invited to where they now carried him up and down stairs was a gradual transition that started with me teaching them how to transfer him in and out of the car, teaching them how to fold up his wheelchair, and getting him ready for bed at night.

His friends from home hadn't been around him as much as his college friends. The kids from Luther, even though they weren't caring for him yet, were more comfortable handling him and helping out when needed. Being vocal with his hometown friends was good training for Chris for when he went back to school in terms of telling people what he needed and directing his care.

Deb and I decided that when Chris came home, he wasn't going to sit inside watching TV all day. We were going to make things happen so he could participate in any activity to the fullest. Life wasn't going to stop because of his injury. Deb carried a lot of her work strengths into lining up home healthcare so Chris had the ability to travel. Whatever needed to be done, our attitude was always that come hell or high water, we'd make it happen.

The temporary nature of his stay at home made planning difficult, because while trying to figure out a system for when he was home, we were also making plans for him to return to college in the fall. Returning to Luther never felt unobtainable, but it was scary, especially for me with my focus on logistics. I was so overwhelmed with all of the challenges he faced when going back to school, at one point, I wanted him to delay his return. I felt he'd be that much stronger if he waited one more semester.

Deb was the voice of reason. "We'll make it work," she said. Where I wanted to know how everything was going to flow, she calmly said, "We'll get there and figure it out. It's going to work out fine." She was right, and I tried really hard not to look too far out, but that was easier said than done.

I was anxious about Chris going back to school because I'd been there since his accident, making sure he was taken care of, and I felt he should live with Alex. On the flip side, I knew he wouldn't integrate or be immersed in the college experience if he lived off campus. I knew it would be better for him to live as one of the guys in the dorm, so we compromised by finding an apartment for Alex only five minutes from campus.

I drove everybody nuts during that time because I liked to have my *I*s dotted and my *T*s crossed, with everything planned out in advance. I stewed over every little detail.

How's he going to get to each class? Who's going to open the doors for him? Is each building accessible? Will there be somebody there to take notes for him? How will his textbooks be delivered? He can't hold a textbook or turn a page, so his books will have to be e-books. How will he take his tests? Who's going to get him ready every morning? Who's going to put him in bed? Who's going to be there to help him at night?

Deb reminded me that we couldn't anticipate every issue or plan each minute of his day, and she reassured me that most things would take care of themselves. I had to come to terms with the fact that we weren't going to have it all figured out, and that was okay.

We talked through our concerns with several of Luther's staff, Chris's roommates, and friends of ours who lived in the area. Football coach, Mike Durnin, helped us find Alex an apartment, and friends who lived in Decorah let me store some of our stuff in their garage and were available as a safety net if Alex had any problems.

Alex volunteering to help her brother was a tremendously generous gift to our family. Deb and I would never have asked her to do it, but Chris couldn't have made the transition without her. Even when we thought we had everything covered, there were times when something came up and she was there for him in a way no one else would have been. She never saw it as a sacrifice, and she'll never know the depth of our gratitude.

About two or three weeks before Chris went back to school, I was so consumed with the details that I realized we hadn't considered Alex's emotional well-being. What would she do when he was in class? What would she do at night when he was with his friends? We were so focused

"For some reason, I wasn't nervous about moving to a town three hours from home, not knowing anyone, living in an apartment by myself, and not having my usual support system around. But I didn't even think twice about it, which surprises me with how shy and how much of a homebody I really am now. I honestly couldn't stand the thought of not being near my brother, and feeling powerless, and not being able to be right there if he needed something."

Alex Norton, Chris's sister

on getting him moved back that we temporarily lost sight of

282

what *her* life would be like when she wasn't helping make life easier for Chris.

Once they were in Decorah, Alex asked Chris to join her at the apartment each week for dinner so he could be there for her in the same way she was there for him. During the day, she had her hands full getting him to class, picking up medications when needed, taking care of his laundry, making sure he got his lunch, and a thousand other things, but at night, he was with his buddies while she was in a new town and didn't know anyone.

Chris often brought his buddies over, and Alex cooked for them too. Since there was only a one-year age difference between Alex and the seniors at Luther, she became friends with some of the guys from the football team and their girlfriends. She soon had her own social group to hang out with when she wasn't helping Chris.

When fighting for Alex to get paid for helping Chris, I had to play the heavy again with the insurance company. Alex was a registered nurse working for fifteen dollars an hour when they normally paid an RN twenty-five dollars an hour, and the insurance company didn't want to pay her at all because she was family.

I put my foot down and said, "No. We're not going to find somebody who doesn't know Chris, who isn't a family member, and isn't as skilled." We were so grateful for the policy, but wished we didn't have to battle to receive the benefits.

Chris went back to school early to report in with the football team. Luther's head football coach, Mike Durnin, did a wonderful job of making Chris feel like part of the team, and we liked the idea of him moving in two weeks before school started so he could get back into a routine, become used to dorm life, and figure out how to maneuver around campus. Nolan came with us and stayed in the dorm with Chris the first couple nights to help with the transition, while Alex moved into her apartment.

We were blessed to find a home health care nurse, Nancy, who took excellent care of Chris. She came in three or four times a week to do his personal care, but she also made sure his medications were organized, picked up his room, put away his laundry, and did all kinds of extra things she didn't have to do. She was wonderful, Chris thought the world of her, and Deb and I couldn't have been happier to have her in his life.

Before Chris went back to school, we knew the character of his college friends based off his experience playing football and when he was in the hospital, but we had no idea how that would transfer once he returned. It was one thing to be a good friend and have fun with him, and another altogether to meet his needs and basically serve him. To our great relief, Chris's friends embraced him and made him a part of the group. As a parent, seeing how his friends took care of him and loved him eased our minds so much, and it gave us faith in the improperly dubbed "me" generation. Not only did they help him in the dorm and on campus, but they also took him tubing down the river, to concerts, camping, and on a spring break trip to the beach.

One of the benefits of the NCAA policy was that it paid for non-skilled care. If a friend wanted to help Chris get ready for bed, do his laundry, or take him to ride the exercise bike, we could pay him through our insurance. At first, a lot of his friends didn't want to get paid to help. We understood and respected their attitude, but we also wanted to have someone there at all times whose job it was to help. He needed assistance and somebody had to do it, so getting paid made it mutually beneficial. Several of his friends quit their work-study jobs or their part-time jobs because we were able to supply them with a steady income.

We didn't want Luther to hand Chris anything, or make it easy for him, but we hoped they would work with him in doing his schoolwork a different way. For example, he couldn't write with a pen and paper or fill out a test. My hope was that they'd make adaptations so he'd get the same educational opportunities as everyone else in a way that kept the playing field level, yet didn't put him at a disadvantage.

Fortunately, they had most of that worked out prior to him starting classes, and what they didn't, they were able to work through as they went along. Student services coordinated the effort to have someone in Chris's class take notes, put his tests on the computer so he could take them in the library, and download his textbooks to his iPad. They were really good about getting that set up and working with his instructors.

Luther's head athletic trainer, Brian Solberg, allowed us to keep the RT300 bicycle in a special room, and he made his staff available to help Chris, which was a huge help in making sure Chris continued his therapy. Brian also advocated for sidewalks and helped with different areas on campus that weren't conducive to a wheelchair. He pushed for fixes to routes Chris routinely traversed.

We contacted the rehab places Mayo had recommended in Decorah and explained Chris's situation. We asked if they'd worked with someone with his injury before and if they'd be able to take him on as a patient. Most therapists saw a patient three times a week for forty-five minutes, but Chris wanted therapy every day for several hours a day, so he would significantly add to a therapist's schedule. We didn't want to bounce around from place to place and therapist to therapist, but after our experience in Des Moines, our expectations were pretty low.

The first time we took Chris to meet physical therapist Lisa Kreig at Euro-Team, she wanted to check him out, so she grabbed him, stood him up, strapped a harness on, and started walking him around as if she'd been working with him for years. My fears about the quality of therapy in Decorah went out the window when I saw she wasn't afraid to jump right in.

Deb and I knew right away he'd be in good hands. Chris loved working with Lisa because she was go, go, go for two solid hours. Lisa, along with Jennessa Luzum, his OT at Winneshiek Medical Center, were true blessings because getting the right therapy was just as important to Chris as getting back to college.

Chris was worried about fitting everything in between school and therapy. At that point, he'd been out of school for a year. Suddenly, he was a full-time student doing full-time therapy, and it was a lot. Deb and I were worried about him trying to do too much. After an adjustment period, he settled into a manageable routine.

It meant a lot to us when Coach Durnin called and told us Chris would be an honorary team captain at the first home game. It was an honor to our family, as well as a testament to Mike's hard work at making us feel connected and Chris feel special and a part of the program. Chris had left the field in a helicopter, so coming back and being able to stand on the field made for an extraordinary and bittersweet day.

> *"It was fun tailgating with them at the first home football game of the 2011 season. Chris was named an honorary captain. A tremendous applause and a standing ovation came from the crowd as Chris appeared on the field with the help of two of his friends — members of the Luther football team."*
>
> Luann Smith, Retired Luther Employee

Three or four of his Mayo therapists came wearing T-shirts that said "Team Norton," and that really meant a lot to our family. I tried to ignore the ache in my heart and focus on Chris standing for the National Anthem and the coin toss, and appreciate the crowd's standing ovation. Our family beamed with pride on the sidelines—Chris had come so far in a very short period of time.

The following Saturday, we went to Central College to watch Luther play the team Chris went up against when he was injured. After the game, Central's coach, Jeff McMartin, presented Chris with a football, while the Central players acknowledged Chris individually. When the players went to the locker room, I noticed a Central player standing off to the side, looking a little emotional. Some parents came up and introduced themselves, waved the player over, and explained that he was the boy who'd collided with Chris on the play when he was injured. It wasn't until he and his parents hugged Chris that I realized the weight he must have carried with him over the past year, even though it was just a freak accident and it wasn't his fault. I was glad he came over, because it was a tender and meaningful moment that I hope helped put his mind at ease.

Back home, with Chris and Alex in Decorah, Deb, Katie, and I heaved a sigh of relief. Within months, we'd made two huge transitions, and with the help of family and friends, we'd somehow made it work. One of the things Deb and I continuously battled internally was not putting everything on Chris's injury. When we worried if he'd meet the right girl, or take care of himself when he was away, or get a good job, we tried to remember that we had the same worries for Alex and Katie. It was too easy to place, "because of his injury" on the back of normal parental fears. Armed with that knowledge, we thanked God for our blessings and kept on praying for the future.

CHAPTER 23

I keep my eyes always on the Lord.
With him at my right hand, I will not be shaken.

~Psalm 16:8 NIV

CHRIS

When I was in high school, I had no idea about my future. I loved the lake and I wanted to make enough money to have a lake house. I thought becoming a lawyer would be a natural fit because lawyers made a lot of money, and I enjoyed a good argument. As a lover of the stock market, I also considered business and finance. Like most kids my age, all I knew was that I wanted to make money while somehow making a difference.

When I started back to school in the fall of 2011, I was intent on going to law school to possibly become a lobbyist or an advocate for people with spinal cord injuries. I wanted to do some sort of legal work to help injury victims who needed assistance with funding and working with insurance companies. By then, I knew the system was broken for most patients forced to stop rehab when their insurance ran out, and I longed to improve the system any way I could.

As I made progress in therapy, my plans for the future changed accordingly. I considered becoming an engineer when I saw a need for better, more affordable equipment and technology for spinal cord injury patients. I hadn't totally given up on the law, as the need for improved insurance coverage for injury victims and advocates for people in my situation was great. My injury and recovery dominated the career avenues I explored, but I eventually circled back to business.

The student academic support center at Luther was a big help to me. For instance, they coordinated a system where students were paid a small stipend for taking class notes, typing them up, and then e-mailing them to me. I was able to pay attention to what the teacher was saying instead of worrying I wasn't getting it all recorded. Once I knew my way to each classroom and had someone lined up to take notes, I was able to relax and concentrate on my studies.

My teachers were given advanced notice about my presence in their class, and I communicated with them about some of my needs and how they could help me succeed. For example, instead of handing out a paper copy, teachers scanned the handouts and e-mailed them to me so I could do worksheets and readings on my iPad. The teachers were all very flexible in allowing me to turn in my work electronically.

Having Alex around school really put me at ease, especially during the transition. If it wasn't for her willingness to put her life on hold for me, I wouldn't have been able to live on campus and continue college at Luther. Before Alex and I moved to Decorah, I was nervous for her. She was going to be living by herself, she didn't know anyone but me, and I started to feel badly that she was coming to help me without any friends of her own. If she was with me all the time, how was she going to make friends? I was worried and scared for her emotional well-being.

In the beginning, I could tell she was nervous about the isolation. We hung out a lot because she was involved with pretty much everything in my life, especially that first semester. Alex was a social person who didn't want to hang with her brother all the time, so it didn't take long before she began making some good friends of her own. A lot of people knew she was living alone, and they took it upon themselves to include her. Eventually, I was asking her to hang out with me because she'd made such good friends from Luther that when she wasn't helping me, she was having fun with them.

I had scheduled patient nursing care for Monday, Wednesday, Friday, and Saturday mornings to help get me out of bed, go to the bathroom, shower, shave, and cut my hair. At first, the nurses rotated, but soon Nancy became my main nurse, solidifying her status as my mom away from home. She took really good care of me and even did things for me outside of her nursing responsibilities, like picking things up for me at Walmart, making my bed, cleaning my room, and sometimes doing my wash. She made me feel special, and I was blessed to have her.

When Nancy's aide, Sandy, moved from Decorah to New York, Kaitlyn took over for Sandy, helping me for over two years. She did all the extra stuff like Nancy—picking up things at Walmart, keeping my room orderly, and driving me to appointments.

I always knew my college friends were unique in how supportive they were, but when it came down to really depending on them at school, I could count on them for anything. I trusted them, they always looked out for me, and they tried to include me whenever possible. It was one thing for my friends from back home to be there

"I still remember the very first visit with Chris. I was very impressed with how he arrived with two big football buddies. I was amazed at how kind, caring, and helpful they were. The support he had from friends and family was unmatched. His personality and demeanor was also unmatched."

Jennessa Luzum OTR/L CHT, Winneshiek Medical Center

for me because we'd grown up together, but I'd only known my college friends for a short time before my injury. They went out of their way to help with unexpected loyalty, sacrificing for my benefit, and were willing to take on the added responsibility of caring for me. I depended on them, they understood that, and selflessly helped as if it were no big deal. My college buddies became my brothers.

As much as my friends tried to include me in everything, I sometimes declined their invitations. For example, I desperately missed playing basketball and shooting baskets, so whenever my friends said they were going to play a game of pick-up basketball and asked if I wanted to go with them, I'd tell them to go ahead without me. They wanted to include me, which was awesome, but I would have given anything to play a game of pick-up basketball and it hurt to even watch. Whenever my friends told me they were going to the rope swing in town and they'd be back in a couple of hours, I acted like it was no big deal so they didn't feel uncomfortable. I didn't want them to not go just because I couldn't, but I really wished I could've gone. It was hard on all of us because I think they knew I felt left out, but I had to accept there would always be things I couldn't do. They did the best they could to include me, and for that, I was grateful.

Thanks to Luther's head trainer, Brian Solberg, I was able to do extra workouts with the training staff. Most of my friends were busy at football practice, and after the first semester, Alex was busy working part time and doing schoolwork, so Brian showed the student trainers how to help me with the bike. A lot of the student trainers wanted to be physical therapists, so helping me was great experience, and I became really good friends with them. Some of them even went to PT with me and assisted me in the pool. The student trainers were eager to help, they kept me focused, and they saved me from bugging my roommates all the time.

I marked the one-year anniversary of my injury by going out with friends. I felt a lot of emotions that day, more than I ever thought I would. I couldn't believe it had been a year, and yet it seemed like a lifetime had passed since my injury. I took the time to reflect on how far I'd come in a year, and eagerly anticipated where I'd be the following year. The one-year mark was especially hard because at the time, I didn't know my path. Even though I was inspiring and motivating others, I still felt a bigger purpose and meaning waiting just out of reach. The uncertainty about my future made it scary.

The Saturday after I served as honorary team captain for Luther's first home game, my parents and I went to the Central vs. Luther game at Central College. After the game, my family and I were really touched when the Central team came over to shake my hand and the coaches told me they were praying for me. Later, a Central player and his family approached and asked to take a picture. There was no doubt in my mind that the player with the pale face and glassy eyes was the kid involved in the play where I broke my neck. After a small exchange and the picture, they walked away. My dad confirmed he was the kid whose leg my head collided against.

If we'd spoken about the play, I would have told him it

didn't matter whose leg my head hit that day. It wasn't his fault, and it wasn't my fault, it was just an accident during a football game. I never once wondered who he was or felt any resentment or anger toward him, but I could tell he was shaken by what happened. I hope he found some peace after our exchange.

I was incredibly surprised and honored when my football coach, Mike Durnin, nominated me for the 2011 America's Choice for Courage in Sports award. I was doubly excited because if I won, I'd get to make an appearance on the *CBS Early Show*. I thought there was no way I'd win, but after a big voting push by my family and friends, I made it into the finals. I found out I'd won a month and a half before they released the names to the public, and I was so pumped, but I had to keep it a secret. Winning meant my family and I would get to fly to New York City for the official announcement.

Flying for the first time since my accident made me nervous because I didn't know what to expect. I'd flown before, but I couldn't recall ever seeing anyone in a wheelchair on an airplane. After struggling to maneuver through stores and even our home, I knew airplane aisles were too skinny for a wheelchair.

At the airport, I transferred to an aisle chair, a really narrow wheelchair, and loaded thirty minutes before anyone else because it took some time to slide in between the rows and transfer into the seat. I was nervous for takeoff and landing because I felt as if I was going to slide out or fly forward with the momentum, but between the seatbelt and my dad's arm, I stayed put.

My friends Shawn and Nick from West Point met us in the city, and we felt like kings being picked up by Escalades and Mercedes and driven around while Jay-Z and Alicia Keys' song "New York" blared from my phone. I'd never been to New York City, and the sights and sounds made me feel as if I'd landed on cloud nine. They even put us up at a nice hotel downtown.

My family and I got up early the next morning to be at the CBS Studios where the makeup and hair people treated us like stars. No one really explained exactly what to expect on the show, and the next thing we knew, we were in the studio, and they announced we'd go live in ten seconds. My stomach curdled with nerves as the countdown began. With no idea what questions were coming, or what we were supposed to say, we answered without thought. Minutes later, when the segment was over, I thought we'd handled it well.

CBS and Intersport, the company behind the award, gave us tickets to the Rutgers-Army game at Yankee Stadium where they treated us to a tour of the new facility and the Yankees' locker room. Yankees General Manager, Brian Cashman, also gave me a baseball signed by closing pitcher and future Hall of Fame inductee, Mariano Rivera. In addition to the tour and the ball, the Yankees gave us sideline passes and suite tickets with access to a VIP lounge and dinner.

We also met with Eric LeGrand at the game because we

were both in the running for the Courage in Sports award and he was there supporting his alma mater, Rutgers. Eric was upbeat, happy, and optimistic, and his family was very nice and down-to-earth, but meeting him was very humbling. His family kept asking me questions because the location of our injuries, between the C3-C4 vertebrae, was the same, and yet I could tell they were wondering how I had regained so much more strength and movement than Eric. Despite everything we had in common, our recovery was very different.

Eric was so happy and full of life that I understood how people were motivated by him and found inspiration in how he handled his injury and recovery. I totally understood when he said he was thankful for what he did have, as I tried not to dwell on what I didn't have, but focused on what I did have and stayed positive. Like me, he was also very grateful for his family and support system. Meeting Eric reminded me to be thankful because my situation could have been worse.

"I saw the news on Sunday of Eric LeGrand of Rutgers University. I couldn't believe 'it' could happen to two young men on the same Saturday in October. I made a point of calling the Rutgers football office on Monday morning to offer my thoughts & prayers to them and to share Chris's story."

Mike Durnin, Former Head Football Coach at Luther College

During our time in New York, we visited the Statue of

Liberty and went up to the top of the Empire State building. On our last day, I really wanted to go to Rockefeller Plaza to see the *Today* show. My family wanted to sleep in, but I pestered them until they relented. We arrived early to get a good spot along the roped off area, and my dad, never one to stand quietly, began talking to someone with security, telling him about my injury and how I loved the *Today* show and how watching it really boosted me up when I was in the hospital.

The security guard started whispering to someone else, who whispered to someone else, and before I knew what was happening, the security guard pulled aside the rope and my dad pushed me right next to the opening where Matt Lauer, Ann Curry, Natalie Morales, and Al Roker walked out. The *Today* show stars came outside and filmed their segment, and as they walked by to go back inside the studio, they all shook my hand and greeted me. We took a couple of pictures with them, and then as if in a dream, Ann Curry asked who was with me and if I wanted to go inside.

We all looked at each other as if Santa Claus had magically appeared and offered us a tour of the North Pole. With the wave of her hand, Ann gestured for my whole family to follow her inside the building, and then she just started giving us her own personal tour of the studio. She showed us the green room and offered us food. We followed her to another set where she had a segment with an author who looked nervous enough to puke.

It was surreal for us to be in the studio watching the show

being taped right in front of us, especially because it was so unexpected. We all squeezed into an elevator and followed Ann upstairs where they were taping a food segment. Someone in my family made an offhanded remark about wanting to try the food they made because it always looked good, and the next thing I knew, they handed me a plate of food. It was like a dream come true.

Ann was all set to take us to the control room, but unfortunately we had to leave to catch our flight. I was really disappointed we had to go, and so thankful to her for the spontaneous hospitality. We made our flight, and everyone was glad we got up early and made it to the show. We couldn't have had a better experience in New York.

Back at Luther, even with my hectic schedule, I always did well in school, mostly because of my work ethic. Someone once told me the phrase, "Work hard, win easy," and I kept repeating it because it just stuck. Something about it really spoke to me, and I felt it summed up in the simplest way possible what I believed to be true. By working hard and putting in the time, the results would follow. The phrase basically meant success by preparation, capturing everything I ever felt about life and how life worked. It was smooth and easily flowed off the tongue, so "Work hard, win easy" became my catchphrase.

I took every opportunity to work my muscles, like purposely eating with my right hand because it was weaker than my left, and doing mini sit-ups whenever I found the time. I would type with my left hand until it fatigued, and then start typing with my right. I tried to think of new ways to push myself because I'd get restless and feel like I needed to be doing something constantly. If I dropped my jacket on the ground, for example, it was pretty easy to get one of my nine or ten roommates to come and grab it for me. There were times when I didn't want to ask, so I'd try to pick it up, and sometimes I'd surprise myself. While watching a movie or TV show, I'd put hand simulators on my forearms that stimulated my hands to open and close, or I'd squeeze some foam blocks I borrowed from OT to work on my hand grip. My therapists gave me suggestions for things I could do on my own, and because every single part of my body needed work, I could always find something to do.

Because of the damage to my spinal cord, my body would often spasm. The spasms were kind of embarrassing because my whole body would start to shake as if I were having a seizure. There was no way to tone it down or warn friends. Stretching and exercise helped calm the spasticity, but sometimes I'd have a spasm in my rib cage that would bend me over and knock me off my chair.

One afternoon when my sister dropped me off at Mayo for therapy, while waiting for her in the lobby, a big spasm surged through my whole body and jolted me to the side. I was stuck in the public area of Mayo hanging off the side of my chair, trying desperately to get someone's attention to help me sit up. The receptionist at Mayo thought I was having a seizure or a heart attack, so she called a "45-code blue," throughout the hospital, indicating the most serious emergency. Mayo's EMS team ran over and sat me up, and when I saw the defibrillator and the syringe in their hands, I suddenly found my voice.

"I'm fine," I said. "I had a spasm, not a seizure. It's completely normal."

There were almost a dozen people standing in a semicircle around me, staring at me with equipment at the ready. Of course, Alex arrived when it was over, so I had to explain to her what had happened as people continued to run to the area in response to the code. When I got to the rehab floor and told them what happened, they thought it was funny, especially Amy.

Around Christmas time of 2011, I started receiving requests to speak at events. In January, I gave my very first speech to the senior class at Decorah High School. It was especially bad—a lot of stammering—because I hadn't taken the time to prepare. In February, I spoke at the Chapel at St. Mary's Hospital in Rochester, Minnesota.

I always felt nervous when giving a speech or a presentation, but I'd taken a lot of speech classes and done theater in high school, so it wasn't extreme or unhealthy. Whenever I spoke about my injury and recovery, the room would go silent, no one moved or fidgeted, and it seemed as if everyone held their breath as they watched me with watery eyes. It was like nothing

I had seen before, and the experience opened my eyes to the appeal of my story.

Our first family vacation after my injury was taken during spring break, and I was nervous about being a nuisance on our trip to Florida. Fortunately, my roommate, Richie, came along to help, and we quickly discovered that wheelchairs didn't work in the sand. Richie did everything he could to push me in my chair, but we gave up after fifteen feet. The hotel told my mom they had a public beach chair with giant inflatable rubber tires that rolled smoothly over the sand. While we did encounter some challenges, overall we had a really nice time.

Every day I learned ways to adapt to situations, like going to the beach, maneuvering stairs, and flying on airplanes. My friends were great about pushing me to try new things, like floating down the river. When they first suggested the outing, I told them no way. I was scared of getting hurt, but they said they'd make it work by getting a raft that had a backrest, sat low in the water so it wouldn't tip over, and by hanging on and not letting go. It sounded crazy, and my parents thought the same, but my friends insisted.

The trip was nerve racking. We had to park a long way from the access spot, so my friends had to carry me to the river. Getting the raft set up was stressful and strenuous on everyone, but once we got situated, the water felt great. I was nervous at first and remained adamant that someone stay on each side of me, but it didn't take long to realize how stable and comfortable the ride was and how little need there was to worry.

Floating along with my friends by my side felt normal and liberating. I blended in and looked and felt like anyone else on the water, relaxing and enjoying the outdoors—something I hadn't been able to do much since my injury. It felt wonderful to be out in the sun and yet not get dangerously hot, as the water kept my body from overheating. Tubing down the river was one of the best experiences I had since my injury, and made me realize that sometimes, out of fear, I over-reacted to things that weren't a big deal.

I had established a firm trust in my friends, and in the end, that trust overruled my anxiety and enabled me to try a new experience. Not everything in life was accessible, but with a little brainpower and some brawn, I didn't have to miss out. Trying new things, and taking leaps of faith with my friends and family by my side, helped pave the way to my future.

CHAPTER 24

I have learned a lot from Chris over the last nineteen months, primarily about faith and trust. What it means to believe there is a plan for you when you go six weeks without being able to move your legs or nineteen months without walking. About perseverance — having to work for hours on end both in school and therapy to try and get a little better each day. About perspective — realizing all of the blessings we have and we take for granted, and appreciating the little things in life, and that the word "can't" really means "won't." Because the fact is that there is nothing you "can't" accomplish with faith in God, prayer, and determination. A good friend of mine recently said it best. "Chris just won't be denied!"

~Terry Norton, CaringBridge, May 31, 2012

TERRY

On the one-year anniversary, while Deb and I wished Chris had never been hurt, we couldn't ignore all the blessings that had occurred along his journey. We looked back at our lowest point on the day Chris got hurt, and we realized the positives had simply multiplied since that horribly uncertain time. Whether it was the medical professionals at Mayo who touched his life, the strangers who renewed our faith in humanity, the friends who kept us afloat, the opportunity for his return to college, the therapists he found in Decorah, his beloved nurse Nancy, his sisters' sacrifices, his college friends' dedication, the list went on and on. Along with the progress he'd made, we focused on the blessings of the people put in our path.

We communicated with either Chris or Alex daily through text. We didn't talk on the phone much because they were so busy, and typically with Chris, communication was feast or famine. When he had a lot of stuff going on, we didn't hear from him often. When he was on a roll about something with school or rehab, we'd hear from him multiple times a day. It was nice to have Alex there to fill in the gaps.

As a testament to his hard work and effort, Chris made the dean's list his spring semester of 2012. We were really proud of him because we knew the extra things he went through every day just to make it to class. Everybody else at Luther rolled out of bed and off they went, but Chris had to start his day an hour early, and it took him a lot more time to take a test and to complete his schoolwork. We never expected him to hold that high standard during his entire college career, but it was something to be proud of because we knew what it took for him to achieve it.

To be honest, Chris's success in college changed my perspective in general. In my job as an educator, whenever I encountered students who had thousands of excuses why assignments didn't get done, I had little patience knowing how hard Chris worked to be successful. Life is difficult, and those who do well put in the time because they want to succeed.

Chris never focused on excuses, he focused on making things happen, and if *he* could do it, so could anyone else.

One of the things Deb and I talked about when Chris returned to college was that he couldn't be under the microscope all the time—he was still a college kid. With all of the attention he received, we didn't want him to be held to unrealistic high standards when he was a nineteen-year-old student who was going to make mistakes. He was in a position to demonstrate some of his better qualities and be a role model, but he wasn't perfect, and we didn't want anyone having unfair expectations of him.

Chris worked diligently to become more independent. He wanted to be able to go to the wellness center, the student union, and the cafeteria on his own whenever possible, and having specific goals helped motivate him. There were little hills and different areas he began navigating himself, and Luther also recognized the locations where needed improvements would help his accessibility. It was a big deal for him to be able to get around campus on his own.

By February of Chris's second semester of college, as he got stronger and continued recovering, and his friends learned his system and needs, Alex was able to start paring back her time with him. All along, our plan was that between his friends and his recovery, he'd eventually transition out of her care. That was a good sign of his progress, and it allowed Alex to get a part-time job in a doctor's office.

Going back and forth to Mayo twice a week was wearing on Alex and Chris because they were giving up three hours a day every time they made the trip. Between the lost time, his progressing past the need for Mayo's specialized equipment, and becoming more comfortable with Lisa Kreig at Euro-Team and what she was able to do with him, it seemed logical for Chris to transition to Lisa full time at the end of his first year back at school. He also received excellent OT from Jennessa Luzum at Winneshiek Medical Center in Decorah. Mayo remained his medical and therapeutic headquarters.

The second year was a lot harder for Alex because the friends she'd made at Luther had graduated. At the same time, Chris's friends were taking on more and more responsibility for his care, and Chris needed her less and less. With only a part-time job in a doctor's office keeping her in Decorah, and her family, friends, and boyfriend back home, by the end of Chris's second year at school, Alex was ready to come home.

Alex never expected praise for helping Chris, and she never begrudged living in Decorah because she did it out of love for her brother and knowing there was no way we could have gotten him back to college without her. She taught his friends how to care for him, drove him back and forth to Mayo, and did a thousand other things too numerous to list. When she moved back home, I couldn't help but feel a little worried about Chris being in Decorah without family. What if he got sick? What if he wanted to come home for a weekend? His needs changed,

Alex needed to get on with her life, and I had to trust that Chris would be fine on his own.

In the end, I think Alex's time with Chris made her a better nurse. She understood what a family went through, not just from the medical side, but also the accompanying emotions and the importance of hope in a patient's recovery.

Alex wasn't the only one who benefited from helping Chris. One of the moms on the football team really touched my heart when she said she loved watching the interaction of the young men attending Luther and how they took care of and supported Chris. She thought it made them all more compassionate, and I think she was right. I liked to think that being around Chris every day helped his

"These guys were so good to Chris and always willing to help him in many ways. They drove the van, helped him daily, and also helped him with his wheelchair on campus getting to classes in all kinds of weather. They truly played the role of big brothers. I often thanked them for what they were doing for Chris. They were an important part of Chris's recovery."

Luann Smith, Retired Luther Employee

friends have a better appreciation for the disabled or someone battling an injury. I think the ripple effect among his friends and acquaintances was huge, as I personally believe serving others impacts everyone for the better.

Chris's friends were just phenomenal because they helped

him have the college experience that everybody else did, and that was something Deb and I always tried to focus on when we'd start to feel bad. We'd think about the college student who was depressed, or suicidal, or miserable because they were lonely. Chris had hundreds of friends who loved him, cared about him, and took care of him. Despite his physical limitations, in many respects he was better off than a "normal" student whose problems remained undetected. Deb and I couldn't have asked for kinder, more caring friends for Chris than the special group of guys at Luther.

Our blessings continued when Coach Mike Durnin told us personally that Chris had won the 2011 America's Choice Honoree for Courage in Sports award. Of course, we couldn't reveal the winner until they announced it on the *CBS Early Show*.

After a lot of consideration, I went to Lauren Price from Intersports, the company out of Chicago that put on the award, and told her that it was planes, trains, and automobiles for us to get Chris from school and fly to New York for only one day, and that we really needed our two daughters to come along because Chris's story was about family. To make a long story short, Intersports flew our entire family of five out to New York City, we stayed three nights, and they had two vehicles pick us up at the airport and stay with us during the trip. Intersports totally took care of us when they recognized the importance of us being together.

Our trip to New York City was Chris's first time on an airplane since his injury, and we were a little nervous about the logistics. We checked his chair at the door, they transferred him to a narrow chair that fit down the aisle, and Alex transferred him from the aisle chair to the airplane seat. Flying to New York really proved to us that there was nothing we couldn't do with a little planning.

All five of us appeared on the *CBS Early Show*. After we went through hair and makeup, mics were attached. Then they revealed Chris as the winner, showed some footage, and interviewed Chris and our family. While there was just one person interviewing us, there were probably fifteen or twenty people present on the set that day. When the interview was over, everybody clapped. Lauren from Intersports said she'd never seen anything like that before.

Our next stop was the Rutgers vs. Army game at Yankee Stadium. Lauren had worked with the New York Yankees to give us a tour of their facilities, as well as an opportunity to meet Eric LeGrand and his family who were in town for the Rutgers game. The Yankees also gave Chris a ball signed by Mariano Rivera, lighting him up from ear to ear. The Yankee organization couldn't have treated us better.

We met Eric LeGrand and his family at the stadium, and I couldn't possibly describe that surreal experience. Chris and Eric couldn't have looked more different on paper. Chris was a white kid from the Midwest playing Division III ball, and Eric was an African American kid from New Jersey playing Division I ball. Yet, they had so much in common. Our families instantly connected—Chris with Eric, Deb with Eric's mom, and Alex with Eric's sister—drawn together by an almost palpable force in the room.

Lauren kept telling us we had to leave, but nobody wanted to break the connection. Eric and Chris got hurt the exact same day, on the exact same play, and they'd been through so many of the same experiences. Eric had a very tight knit family like ours, and his family was a big part of his story. There was a vibe in that room, a closeness that was hard to describe.

When we finally broke apart, we continued our whirlwind sightseeing circuit. In a three-day period, we'd appeared on the *CBS Early Show*, went to Times Square, toured Yankee Stadium, visited the National September 11 Memorial, and from Battery Park, we saw the Statue of Liberty. The impromptu tour of the *Today* show capped a fantastic weekend in New York City.

When spring break rolled around in March 2012, we decided to get out of cold Iowa and head to sunny Florida. After traveling to New York, we were familiar with the logistics, like making sure we had a handicap-accessible room and arranging home healthcare. The trip went really well, and it proved that with a little planning, we could still have great family vacations and do the things we wanted to do.

I felt honored to be a guest speaker at Luther Senior Athletes Awards Ceremony in the spring of 2012. All of the senior athletes were aware of Chris's injury, especially the football players, and I really wanted to make an impact on the fine group of young athletes. I practiced and practiced and really prepared for the presentation where I told the seniors to make the most out of their lives and not to settle for less. I felt really good about the speech because I spoke from the heart, and it was very emotional. Later, Chris told me that one of his marketing professors told him it was the best speech he'd ever heard in his life.

As we got further along in Chris's recovery, I changed my mind and wanted to talk to the people who'd reached out earlier about their spinal cord injuries, the same folks I'd politely put off after Chris's injury when I wasn't ready to face the reality of his future. I contacted Greg Young, a gentleman from Chicago who'd suffered two spinal cord injuries, and whose son played football for Central College. I ended up communicating with him a lot. I also spoke to Tyson Gentry, the Ohio State football player who broke his neck in 2006, and his dad, Bob Gentry.

Chris received calls and messages from several sports celebrities. Former Pittsburg Steelers' player Ryan Clark didn't have an injury, but he did suffer an altitude related setback due to his sickle cell anemia. He contacted Chris on a regular basis, texting him from the locker room at the Super Bowl and trying to arrange a meeting when they played in Kansas City. Some people made initial phone calls or left messages, but Ryan stayed with Chris and really lifted him up. Tim Tebow also regularly encouraged Chris through tweets, texts, and phone calls.

Chris was a huge Iowa Hawkeye fan, and at the time, Ken O'Keefe was their offensive coordinator. He called Chris every Saturday after the Iowa football game and put one of the players on the phone. Ken even invited Chris to visit the University of Iowa where he met Coach Ferentz. Chris also attended a practice where the football players acknowledged him as they headed into the locker room. Iowa State's football coach, Paul Rhoads, invited Chris to speak to the Iowa State football team, and then he gave Chris sideline passes to several games and contacted Chris whenever an article about him came out in the local media.

One of our biggest supporters was Ohio State football coach, Urban Meyer. In trying to contact Tim Tebow, a friend of a friend of a friend knew Urban Meyer. One morning, I got a text from Coach Meyer saying he'd heard about Chris's story and that he was praying and thinking about us. I messaged him back, and from there, Urban started keeping in touch with us, and he connected Tim and Chris.

Coach Meyer invited Chris to Ohio State, and Chris and his buddies visited him twice. The first time, Chris described the visit as a dream come true. He took a picture with the Heisman Trophy, and stood in Ohio Stadium, also known as The Horseshoe. Chris and his buddies even went with Urban Meyer and his family to watch his son play baseball. Another time Chris and his friends visited with Coach Meyer in his office, watched a practice, and attended a game.

None of those guys—Urban Meyer, Tim Tebow, Ryan Clark, Ken O'Keefe, Paul Rhoads—reached out to Chris for a picture opportunity, an endorsement, or any benefit to them. They all connected with Chris because of their character. They were really good men who, despite their busy schedules and how many people wanted a piece of them, took the time to make a difference in Chris's life.

Even though their trip to Ohio State was a dream come true, Deb and I still worried. The boys were in the car for a long time from Decorah to Chicago, and then on to Columbus, Ohio. We were apprehensive about the logistics, but a lot of our concerns were just normal mom and dad fears about college boys on a road trip. Because of Chris's needs, we arranged the hotel in Columbus and contacted a local home healthcare agency to come to the hotel room. That was the first time we'd arranged an out-of-town agency when we weren't present.

While visiting Ohio State, Chris and his friends stayed at a hotel, but they also spent time with Megan and her friends. Megan, a soccer player for the university, had gone to high school with Chris. She sent me a message after they'd left telling me what a neat group of friends he had. She and her friends were in awe of how they cared for Chris and how they took care of him. Without a word being spoken, they just did what needed to be done. She said it was incredible to witness, and that I should feel good about the care they gave him. Her unsolicited note really warmed our hearts and confirmed what Deb and I already knew about Chris's friends.

"I have never seen 18-22 year old males so mature, respectful, and dedicated to a friendship. My father always told me 'if you want to take a look at yourself, look at your friends.' Chris Norton has great friends because he is a great man."

Megan Gill, PT, DPT, Clinical Lead Physical Therapist for Spinal Cord Injury, Mayo Clinic

Despite our trust, when Chris wanted to go tubing over Memorial Day weekend with a big group of guys, Deb and I were concerned. Chris could get sun burnt, dehydrated, or if they didn't watch him closely enough, he could tip over and drown because he couldn't protect himself. Deb and I remembered all too well how young and careless we were in college, and Chris had to rely on other people to look out for him while having a good time. We were scared.

We talked to Chris, we talked to his friends, and I reminded them that his body didn't sweat and couldn't cool itself down. I knew Chris was tired of us worrying about every little detail when things managed to take care of themselves, but the truth was, we'd worry whether he was hurt or not, because that was our job as his parents. It eased our minds knowing that by that point, Chris's friends had taken care of him for a year. They knew he needed a home healthcare person, and they recognized his additional needs, so they took our hovering in stride. Taking care of Chris wasn't a big deal to them, and they made it work.

Every summer when Chris was at Luther, he stayed in Decorah because he had a great system worked out with PT and OT that we couldn't replicate at home. He also felt a little claustrophobic at our house because we lived in the country where we didn't have sidewalks, so at home, he couldn't go anywhere on his own. On campus, he could go out his door, get onto the track around the football field, and do laps. He could go to the wellness and athletic center where his RT300 bicycle was kept, or have someone help him get into the pool. He could also access the student union and the rest of campus. Plus, all of his college buddies were in Decorah.

When Chris was unable to accept his Heroes of the Heartland award because he was busy with school, Deb and I were honored to take his place. When we were contacted by the American Red Cross and looked at the other "heroes" being honored, we were really humbled for Chris to be recognized and included in such a fabulous group of individuals. We all felt truly blessed that his story had touched so many lives.

I had other speaking engagements that came out of my experience with Chris. I was the first non-Mayo employee asked to speak at their annual meeting. That was really special because they telecast the speech to their thirty-six thousand employees throughout the country. They wanted me to share Chris's story and our experiences at Mayo. I also spoke at the 2012 Fields of Faith event in Bondurant, and I delivered a meaningful message about overcoming adversity and facing challenges. Even though Chris was hardwired to be optimistic, and he faced each day with a sense of hope and joy, faith was what got him through. I wanted the students to trust God, and to reach out to friends and support groups in order to face and overcome their individual challenges.

Before Chris initially returned to Luther, Sandy, a local certified nursing assistant who insisted on helping when Chris went back to school, volunteered to help Chris every Saturday. She just fell in love with him and his story. Sandy wrote us a card that said she'd volunteered with the idea of helping Chris, but in the end, he helped her. She'd looked at her life and compared it to what Chris dealt with, and the fact that he never had a bad day made a real impact on her. His attitude was truly contagious, and we did our part in spreading his good news.

We'd come a long way and had further to go, but we'd reached a point where looking back and taking stock helped keep our feet on the ground and our eyes facing forward. Sharing our experiences with others while retaining faith and hope for Chris's continued improvement helped Deb and me accept the reality of his situation and spread his message of hope.

CHAPTER 25

For I know the plans I have for you," declares the LORD, "plans to prosper you and not to harm you, plans to give you hope and a future.

~Jeremiah 29:11 NIV

CHRIS

God kept putting people in my path who changed my life for the better. The Lynch family altered my career trajectory when they invited me to speak at their annual Lynch Family Foundation benefit and golf outing in June 2012. When I pressed them for details, they said they wanted me to share my story and tell people a little bit about myself.

I was nervous because I'd given two prior informal talks that I felt weren't very good or my best, but I really wanted to do well, especially when I found out that Paul Rhoads, Iowa State's head football coach, and another professional speaker would be in attendance. This was the first speech I took seriously and practiced for, not only because of the other speakers, but because I thought sharing my story could help advocate for change.

After my speech, I was totally blown away when the Lynch Family Foundation presented me, as the event beneficiary, with an accessible tandem bicycle and some money. When we first met, I mentioned a goal of mine was to purchase an accessible bike, get outside on Decorah's trails, and eventually participate in the Des Moines Register's Annual Great Bicycle Ride Across Iowa (RAGBRAI). The event went really well. I was so grateful for the bike, and I think the speech was well received.

Later, at the event recap with Gary Lynch, and Jason and Erin Golly of the Lynch Family Foundation, Jason said if I wanted to put on my own charity fundraiser, they'd be happy to help. They offered food and support for whatever I needed; they would back any cause I wanted to support. His suggestion made something click in my brain, and I thought, *yeah, there's a lot of need, and I really want to help.*

When I first came home from Mayo and had to drive two hours from Des Moines just to use the RT300 bike, I began to understand what most spinal cord injured people faced every day. I had a friend from rehab, for example, who drove two hours to Mayo and back just to use the bike I had in my own room. Going through the whole injury and rehab process, I saw so many people get left behind or plateau because their insurance stopped paying for therapy. They weren't blessed with the human or financial resources I had due to my friends, my family, and the insurance policy. I felt humbled and sad for those without the same opportunity to get better. The need was huge, and thanks to the Lynch Family Foundation, I was suddenly in a position to help.

Whenever I thought about what life would look like if I'd gotten hurt at Central College and had been flown to a local hospital instead of Mayo, I cringed. At Mayo, I had access to the people, the resources, and the equipment to recover as much as possible, and thanks to my insurance, I had the means to continue rehab. The rehab clinics I'd been to around the state of Iowa lacked the better technology and equipment to help people with more severe injuries. There were numerous people who needed better equipment and wanted to get better, so if we could get more advanced equipment into existing rehab clinics in locations where people with spinal cord injuries needed it, we'd make a difference in the community.

My parents were the first ones I talked to about starting a foundation. They both had business degrees, my mom worked with a foundation back home, and they had friends with experience, connections, and a good understanding of how foundations worked. At the time, I had yet to take my first business class, so I had no idea how to get started other than my own research. I was intimately involved in creating the name and the mission, as well as determining the direction of the foundation and the people we wanted to help. My family worked to file the paperwork with the government for our 501(c)(3) status, figure out how we should run the foundation, and brainstorm who would serve on the board.

With the support of my mom and dad, the SCI CAN Foundation was born with the mission to aid in providing equipment to facilities where people who wanted to use it would have access. SCI CAN stands for Spinal Cord Injury (SCI) Christopher Anderson Norton (CAN). Our focus was to locate clinics and assist them in paying for advanced equipment that could help people with their health, recovery, and wellness. At that point, I never saw making a career out of the foundation, I just wanted to organize and influence people to contribute to the cause.

After the Lynch Family Foundation planted the idea, and with my family and friends behind me, we decided to hold an event in Decorah to raise funds to purchase an RT300 bicycle for Northeast Iowa. Because I received occupational therapy at Winneshiek Medical Center and I was familiar with their rehab facility, I knew they were a good choice because of their client base, neutral location, easy access, available staff, and flexible hours. We wanted to purchase the bike because it could not only help with spinal cord injuries, but with strokes, Parkinson's, multiple sclerosis, and cerebral palsy. We concentrated on equipment that served a broader range of ailments, especially in more rural areas.

Holding an event in Decorah made sense because I spent the summer there focusing on therapy, and I wanted to give back to the town that had been so supportive of me in my recovery. We organized a bike/run/walk on the trails around town, and with the help of friends, family, the Lynch Family Foundation, and Winneshiek Medical Center's marketing department and foundation, we started marketing the event. We distributed fliers, and talked to local businesses, radio stations, and the newspaper to spread the word.

We intended to raise money through free will donations to SCI CAN, by selling T-shirts and wristbands, through sponsorships, and a silent auction. We set up tents along the trail with activities to make it as fun as possible for the participants. There was no RSVP, and no official start time, it was just come ride, run, or walk. The event went great and we raised enough for the bike, but there was so much need that a one-time event didn't make a dent.

We started out small with the bike event in Decorah and set our sights on Des Moines. The following winter, my parents set up a dinner event in Des Moines with speakers, entertainment, and an auction that was very successful and much easier to run than an outdoor event. So, we stopped doing the bike/run/walk and switched to having dinners in both Decorah and Des Moines. Iowa was our first priority because we knew firsthand how great a need there was for advanced technology, equipment, and facilities in our home state.

A natural progression was to grow our foundation throughout the region, then eventually coast-to-coast because the need existed everywhere. However, our focus remained helping those with spinal cord injuries find help close to home so they didn't have to relocate outside of Iowa. I knew from experience that while going to Denver, Chicago, New Jersey, or Atlanta were all good options, the ability to stay in a person's home state where they could receive support from family and friends was vital.

After reaching out to different rehab facilities and reviewing the equipment they had onsite, we set up an application process for clinics to apply for grant money to purchase needed equipment. In choosing our subsequent recipients, we asked the facilities to tell us what they thought they needed through a grant application. Then our medical professional board members assessed the applications. It felt awesome to award the first grant and to set a goal, work hard, and provide equipment to a facility that really wanted and appreciated our help. The applications weren't rolling in at first, but through media coverage of the events, word of mouth, and social media, we raised awareness on a grass-roots level.

As I started to get more and more requests for speaking engagements, and I got a little more comfortable with the prepared speech that evolved from the one I gave at the Lynch Family Foundation event, I began to get excited about speaking. After seeing the impact and the response I got when I first presented that speech with everyone jumping up to give me a standing ovation and people crying in the audience, I felt confident spreading my message of hope and faith.

While in school, I operated as the face of the foundation and shared my vision with the board. I did a lot of the marketing, event planning, and speaking on behalf of the foundation. My public speaking and the foundation complimented each other. While I tried to separate my motivational and public speaking from the foundation, starting the foundation was a part of my story, so that always came up when I gave a speech. A lot of the people who wanted to help SCI CAN were influenced by my story, and public speaking was a huge part of being the face and the overall leader of the organization.

It was a heady rush to meet other people, share my story, and then have kids and adults tell me how inspired they were, and how my message changed their lives and gave them a new attitude on a deeply emotional level. Seeing the impact of my story on people's faces made me think that maybe I could make a career out of speaking, which was ironic considering I used to have a really bad lisp and my worst grade in college was in my public speaking class.

From talking to others, like Iowa State's Paul Rhoads, Iowa educator, coach, and speaker, Aaron Thomas, as well as Ohio State football coach, Urban Meyer, I learned that as long as I had a good story to tell, how I presented it wasn't as important as the story and the message, but I knew I could improve. People enjoyed my speeches even when I felt they weren't my best. Knowing I could do better really spurred me to make improvements and attempt to be more impactful.

If I could share my message, empower others, and travel,

I felt like I was doing something to help others. I talked to my mom and dad about my future, and they agreed it was a good idea and the right direction for me. My message covered a broad range of people and demographics—middle school students, high school students, college students, business people—so it was something we were excited to share.

My path developed slowly at first because I was still in school. People and organizations asked me to speak at events or to different groups, so I wasn't actively marketing myself, but through word of mouth, I was asked to do more and more speaking. It started with Fellowship of Christian Athletes' sports camps in Minnesota. They really liked how I spoke at one camp, so they asked me to speak at another, and then a banquet, and then a fundraiser, so I stayed busy with FCA. They loved how the kids responded to my message and after doing it more and more, I got better and better.

> *"The message that Chris has is special because overcoming adversity is so universal. Everybody has adversity in their life, everybody gets discouraged."*
>
> Joe Gilson, Lifelong friend

I offered to speak at my hometown high school and middle school, and through personal connections of my parents and friends, I was asked to speak on a pretty regular basis at churches and schools. Those events were a great training ground because I didn't want to start a professional career until I had enough practice and had established some credibility. Once we started the foundation, we set up a website with a page where people could request me to speak, but most requests came through people who followed me on CaringBridge, people who followed my Twitter or Facebook posts, and people who'd heard about me through articles in the newspapers and stories on TV. They'd hear my story, go to my website, find my contact information, and send me an e-mail.

As time went by, we started to realize that what we were doing with SCI CAN was great, but a lot of people needed more than just equipment. Transportation was a huge issue, as some people needed a driver and a helper to get them set up on the equipment. Our mission's focus on placing advanced equipment in rehab facilities didn't allow us to help people who felt depressed or unmotivated, or those who didn't have resources, insurance, or friends to take them places.

We expanded our mission to include improving quality of life, health, wellness, and recovery of those with neurological disorders so we could serve those with the greatest need. For example, we took a girl who really needed an uplifting experience to Ironwood's Sports Wheelchair Camp where she was able to meet other people in similar situations, do something fun, get out of the house, and step out of her comfort zone. The experience opened my eyes to the endless activities that were accessible like boating, kayaking, and zip lining.

SCI CAN continued as a family operation. I focused on

event planning, meeting with businesses, acquiring sponsors, grant writing, and public speaking. My dad continued to do the financial accounting and a lot of the behind-the-scenes work. My mom had a lot of great ideas for the events, she designed our brochures, and she helped manage and run our events and fund-raisers. My sisters, particularly Alex, took an active role in marketing and in getting the foundation's message heard.

I constantly met people and heard stories about spinal cord injuries and people in need, it was just non-stop. Every story compelled me to keep helping others and expand our reach. Spinal cord injuries and recovery problems wouldn't be fixed overnight or even within a couple of years, which was why I wanted to make raising money and awareness a lifelong mission.

SCI CAN was blessed to have the support of the Fellowship of Christian Athletes, and we were grateful to Courage in Sports for their continued support of our foundation. The Lynch Family Foundation was our biggest supporter. The year after the event where they surprised me with a tandem bike, they asked me back to give a speech, recap what I'd done in the past year, and surprised me again with a $10,000 check for SCI CAN.

Urban Meyer kept in contact with me after I talked with Tebow and after I left the hospital, something he didn't have to do. Once he landed the Ohio State head coaching job in 2012, I figured we'd get disconnected. Instead, we became closer and he even invited my friends and me to Ohio State. We visited him in his office, toured the facilities, the stadium, and held the Heisman trophy.

That experience alone was worth the twelve-hour road trip, but then Coach Meyer invited us to his son's baseball game the next day. We had a great time shooting the breeze with him, and he seemed very intrigued with my story. Prior to leaving the game, he said he wanted therapy updates from me at least one a week. I felt honored and humbled he took such an interest in supporting me.

The Des Moines event site, Prairie Meadows, as well as Luther College, Craig and Lea Culver, the Lohse Family Foundation, and my family have been huge supporters. I could go on and on about all the people who were there for me. For instance, I won't forget all my friends who aided by driving me around, talking to businesses, passing out fliers, and spreading the word. It didn't take long to realize the world was full of wonderful, caring, selfless people willing to help on a regular basis.

When I was in school, I wanted to have a bigger role in the foundation, but between classes and therapy, it was hard to devote as much time as I would have liked. I had my hands in so many different projects, I couldn't do anything full speed the way I wanted. Additionally, as a board member of the Neurological House Foundation, I offered to help run another event in Rochester, Minnesota, to raise money to establish the first ever Neurological Recovery House, a hospitality house for those with neurological issues and their families near the Mayo Clinic.

As my family quickly discovered after my injury and hospitalization, it was too expensive to stay at a hotel for months on end while doing outpatient rehab at Mayo, and my rehab options at home didn't fit my needs. If I hadn't squeaked in under the eighteen-year-old age limit, I wouldn't have been able to stay at the Ronald McDonald House and continue getting care at Mayo. A Neurological Recovery House provided people of all ages who wanted to stay and continue to receive care at Mayo an affordable and accessible option.

The idea for NRH and the foundation were established by some of the doctors and nurses in the neurological field at Mayo because they saw a huge need. After I left Mayo, was at school for a while, and had started my foundation, they reached out to me about the project and asked if I'd apply for a board position because of my rehab, foundation, and fundraising experience. My role as a board member was to give patient and family insight because they had the medical professional side covered. I never considered not taking part, even though my schedule was jam packed, because I was very passionate about helping others in need. The goal remained to establish Neurological Recovery Houses all over the country, modeled after the Ronald McDonald Houses.

I definitely took school seriously. I loved the liberal arts idea and philosophy, and I attended Luther College expecting to get a broad education in a lot of different fields. My official major became business management, as I felt that major best suited my needs for the foundation. While I took my business classes seriously and I wanted to learn as much as I could, when I figured out what I wanted to do with my life, taking the odd language, religion, art, and science classes made it a lot harder to stay focused and motivated to do well in those classes.

After discovering a passion with the foundation and speaking, school kind of took a back seat. If I had a big speaking engagement where a lot of people with networking ties could help SCI CAN well after school was over, and I had the opportunity to reach and influence lots of people, I ended up missing classes for the day. Most of my teachers understood. It didn't hurt that I felt sort of like an unofficial ambassador for Luther College during my speaking engagements.

I was honored as one of Central Iowa's 2012 American Red Cross Heroes of the Heartland after my dad and a girl from Luther nominated me for the award. I couldn't make it to the banquet because it was on a school day in the middle of the week, but my family went in my place. Designations like the Heroes of the Heartland award and the Courage in Sports award helped give credence to my foundation and my message, as well as spread the good work we were trying to accomplish.

Thanks to Mayo, I got to throw out the first pitch at a Minnesota Twins game in September, 2012. My friend Tanner went out to the mound with me, and I wanted to stand up to throw the pitch because I didn't want to do it sitting down. *Go big or go home!* For a month, I worked on throwing a baseball and figuring out the best way Tanner could stand me up and be out of my way so I could throw the pitch. A lot of thought and practice went into it, and I was pretty nervous because sometimes my hands couldn't get a good hold of the ball.

I told Tanner that if I stood and dropped the ball, he should sit me back down and I would throw it from my seat. I was worried that if he tried to retrieve the ball from the ground, I might lose my balance and fall down. So, of course, I got up and dropped the ball right away. Without hesitation, Tanner bent down, picked up the ball, and popped it right back into my hand like it was nothing. I was so glad he didn't stay with our earlier plan because when we tried it again, it went fine.

It took me two years to walk unassisted with a walker in therapy only, and achieving that goal definitely motivated me to keep working hard. It made me reflect back on how far I'd come and how far I had yet to go before I could lose the walker. For better or worse, I was on to the next thing. Sometimes my reaction frustrated my parents and therapists because I didn't get overly excited about accomplishing something new. I'd get excited when they got excited, but I was always looking ahead to the next goal.

By the two-year mark, I felt confident saying my injury was without a doubt a blessing. At the one-year anniversary, I could somewhat see it as a blessing, but living life was still so hard, and thinking about my future filled me with fear. There were a lot of question marks in my life about what I was going to do and if I'd find someone to share my life with. By the second year anniversary, I was looking forward to the opportunities with the foundation and speaking engagements, and there were a lot of different things happening in my life that were exciting.

> *"Everyone always asks me what I thought about dating someone in a wheelchair. From the beginning I haven't even seen his chair. I've seen who he is as a person because that's what shines through to me. He was confident in his own skin and never made his chair an issue or a concern."*
>
> Emily Summers, Chris's girlfriend

At the three-year mark, without a doubt, I knew 110 percent it was a blessing. Life was great, I was getting stronger, the foundation was making a difference, speaking was still fulfilling, and I met a great girl named Emily through social media. As our conversation developed, our interest seemed mutual. I worried that when I told her my story, she'd get scared and end our conversation, but she seemed intrigued and wanted to meet. I definitely wanted to meet her, but we took it nice and slow. We became Facebook friends, and we went from there to texting. Emily attended Iowa State University in Ames, Iowa, and we decided to meet when I visited a friend on her campus. We hit it off right away, and we haven't slowed down since.

Emily was instrumental in my recovery, both physically

and mentally. As a passionate, driven person, she recognized my passion and drive to get better and stronger. She helped me achieve my goals by learning how to transfer me, how to stand me up, how to walk me in my walker, and how to do all the things my guy friends did to help me with therapy. When she visited me at school on the weekends, she assisted and encouraged me during workouts.

People have often asked if I could go back and change the play, if I would, and the answer has always been no. I wouldn't change anything about it. It was impossible to look back and not see the countless blessings that were a direct result of my injury and the wonderful people I'd met along the way. My journey from injury to recovery and beyond was a gift, and even though it would make life easier, I'd never go back and change a thing.

CHAPTER 26

The point of "faith" is believing and trusting in things we cannot see or understand. The last three years have been filled with moments of hurt, pain, sadness, anger, and disappointment, and at the same time joy, love, encouragement, and hope. Trials refine us, and they make us grow in our faith and determination.

~Terry Norton, CaringBridge, October 16, 2013

TERRY

While Chris was at Mayo, the whole family recognized that other people with spinal cord injuries didn't have the same advantages as Chris. We learned very quickly that our insurance, both our primary insurance and the NCAA policy, afforded us more benefits than others. Chris didn't feel it was fair, but we didn't have any idea how we could help other people. Then Chris spoke at the Lynch Family Foundation event, and Jason Golly asked Chris what he was going to do with the money they gave him. The idea that had been brewing all along to assist other people with spinal cord injuries get equipment fused into a plan.

Chris knew he wasn't the only person with the drive, determination, and desire to get better. Most people wanted the opportunity, but were denied because of forces outside their control. I gave Chris a lot of credit for acknowledging his advantages and wanting to do something to help. Our foundation came into existence because while the thought lingered in the back of our minds, when Jason Golly pressed Chris, he provided the impetus that made us pull the trigger.

I believe the Lynch family saw a lot of potential in Chris, and they wanted to support him by maximizing that potential in order to bring about change. Even the tandem bike he received at the fundraiser represented yet another gift that made him feel blessed, and it fueled his desire to aid others. God's work was in action again, placing people in Chris's path to guide him when he needed it most, stoking his excitement about the foundation as a meaningful way to bring about change in our community.

When Chris presented the idea of starting our own foundation to Deb and me, I was kind of surprised. He was only twenty years old, and most twenty-year-olds don't start foundations to help other people. In his situation, for Chris to be focused on others made me very proud, but in the back of my mind, I thought, *oh, boy.* I was worried about him adding something to his already crowded plate. He was a full-time student, in therapy full-time, and he wanted to add a foundation to his schedule.

When I stepped back and looked at the big picture, I realized that if he had something he was focused on, passionate about, and believed in, it would maintain his perspective and his attitude on the rare occasions he got down. In the long run, if starting a foundation was really important to him and something that drove him, it would be a real positive in his life, especially at a time when his future seemed so uncertain.

Getting the family on board was the easy part, and boy did we have work to do. We formed a corporation, filed for non-profit status, created our bylaws, and began focusing on our mission statement. Fortunately, I was able to use a local foundation's paperwork as a guide. In what would become our *modus operandi*, Chris came up with the idea, and Mom and Dad did the paperwork and executed the plan.

After incorporation and filing for non-profit status, we needed to put together a board of directors. Chris and I talked at length and decided that in order to give us legitimacy and for our mission to work, we wanted approximately eight board members comprised of business and medical professionals. We wanted people who'd feel passionate about our mission, take the position seriously, and be good contributors.

We first approached attorney Pat Vickers, Chris's roommate's father, who'd been with us from the get-go, and who enthusiastically joined. We asked Scott Atzen, a supervisor at Des Moines Waterworks and a longtime friend of our family, to become a member. Scott fit our needs because of his proximity to home, event experience, business experience, and his connections in the community. With Chris, Pat, Scott, and me in place, we then approached Mike Durnin, Luther's head football coach, as a Luther representative. Fortunately, he accepted with honor.

When we weighed our medical professional options, we wanted to keep Mayo in the loop, so Chris's PT, Megan Gill, was a natural choice. We also wanted to ask someone from Decorah. Hannah Gaveske had worked at Winneshiek Medical Center as an athletic trainer, but was utilized as an athletic trainer by Luther College at the time she joined our board. She was a great fit for our foundation, especially since she went on to become a trainer for the US Olympic Training Center in Chula Vista, California. We also asked Jennessa Luzum, Chris's OT at Winneshiek Medical Center.

I was thrilled with the group we'd assembled representing exactly what we wanted from the business, legal, and medical fields. About a year after we formed, we asked former University of Iowa basketball player and Iowa City businessman, Mark Gannon, to join us. He was a good addition to help broaden our base throughout the state of Iowa.

As we assembled our board of directors, we began focusing on our mission statement. From the beginning, we knew we didn't want to own the therapy equipment, the therapy facility, or run a therapy program because we didn't want to deal with insurance, maintenance, laws, and regulations. Also, we talked about getting the biggest bang for our buck in order to multiply the equipment's impact. The money we raised would go to organizations, achieving our goal of impacting multiple individuals. We aimed to keep the money raised in the community as much as possible. If we raised money in Decorah, for example, we'd grant the money to an organization in or around Decorah.

When we started, Chris and I had different unstated visions for the direction of SCI CAN. I envisioned doing one event per year, picking out one piece of equipment to raise money for, coming together as a group, and raising anywhere from fifteen to fifty thousand dollars to achieve our goal. Chris had a different vision because he was a "go big or go home" kind of guy. He thought big, he dreamt big, and he shot big.

Our initial plan was to hold an event in Decorah raising funds for an RT300 bicycle because there was nothing like it in the northeastern part of the state. The whole family helped with the first SCI CAN event. Because Winneshiek Medical Center already knew they were going to receive the bike, their marketing department helped with posters and promoting the event to their employees. Having the recipient's help was huge, and we weighed the effect of that when we decided to change the way we allocated funds. For the sake of logistics, and after continued discussion and debate, following recipients were not picked in advance.

We eventually decided to award the money through grants, allowing the facilities to buy the equipment after defining through the application process what they wanted, why they wanted it, and how they planned to maintain it. After the fundraiser, we'd present them with a check, along with the agreement that they would use the money to purchase the stated equipment.

Our resident attorney, Pat Vickers, helped draft the application and awarding agreement that relinquished us from liability and any responsibility for the training, maintenance, and upkeep of the equipment. Because we were all working professionals with other jobs, we couldn't assume the responsibility of the equipment once the money was distributed. Thus, our mission was born.

Before we decided to form the foundation, Chris wanted to go to law school or possibly get his MBA and do something business related, but he never really saw himself inside an office. He wanted to be out and about, meeting people and networking. When he was injured, he thought about careers in terms of what he could do to help and serve others. After being asked to speak at different events, his speeches evolved from just telling his story to a message of hope that resonated with people in their businesses, marriages, faith, or whatever challenge they faced. As his message began to have a real impact, he realized that speaking afforded him the opportunity to help others and that perhaps God's plan was for him to focus on speaking and the foundation.

Every time Chris spoke about his injury, he credited faith, hard work, determination, family, and friends for his success. He didn't want people focusing only on the facts of his injury, because his message was about responding to life's challenges, not the specifics of the challenge. Everyone faces challenges, and everyone who heard his message of faith, family, and determination also had the ability to make something good out of a bad situation.

I was always a little concerned about his future, but I knew he was going to have a positive impact on the world. I looked at him and knew he was already having an influence on lives, even before he was cut loose from college. He was destined to do amazing and unbelievable things, and knowing that brought me

"Throughout the years that I have known Chris, I have learned a great deal by being a part of his journey. I have learned from him that our path in life is dictated less by the events that unfold, and more by how we choose to react during the succession of those events."

Rich Holton, Luther classmate and friend

peace. The more his story was told, and as more people got to know him (faults and all), his impact on others continued to grow. The scale by which he measured his goals and outlook only got bigger, to the benefit of others.

With so much of his time spent in Decorah and not seeing him every day, we didn't realize all the improvements Chris was making. For example, during the summer of 2013, Chris, my mom, Alex, and I drove to my nephew's wedding. Chris sat in the front passenger seat. For the longest time, he couldn't raise his arms over his shoulder, but when the sun shone on his face, to my great surprise, he reached up and pulled the visor down. Later that evening, he reached across the table for the pepper, a task he hadn't been able to do before on his own. He'd come a long way from when I had to feed him every bite, and it felt encouraging to witness his progress toward independence.

Chris defied the odds and regained more movement than the doctors ever expected. He didn't just pop up and take off, but he continued to make gains and surpass his prognosis. Whenever I got impatient with Chris's recovery, I thought back to where he was one, two, or three years prior and it helped, because sometimes I needed a conscious reminder of how far he'd come. I couldn't compare post-injury Chris to pre-injury Chris, because if I tried, I'd never have found peace until he was 100 percent recovered. I had to adjust my mind and be thankful we didn't lose him that beautiful October day. Chris Norton was Chris Norton, regardless of his level of recovery, because he never let the accident define him.

Since he missed a year of school, Chris's original class of friends graduated a year ahead of him, and when they moved out of the dorm their senior year, as a testament to their character, they checked in with Chris first. Deb and I naturally worried how Chris would do with the change.

"I'll be fine," he said. "We'll get some new guys in here, no big deal." And he did.

When Chris initially went back to college, we taught one or

two kids how to help him, two or three more learned, and each year, that number multiplied. His friendship circle eventually grew to include a number of younger kids who moved into his dorm cluster, so his friends handed off the torch before graduation, easing our minds.

While in college, Chris had more on his plate than most adults. I encouraged him to find a balance between school and speaking, but as he matured and got older, it was harder to focus on school. When he looked at what was more important—an A versus a B and the opportunity to speak to and potentially motivate someone—there really was no choice. His goal was to succeed at school the way he succeeded in all aspects of his life, but he understood that his message of hope meant more than his GPA. Despite everything on his plate, his grades suffered only slightly due to his therapy hours, motivational speaking, and the foundation. Chris continued to achieve high marks, spending several semesters on the Dean's List and graduating with a cumulative 3.4 GPA.

Chris continued to live life to the fullest. During his junior year, he went to Panama City Beach for spring break with his buddies. When his doctor asked how he got everything arranged, Chris answered, "My parents just make it happen."

Luther offered a January term between the end of the first semester and the beginning of the second semester where students did an internship or studied abroad. Chris flew to Seattle and spent three weeks at Microsoft, Google, Facebook, and other high tech companies up and down the west coast. When he first mentioned the idea of going, we knew it would take some arranging, but we didn't want him missing a fabulous experience just because it required some effort.

I worried about Chris's perfectionist tendencies. Already carrying a lot of responsibility and a full schedule, in his senior year, he also served on the board of directors for the Neurological Recovery House in Rochester, Minnesota, a foundation started to provide accessible housing for people with neurological disorders. Toward the end of his college career, I told him to slow down, put everything else on the back burner, and finish strong in school.

Chris continued to have an amazing attitude and a thoughtful process for determining what he wanted to get involved in. He literally wore me out in a good way because there were days or weeks where he'd call, e-mail, or text me three or four times a day, and never about himself.

Here's what we need to do for the neurological recovery house.

Here's a situation going on with this individual.

Here's a thought for our next fundraiser.

His mind was going all the time, and I spent many days trying to reel him in because he was spreading himself too thin. Given the alternative, I'd rather try to reel him back than try to light a fire under him, but the realist in me always attempted to cool his flames. His energy, drive, and passion for others inspired a lot of people.

Once the foundation began receiving grant requests and our knowledge increased on how much need was out there, our goals kind of exploded. Before Chris's injury, I didn't know anything about spinal cord injuries, and I had no idea how far behind so many rehab facilities were in terms of equipment. Our goals went from doing one event and purchasing some equipment for facilities in our area to realizing the global nature of the issue. People in Las Vegas, Florida, as well as Canada, Australia, and Sri Lanka contacted me about putting in applications.

The scope of need was overwhelming. We had to pick what we could bite off and chew, but it helped expand our thinking and broaden our mission and goals. There were other non-profits geared toward spinal cord injury research, some geared toward providing direct therapy, and some provided needed funds to individuals. SCI CAN was pretty unique in that we didn't give to individuals, but to organizations to provide therapy to as many people as possible.

Our ultimate goals for SCI CAN included getting to the point where we could pay Chris as executive director and hire additional staff as needed. The time commitment continued to grow more than full-time working people could reasonably handle. Other goals remained to support buying much-needed equipment on a local, regional, and national level; the establishment of a much-needed state-of-the-art facility in Des Moines; and to make sure the Neurological Recovery House in

Rochester got started and grew nationally. While there was no official connection between the Neurological Recovery House and SCI CAN, we partnered together to run their first event and supported their efforts to get the house started.

Deb and I had a path we were on at the time of Chris's injury. I pictured us watching Chris play Saturday college football games, Alex graduating from college, and Katie finishing high school. God had other ideas. Chris's injury sent us down a road we hadn't anticipated. I never expected we'd start a foundation, or in two and a half year's time, Chris would have spoken to over forty different organizations, and we would have raised over $375,000 to benefit others.

The sense of accomplishment we felt from conceptualizing the foundation to executing the fundraiser to presenting the money was indescribable. Every time we distributed grant money, I was overwhelmed by our good fortune. Whenever I focused on day-to-day worries with Chris's recovery, wishing he'd go further and that his path was smoother, I'd take stock of the equipment we'd provided and the impact we'd made on people, most of whom we'd never meet. It really helped me find a purpose behind his injury.

People often asked, "How do you work all day and then spend almost every other moment working on the foundation?"

My answer was simple. "We take one day at a time."

Every Saturday morning, Deb and I worked on the foundation over coffee, and I'd also work at night. Hearing the positive impact from others kept me going when I started to wear down and feel like I was burning the candle at both ends. For instance, when a grandmother told me how much her six-year-old granddaughter's handgrip had improved because of the equipment we'd provided, she gave me that extra boost of energy to power through, and I felt so grateful for God's plan.

When Chris was first injured, our focus in terms of his quality of life, level of accomplishment, and success was based mostly on the physical. I was ultra-focused on Chris becoming functionally independent, meaning Chris would walk again and basically make it back to 100 percent. Over time, by simply watching the impact he had on others, I learned to appreciate that the quality of his life wasn't tied directly to his physical recovery.

I still prayed and hoped every day that he'd continue to recover and eventually walk, but my focus shifted from the physical to the emotional. Chris's quality of life came to mean more about him being surrounded by people who loved him, being in a position to make a difference and have an impact, and being a role model for others. It didn't happen overnight, but the shift represented our acceptance, peace, and deep awareness of the value of every human life.

By the two-year anniversary of Chris's injury, I realized in many ways the accident was a blessing. Chris really helped me come to terms with that when he said if he could go back and change the play, if he could go back and change those few seconds that altered his life so drastically, he wouldn't because he was a better person because of it. Hearing those words really encouraged me because I needed to know that he was okay with his life.

When I thought about everything that had happened to us since his injury—the foundation, the growth of Deb's faith, and a profound change in my own faith—none of those things would have happened if it weren't for the accident. If *Chris* could look back and take stock of his life before and after and appreciate all the good that had come out of his misfortune, *I* could certainly do the same. And when I did, it was easy to see the blessings and God's hand at work in our lives.

On the three-year anniversary of Chris's injury, he tweeted: *Three years today is when my life changed forever but changed for the best. This has made me a better person.* Honestly, I didn't know if that statement was prayer driven, but the person who needed to hear that the most was his dad.

In my mind, by three years out, he was supposed to be 100 percent. So for me, each year was harder as I realized the severity of his challenge. It was harder for me over time, while it got easier for Deb. Reading his tweet was a crucial moment for me, because I really needed to hear that in the totally unsolicited manner in which it came.

Knowing he felt blessed was an extraordinary gift because it lifted a burden from my shoulders. When Chris said something, he meant it—he wasn't blowing smoke or doing it for attention.

Considering the day-to-day physical challenges he faced and the fact that people were hardwired to be self-centered, his was a pretty tremendous statement.

One of Chris's main goals was to drive. He longed to do the most mundane tasks on his own, tasks most of us took for granted. Relying on others hindered his independence, especially as graduation loomed. The biggest hurdle in his quest to drive wasn't physical, but financial. Our insurance covered a third of the cost, but the remainder needed to come out of our pocket or through fundraising, and Chris didn't want to focus our efforts inward.

While it was easy to solicit money for the foundation or to fund raise for somebody else, we weren't going to organize a fundraiser to purchase a van for our son. Not long before Chris graduated, a Decorah restaurant owner told Chris it was time for the restaurant owner to get some people in the community together to start working toward raising money for his vehicle. His comment was representative of how supportive and loving the Luther College and Decorah area were to Chris and our family. Our gratitude for that town continued to run wide and deep.

If everything that happened to Chris was only about seeing him graduate from college and making some progress in therapy, I wouldn't have had the peace and optimism I had about his future. About all of our futures. I liked to think that the equipment we gave changed people's lives, and maybe

349

somebody out there who was discouraged and ready to give up heard Chris's story and turned their life around because of it.

As a result of our journey, we were more compassionate. We suddenly looked at people and asked, "How can we help? What can we do to make a difference?"

I like to think that while we benefited, so did all the friends Chris had in college, those who helped take care of him and returned to their hometowns with a better sense of community and knowledge that people with injuries, disabilities, or handicaps were no different than others. They learned that Chris was just like everybody else, and that in a split second, they could be in the same situation.

"We have such a strong connection and I could tell when I first met him how incredible of a person he was. He is so determined, funny, caring, and he has such a strong faith. I wasn't going to pass up all of that because he was in a wheelchair."

Emily Summers, Chris's girlfriend

Chris's beautiful girlfriend, Emily, didn't know him before he was hurt. Their relationship alleviated two of my biggest fears—that women would care too much about his physical limitations and not see him for the person he was. Emily saw Chris for Chris; she never saw the chair, and she wasn't

intimidated by his circumstances or uncomfortable around

him. That meant the world to Deb and me, especially because she was such a wonderful person.

Like Chris, Emily wanted to make a difference in the world. She always thought about what she could do for other people and how to get involved. Deb and I loved Emily for the wonderful person she was and for the way she cared deeply about Chris. It was a true joy welcoming her to our family and watching their relationship blossom.

Chris's story touched people in many different ways. People battling depression, people who'd given up on going to church, people who'd given up on therapy all told me what a difference Chris's story made in their lives. Some told us about their co-workers or relatives struggling with a variety of ailments — physical and emotional — who took Chris's story and used it as inspiration to follow a different path. A guy I used to work with had a sister who'd given up on the church. She'd faced challenges in her life and felt as if God wasn't there for her. He used Chris's story as a gentle nudge that helped get her back to church.

So many stories were shared with us along the way — people from all walks of life and from all over the country — at times when we were fighting the battle and feeling a little down. I watched people treat Chris with compassion and caring in ways I never realized were possible. Our family's experience renewed our faith in the goodness of people and the ability we all had to make a difference.

I do believe what happened to Chris happened for a reason, because it was impossible to think otherwise when I examined the spider web of how everything seemed inter-connected. His injury afforded an opportunity to provide better services and care for so many people with spinal cord injuries. For example, I know that within two years of SCI CAN's formation, over three hundred people had benefited from the equipment. When the ripple effect was taken into account, the number increased exponentially.

After Chris spoke at Loras College, he received a message from a girl whose sister was contemplating suicide. She was so moved by his speech, that she called her sister and shared his story, and it changed the course of her life. We couldn't look at the examples we received on a weekly basis and say there wasn't a purpose behind what happened. Our minister once said that events in our lives could either define us or inspire us, and I truly believed that event did not define Chris, but inspired him.

CHAPTER 27

Trust in the LORD with all your heart and lean not on your own understanding; in all your ways submit to him, and he will make your paths straight.

~Proverbs 3:5-6 NIV

CHRIS

With the foundation up and running, my plans for the future taking shape, and a beautiful, caring woman by my side, I set my sites on graduation. Convinced I'd walk out of the hospital after months at Mayo, I was forced to readjust my plans and set more achievable goals. Years later, after four years in therapy, I publically set a new goal on my blog that received front page coverage from The Des Moines Register: to walk across the stage at graduation in May 2015.

I continued to improve in weekly therapy with Lisa Krieg at Euro-Team, but I knew in order to succeed, I needed more than the four hours of training I was getting and to think outside the box. Emily heard of an intense trainer, Mike Barwis, who'd helped two paraplegics walk again. While I'd seen the story of Brock Mealer, one of the paraplegics Barwis helped, on

ESPN and the Big Ten Network, I never looked into it. Emily discovered that Mike Barwis had his own gym called Barwis Methods Training Center in Plymouth, Michigan, and she encouraged me to contact him, but I wasn't sure how to connect.

After e-mailing Barwis Methods through their website in February 2014, I was added to their year-long waiting list. Determined and impatient to make contact, I reached out to Brock Mealer through Facebook. I messaged him and introduced myself, told him my story, and shared my desire to work out at Barwis Methods. I wasn't trying to cheat the system, but intuition told me I had to go to Barwis Methods at whatever cost. Brock helped connect me to the right people in order to get on the schedule for an evaluation, and not a moment too soon. A reality TV show, *American Muscle*, based out of the gym and the work done there, aired on the Discovery Channel in July 2014, bringing Mike and the facility much deserved attention.

On August 18, after months of trying to sync our schedules, I got an e-mail from the gym saying there was a time slot available in the morning on August 21. Despite having to make the twenty-hour round-trip drive on a few days' notice, I agreed to the appointment. After lining up a ride from Decorah to the airport in Cedar Rapids, Iowa, to pick up Emily upon her return from Florida, we drove to Michigan for the one-hour evaluation. After the session, we drove to Rochester, Minnesota, because we had a big fundraising event for SCI CAN on Saturday night.

The session went better than I could have imagined. Mike

was intense and intelligent. Without knowing my background, or me, he demanded I give him my all. I knew he was going to push me past my limits, which I desperately wanted, and I also learned that the number of people he'd helped walk again were not a few, but over fifty. The one-hour session soon turned into a four-hour intense workout. He confidently told me that after four to five weeks in his program, I'd be a changed man. I was sold, exhausted, and unbelievably optimistic.

Mike Barwis had a great understanding of how the body worked and the motivating factors to push patients to the extreme. After the evaluation, I made plans to finish school early and start my training in January 2015. Upon completing my graduation requirements in December, I eagerly anticipated the move to Michigan and the ability to focus on rehab through the winter and spring. Emily and I found an affordable two bedroom, one bath accessible apartment, packed a U-Haul trailer, and made the eight-hour drive to begin the program.

My first day at Barwis Methods, I had a two-hour appointment. I'd hoped to work with Mike Barwis, but he was in Florida training the New York Mets and wouldn't return until February. My first workout with two of his trainers went well, and the atmosphere, while intense, seemed friendly. The music blared loud, and the walls were littered with jerseys from professional athletes who trained at the gym.

Also displayed on the walls was an array of quotes, like the one from General George S. Patton next to a gigantic American flag. "May God have mercy on my enemies, because I won't."

My favorite Mike Barwis quote, "If the people we work with today mean more to us than ourselves, we will be good at our jobs," embodied what he and the family-like atmosphere of the gym was all about. The gym drew people of varying ages and performance levels, so the facility exuded a busy and enthusiastic vibe. After a quick glance around, I spotted some professional athletes, some disabled people like myself, and even some average athletes.

The trainers first tested my range of motion and strength as I lay on a mat table. It became routine to start there and perform various exercises to isolate different muscles in order to strengthen them. I pressed down against the pressure of the trainer's hand with each foot ten times, and then I pushed my toes up against the pressure of the trainer's hand. We did similar exercises with my quads, hamstrings, hip flexors, and eventually all the muscle groups.

After the mat exercises, we tackled the squat rack where I was placed in a harness attached to a weight suspension system that assisted in keeping me upright. The system took weight off my body, so I didn't have to squat my full body weight, which I was unable to do at the time. I started with fifty pounds and was slowly lowered to forty-five pounds. The trainers instructed me to squat below ninety degrees, a very deep and difficult squat for me. In addition, I had to stand in the correct position—upright with my hips underneath me—before going back down for another repetition. My legs began to burn after four sets of squats. We wrapped the session with a fifteen-yard walk using a walker. I was used to walking on a firm surface like tile or a track, and the turf floor covering turned the routine exercise into a challenge, making my ankles work extra hard to stabilize my body.

Once home, I followed up with a biking session, worked with my Bioness hand stimulator, and did balancing exercises with Emily before bed. I practiced free balancing (not holding or touching anything) to see how long I could stand before falling over, and I only managed five seconds before Emily had to grab me. Between the gym's emphasis on technique and the turf walking exercise, I went to sleep knowing I was in the right place to progress and help me achieve my goals.

On my second day in Michigan, I was assigned to a new trainer, Mike Rhoades, who was extremely knowledgeable but new to neurological training. The session didn't go as well as I wanted, and I became frustrated with myself. Later that night, after a day spent allowing doubt to fester, I questioned my decision to move to Michigan. Was it the right place? Would I ever be able to walk again? Had I set an unattainable goal? Would I get better? Would I let others and myself down by not walking? I stewed in uncertainty and fear.

"What's wrong?" Emily asked. Obviously, she could tell I was troubled.

Worry jelled into frustration. "I just want to beat this," I said, frustrated to the point of tears.

Knowing I wouldn't be able to sleep, Emily suggested I try walking from the kitchen into the bedroom. I used my unsettled emotions to fuel my walk to bed, walking so well we did it a second time, my best walk yet. Satisfied and encouraged to keep working, I banished the fear and fell into an exhausted sleep.

The next day of training went better. Every single transition I'd made since the injury took time and patience to adjust to, and with that in mind, I resigned to let things happen and not get stressed. By the second week, my trainer figured out how my body responded to different positions and exercises, and our time together went much smoother.

> "*My heart sank. In that moment I knew I was going to do everything that I could to help him reach his goals. I believed in him and knew he would accomplish anything he set his mind to.*"
>
> Emily Summers, Chris's girlfriend

However, a urinary tract infection caused my body to weaken and spasm, minimizing my gains. Despite the setback, my squats were down to thirty-five pounds of assistance instead of forty-five to fifty pounds, I started a new leg press machine called the shuttle, my walking improved, and I could balance with Emily for a maximum of five to ten seconds before completely losing my balance.

On January 11, a phone call woke me early in the morning. "Hello?" I said, my voice groggy from sleep.

"Hey, buddy," Dad said, as if calling at the crack of dawn were normal. "How are you doing? "

"Good. What's up?" *Something must be wrong. He would never call me this early unless he had something important to tell me. Please no deaths...*

After a deep breath, Dad said, "Mom's doing just fine, and she'll be okay, but we had to bring her to the emergency room last night, and she had a stent put in her artery."

"Mom had a heart attack?"

"Yes. She's in the ICU recovering."

I couldn't believe what I'd just heard, and I didn't know what to say. All I could do was thank God my mom was alive. I never would have expected my extremely health conscious mom to suffer a heart attack. My dad assured me I didn't need to go home and that she'd be okay. I hated that I was so far away, and I desperately wanted to see her and be there for her, but my dad insisted I stay put. With his assurance that Mom would want me to stay, I remained in Michigan and continued with therapy, checking on her every day by phone.

I saw a massage therapist at the conclusion of the second week because the workouts caused my muscles to stiffen and become so sore I could barely lift my head off the pillow. The massage helped loosen my muscles, time eased my worries, and the third week of training went even better than the second. My body responded well to the therapy and my trainer and I were in sync with what was needed to make greater strides in my progress.

By the end of week three, I was able to tolerate three and four hours of therapy at a time, and I improved significantly. I was down to squatting with the assistance of fifteen to twenty pounds, I increased the number of resistance bands when using the shuttle, and I was able to walk twenty-five yards instead of fifteen yards with a walker before taking a break.

Emily and I enjoyed our time together and the weeks flew by, but it didn't take long for me to become concerned about the amount of time she spent tending to my needs. She never complained or made me feel like a burden, but her life revolved around me 24/7, and I felt guilty for keeping her from her passion of working with at-risk children and others in need. She routinely mentored eight or more kids, her phone constantly rang with calls from kids who needed to talk to her, and yet her life took a back seat to mine, and it couldn't go on forever. I loved her too much to stifle her dreams while reaching for my own, so I hoped and prayed an opportunity would present itself in Michigan where Emily could utilize her life's passion and feel fulfilled.

Our prayers were answered after a meeting with the director of development at Barwis Methods to discuss how we could help their First Step Foundation. When we learned they had another foundation called Athletic Angels helping at-risk children through mentoring, athletic, and academic opportunities, Emily turned to me wide-eyed, thrilled beyond belief they had an organization to benefit those she loved to serve. She had to get involved. The next day, after a three-hour conversation with Mike Barwis about why he started the foundation and how they could benefit more children, Emily was offered the opportunity to help expand and grow Athletic Angels!

With my concerns for Emily abated and my mom on the mend, I saw even greater improvement in week four of training than in week three. I squatted with no weight assistance, brought my hips underneath me much easier, added more resistance bands on the shuttle, and walked a forty-five yard straightaway while raising my legs higher with my steps. Things were coming along. While Emily helped me walk to bed, I was able to take a step with her using one arm to hang onto me, and balancing in the twenty to thirty second time range.

Fortunately, during our short time at Barwis Methods, we made friends through our time at the gym, and we even got to hang out and attend the Detroit Pistons vs. Cleveland Cavaliers basketball game.

By February 2, I felt really strong. I tolerated more sets and repetitions of mat exercises, went right from those exercises to the leg press machine and cranked out four sets of ten reps, and went straight to walking. Instead of fatiguing and my energy and strength slipping at the end of the workout, I excelled.

Emily and I walked 150 yards with a walker after my session. I couldn't believe how well I'd performed on a Monday.

Tuesday went great too. I squatted with no weight assistance with improved positioning. My walking typically struggled after squats, but this time my walking felt its best. I walked twenty-five yards without a break at the end of my session and in a faster time than before. That night, we timed my balancing at a minute, forty-five seconds. Encouraged by my progress, I tried again for two minutes, and made it four! I was shocked and beyond excited about how far I'd come in such a short amount of time. By the end of the week, I'd walked fifty yards.

The following Monday, the trainer let me squat without the harness. I would get as low as I could with my squat, but without the help of the harness, I would hit a point where the nerve signal would just turn off and my legs would give out. Whenever I got to the point in my squats where my legs gave out, one of my trainers stood behind me to break my fall until I regained the connection. A second later, I shot back up to standing. The point of the exercise was to get my body used to squatting lower and to gradually lower the spot where I would lose the nerve connection.

On "Walking Wednesday," I tried to walk five more yards than the previous week. We decided I might as well walk sixty yards, which I accomplished, but it took an hour and ten minutes. I was dead on my feet after and still had two more hours of training. After working on my upper body for one hour, I finished my session on the shuttle with a record number of resistance bands. After four hours in therapy, I was exhausted.

The next day, I squatted again without a harness, and went lower and slower than the day before. My first three sets were so strong, they put on a ten pound weight vest for my fourth set and I still did really well. I was amazed by my progress. Later that week, needing a break, Emily and I hung out with fellow gym member, Claudia, and her mom, Deb. We went out to dinner and played cards with them after.

I had my best day on the leg press on a Monday in mid-February, pushing more weight and needing less assistance than ever. I remained strong through the four sets, though fatigue usually settled in on the last two. I went from the highest of highs to the lowest of lows when, while walking, I struggled to go twenty yards and then fell. My trainer and I typically talked trash and teased each other throughout my workouts, but I got to the point where I was so angry about my performance that he noticed and backed off the banter. I always shielded my true feelings of disappointment whenever I was having a bad day, especially during workouts, but there wasn't any way to mask my frustration.

I couldn't accept bad days because every day was so important for me in reaching my goal. The fear of plateauing lurked in the back of my mind at all times and pushed me harder in my recovery. On bad days, it felt as if I'd reached a plateau, indicating my recovery was over. Fortunately, that never happened and I always bounced back stronger, but I was in such a vulnerable state that the logic of having an off day didn't matter. It kept me hungry for the next workout. Even though I'd had my best day on the leg press, walking was most important, and my performance sent me spiraling downward. I put a lot of pressure on myself to get one small step closer to my goal every day. Mercifully, each time I took a step back, I ended up taking two or three steps forward, so with that in mind, I accepted the fall as a molehill and not a mountain.

Tuesdays and Thursdays were squat days. Growing up and prior to my injury I *hated* squats. I was bad at them, mostly because during my growth years, I had Osgood-Schlatter, a disease that caused inflammation in the bone, cartilage, and/ or tendons of my legs. I suffered through a lot of pain from OSD my eighth grade and freshman years of high school—the same time when weightlifting became an integral ingredient for improvement in sports. The slightest touch had me wincing in pain.

For spring baseball, I had to put a sweatshirt under my knee for kneeled throws in order to minimize the pain. Squats were excruciating, but I did them because I wanted to be the guy who fought through the pain and never sat out. Doing one-legged squats for two years on my left leg caused a major strength imbalance, which meant I lagged behind everyone else in squat strength, and my form was awful. While attempting to alleviate the pain, I caved my right knee inward to limit the pressure and shifted all my weight to the left side, a habit that continued once the pain went away.

Doing squats at Barwis Methods Training Center felt normal, as if I were able-bodied. Exercises where I could see improvement in my strength and movement made me feel great, while exercises where I couldn't tangibly see strength or movement improvement were frustrating. I felt defeated whenever I couldn't activate a muscle group, no matter how hard I tried. I knew I had to start somewhere, and I needed to work on my weaknesses, but it was mentally hard to muddle through when things weren't going well. I performed best with a balance of exercises where I could excel on some and challenge myself with others.

The squats on the day after my walking fiasco went very well. I went low and held for three seconds before coming up, did two sets without weight, and completed the last two sets with a weight vest. The next day, "Walking Wednesday," I had a four-hour workout session where I knew my walking endurance would be tested. I was nervous due to how poorly I'd performed on Monday. Each week, I walked farther, and the idea of walking farther than last week seemed impossible. With God's help, I walked the full length of the turf in the gym, a total of sixty-five yards, with only two short standing breaks, and no sit-down breaks, in a total time of forty minutes. The prior week, I walked five yards less in seventy minutes, a marked improvement that really lifted my spirits.

Right after my session, Emily and I left for the airport to fly to Moline, Illinois, where Emily's family picked us up so I could speak the next day to more than twelve hundred North Scott High School students. During my last semester of school, I turned down many speaking requests in order to concentrate on school and enjoy my remaining months as a student. Despite feeling nervous because I hadn't spoken in months, it felt natural to speak again, and I received tremendous feedback from both the students and the administrators. The next day, my nerves spiked again when I spoke for an hour to a Des Moines Area Community College facility at Newton where my dad worked. Fortunately, I once again received great feedback, including from a man who told me he'd heard hundreds of motivational speakers, and my speech was one of the best he'd ever heard.

I then spoke to four hundred sixth graders in Ankeny, Iowa, where every year the teachers presented my story during their lesson on heroes. The kids were great listeners, and the wonderful experience reinforced my desire to spend my life impacting others.

Our SCI CAN fundraiser was held in Des Moines at Prairie Meadows Events Center the following day. The program was well received by the packed house of four hundred guests. We raised $70,000 and gave some of it away in scholarships to benefit kids with disabilities. We flew back to Detroit on February 23rd in order to shoot the First Step Foundation's video with a director from Los Angeles. Emily, in her official role, helped coordinate the shoot.

By February 24, I was up to five sets of squats with a ten-pound weight vest, a feat that seemed impossible only a month before. That day, five minutes into my unassisted standing, Emily said, "Keep going. Mike Barwis is coming over."

I was told there was a chance I'd train with Mike on the twenty-fourth, and I was anxious to work with him. Because he'd been so busy, I hadn't really seen him over the first six or seven weeks in Michigan. I really wanted to show him my progress and have him update my program. Quickly regaining my composure, I stood really well, and felt encouraged when Mike cheered me on. I ended up standing for seven-and-a-half minutes. Mike was so impressed he started working with me on the spot. He wanted to evaluate my progress and see what new strength I'd gained, exactly as I'd hoped. He said he'd stay with me for thirty minutes, but he ended up staying for an hour and a half and missing his video shoot with pro athletes.

Mike was really impressed with how far I'd come and told me exactly what I needed to do in order to walk without the walker. He instructed me to work more on my glutes and to stand more upright so I wouldn't rely on my quad strength. He also told me to focus on my abductors and external rotators, writing up a list of ten different exercises for me to work on using those muscles. Blessed with the eye to know exactly what I needed to be able to walk again, Mike wanted nothing more than for me to get rid of the walker and move unassisted. He showed me what I was doing wrong and said that I was at the point where I needed to change to the correct walking form if I wanted to meet my goal.

Knowing he was the expert and that his advice was spot on didn't alleviate my fears. I knew it would be difficult to make the changes he wanted because I'd been compensating for my weaker muscles and relying on the walker for too long, forming bad habits. I'd neglected the muscles that needed the most work in order to take the next step and stop using the walker. I had to change up my workout and get out of my comfort zone if I wanted to achieve my goal.

> *"He does not take no for an answer. He pushes at the obstacle until he figures out how to get his body and life around, over, or through it — not stop at it!!"*
>
> Lisa Krieg, PT Euro-Team in Decorah

I'd done it before at the three-year mark when I finally decided to stop using leg braces in order to walk and stand. The braces helped support my ankles and knees, but because I relied on the braces, my ankles and knees never had the chance to improve on their own. I experienced some frustrating weeks while trying to get back into the same walking form I had with the aid of the braces. Eventually, my ankles and knees regained the strength I needed, and I made significant progress because I was no longer relying on the leg braces for support.

Armed with the knowledge of what needed to be done, and reminding myself of the patience that would be necessary to see me through, I felt ready to take the next step in my recovery.

CHAPTER 28

As I sat in church and listened to him (Chris) speak, I thought about the doors that have closed, but more importantly about the ones that have opened. I know in my mind that in many ways Chris's injury has been a blessing. That he has an opportunity to shine and to make a difference in the lives of so many people that he would not have had otherwise. To God alone be the glory.

~Terry Norton, CaringBridge, October 16, 2012

TERRY

Chris finished all of his classes in December 2014, and Deb and I moved him out of his dorm for the last time a few weeks before Christmas. Moving Chris out of Luther was like strapping myself in to an emotional roller coaster. I felt so many sentiments on the drive up, thinking about his time at Luther, our expectations for him when we dropped him off the first time, his accident, and the resulting total upheaval of our lives.

He'd lived in his dorm room and in the "cluster" for the past three-and-a-half years, from the beginning of the 2011/2012 school year through the fall of 2014. The cluster provided the only room on campus that was accessible, and because of the quality of therapy available in Decorah, the accessibility he had to the facilities and campus, and the friends he had around him, he stayed every summer. He'd never moved out after getting settled in.

After packing his things in the van and taking a long glance around the empty room and the cluster for the last time, we all stood silent, overcome by emotions, both happy and sad. Chris faced so many hurdles while living on campus and attending Luther College. He'd come there full of hope and excitement, ready to earn a degree and help bring the football program back to glory. He'd left after ten weeks on a stretcher, come back after ten months in a wheelchair, and was leaving campus a full grown man, ready to face whatever life threw his way.

Pulling away for the last time, I knew Luther would always trigger a colossal range of emotions for me. As a family, we'd experienced every emotional peak and valley during his more than four years at Luther.

As with most kids moving out of college for the last time, Chris was a different person than the one we'd dropped off in the fall of 2010 — not just physically, but in every way possible. During his time at college, he'd learned to live as a

> *"If he had not been injured, he probably would not have met Emily, started a foundation, and been an inspiration to so many young people. God is using Chris, working through Chris for His will."*
>
> Connie Norton, Chris's Grandma

physically handicapped person, discovered his career passion, made more friends than I'd ever have in my lifetime, touched lives, impacted thousands, and fell in love. It was hard not to see the blessings that walked hand in hand with the heartache on our journey down memory lane.

We had lots to look forward to, not only the upcoming Christmas holiday with family, but also our oldest daughter, Alex, getting engaged to her longtime boyfriend, Bill McManus. Bill asked my permission and blessing to propose on their New Year's ski trip. It was really difficult to keep the news a secret for several days.

Deb, Chris, Katie, Emily, and I also visited my mom in Iowa City the day after Christmas. We had a great time visiting with Mom, shopping, eating out, watching movies, and playing cards. We weren't expecting the van to break down on the way home from Iowa City, or having to tow it back home. Alex, who hadn't made the trip because of work, had to come and get us. The two-thousand-dollar bill to have the van fixed ended up being a very painful but necessary expense.

Unfortunately, the van wasn't ready when it was time to move Chris and Emily to Michigan where he'd planned to work with Mike Barwis at Barwis Methods for the winter and spring. Chris had spent nearly a year communicating back and forth with Barwis and researching the facility, Mike, and their clients. He felt time spent there was vital for reaching his next goal of walking across the stage at graduation in May.

I had watched a YouTube video with Mike Barwis speaking and introducing a client of his who later walked. From the video, I knew Mike was Chris's type of guy—inspirational, a motivator, and a positive person. Knowing the environment Barwis created and the outcome they typically achieved, I knew Chris would love working with Mike to realize his goals. Chris responded well to encouragement and sports/coaching type people and environments. He loved being pushed hard and was willing to do his part.

After Chris researched Barwis Methods thoroughly, and made the trek for a face-to-face visit and assessment, we knew Barwis Methods was the right place for Chris and our best option for him progressing to the level he wanted to attain.

Chris, Emily, Chris's friend Brock, and I left home with a U-Haul trailer, stopped in Emily's hometown to get Emily's possessions, and stayed overnight in Chicago. Deb left later and met us in Chicago after the van was repaired. We all drove to Michigan the following day through rain, sleet, and a little snow. The apartment they'd rented was nice, but it wasn't much fun moving in during a rain and sleet storm. Deb, Brock, and I left for home a few days later, and we drove through a terrible snow storm with visibility so poor that we ended up staying overnight in Iowa City at my mom's and driving home the following day.

Once home, my parental worries reared their ugly heads, worries I'd buried under the mountain of details it took to get Chris and Emily moved to Michigan. My biggest concern about them spending the winter and spring in Michigan at Barwis

Methods was how far they would be from home without a lot of support from family and friends. Deb and I worried about Emily shouldering everything herself without us there to provide some relief.

By January, winter was in full swing, and I felt uneasy about Chris and Emily getting around in bad weather in a new and unfamiliar city. Chris also had lofty expectations for his progress under Mike's tutelage. As his father, I was concerned he'd be discouraged if he fell short. I knew he'd give it his all, but I couldn't stop the anxiety train that began its journey the day he was born. Because it was important for Chris and Emily to move to Michigan and face this challenge together, I wasn't willing to put a damper on their enthusiasm and voice my concerns.

One Sunday night early in January, not long after moving Chris and Emily to Michigan, Deb gave us a scare. Just before ten o'clock, we were getting ready for bed when Deb said her jaw hurt and she felt a little nauseated. She asked Alex for some aspirin, and in discussing Deb's symptoms, Alex immediately recognized that Deb was exhibiting the classic signs of a heart attack in a woman. Deb was a health nut who ate right and worked out a lot, so my initial reaction was disbelief, but I knew not to question the nurse in the family, so we went to the hospital right away. As we got close to the hospital, Deb started feeling pain under her arms, and she became hot and restless.

Things progressed quickly at the ER. They ushered her

through admissions, performed an EKG, and determined she was in fact having a heart attack. I thought *I* was going to have a heart attack when the ER doctor gave me her diagnosis and told me if we had kids close by to call them and have them come to the hospital right away. As if living in a nightmare, I called Alex and Deb's sister and brothers, alerting them to Deb's condition, but I waited until the following morning to call Chris or Katie. Chris and Emily were too far away to make it home, and Katie was hours away at college. I knew they'd both be upset and want to come, and I couldn't take the chance of them driving late at night while emotional.

Doctors surgically implanted a stent in Deb's artery, clearing the blockage. Deb awoke from surgery groggy, but alive and kicking. The stent did the trick, and after extensive testing and four days in the hospital, she was released to go home with a laundry list of precautions, new medications, and a renewed appreciation for everyday life. I made sure she got plenty of rest, tried to do more around the house, and farmed out her duties for February's SCI CAN event in Des Moines to willing friends.

Deb continued to improve, the SCI CAN event went well, and we raised over $70,000. We enjoyed visiting with Chris and Emily at the event and seeing for ourselves the progress he'd made in the month and a half since we'd dropped him off. Before they left to go back, Deb and I felt good knowing Chris and Emily had adjusted to life in Michigan, they'd made new friends, gotten to know the area, liked where they were living, and Chris continued to progress physically. They'd even gone to two Detroit Pistons games and the Iowa/Michigan basketball game in Ann Arbor.

In early April, Deb and I went to visit Chris and Emily for a long weekend. I was really pleased to see how happy they were and how good they felt about Chris's progress during his time at Barwis. Deb and I watched Emily take care of everything Chris needed effortlessly. Seeing how happy and contented they were together filled us with joy. Physically, Chris's posture and balance had improved significantly. He stood in the family room of the apartment with Emily a few steps away, and if I didn't know any better, I'd have thought he was a college athlete standing there like anybody else.

"I've often asked myself, 'How would I respond if I was in Chris's shoes?' I don't know that I would have his strength, determination, grit, and faith."

Benny Boyd, Former Assistant Coach, Luther College

On the trip home, Deb and I were filled with optimism for their future. Our son was happy and in love, making great strides in his recovery, and filled with hope. We wouldn't see Chris until graduation at the end of May, and while we prayed he'd meet his goal, we knew the journey was worth the effort no matter the outcome. I reached across the console and grasped Deb's hand, our eyes meeting before I looked back at the road, and with that brief glance I felt at peace, enveloped in our heavenly Father's loving embrace.

CHAPTER 29

"I have told you these things, so that in me you may have peace. In this world you will have trouble. But take heart! I have overcome the world."

~ John 16:33 NIV

CHRIS

By the end of February, we began focusing on the different muscle groups Mike advised. We had worked on those muscles during my time at Barwis, but not with the emphasis that was necessary. I was able to squat with twenty-two pounds on my back, and I worked on standing straight up-and-down, bringing my hips underneath me because I had a tendency to lean forward and utilize my strongest leg muscles — my quads.

Walking with the correct positioning, with my hips and back in a straight line, was really difficult. My muscles were weak, and elongating my upper body made it difficult to breathe through my diaphragm. Hunching over made it easier to get air in and out of my lungs, and standing up straight with my abs firing compressed my breathing, making me light-headed. It felt as if I'd regressed when I was struggling to stand correctly, let alone take a step. I fought the urge to throw my hands in the air, relying instead on my faith and my belief in Mike as the expert.

By the first week of March, I wasn't straining as much to breathe when I stood using the correct posture, but taking steps was still a trial. I thought I was ready for the challenge, but it seemed absurd to struggle while standing when only a week ago I'd been able to walk sixty-five yards. I felt trapped inside my body, unable to walk and fire my hip flexors, crushing the sense of freedom I received from making progress, and frustrating me to no end.

By the end of the week, I'd started to walk using the correct position, but still struggled to make it five yards. Fortunately, I continued to increase my leg press resistance and squatted for two sets wearing the weight vest, while my weakest muscles, like my external rotators, started firing on a more consistent basis during the mat exercises.

"The most remarkable thing about Chris is his passion for life, his unshakeable attitude, and above all his spirit. The real story of Chris Norton is not a story of tragedy, but a story of healing. And the pages are still being written."

Rich Vickers, Chris's college roommate and close friend

Slowly but surely, the essential yet underused muscles began to strengthen. As with all of my recovery, patience was a vital component.

I made the tough decision to cancel my spring break vacation plans to Arizona. I'd been looking forward to relaxing with my family away from cold Michigan, but with my goal to walk across the stage in May, I needed to stay in Michigan and train. I couldn't sleep at night if I felt I hadn't worked hard enough that day to reach my goal, and spending a week of vacation had the potential to haunt me for years if I wasn't where I wanted to be at graduation. There would always be plenty of time to vacation with my family, but I only had one college graduation. In order to accomplish my goal, I had to make sacrifices, and I decided vacation could wait.

Emily had planned her own vacation with her family over spring break, and once again friends came to the rescue. My good friend, John Schram, flew to Michigan to stay with me for the week while Emily was gone so I could continue training. While my underused muscles were getting stronger, they'd quickly fatigue, which made walking tough. During my week with John, I walked ten yards consistently, but it was still a struggle.

When Emily returned from visiting her family, we went to Cleveland to visit Dr. Issam Nemeh, after several people at Barwis with similar injuries recommended him. At first, I was skeptical about Dr. Nemeh and didn't investigate his practice, but after several other people I knew went to see him and saw some pretty phenomenal results, I changed my mind, did some research, and decided to make an appointment.

380

Dr. Nemeh was featured in a number of news programs, TV shows, and articles due to his innovative and highly effective methods of treatment. Emily and I found Dr. Nemeh to be a very nice and religious man who was fun to talk to and extremely optimistic. Dr. Nemeh performed acupuncture with electrical stimulation and used various instruments to stimulate my nervous system.

After our visit with Dr. Nemeh, Emily and I went to get pizza near his office at a restaurant that advertised accessibility. To our great dismay, the restaurant's narrow hallway and step-up seating wasn't anywhere close to accessible. While I was able to maneuver up the step and squeeze through the hallway, Emily and I were disappointed because we knew lots of people who were already self-conscious in their chairs and who'd be emotionally crushed if they went to a restaurant only to be turned away because they couldn't get in the door. Despite the disappointing restaurant experience, we considered our trip a success.

After Dr. Nemeh's treatment, my hands were more relaxed and not as closed as they usually were, and I also regained more sensation in my upper and lower body. To test my increased sensitivity to pain, Emily started pinching me all over my body. I'd lost the feeling of pain below my chest after the accident, and to my great surprise, the pinches hurt! Unfortunately, my heightened sensitivity decreased a bit the following week, but that only increased my desire to pay the doctor another visit.

By the end of March, my walking had improved. At night, Emily and I worked on standing balance, and I stood for over ten minutes on my own.

One night, while balancing with my left hand grabbing onto Emily's hand, she said, "If you can take a step right now, I'll give you five hundred dollars."

She was kidding, as she felt sure I couldn't step with so little assistance. Never one to ignore a challenge, I took a step, and then two more just like it! We felt ecstatic watching prayers answered, and our enthusiasm carried us through the whole week.

During the first week of April, while sitting on the mat table during a session, Mike Barwis came over, hoisted me into a standing position, and said he wanted to observe me in action. I didn't know what he was checking for, but he tried to get me to take a side step. I tried, but I didn't get very far to the side. My legs pulled to the inside, which made taking steps to the outside very difficult. He laid me back down to stretch my hips and groin, and he noticed that my nerves and tendons were locked up tight from my legs pulling to the inside.

Thinking that the tightness was blocking the nerve signals and feelings to use the muscles to move to my legs to the outside of my body, he used his fingers to dig in on a certain point on my hip where the tension was the most concentrated. At the same time, he had someone put my leg into position to release the tension, and the next thing I knew, I felt more sensation on the outside of my hip, and I was able to fire that muscle much stronger. When he tried explaining what he'd done, he talked fast and was so detailed that all I knew was that I was in the right place to achieve my goals.

By the next week, I was walking farther and with less help, even walking a few steps with my left foot by just holding onto Emily with one hand. The progress I'd made gave me a huge push. With less than forty-six days until graduation, I felt very optimistic about my gains.

Even with my exceptional progress, I was nervous whenever I thought about graduation. How would I do it? With my walker? With Emily? With crutches? I worried about how long a walk I could do, if the gown would affect my walking, and if people would be able to see my gains and how hard I'd worked. The only thing I could do was work through the doubts, but at night I grew restless lying in bed with those thoughts flooding my brain.

Like clockwork, Mike Barwis called one morning to discuss how I was feeling about my graduation walk and if I had a plan. When I explained my doubts and concerns to him, he reassured me that no matter what I did on stage, people would love me and be proud because of how far I'd come. He encouraged me not to worry about what people thought and to just give it my all, reminding me I could only control my attitude and effort, and suggesting I focus on those two things.

Mike recommended I try the forearm crutches Brock Mealer

used years ago when he first relearned to walk. We located the crutches, but I was nervous because I hadn't used crutches for months, not since working at Euro-Team in Decorah. Despite my apprehension, when I tried the crutches, they worked really well, so well that I was close to taking a step with no one's help. That night, I took the crutches home to our apartment and by using them, was able to take several steps all by myself.

Ecstatic and very encouraged by my progress, I also knew that my strength was ten times stronger at night than in the morning. For some unknown reason, as a day progressed, my strength increased. So mornings were tougher. Unfortunately, graduation was scheduled to take place in the morning, but I had a month to turn a few independent night steps into lots of great steps by the morning of May 24, 2015.

By mid-April, my gym time increased from three hours a day to five hours on Tuesdays and Thursdays, in addition to my night work with Emily. Although crutch walking was going well, I decided to walk without crutches. I didn't want my graduation walk to take up too much time, and I knew I'd take longer than any other student. Considering the additional setup time necessary to get the crutches on and off, I decided to walk with Emily, whom I was most comfortable walking with anyway.

As April slid to May, I began taking a nighttime supplement to aid sleep, recover muscles, and rest my nervous system. With the countdown marching onward and my focus solely on graduation, I also added an additional trainer to my workouts. With the clock ticking, whenever I struggled to walk, disappointment triggered a film loop of failure inside my head, and swung the door open to crippling anxiety. Like a self-fulfilling prophesy, my body stopped reacting and responding the way it usually did. My walking got worse, and I fatigued much quicker.

Desperate for answers, I decided all the extra hours of therapy coupled with never taking a break had taken a toll. I took the following Monday, Tuesday, and Wednesday off for physical and mental rejuvenation. My brain was fried from concentrating so much while trying to initiate different muscles throughout my body. In the past, any breaks I took were for necessities like speaking engagements, travel, and school, but this time I needed to take the initiative. I just knew my body would feel stronger after a break, but to my utter confusion and frustration, my body felt even worse after coming back. Why was this happening, and why *now* with graduation only weeks away?

I fought the urge to break down into tears every time I attempted to walk, because only weeks ago I'd been capable of walking so much better. What had changed? When I saw Mike Barwis, I explained the situation, and he gave me a few suggestions, one of which was to stop taking the nighttime supplement.

The following weekend, I felt my body starting to wake

back up, but I still felt worn down and dehydrated. We went to see Dr. Nemeh again, hoping to get back on track. By Monday, my walking was much better — still not to where I wanted — but I felt relieved to be able to lift my legs again. As the week progressed, I felt more like myself, and my stress leveled back to normal.

By the middle of the month, I had my best walk with Emily — ten strong and fluid yards — and once again felt confident about the five-yard graduation walk. On the nineteenth, because of dehydration, my walking didn't go well. The gym didn't have air-conditioning or fans, and temperatures in the building reached the upper 80s. My body overheated, causing my legs to lose nerve connection, and I got lightheaded while standing. While uncomfortable, it was a good reminder to make preparations for graduation and the possibility of spending a hot day on Luther's football field or being indoors due to inclement weather. The last thing I wanted to do was pass out on stage!

On Wednesday, my walk went well, and I felt ready for the ceremony. I purchased dress shoes that would help with ankle stability to wear on graduation day and practiced with them during the week. We left on May 20 for Emily's hometown, Muscatine, Iowa. After a couple of peaceful days at the Summers's home, we left for Decorah on May 22. On the drive to Decorah, I worked on my speech for the Luther Senior Sports banquet held the next morning and practiced it the whole way.

The presentation served to distract me from the surprise I'd planned for Saturday afternoon and graduation on Sunday morning.

For three months, I'd plotted and planned the perfect marriage proposal for Emily. Both of us were ready to take our relationship to the next level, and I racked my brain thinking of a romantic way to surprise her. Emily loved watching proposal videos on YouTube, and the pressure was on to make her proposal memorable. Emily would be the first to admit I'm not the most romantic guy, but I knew I could make up a lot of ground by creating a proposal she'd never forget.

Between March and May, every time Emily and I weren't together, I was on the phone with my family coordinating aspects of the proposal. I carried a checklist in my head of things I knew she liked: family involvement, videotaped, and pre-planned. My friend, Michael Crocker, flew in from California to film the proposal, and another photographer friend, Tyler Rinken, was on hand to capture the moment as well. My family bought rose petals and roses to scatter on the floor, placed a bunch of photos of Emily and me around the room, and set up a speaker to play our song, "All of Me," by John Legend. They spelled, "Will you marry me?" with candles on the floor of the back room to our favorite restaurant in downtown Decorah, Rubiayat.

I knew the owner really well, so when I told Emily that the owner had a graduation present for me that I needed to pick up before they opened at 4:30 p.m., she didn't blink an eye. Emily and I were conveniently dressed nicely from my speaking engagement that morning, and I told her we had a video interview with the news station afterwards, so she touched up her makeup before we left.

That day, I couldn't eat a thing because I was so nervous, and Emily kept asking me why I wasn't eating. She was worried about keeping my strength up for the walk the next day. I wasn't nervous she would say no, but I wanted the proposal to be perfect.

After lunch, we went to our room to practice standing and walking, and my parents left to go shopping, which was code for "get the restaurant ready." Emily was totally thrown off that my dad went shopping with the girls because she knew he hated to shop. Finally, I got the call from Kim, the restaurant owner, which meant the room was ready and everyone was in place, including Emily's family. I didn't say a whole lot on our way to the restaurant, as I tried to prepare how I would ask her to marry me and control my racing heart.

We got to the restaurant, Kim let us in, escorted us to the back room, and slipped me the ring. Emily read the lettering on the floor, realized what was happening, and said, "Oh my gosh, oh my gosh, oh my gosh," before starting to cry.

Seeing Emily so emotional got me choked up, but I collected myself and asked her to marry me. She said yes, slipped the ring on her finger, and my cameraman and videographer captured the whole event. Shortly after, all of our family came out of hiding to smother us with hugs and congratulate us on making our plans official. I'd arranged for friends to come to celebrate with us as well. Everything went as planned.

After celebrating with family and friends that evening, Emily and I called it a night because we had to get up early the next morning for graduation. While sad to leave early with so many friends in town, the most important thing was to accomplish my goal—the *other* event everyone came to town to witness.

We woke up at 5:00 a.m. so my body would have six hours to adjust and be strong for the graduation walk. We started the day with some exercises, a short walk to warm up, and then waited anxiously for the commencement ceremony.

With my presentation complete and my future with Emily secure, my nerves returned with a vengeance. I'd set out to accomplish a huge goal in a very public setting, but I couldn't predict how my body would respond when it came time to walk. *I* knew I'd already succeeded from the gains in strength I'd made and from the focus I'd put into making my graduation walk a reality, but I wanted everyone else to see how far I'd come too. The keynote speaker helped to ease my nerves with one of the funniest speeches I'd ever heard, but once the graduates started walking across the stage to collect their diplomas, my stomach fell to my knees.

As we approached the stage, Emily in front and my

friend, Tanner, pushing the chair from behind, the dean read, "Christopher Norton," signifying game time. Like the athlete I'd always been, I focused on my training and the task at hand, and didn't worry about anyone or anything else. Emily and I knew I was ready. I put a smile on my face, looked up at the woman I loved, and said, "Let's do it."

Everyone in attendance rose to his or her feet to cheer me on as I made my way across the stage. The excitement and emotions of the crowd really caught me off guard and pushed me forward. The walk went well, and I only stepped on Emily's foot once. As I got close to the president of the college, with Emily's help, I lined up my feet to shake her hand. I pumped my fist in the air to acknowledge the crowd's support, and the resounding applause echoed across the basketball gym. Quite a few people on stage had tears in their eyes.

Tanner wheeled me off stage where family and friends were there to greet us, right where they'd always been. There wasn't a dry eye in the crowd. I didn't realize the magnitude of what I'd accomplished or how many people were emotionally invested in my walk until I finally got back to my spot for the ceremony and took stock of the last few months.

> *"Walking across the stage with Chris was the best moment in my life, which is saying a lot since the proposal happened the day before and was absolutely perfect."*
>
> Emily Summers, Chris's fiancé

While so relieved it was over, I also felt extremely proud of accomplishing the goal I'd set out to achieve with everyone I cared about by my side.

I didn't walk alone. God was with me from the very beginning, and I had Emily by my side, my family cheering from the audience, and all of my friends for support. So many people contributed to make my graduation walk a success. As with so many things in the adventure called life, I was forever grateful. At twenty-three, with the woman I loved by my side, surrounded by family and friends, I was truly blessed and ready to face whatever came next. Bring it on, God.

CHAPTER 30

There are so many wonderful people out there, and the generosity we have felt along the way from friends, family, and complete strangers has just been amazing. You see God here on earth in the faces of the people your lives touch.

~ Terry Norton, CaringBridge, October 16, 2012

TERRY

In true Chris fashion, he and Emily made friends, loved their time in Michigan, and just made everything work. My doubts about the obstacles they'd face while there were for naught. From the moment he went back to college after his injury, I witnessed the same pattern time and time again. I'd worry about every possible pitfall, and Chris would find a way to make things work just fine.

Chris and Emily also became very involved in the foundations Barwis Methods operates, First Step and Athletic Angels. Both Chris and Emily, so driven to help others, were drawn to the foundations and the work they did for people in need. Their time at Barwis Methods fulfilled every one of their needs.

Chris loved his therapy at Barwis Methods and made so

much progress. When he first arrived in Michigan, he couldn't balance on his own without leg braces for more than four seconds. Soon, he was able to balance for up to ten minutes. As another example of his progress, at first, he had to have fifty pounds offloaded in order to perform a squat. Through hard work and with the expertise of his trainers, he soon progressed to not only

"There are few people in life that can deal with adversity in a way that is truly uplifting and something that will drive other individuals to achieve success."

Adam W. Busch, Former head football coach at Bondurant-Farrar Community Schools

squatting his full weight, but also adding thirty-three pounds of resistance!

From the moment Chris introduced us to Emily, we knew she was something special. Gradually, Chris came to depend on Emily in the way he'd counted on his friends at school. It didn't take long until she was the one helping him work out on the weekends and traveling with him to speaking engagements. Deb and I witnessed another prayer answered as we watched our son fall in love with a beautiful woman who loved him for who he was.

The challenge of planning and preparing for Chris's surprise proposal was fun and exciting, as we were extremely pleased for both of them. But it was also very stressful. Trying to keep the planning quiet was tough. We had to be sneaky when sending Chris any type of text or e-mail related to the proposal in case Emily happened to see it, so we often disguised our communication as SCI CAN financial information. It was really hard not to shout from the rooftops or tell any of our friends, but we just couldn't take a chance that word would spread.

Chris was very specific about the setup for the proposal. He wanted the room scattered with flowers, flower petals, candles, and pictures. His sisters made a poster that spelled out, "All of me loves all of you," quoting the John Legend song they'd adopted as their own. We fashioned, "Will you marry me?" with candles and flower petals on the floor, and had their song playing in the background.

The owner of the restaurant, Kim, called Chris and lured them to the restaurant under the guise of a graduation present he needed to pick up before a big group arrived. Thinking they were heading to a TV interview after they picked up the graduation gift, Emily wore a pretty dress, and they both looked picture perfect. Emily's family was present, and so was ours, hiding in the restaurant's kitchen while the actual proposal took place. Emily was totally surprised, very emotional, and thankfully agreeable to becoming Mrs. Christopher Norton. After the proposal, a handful of his friends arrived to celebrate with our two families, capping the evening with laughter and love, so appropriate for Chris and Emily.

With the most important part of Chris's future secure, we all set our sights on his graduation walk. While exciting, graduation was also very nerve racking because I knew how hard Chris had worked day in and day out for four-and-a-half years to accomplish his goal. More importantly, I knew how much it meant to him and to those who'd followed his journey.

I'd spent the prior year praying daily over his graduation walk and that he wouldn't be disappointed, no matter the outcome. I knew firsthand how far he'd come in his recovery and the effort he'd expended to get there. As his harshest critic and most ruthless trainer, Chris set high expectations for himself.

I didn't want what he'd already accomplished — his recovery, the inspiration he'd provided to thousands, and the creation of a non-profit that was already helping so many — to be diminished by whether he walked, crawled, danced, or skipped across the graduation stage. As his dad, I probably knew Chris better than anyone, and he had his heart and mind set on walking. When he said he was going to do something, he planned to do it no matter what.

Worrier that I was, I also fretted about the crowd. Chris's "actual" class had graduated the year before, he'd finished school in December in order to train in Michigan, and that meant he hadn't been on campus the whole spring semester. In the back of my mind, I worried over how people would feel about him taking too much time or taking the spotlight, even though it wasn't intentional.

My concerns vanished as soon as his name was called and

the room erupted into thunderous applause. Everyone leapt to their feet, and I felt the surge of energy from the audience guiding Chris and Emily along every step. They clapped and cheered for two minutes straight while he walked and received his diploma. Being in that gymnasium, with the crowd radiating joy, was one of the most incredible atmospheres I have ever experienced.

> "I am blown away by how fortunate I am, from the first days of ordering those bracelets, to recently witnessing Chris walk the graduation stage and propose to his girlfriend, to have been a part of everything that has transpired between those two points. I have seen Chris's story bring out the best in others, the best in myself, and serve as evidence that no matter what road — however dark — life decides to send us down, the choice to see the light is always ours to make."
>
> Rich Holton, Luther classmate and friend

Immediately afterwards, Chris's face revealed every emotion we felt as he smiled from ear to ear. We all heaved a collective sigh of relief that he'd achieved his goal in the warm embrace of over forty family members and friends in attendance. At lunch after the ceremony, we had much to celebrate and thanked God for our blessings.

Looking back on the day, I remember feeling disappointed when our local TV station cancelled the interview they'd scheduled with Chris the morning of graduation. They planned to stay and cover the event, so when they withdrew, there was no one there reporting. The absence of the media didn't take anything away from what Chris had accomplished, but I thought it would've been nice to have his story shared to possibly inspire others.

It wasn't long before the media maelstrom began, starting with an online article that garnered many hits and caused the station that cancelled to do a follow-up. The next day, Memorial Day, they sent a TV crew to our house. From there, the story went viral, reaching surreal proportions. *CBS Evening News* asked for permission to run the story, Chris and Emily appeared on *Fox & Friends* with Elizabeth Hasselbeck, *NBC Nightly News* came to our house, followed by an out-of-the-blue flight to New York City to appear live on ABC's *Good Morning America*.

Along the journey to New York, major media outlets in Japan, Australia, and the UK contacted Chris requesting to run his story. Every major online media outlet ran his account as well. I went from being disappointed that his inspirational milestone was getting overlooked to feeling humbled by our blessings as his tale went viral. Once again, God had bigger plans than I did.

While graduation ended one chapter of his life, it marked the beginning of another. For the first time in a long time, Chris had the world by the tail, and no matter what came, we all knew he could handle life's ups and downs.

By the grace of God, "Team Norton" was ready for anything.

ACKNOWLEDGMENTS

First we would like to thank God because all things are possible through Him. We would also like to thank Christy Hayes for her expert advice, dedication, and tireless work on our behalf to make this book a reality. We had dreamed of someday writing a book together about our journey, but this would have stayed only a "dream" without Christy and her expertise. Our paths crossing happened for a reason, not by chance.

We would like to thank our family; Deb, Alex, Katie, and of course Grandma Connie, for being there every step of the way from the beginning. This journey would have been impossible without their love and continuous support.

We can't begin to thank all the family and friends who have supported us through this experience. Chris would like to thank his college friends who took him to therapy, worked with him daily, helped not only make the college experience possible, but memorable. In addition, thank you to all of Chris's caregivers, nurses, therapists, and doctors who took excellent care of him. Thank you to our hometown friends and family who organized fundraisers, remodeled and repaired our home, and made countless trips to Rochester to support us. For all of those people's love and support we dedicate this book in their honor.

Lastly, Chris wants to thank Emily for her devotion, care, and love for him. Without her, Chris would not be where he is today.

We pray the message that comes through from this book is the power of faith, family, and friends, and that your responses—not your circumstances—determine your outcome in life.

ABOUT THE AUTHORS

CHRIS NORTON is a motivational speaker and founder of the SCI CAN Foundation. Chris suffered a severe spinal cord injury playing college football in 2010, losing movement and feeling below his neck. Through faith, family, and unwavering perseverance, Chris came back from his injury stronger than ever, receiving his business management degree from Luther College.

Chris has appeared on ABC's *Good Morning America*, Fox News' *Fox & Friends*, NBC *Nightly News*, CBS's *The Early Show*, and his story has been featured in *TIME, USA Today, E!, People,* and *Cosmopolitan.*

Chris speaks regularly to students and organizations about overcoming adversity and achieving goals. Currently residing in Michigan with his loving fiancé Emily, Chris wouldn't take back the play that left him paralyzed due to the positive influence his story has had on millions of people worldwide.

Learn more about Chris at https://nortonmotivation.com, or follow him on Twitter @chrisnorton16.

TERRY NORTON is the Director of Des Moines Area Community College Jasper County Career Academy. Terry has over twenty years of experience in education and training, both in the corporate sector as well as K-12 and post-secondary education. Terry earned a Bachelor's of Business Administration from the University of Iowa and a Masters of Art in Teaching from Drake University. Terry is the proud father of three children and has been married to his beautiful wife, Deb, for over thirty years. Terry has served as board president for the SCI CAN Foundation since it's inception in 2012.

CHRISTY HAYES is a *USA Today* bestselling author from Atlanta, Georgia. She earned a bachelor's degree in journalism from the University of Georgia, has been married to Chris for more than twenty years, and they've been blessed with two wonderful children, Charlie & Lindsey. Learn more about Christy at www.christyhayes.com.